The Design of OS/2

H. M. Deitel

Nova University

M. S. Kogan

IBM Corporation

ADDISON-WESLEY PUBLISHING COMPANY

Reading, Massachusetts • Menlo Park, California • New York
Don Mills, Ontario • Wokingham, England • Amsterdam • Bonn
Sydney • Singapore • Tokyo • Madrid • San Juan • Milan • Paris

Sponsoring Editor: Keith Wollman
Electronic Production Administrator: Beth Perry
Text Designer: Herb Caswell
Technical Art Consultant: Joe Vetere
Illustrators: Tech-Graphics
Cover Designer: Peter Blaiwas
Manufacturing Coordinator: Judy Sullivan

Library of Congress Cataloging-in-Publication Data

Deitel, Harvey M., 1945–
    The design of OS/2 / H.M. Deitel, M.S. Kogan.
      p.   cm.
    Includes bibliographical references and index.
    ISBN 0-201-54889-5
    1. OS/2 (Computer operating system)   I. Kogan, M.S. (Michael S.)   II. Title.
QA76.76.063D455   1992
005.4'469—dc20   91-17015
                                                         CIP

2 3 4 5 6 7 8 9 10-DO-9594939291

To the designers, implementors, and testers of OS/2:
For bringing edge-of-the-art distributed computing
capabilities to the desktop of the 1990s

To Dean Edward Simco:
For his indefatigable efforts in creating and nurturing the
Center for Computer and Information Sciences at Nova University

Foreword

It is a pleasure to write these opening comments for Deitel and Kogan's, *The Design of OS/2*. We at IBM believe strongly that the new 32-bit OS/2 2.0 will have an important place in the market for personal computers, workstations, and network servers. The book clearly and thoroughly explains the architecture of the operating system in a manner appropriate both for technical professionals who want to understand OS/2's internal structure, and for software developers considering investing in OS/2 applications development. It provides insights into *why* various key design decisions were made.

Dr. Michael Kogan is the chief architect of OS/2 2.0; Dr. Harvey Deitel is the author of one of the world's most widely used operating systems textbooks. Their combined experience covers every major current IBM operating system, as well as the UNIX system, networking, multimedia, and open systems. Dr. Kogan, through his position at IBM, is well apprised of IBM architectural trends. Dr. Deitel consults in the open systems arena with activities related to open operating systems, object orientation, OSI protocols, and international computing and communications standards.

Why OS/2?

Computer systems are evolving rapidly, and OS/2 is designed to support these changes. There are radical changes in hardware, from older systems supported by modest 8- or 16-bit microprocessors, to newer high-powered 32-bit microprocessors such as the Intel 80386 and 80486. RISC systems and multiprocessing systems offer the potential for massive increases in net processing power.

Radical changes in user support also are demanded. The personal computers of the early to mid-1980s tended to be standalone systems. In the 1990s, personal computers will be networked in local and wide area networks. OS/2 is designed to support mission-critical applications—that is, applications that must function continuously and reliably to support key activities of businesses and other organizations. OS/2 is designed to enhance personal productivity. End users working in OS/2 environments can get more done because of the ease of use, high performance, high reliability, information accessibility, and system integrity provided by OS/2.

The shift in application development toward object-orientation is gaining momentum. To become more productive software developers need to reuse components, to develop prototypes more rapidly, and to implement polished and tuned applications faster. OS/2 provides an environment conducive to object-oriented systems development.

The following sections briefly describe OS/2 2.0 and its capabilities. As you read this book, you will come to understand what is "under the hood," and how these capabilities are implemented.

The Integration Platform

We call OS/2 2.0 the "integration platform" because you can run your existing DOS applications, DOS extender (such as the popular Windows) applications, and OS/2 1.3 applications on OS/2 2.0, and they will run more efficiently on the same hardware than they do under their originally intended operating systems. You can also run the new, high-performance 32-bit applications designed to take advantage of 32-bit architectures. Applications run better from the standpoint of performance, integrity, and usability, translating into productivity gains.

Protected Multitasking

OS/2 2.0 represents the evolution of DOS into the world of protected multitasking. It uses the protection mechanisms of the 80386/80486 architecture to ensure robust operation. It runs many applications simultaneously without the danger of misbehaved applications destroying one another or the operating system—precisely what is needed in mission-critical application environments. An application may not access the private data of other applications. This level of protection is facilitated by the fact that OS/2 applications execute in separate address spaces; DOS extender applications, on the other hand, share a single address space. An errant DOS application may destroy a DOS extender's kernel, thus requiring a reboot, and work may be lost; the OS/2 kernel is protected from errant applications. OS/2 can run multiple versions of the same software simultaneously, making it ideal as an application developer's platform. Its multitasking capabilities make it appropriate as a network server. It uses preemptive scheduling, so it offers good responsiveness to applications of differing characteristics. Priorities are calculated dynamically, so OS/2 can multitask timing-critical applications in both the foreground and the background.

Mission-Critical Systems

OS/2 has many features that support mission-critical business applications. It provides protected multitasking, processes, threads, interprocess communication, and virtual memory, as well as reliability/availability/service (RAS) features that help to isolate software problems and to ensure robust operation.

Applications

There are already 2500 OS/2 software applications announced or available, including 300 Presentation Manager applications. Popular software packages are available, such as Lotus 1-2-3, DBase, WordPerfect, and many others. Many 32-bit OS/2 applications have appeared, and hundreds more are under development. OS/2 2.0 is a critical platform for

IBM's Systems Application Architecture (SAA), our plan for integrating the IBM mainframe, minicomputer, workstation, and personal computer product lines. OS/2 2.0 is designed for machines based on Intel's 32-bit 80386/80486 architecture. In particular, 80386-based systems have proliferated, creating the installed base needed to attract the resources of the independent software vendors. With the appearance of 32-bit OS/2, major user organizations and independent software vendors are making substantial commitments to developing OS/2 applications. OS/2 2.0 provides a powerful base for future growth; 32-bit applications provide dramatic performance improvements over their 16-bit counterparts. Our PMREXX application, for example, demonstrated a 60 percent improvement when used in the 32-bit programming environment.

Memory Management and Virtual Memory

OS/2 2.0's virtual memory model provides 4-gigabyte addressing. The large, flat, paged 32-bit memory model frees the application developer from the memory constraints of the 16-bit segmented model, and from the complexity of managing memory in the 16-bit environment. The 32-bit paging model achieves better utilization of memory and higher performance. The DOS extenders that use virtual memory are typically constrained to a small virtual space; Windows 3.0 applications, for example, share a virtual memory no larger than four times the size of physical memory. In OS/2 2.0, each application has a 512MB virtual memory limit, so the key memory limit is the available disk space. DOS extenders generally use the segmented memory model, in which each piece of memory can only be as large as 64KB; in OS/2 2.0, memory objects can be as large as they need to be (up to the limits of virtual memory). OS/2 runs multiple DOS applications, each with more real memory and far more virtual memory than is available through DOS extenders such as Windows, and each protected from the others to ensure more robust operation. DOS applications can use the DOS Protected Mode Interface (DPMI) to access up to 512MB of extended memory.

Productivity and Ease of Use

OS/2 2.0 provides numerous productivity and ease-of-use improvements. It provides a graphical installation procedure, and it uses an object-oriented, graphical user interface with the drag-and-drop environment implemented consistently across the entire system. Local area network requestor capabilities are integrated into the shell. Intelligent font technology is employed. OS/2 2.0 supports a great variety of printers. It provides an on-line, interactive tutorial, and includes various utilities, games, and productivity applications to help the user become familiar with the system quickly. Extensive on-line help capabilities are provided. In a typical OS/2 environment, the operating system manages the environment transparently to the user. OS/2 worries about the network, and determines whether it has the latest software updates and data updates. The user does not see all that activity. Rather, the user sees only the graphical user interface, which will continue to be enhanced.

Workplace Model

OS/2 2.0 implements the SAA Common User Access Workplace model, which uses the desktop metaphor of how people work. It derives from our OfficeVision system, and works in the object-oriented paradigm. The Workplace model provides an intuitive user interface for managing any objects, including programs, files, and devices.

Presentation Manager

Given that we can run Windows applications out of the box, why do we encourage the development of Presentation Manager (PM) applications? PM applications offer better integration with the Workplace model. Threads can be used to maximize the advantages of multitasking, and to increase system responsiveness. PM applications can take advantage of the capabilities of the OS/2 Database Manager and Communications Manager. In general, PM applications can use the more powerful capabilities provided in OS/2 2.0 for interprocess communication, tasking, semaphores, multithreading, and graphics. The High-Performance File System (HPFS) offers greater data integrity, minimizes disk fragmentation, exploits SCSI performance features, uses sophisticated input/output caching algorithms, and supports huge disks and long filenames. Finally, OS/2 2.0 uses installable file systems, which makes it easy to support new kinds of media, such as CD-ROM.

Portability

The popularity of flat, 32-bit virtual address spaces across many platforms facilitates porting OS/2 to those platforms. This portability enables OS/2 to compete effectively with UNIX in the workstation marketplace. Porting to RISC platforms is underway. The 32-bit API is portable to multiprocessor architectures, as well as to uniprocessor architectures.

Multimedia

OS/2 2.0's exploitation of the 80386/80486 architecture is important for high-performance applications, such as speech synthesis and recognition, full-motion color video with sound, and the integration of these technologies under the rubric of multimedia. OS/2 is a particularly strong system for multimedia applications. It encapsulates system resources, freeing the developer from having to control them directly, and it offers powerful graphics capabilities. Multitasking supports the multiple data streams common in multimedia applications. OS/2 2.0 supports the notion of fast threads specifically for multimedia applications. Multimedia also demands the manipulation of huge objects such as bitmaps; this capability is facilitated by the large, flat, 32-bit virtual addressing model.

Object Orientation

Through extended attributes, OS/2 provides file-system support for object-oriented capabilities, and we are enhancing support for object-orientation. The motivation for this support is clear. Object orientation enables developers to write collaborative software without having a detailed understanding of all components. It yields reusability of substantial functions, dramatically improving the productivity of developers working on sophisticated new applications—surely a source of excitement in our industry. Projects underway emphasize the use of object-oriented programming techniques and of other edge-of-the-art technologies (such as multimedia, expert systems, and visual programming) to create applications useful across a wide range of hardware and operating system platforms. These efforts focus on developing applications by combining reusable software objects. Their work products will become available on OS/2, AIX, UNIX, and Macintosh systems, among others, ensuring wide distribution.

Networking and Distributed Computing

IBM has endorsed the Distributed Computing Environment (DCE) of the Open Software Foundation. DCE supports heterogeneous, multivendor distributed computing. IBM's SAA is being extended to include DCE. OS/2 is a key SAA system and will support DCE. In particular, OS/2 will include remote procedure calls (RPCs), the distributed naming service (in conformance with OSI's X.500 standard), the time service, the security service, the threads service, and the distributed file system. OS/2 provides many features that support networked environments, DCE, and cooperative processing. Perhaps most crucial is OS/2's support of key networking standards, such as SNA, TCP/IP, and OSI. OS/2 LAN support includes key local area networking standards, such as token ring and Ethernet, and wide area networking standards, such as X.25.

Overview of the Book

Deitel and Kogan describe the evolution of personal-computer operating systems through the early years of DOS and its various versions, and the development of OS/2 through its 16-bit and 32-bit versions. They discuss the microprocessor architectures, hardware system architectures, and operating system architectures of the IBM-compatible, personal computing marketplace. They explain how protected multitasking is implemented, and provide insights into the relationships between threads and processes. A detailed discussion of memory management is presented, including explanations of the segmented model of OS/2 1.X and the flat model of OS/2 2.0. The various interprocess communication mechanisms are considered, including shared memory, semaphores, signals, queues, and pipes. The I/O management chapter explains the notions of files, devices, installable file systems, device drivers, and DevHelp services. With all the attention on graphical user interfaces today, the reader will appreciate the discussion of the Presentation Manager and windowing concepts. The book's highly detailed treatment of providing compatibility for DOS, Windows 3.0, and OS/2 1.3 is superb. The communications features of OS/2—including OSI, X.25, LANs, SNA, and TCP/IP—are covered in depth. The book concludes with a look to the future, considering such important topics as open systems, competition and cooperation between OS/2 and UNIX, IBM's Systems Application Architecture, multiprocessing, security, and multimedia. Deitel and Kogan have written a clear, thorough, well-illustrated, frank, and insightful analysis of the architecture of OS/2 2.0. Their work is an important contribution to the operating systems literature.

James A. Cannavino
IBM Vice President and
General Manager, Personal Systems

Preface

The goal of this work is to provide insights into the design decisions and philosophies of the OS/2 operating system. We discuss the motivation, architecture, and realization of OS/2 in the personal computing marketplace. The designs of the major components of OS/2 are described. Each area bridges operating systems theory to the design and implementation of OS/2. Where appropriate, a comparison of the technical aspects of OS/2 and UNIX is provided. The evolution of personal computer operating systems from DOS through 16-bit OS/2 and 32-bit OS/2 is presented.

Chapter 1 recounts the history and evolution of the DOS and OS/2 operating systems. It sets the stage as we illustrate how the OS/2 development teams reconciled real-world development constraints with providing the functionality and performance demanded by a maturing PC industry.

Chapter 2 describes the microprocessor architectures on which the DOS and OS/2 systems execute. We consider the 8088/8086 processor family, the 80286, the 80386, and 80486 CISC-style processors. Looking towards the future, we consider RISC-style processors such as the Intel 80860 and the IBM POWER architecture used in IBM System/6000 workstations.

Chapter 3 presents the hardware system architectures of the personal computer systems that use the processors discussed in Chapter 2. We consider key personal computer bus architectures—the original Industry Standard Architecture (ISA), the Micro Channel Architecture, and the Extended Industry Standard Architecture (EISA). Uniprocessor and multiprocessor configurations are discussed. The programming tools available for the various hardware architectures are described, and the evolution of these is traced across the operating system platforms.

Chapter 4 overviews the architectures of 16-bit and 32-bit OS/2 systems and programs. A discussion of the DOS system gives the technical foundations of the precursor to the OS/2 system.

Chapters 5 through 10 describe the architecture and design of the major components of the 16-bit and 32-bit OS/2 systems. When a component provides the same functionality in both the 16-bit and 32-bit systems, a single discussion is rendered and differences in the two versions of the component are noted where significant (as in Chapter 5 on multitasking). When the 16-bit and 32-bit versions of a single component are substantially different, separate treatments of the component are presented for each version (as in Chapter 6 on memory management). Each major component is discussed in terms of its API calls, internal algorithms, and data structures. These specify the behavior and content of 16-bit OS/2 and 32-bit OS/2.

Chapter 5 discusses OS/2 multitasking. The overall architecture, internal data structures, and major algorithms that compose the OS/2 task manager, dispatcher, and scheduler are detailed.

Chapter 6 describes OS/2 memory management. Both the segmented 16-bit memory model and the paged 32-bit memory model are discussed.

Chapter 7 deals with interprocess communication issues in the multitasking environment. Shared memory, semaphores, signals, pipes, queues, and exceptions are examined in both the 16-bit and 32-bit OS/2 systems.

Chapter 8 describes the I/O components of OS/2. The architectures for devices, file systems, and device drivers are elaborated along with their respective APIs or interfaces.

Chapter 9 describes the presentation management aspects of OS/2. The roles of the keyboard, mouse, and screen devices are examined and analyzed with respect to OS/2's session management architecture. The function and design of the graphical user interface of OS/2, as provided by the Presentation Manager, are also described.

Chapter 10 explores issues in providing compatibility. Both the 16-bit and 32-bit versions of OS/2 provide DOS compatibility. The 32-bit version also provides Windows 3.0 compatibility and 16-bit OS/2 compatibility.

Chapter 11 examines the role of OS/2 in the communications arena. IBM's System Application Architecture and the ISO Open Systems Interconnection reference model are described, as well as OS/2 Extended Edition and LAN Manager. The role of OS/2 in networked workstation and multiuser environments is also considered.

Chapter 12 discusses future issues for OS/2. We examine the technical requirements placed on OS/2 to support open systems, RISC architectures, multiprocessor platforms, and multimedia.

It is a pleasure to acknowledge the people who helped us throughout the writing, review, and production phases of this project. Thanks to the individuals in IBM management, communications, and legal areas for their support in this endeavor. We are also grateful for the comments of many IBM OS/2 designers, testers, planners, and developers.

The book was reviewed by many people, including

Jack Boyce (IBM Corporation)	Byron Pazey (Consultant)
Glenn Brew (IBM Corporation)	Raymond Pedrizetti (Microsoft Corporation)
Ross Cook (IBM Corporation)	Dr. Freeman Rawson (IBM Corporation)
Greg Gruse (CITRIX)	Dr. Edward Simco (Nova University)
Edward Iacobucci (CITRIX)	Dr. Raisa Szabo (Nova University)
Dr. Edward Lieblein (Nova University)	Raymond Westwater (FutureWare)
Jim Macon (IBM Corporation)	

Iris Boshell took dictation of major portions of the first draft of the manuscript.

Our efforts were encouraged by IBM managers including Lee Reiswig, Tommy Steele, Roy Clauson, Oscar Fleckner, Janis Walkow, and Shon Saliga. We are especially grateful to James Cannavino for taking the time out of an incredibly busy schedule to prepare the foreword to the book.

Special thanks are due to Ross Cook of IBM for many insights into the intriguing subtleties of the operating system design process, and to Glenn Brew of IBM for serving as a constant technical sounding board, for his friendship, and for his encouragement.

Thanks to Barbara Deitel for handling the development of the manuscript from the author's side, and for coordinating the production of the book with Addison Wesley. Her tireless efforts enabled us to concentrate on preparing the technical material.

Framingham, Massachusetts   H. M. D.
Delray Beach, Florida   M. S. K.

Contents

Illustrations

ABOUT THE AUTHORS

Dr. Harvey M. Deitel has 30 years experience in the computer field. He participated in the research and development of several large-scale operating systems and in the design and implementation of numerous commercial systems. His current research is in the areas of open systems and open systems interconnection (OSI)—the emerging international standards in computer networking. He received the Bachelor of Science and Master of Science Degrees from the Massachusetts Institute of Technology where he did extensive development work on the Multics operating system. He received the Doctor of Philosophy Degree from Boston University where his dissertation research examined the problems of developing very large-scale structured software systems.

Dr. Deitel has been interested in operating systems since 1963. He worked on the pioneering teams that developed IBM's OS, IBM's TSS, and M.I.T.'s Multics; these systems led to today's MVS, VM, and UNIX operating systems. He has consulted for Epson, Advanced Computer Techniques Corporation, Computer Usage Corporation, Harbridge House, American Express, IBM Systems Development Division, IBM Advanced Systems Development Division, IBM Thomas J. Watson Research Center, M.I.T.'s Project MAC, Microsoft, Apple, Digital Equipment Corporation, Sun Microsystems, and the Corporation for Open Systems International (COS).

Dr. Deitel is the former chairman of the Computer Science Department at Boston College where he developed and implemented the graduate program in computer science. He currently serves as Full Professor of Computer Science and Full Professor of Computer Information Systems at Nova University in Fort Lauderdale, Florida, where he has been involved in the implementation of Nova's Master of Science Program in Computer Science at IBM's Entry Systems Division in Boca Raton. He has received numerous teaching commendations, and has been rated nationally among the top computing educators in the country.

Dr. Deitel is a member of several professional honoraries including Tau Beta Pi (engineering), Eta Kappa Nu (electrical engineering), Sigma Xi (scientific research), and Beta Gamma Sigma (management). He holds the CDP certification of the Institute for the Certification of Computer Professionals, and is a member of various professional societies including the Association for Computing Machinery, and the Computer Society of the Institute of Electrical and Electronics Engineers.

Dr. Deitel's publications include *Absentee Computations in a Multiple-Access Computer System*, MAC-TR-52, Advanced Research Projects Agency, Department of Defense, 1968; *Introduction to Computer Programming*, Prentice-Hall, 1977; *Structured Software Development*, Ph.D. dissertation published by University Microfilms, 1980; *Operating Systems* (with H. Lorin of the IBM Systems Research Institute), Addison-Wesley, 1980, "Functions of Operating Systems," (with H. Lorin) *Software World*, Vol. 12, No. 2, 1981, "Computers and Communications: Improving the Employability of Persons with Handicaps," *Journal for Vocational Needs Education*, 1984; *An Introduction to Operating Systems*, Addison-Wesley, 1990 (Second Edition); *VAX-11 BASIC*, Prentice-Hall, 1985; *Computers and Data Processing* (with B. Deitel), Academic Press, 1985; *An Introduction to Information Processing* (with B. Deitel),

Academic Press, 1986, *Microsoft Macintosh BASIC* (with P. Deitel), Prentice-Hall, 1988; *Microsoft IBM QuickBASIC* (with P. Deitel), Prentice-Hall, 1989.

Dr. Deitel is currently writing four other books including: *C Programming* (with P. Deitel) (Prentice Hall), *SPARC System Software and the Sun Operating System: UNIX System V Release 4* (Addison Wesley), *SunNET: Sun's Approach to Distributed Computing* (Addison Wesley), and the third edition of his book, *Operating Systems* (Addison Wesley)—now considered a classic in the field of computer science—whose previous editions have been used in 1000 universities in more than 100 countries throughout the world.

Dr. Deitel's current research is in the area of open systems interconnection (OSI)— the emerging worldwide standards for computer networking. He is the series editor of the *Open Systems Series* sponsored by the Corporation for Open Systems International (COS) and published by Addison-Wesley. This series includes advanced texts on key aspects of OSI and the Integrated Services Digital Network (ISDN). He is currently writing the lead text, *Open Systems Interconnection*, for this series. He has given operating system seminars at the International Congress Center in West Berlin. His books have been translated into Japanese, Chinese, Spanish, and Russian.

Dr. Michael S. Kogan has 10 years of experience in the computer field. In 1984, he received the Bachelor of Science degree in Computer Science and Mathematics from Emory University in Atlanta, Georgia. At Emory he work in Berkeley UNIX and CP/M environments on VAX and 8080-based systems. In 1986, he earned the Master of Science degree in Computer Science from Nova University in Ft. Lauderdale, Florida. In 1991, he received the Doctor of Science degree in Computer Science at Nova University. His dissertation examined the motivation and design of 32-bit OS/2.

In 1984, Dr. Kogan joined IBM in Boca Raton, where he developed and tested several products in the IBM Engineering/Scientific software series. This experience included the testing of a DOS-based FORTRAN compiler, and the development and testing of DOS device drivers for hardware cards used to interface with engineering devices. He led the effort to redesign the device driver architecture of XENIX 2.0 for the 80286 processor, and developed and tested several XENIX device drivers.

In 1985, he was drafted into the OS/2 project. He was a lead developer for two and one half years during the design, development, and testing of the 16-bit versions of OS/2. He had responsibilities in many areas of the 16-bit system including device drivers, memory management, debugging, queues, DOS compatibility, and system initialization. This was followed by another two and one half years as the principal architect of the 32-bit version of OS/2.

Dr. Kogan has published articles on OS/2 in the *IBM Systems Journal* (Ko88) and in *IBM Personal Systems Developer* (Ko90)(Ko90a)(Ko90b). Several of these articles have been reprinted in other publications worldwide. Dr. Kogan is also credited with numerous software inventions, and has several patents pending for technologies he developed for the 32-bit OS/2 system. He frequently represents IBM internationally in a consulting capacity to IBM customers who are moving to the OS/2 platform.

1
Historical Background

Nothing endures but change.

Heraclitus

It is always good when a man has two irons in the fire.

Francis Beaumont and John Fletcher

That's a better hardware base [the PS/2] than what UNIX started with, and there's a good possibility that OS/2 will be better than UNIX.

Dan Bricklin

Outline

1.1 INTRODUCTION

This chapter reviews the history of personal computers and operating systems. It traces the evolution of personal computer hardware from the original IBM Personal Computer to the latest IBM PS/2, and examines how this process has affected the content and design of DOS and OS/2.

Before 1980 most computers were mainframes and minicomputers, large computing resources that were mainly job- and transaction-processing systems. Operating system technology had evolved from its early simplistic control program stages to sophisticated multiprogrammed virtual memory systems such as VM, MVS, and later versions of UNIX. In the era of large, centralized computing resources, computer time was expensive, learning was time consuming, assistance was difficult to obtain, and computing resources were scarce. Users rarely had opportunities to interact privately with a local computing resource.

The advent of the microprocessor and of inexpensive, off-the-shelf computer components enabled the creation of the first microcomputer systems. The Altair, a primitive computer kit based on the Intel 8080, was one of the most popular early systems. The Altair was surpassed by the Apple I and II computers created by Steve Jobs and Steve Wozniak. The Apples used the MOS Technology 6502 chip and included a keyboard and display. Also gaining acceptance were microcomputer systems configured with the Intel 8080 and Zilog Z80 processors. Besides the Apple, which had its own proprietary operating system, the Intel and Zilog systems principally ran the CP/M operating system. CP/M was primarily designed for 8-bit single-user microcomputers that had floppy-disk drives.

At this point, during the late 1970s, IBM decided to spin off an independent business unit (IBU) to investigate the potential of an IBM microcomputer system. In the late 1970s, IBM used IBUs to respond rapidly to new opportunities, and granted them considerable freedom within IBM's business processes. An IBU is similar to a venture capital operation that attempts to exploit evolving technologies. The IBU ultimately became the current Entry Systems Division (ESD) of the IBM Corporation, which is responsible for personal computer hardware and operating system development.

1.2 DOS HISTORY

The DOS era of microcomputer operating system technology began when the first IBM Personal Computer (PC) was designed. The first IBM PC went beyond the current 8-bit technology available and used the then-new 16-bit Intel 8088 processor. This choice was made because the current 8-bit systems were being eclipsed by the newer 16-bit systems, and the 16-bit system architecture provided a base for more robust software. The 8088 and 8086 processors are functionally identical, but the 8088 was used in the IBM PC since it was cheaper to configure in hardware. The 8088 processor could address up to 1MB of memory; few designers could envision using all that memory in a desktop personal computer in 1979. IBM also chose the 8088 microprocessor because porting software from existing 8080-based systems to the 8088 would be relatively straightforward.

With the hardware for the first PC under development, IBM sought to adapt existing software for the system. Developing a new operating system and software tools would have taken too long. IBM contracted Microsoft, at the time a new company, to provide a BASIC interpreter, assembler, and link editor for the machine. IBM chose Microsoft because of Bill Gates's experience in writing the most popular BASIC interpreter to date for the Altair systems.

Since many CP/M-based programs were available, IBM initially attempted to interest Digital Research, Inc. (DRI) in providing a 16-bit version of the CP/M operating system for the IBM PC. However, DRI did not foresee the success of the 8088 microprocessor and declined to participate in the venture. IBM then approached Microsoft and, after explaining the requirements, asked Microsoft whether it was interested in providing the operating system software as well as the tools. The main concern of both IBM and Microsoft at the time was whether Microsoft had the resources to develop both the software tools and the operating system in the time required. Realizing that writing a new system was not feasible due to the schedules, Microsoft acquired from Seattle Computing Products a CP/M clone called SCP-DOS. With the SCP-DOS technology as a base, Microsoft predicted that it could complete the operating system, and the original operating system agreement between IBM and Microsoft was established.

In 1981, the first version of the DOS operating system, 1.0, was shipped for IBM PCs. The system supported PCs with up to 256KB RAM, two 180KB floppy-disk drives, and included a Basic Input Output System (BIOS) built into the system ROM. DOS 1.0 was similar to CP/M in the way it managed the diskette devices and files, and it provided the base platform for the first 8088 DOS applications. Since the primary data structure used by the DOS file system to map file blocks to diskette addresses was the *file allocation table (FAT)*, the DOS file system became known as the FAT file system. Figure 1.1 illustrates the DOS system structure.

In 1982, IBM began shipping PCs with 360KB floppy disk drives. Since the new diskette medium had a format different from that of the 180KB diskettes, DOS had to

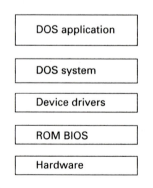

Fig. 1.1   DOS system structure.

be updated. IBM shipped DOS 1.1 when the new diskette drives became available in 1982.

IBM next enhanced its PC line in 1983 with the addition of the IBM PC/XT. The PC/XT had a hard disk that could store far more data than could traditional floppy diskettes. This development illustrates how mainframe technology was becoming less expensive and more widely available in the PC market. The IBM PC/XT also included a new system board that allowed 640KB of memory to be installed.

At this point, a trend emerged that continues to this day in the computer industry: The hardware drives the software. The addition of a hard disk to the PC was a problem for DOS 1.1, since the FAT file system was written for floppy-disk systems in which a single 360KB diskette could contain a maximum of 64 files. This limitation had to be removed; even the smallest hard disks could hold 10MB of data.

Responding to this requirement, the DOS team at Microsoft explored different hard-disk and file-allocation strategies to select one that would enable DOS software to exploit future improvements in storage technology. Merely extending the limit of 64 files per disk would yield too many files to manage in a single file space, so the Microsoft team chose a hierarchical file-management approach similar to the one found in UNIX. They implemented this approach to support both diskettes and hard drives.

Another requirement for the next version of DOS was an architecture for extending the system to support different peripheral devices. This support took the form of *device drivers,* user-installable program modules that interface the DOS system and applications to devices. The version of DOS that included the hierarchical FAT file system, support for hard disks, and a device-driver model for extending the system was shipped as DOS 2.0 in 1983.

IBM's next PC enhancements involved providing faster systems with larger hard disks. The Intel 80286 chip was selected for the next-generation IBM PC, the PC/AT. The 80286 has two modes of operation called *real mode* and *protected mode*. In real mode, the 80286 functions as a fast 8088. In protected mode, the 80286 allows up to 16MB of memory to be addressed and provides features that support a protected multitasking environment. These protection features allow an operating system to separate the memory spaces associated with different programs. However, since the 80286 was not designed to allow existing DOS applications to run in protected mode, they could neither be executed concurrently, nor use more than 1MB of memory. Therefore, DOS applications used the 80286 as a fast 8088. Other operating systems—such as Intel's RMX or Microsoft's XENIX—used the protected mode of the 80286, but neither of these systems was considered to be a mainstream desktop system due to a lack of applications compared to the number of DOS applications.

The PC/AT was also the first PC to use 1.2MB 5.25-inch diskette drives. Since several modifications to DOS 2.0 were necessary for the PC/AT hardware, DOS 3.0 was not released until August 1984. DOS 3.1 was released in 1985 to provide support for PC local-area networks (LANs). Another update to the system (DOS 3.2) was made for supporting 3.5-inch diskettes in 1986. Table 1.1 shows the evolution of the DOS operating system.

Year	Version	System contents
1981	1.0	IBM PC 5.25" 180KB diskette Single task Single user
1982	1.1	5.25" 360KB diskette
1983	2.0	IBM PC/XT Hard disk FAT file system Device drivers
1984	2.1	IBM PC Jr.
1984	3.0	IBM PC AT 80286/80287 real mode 5.25" 1.2MB diskette
1985	3.1	IBM PC network
1986	3.2	IBM PC Convertible 3.5" 720KB diskette
1987	3.3	IBM PS/2 80386/80387 real mode 3.5" 1.4MB diskette
1989	4.0	User shell LIM expanded memory More user memory

Table 1.1   DOS evolution.

1.3 DOS LIMITATIONS

Between 1983 and 1985, IBM, Microsoft, and most application developers began to be aware of certain limitations of DOS and the 8088 environment. These limitations were in the areas of memory management, I/O management, multitasking, system extendibility, and graphical user interfaces.

1.3.1 Memory Management

The 1MB address space, which seemed large in 1980, became a major limitation for larger DOS programs. Applications such as spreadsheets and database systems allowed users to create large volumes of data that needed to be in memory to be processed. The lack of memory became known as the *640KB barrier*, since only 640KB of the 8088 address space mapped RAM. The memory at addresses from 640KB to 1MB in the PC mapped the system ROMs and memory-mapped I/O devices such as the display buffer. The DOS system used from 50KB to 60KB, and device drivers also consumed a portion of the 640KB address space. Thus, application software had less than 640KB available of the 1MB memory addressable by an 8088. Figure 1.2 illustrates the DOS memory layout.

One of the mechanisms DOS applications developers devised to relieve this memory constraint was the *overlay* scheme. Overlays allowed portions of a program not currently needed to reside on a secondary-storage device, usually a hard disk. Since DOS contains only a primitive memory manager, DOS applications had to provide their own overlay management, further increasing their size and complexity.

These memory integrity problems were exacerbated by the behavior of *terminate-and-stay-resident (TSR) modules*. TSRs are loaded like any other DOS program but stay resident in memory after terminating. A TSR is accessed after terminating by either a hardware or a software interrupt. TSRs that monitor keystrokes by intercepting keyboard interrupts are called *hot-key pop-up applications*. The DOS print spooler is a TSR that intercepts timer and printer interrupts to allow the simultaneous queueing and printing of files.

Since TSRs can never be guaranteed that the memory needed will be available when they are invoked, they must allocate when they are loaded all the memory they will ever need. Also, since TSRs are not aware of one another's existence and resource requirements, they can easily cause the system to behave unpredictably. For example, their behavior may depend on the order in which they are loaded.

The 8088 processor provides no memory-protection features, since it was designed to run one application at a time. All 8088 programs execute using actual physical-memory addresses with no distinction between accessing the DOS system's memory or application memory. This lack of protection allows programs to modify one another and the system inadvertently, often causing the system to hang. In a protected system, illegal memory accesses are trapped by the hardware. The operating system is given control; it usually terminates the offending application.

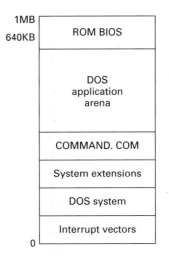

Fig. 1.2   DOS memory map.

1.3.2 I/O Management

Another area in which the DOS environment is limited is I/O control. Any application may read from or write to any I/O device without having access granted by DOS. Although this limitation is really a shortcoming of the 8088/8086 processor, rather than one of DOS, it is still an integrity problem. Application program errors can cause the system to hang, or, even more serious, can cause data on a secondary storage unit to be destroyed inadvertently.

Another I/O problem is that applications have the capability of disabling interrupts to the 8088/8086 processor with a single instruction. If an application disables interrupts and executes a spin loop, the system will remain in the loop forever. Even intermittent disabling of the interrupts to the system can cause applications to behave incorrectly. For example, if an application disables interrupts while a TSR print spooler is using timer tick interrupts to pace its spooling, the spooler will not receive interrupts to continue moving data to the printer. Disabling interrupts can also disrupt communications applications that depend on receiving periodic interrupts for maintaining communications sessions.

1.3.3 Multitasking

DOS was designed to run one application at a time; it is a *single-task* or *single-thread* environment. Even in a single-user, one-program-at-a-time environment, there are requirements for being able to multiprogram the system. A common scenario is using a TSR print spooler to print a file in the background while the user is editing another file from the keyboard. Since DOS provides no multitasking services, programs that require multitasking must do it themselves. However, there is a catch—since DOS is not reentrant, only one program can correctly use the DOS system services at a time. Therefore, competing applications and TSRs can inadvertently both enter DOS, confuse it, and disrupt the system.

A major benefit of building multitasking into the system, instead of into the applications, is that the system can allocate the processor more efficiently than can the applications. When one application attempts to do I/O, it will block, and the system scheduler can resume another application until the I/O is completed. In the DOS environment, an application that requests I/O typically spins in a loop waiting for the device status to indicate that the I/O is complete. This is called *polling,* and wastes many processor cycles that could be spent on other tasks. Since each DOS application that needs to multitask has to do it itself, putting together two DOS applications that need to multitask frequently results in unpredictable behavior.

1.3.4 System Extendibility

DOS applications request DOS system services by issuing *software interrupts,* an 8088-specific form of transferring control between routines. An interrupt causes a transfer of control to an address that is retrieved from an interrupt vector table (IVT) based on the interrupt number invoked. The main difference between a software interrupt and a hardware interrupt is that the software interrupt is caused by the synchronous execution of an

INT instruction rather than by an external hardware-device interrupt request. Figure 1.3 illustrates how the DOS system services are invoked using software interrupts.

Since DOS and BIOS system services are routed through software interrupts, the application requesting the service must pass as a parameter information that specifies which service is desired. Since the information that binds the application with a specific service is hard coded into the application, this is called a *statically linked interface*. DOS and BIOS software interrupt requests specify the software interrupt number and the function code of the service. Thus, there are two levels of decode for each static link. The software interrupt number is decoded by the processor, and the function code is decoded by the software providing the service.

Because all DOS and BIOS (device) services are accessed through the 8088 interrupt mechanism, the memory in which the interrupt-vector table resides is not protected from applications and TSRs. Thus, any application or TSR can *hook an interrupt* and intercept program control when an interrupt is invoked. The result is that the system can be extended by hooking interrupts, but, as more extensions are loaded (usually in the form of TSRs or device drivers), the system's behavior becomes increasingly unpredictable. Also, the order in which the extensions are loaded can change the semantics of the system's behavior. Figure 1.4 illustrates a DOS system with two TSRs loaded.

1.3.5 Graphical User Interface

DOS is packaged with a line-oriented command processor; thus, users must learn DOS commands before they can use the system. New users often find DOS overwhelmingly complex; they complain about the lack of an intuitive paradigm that would make using the system easier. The Apple Macintosh computers were the first microcomputers to exploit successfully the graphical user interface (GUI) technology developed by Xerox at

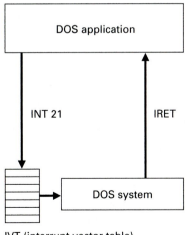

Fig. 1.3   DOS system call.

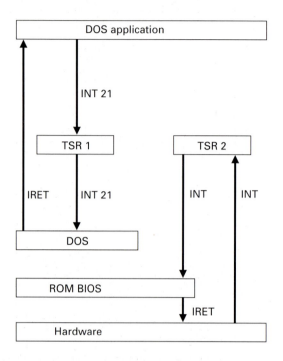

Fig. 1.4   DOS system extensions. (*OS/2 Programmer's Guide,* E. Iacobucci, Copyright 1988. McGraw-Hill Publishing Company. Reprinted by permission.)

its Palo Alto Research Center (PARC) in the 1970s. This GUI technology allows users to interact with the system via a user-friendly pointing device such as a mouse, and visual display keys or icons that parallel the user's tasks. More advanced GUIs provide a *device-independent programming model* that applications use for user I/O functions. This model enables these applications to take advantage of whatever user I/O devices are attached to the system, regardless of the devices' particular physical characteristics. GUIs often provide a *what-you-see-is-what-you-get (WYSIWYG)* capability for displaying graphical information on a variety of output devices.

1.4 OS/2 HISTORY

The need for a more robust version of DOS to provide solutions to these shortcomings was recognized by both IBM and Microsoft, and each company initiated projects devoted to this end. IBM undertook several projects to extend the functionality of DOS while providing compatibility for current DOS applications by using the protected mode of the 80286. Microsoft began DOS 4.0 (not the one that was shipped in 1989) or MT-DOS (for multitasking DOS), a project to define a real-mode multitasking environment that could run on 80286 and 8088/8086 systems. Although none of these projects led to released products in the PC market, both companies learned about the limitations of DOS and of the 80286 architecture and the scope of independent development efforts.

1.4.1 IBM–Microsoft Joint Development

In 1985, IBM and Microsoft signed an agreement to define and ship the operating system that would extend the capabilities of DOS. Under the agreement, both companies would jointly design, develop, and own the resulting product. By 1990 the practice of software companies joining forces to define and develop products had become common in the computer industry. Alliances among computer companies such as Open Software Foundation and UNIX International, and many smaller joint projects among applications developers, are now leading the computer software industry into an era of *open systems*. Emerging software standards will lead to greater software portability and, thus, to better software productivity. Chapter 12 discusses the open-systems platform and the role it will play in the future.

To understand why IBM and Microsoft worked together, we must explore the goals of the product they desired to create and the attributes of both companies' development methodologies. Both companies realized that, if two different advanced DOS systems were developed, the software market would be confused about which was the "right" one. So it made sense for IBM and Microsoft to combine their efforts, and to create a single industry-standard operating system that was endorsed by the two leading companies in the PC market.

IBM has traditionally been known as a hardware company, although it writes most of the software marketed for its larger systems. IBM is by far the largest computer company and wields the most influence in the computer industry. IBM projects are typically large, comprising many layers of management, staff, and technical personnel in the product organization. On the other hand, Microsoft became the leading independent software vendor (ISV) during the 1980s. Microsoft has led the PC software industry in the development of DOS, Windows, and a variety of programming tools. Microsoft also is a leader in applications software for both the Apple Macintosh and the IBM PC systems. Unlike those at IBM, most Microsoft projects are implemented by a small core team of programmers who manage themselves, with extra staff added as needed. Therefore, the combination of the companies created a good team in the design, development, and testing areas.

To facilitate both companies participating in the design and development of the system, they constructed a *software-development process* to describe the methodology for building the product. Figure 1.5 illustrates the general process framework.

1.4.2 Multisite Development

An interesting part of the IBM and Microsoft relationship is that OS/2 was designed, developed, and tested by physically distant partners. Within IBM, there are many sites that work on OS/2 and contribute to the content of the standard and extended editions. The IBM site at Boca Raton, Florida is the sister to Microsoft's site in Redmond, Washington. Together, these two sites are responsible for most of the OS/2 Standard Edition (SE) content and testing. The IBM site at Austin, Texas provides most of the communications and database content for OS/2 Extended Edition (EE). The IBM site at Hursley in the United Kingdom provided the initial releases of the graphics API

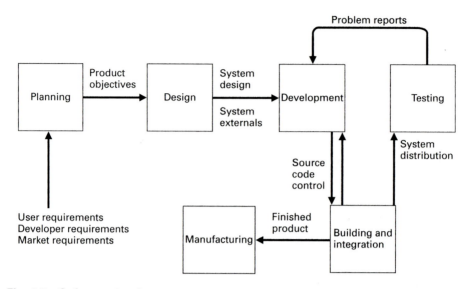

Fig. 1.5 Software development process.

(application programming interface) for the Presentation Manager (PM) and software for supporting IBM's video hardware. The IBM site at Cary, North Carolina provides dialog-management functions for the PM.

All these sites contributing code to a single system created a major problem in source-code control. In a typical single-site development project, a server machine running source-control software is used to ensure the integrity of the source code. The software performs its function by assigning owners to source files, forcing owners to check files out for editing, and to check the files back in when done. However, source-code control is much more complex when a common set of source files must be available to several remote sites that are thousands of miles apart. The solution used in the development of OS/2 is to organize, at each remote site, *build groups* that enforce a *build process* for maintaining a *virtual single-server image* of the OS/2 source code. The build process describes how code is integrated into the system and how the system source-code integrity is maintained across the remote development sites.

The build group implements remote system builds, tracks the build process, maintains backups of all versions of the system, and provides database services to the other development organizations. A database system that facilitates entry of problem reports, design changes, and routing of these items to their appropriate owners is a requirement. All changes to the system and the reasons for the changes are tracked online, so the status of any particular change to the system can be tracked from creation to system integration. This approach allows the system design process to be perceived as a sequence of incremental changes and fixes. Although there are other methodologies, this approach reduces the risk of introducing large numbers of errors into the system at any one time.

1.4.3 OS/2 1.0

The time frame for the development of the initial OS/2 system was from 1985 to 1987. During its design and development, OS/2 assumed many names, including DOS 5, DOS 286, Big DOS, and CP/DOS. The major requirements for OS/2 were these:

- Break the 640KB physical memory barrier; support up to 16MB of physical memory.
- Utilize virtual memory to extend the physical memory resource of a system.
- Provide a protected multitasking environment.
- Provide an extendible, flexible system application program interface (API) architecture.
- Provide a graphical user interface (OS/2 1.1).
- Support DOS application binary compatibility to encourage migration from DOS to OS/2.

Remarkably, OS/2 was originally supposed to run on both the 80286 and the 8088 systems. However, the designers simplified the product to work on only the 80286, since meeting the memory-management requirements for supporting both processors was not realistically feasible. As a result, a subset of the OS/2 API, called the *family API (FAPI),* was developed. OS/2 applications that used only FAPI functions could run on DOS, as well as on OS/2. At this time (early 1985), it was not yet clear what the 80386 would be or when it would be delivered, but Intel assured IBM and Microsoft that protected-mode 80286 programs would run on the 80386, as would DOS programs, if certain guidelines were followed.

From 1985 through 1987, IBM and Microsoft developed OS/2 from the MT-DOS and DOS 3.2 source-code bases. Early prototyping involving the mode-switching capabilities of the 80286 convinced designers that a system could be constructed that multitasked protected-mode applications while running a single DOS application in the foreground. At this stage, it was known that OS/2 on an 80286 would not be able to run multiple DOS applications, or to run a DOS application in the background. CP/DOS 1.0 was nearly complete by late 1986; at that time, however, the next generation of IBM PCs, called PS/2s, was nearing availability, and IBM elected to support the new PS/2 family of computers before shipping OS/2 1.0.

The PS/2 family of PCs was introduced in April 1987. These PCs were of a *form factor* different from that of the original PC and PC-AT, had 3.5-inch instead of 5.25-inch diskette drives, and used a new bus design called the Micro Channel Architecture. (Chapter 3 discusses the Micro Channel Architecture.) The PS/2 family initially included 8088/8086 systems (Model 25), 16-bit Micro Channel 80286 systems (models 50, 50Z, and 60), and a 32-bit Micro Channel system (Model 80). (Chapter 3 describes the PS/2 product line in more detail.) DOS 3.3 was also shipped to enable DOS applications to work on the PS/2 family. OS/2 1.0 Standard Edition was announced in April 1987, when the PS/2s became available; it was shipped in December 1987.

As is true of most new operating systems, OS/2 initially lacked an applications base. Furthermore, OS/2 1.0 did not include the *Presentation Manager (PM)* GUI. Software developers were tentative about beginning OS/2 application development without the GUI. The DOS compatibility of OS/2 did not allow most communications applications to run, and the Extended Edition of OS/2 that provides communications and database support was not available. Therefore the industry did not immediately migrate to the OS/2 platform.

1.4.4 OS/2 1.1

From the time OS/2 1.0 was shipped until late 1988, IBM and Microsoft concentrated on completing the initial release of the Presentation Manager. PM provides a graphical user interface with device-independent graphics in a protected multitasking environment. OS/2 1.1 was delivered in November 1988.

1.5 THE EVOLVING MARKET

The DOS world was not standing still while OS/2 was being developed. DOS application vendors came up with their own ways to extend DOS and to break the 640KB physical-memory barrier. The use of special memory-mapping hardware, and later the 80386, played major roles in extending the memory-management and multitasking capabilities of the DOS environment. Due to concerns about the cost of rewriting DOS applications for OS/2 and the limited size of the initial OS/2 market, many developers opted to use these techniques to extend the life of their current DOS products, instead of immediately porting to OS/2. However, these short-term DOS add-on technologies required DOS applications to perform more complex memory-management and multitasking strategies, resulting in an evolution of more DOS-based limitations.

1.5.1 Microsoft Windows

Prior to and during the development of OS/2, Microsoft designed a graphical user interface for the DOS environment called *Windows,* which was announced in late 1983. Microsoft hoped that Windows would become the standard graphical user interface for DOS systems. However, Windows was not actually shipped until late 1985, and no commercial Windows applications existed when it shipped. By late 1987, Windows 2.0 had been released, and some DOS developers were beginning to migrate their products to the Windows platform.

1.5.2 DOS Expanded Memory

One method of allowing DOS applications to access more than 640KB is called *expanded memory*. Expanded memory works by using a special memory card that bank switches its memory into the 8088 address space through a technique called *windowing* (not to be confused with GUIs that manage windows on the screen). *Bank switching* involves mapping a portion of the memory on a hardware card into a window of the processor's address space under control of application software.

Expanded memory could be used by existing DOS applications with relatively few modifications and gave the user a solution for relieving the 640KB memory limitation. The expanded memory standard, the *Lotus/Intel/Microsoft Expanded Memory Specification (LIM EMS)*, evolved while OS/2 1.0 was being developed. The LIM 3.2 specification allows up to 32MB of expanded memory to be addressed through 16KB address windows in the DOS address space. The LIM 4.0 specification added a 256KB code window. Since DOS applications had to do their own expanded-memory management, expanded memory was clearly not a long-term solution to the problem of the 640KB barrier; however, it did provide programmers with enough relief from memory concerns that they could create applications with better performance in the short term.

1.5.3 DOS Extended Memory

Similar to expanded memory is *extended memory*. Extended memory in general refers to memory that can be added to a personal computer above the 1MB physical-memory boundary that originated with 8088-based personal computers. Extended-memory cards do not have any special bank-switching hardware. A specification analogous to LIM EMS, called *Extended Memory Specification (XMS),* describes the software interface to the DOS-based memory-extending software.

1.5.4 DOS Extenders

DOS extenders utilize the XMS technology to allow DOS applications to run in protected mode and to take advantage of more than 640KB of memory. Although this is transparent to the application user, the program still utilizes real-mode DOS and BIOS for system and I/O services. Extenders provide interfaces that allow programs to switch the processor between real mode and protected mode for DOS and BIOS function calls, and to manage extended memory.

1.5.5   Intel 80386

By late 1987, the 80386 had been shipped, and software vendors were eager to exploit the chip's new features. Significant on the 80386 are its *virtual 8086 mode* (a special mode for emulating 8088 and 8086 environments), a true 32-bit programming model, and a *paged memory-management unit (PMMU)*. The virtual 8086 and paging features of the 80386 made the task of writing a *DOS multitasker*—a system that manages multiple virtual 8086 machines and multitasks them—more feasible than it had been on 80286 machines. The 80386 paging capability also allowed DOS multitaskers to emulate expanded-memory support using extended memory. This resulted in a DOS platform that could run multiple DOS applications that use more than 640KB of memory concurrently.

1.5.6   DOS Multitaskers

DOS multitaskers support the concurrent execution of regular DOS applications, DOS extender-based applications, and applications that use expanded memory. Examples of

DOS multitaskers are Quarterdeck DesqView and Windows 386 (later Windows 3.0). Since these systems are all based on the nonreentrant, real-mode DOS and BIOS, and rely on mode switching between real mode and protected mode, many complications can arise in the multitasking environment. The complications occur because DOS multitaskers and extenders leave the management of memory and the control of mode switching in applications instead of in a protected kernel. The *Virtual Control Program Interface (VCPI)* was developed by a consortium of vendors, including Lotus and Quarterdeck, to address these problems. VCPI specifies an interface that allows EMS emulators, DOS extenders, and DOS multitaskers to coexist correctly in an unprotected environment.

While these DOS add-on technologies that exploit the features of the 80386 were being developed and used by DOS applications, OS/2 was not so quick to exploit the features of the 80386 for several reasons. The investment in the 80286 version was substantial. To keep system memory requirements down and to meet performance goals, the programmers had to write virtually the entire kernel in 80286 assembler code, instead of in a high-level programming language. Although the 16-bit OS/2 system and applications would run as they were on an 80386, redesigning the system and recoding it to exploit the 80386 32-bit programming model and the virtual 8086 DOS compatibility feature was a nontrivial task.

In fact, the task was not feasible, given the limited resources that IBM and Microsoft were able to devote to the project at that time, since both companies had committed to shipping OS/2 1.0 in 1987 and OS/2 1.1 with the Presentation Manager in 1988.

By mid-1989, the PC market had several solutions to the limitations of DOS:

- Expanded memory
- DOS extenders
- DOS multitaskers
- 16-bit OS/2

A factor that inhibited acceptance of OS/2 was the lack of applications. In early 1989, after OS/2 1.1 was shipped with the PM, few applications targeted for OS/2 1.0 were available, and no PM applications were available until mid-1989. Another factor was that the DOS multitaskers provided capabilities that the OS/2 DOS compatibility environment lacked, such as expanded memory support and multitasking of DOS applications. Also, the hardware requirements for OS/2 were larger than were those for DOS extender-based systems, and people began to question how well 16-bit OS/2 could run on an 8MHz 80286 AT-class computer.

1.6 OS/2 1.2

From the end of 1988 through the middle of 1989, IBM and Microsoft worked on finishing the 16-bit OS/2 system. The OS/2 1.2 system was completed by late 1989; it contained the *High-Performance File System (HPFS)*. Recall how DOS 2.0 came out with the hierarchical FAT file system to overcome shortcomings inherited from CP/M. Now, OS/2 needed a new file system that could manage large volumes of disk space more efficiently than could the FAT file system inherited from DOS. In OS/2 1.0, the FAT file system limited each drive unit to 32MB of storage—a hard disk that could contain 90MB had to be partitioned into three logical drive units. With hard disks available in sizes approaching a gigabyte, and with optical media on the horizon, this restriction clearly needed to be lifted. Also, the FAT file system was designed for a single-user single-process environment, and OS/2 needed a more robust file system to support the multitasking server environment. OS/2 1.2 relieved the 32MB per volume restriction for the FAT file system and also provided HPFS.

Another improvement in OS/2 1.2 was in the area of the DOS environment. Although OS/2 1.2 made available more memory for DOS applications, it still neither provided compatibility for many DOS communications applications, nor exploited any of the features of the 80386.

At about the same time as OS/2 1.2 was shipped, DOS 4.0 was released to provide support for FAT-based hard-disk partitions larger than 32MB, more memory to DOS programs, a simple user shell interface, and EMS emulation support on an 80386.

1.7 OS/2 1.3

IBM recognized in 1989, that the OS/2 1.2 product needed to use less memory and to run even faster if it was to meet the commitment of supporting low-end 80286 machines. Therefore, IBM continued to enhance the 16-bit OS/2 1.2 from late 1989 through 1990 to produce OS/2 1.3. This version basically is the same as 1.2, but it runs in less memory and is faster, especially when used in a local area network environment. OS/2 1.3 can run on an 80286 machine with 2MB of memory. OS/2 1.3 became generally available in October 1990.

In September of 1990, IBM and Microsoft also announced a change in their development relationship: The companies decided to discontinue the policy of splitting development responsibility for OS/2 across sites. IBM became solely responsible for the development of 16-bit and 32-bit OS/2, while Microsoft continued work on advanced OS/2 kernel technology and the Windows system. As in the previous development agreement, both companies retain rights to OS/2. Ultimately, the new arrangement allows future OS/2 development to proceed faster than previously.

1.8 WINDOWS 3.0

Microsoft continued enhancing the Windows product while participating in OS/2 development. The Win386 release of Windows essentially added the capability of running multiple DOS applications on an 80386 processor. Win386 also ran existing Windows 2.0 real-mode applications. Win386 was viewed as a stopgap product that would maintain Microsoft's revenue stream until OS/2 caught on. However, Microsoft announced plans to enhance Win386 to provide a third-generation version of Windows that would integrate a graphical user interface with DOS multitasker and extender technology. The announcement of Microsoft's plans for Windows caused further confusion in the PC market concerning what platforms users and programs should migrate toward. Windows popularity was on the rise due to the promises of the unreleased Windows 3.0, and many developers could not afford to build both Windows and PM versions of their applications.

Windows 3.0 became generally available in June 1990 and soon achieved tremendous sales volumes. The product's success can be attributed to two major factors. First, the extravagant marketing blitz by Microsoft for Windows 3.0 had positioned the product as the stepping stone between DOS and OS/2. The Windows 3.0 marketing effort by Microsoft dwarfed the marketing and exposure given OS/2 by IBM and Microsoft combined. Second, there was no other product that exploited all the DOS capabilities of the 80386 while providing a graphical user interface. For these two reasons, many users migrated to Windows, and many application vendors gave up their commitment to PM development in favor of Windows 3.0 development, to maximize short-term profits.

Since VCPI was not compatible with the Windows 3.0 environment, DOS multitasker and extender programs could not run under Windows 3.0. To reconcile the differences in VCPI and Windows, Microsoft introduced the *DOS Protected Mode Interface (DPMI)* standard. It also provided mechanisms for allowing VCPI programs to run in the Windows environment.

Some interesting technical comparisons can be made between Windows 3.0 and OS/2 1.3. Both systems provide support for up to 16MB of memory on 80286 and 80386 platforms. The user shell of Windows 3.0 looks and feels like a modified OS/2 1.2 user shell. To run a single DOS application and a single protected-mode application, Windows 3.0 requires 3MB to 4MB of memory and an 80386 processor, whereas OS/2 1.3 requires 3MB of memory and an 80286 processor.

Both products use protected mode, but Windows 3.0 does not exploit any of the features for protecting the system from applications, and applications from one another. Thus, any Windows 3.0 application can destroy any other Windows 3.0 application and crash the system. Furthermore, since the 16-bit protected-mode API of Windows 3.0 runs on top of real-mode DOS and BIOS, it is easy to write a program that passes a bad pointer to DOS or BIOS, and that therefore hangs the system. Thus, the Windows 3.0 program model is built on the same technology as DOS extender architectures, and has similar shortcomings. On the other hand, OS/2 1.3 is completely protected from applications programs. The Windows-DOS API, compared to the OS/2-PM API, is inferior in many ways—in memory management, in file-system support and I/O controls, in interprocess communication, in the windowing architecture, and in the graphics power and versatility (Pe90).

Another difference in these products, at the design level, is that Windows trades integrity and protection for DOS compatibility, whereas OS/2 does not. The result is that Windows experiences more system crashes due to poorly behaved DOS applications. Functionally, the only advantage of Windows 3.0 over OS/2 1.3 is the capability of multitasking DOS applications when running on an 80386. Except for this capability, Windows 3.0 represents a regression in operating-system technology, compared to OS/2 1.3.

With these drawbacks in mind, it is interesting to theorize why application vendors and users rushed to the Windows 3.0 platform. The multitasking DOS capability and graphical user interface in a DOS environment are the major functional factors that motivated users to migrate to Windows 3.0. However, the major marketing campaign by Microsoft that made Windows 3.0 appear to be more of a DOS-like product than OS/2, and the low price (the product was free, in many cases) of Windows 3.0, also were contributing factors in placing Windows 3.0 on the desktops of many users. This migration occurred without the availability of Windows 3.0 applications that would take advantage of the 16-bit Windows 3.0 protected-mode API and even though Windows 3.0 did not provide any system protection or integrity, a key issue in a multitasking system.

The large marketing push also caused application vendors to plan ports of their DOS software to the Windows 3.0 16-bit API, so as to maximize short-term profits. Many application vendors even gave up previous commitments to OS/2 PM application development, begun in 1988, so that they could concentrate on Windows. This behavior is confusing, especially when we consider that porting applications to Windows is about as difficult as is porting to the PM, that the performance of 16-bit Windows applications is similar to that of their 16-bit OS/2 PM counterparts, and that the Windows environment is much more fragile than the OS/2 environment. Furthermore, the shift in application development strategies came after most developers began working with OS/2. However, we must expect the vendors to migrate their applications to the market with the largest expected volumes.

1.9 OS/2 2.0

While OS/2 1.2 development was drawing to a close, Microsoft and IBM were also designing the 32-bit version of OS/2 that would finally

- Exploit the features of the 80386 and 80486 processors.
- Provide a demand-paged system with a 32-bit programming model that is portable to other 32-bit processor architectures.
- Multitask DOS applications in a protected environment.
- Provide 16-bit OS/2 application binary compatibility.
- Provide Windows 3.0 application binary compatibility in a protected environment.

OS/2 2.0 lays the foundation for the 32-bit operating environment of the future. Like its predecessors, it provides system and application protection for 16-bit and 32-bit protected-mode applications. The major design goals for the 32-bit programming model were to break the *64KB barrier* associated with Intel's previous segmented 16-bit processors, and to provide a portable 32-bit programming model for the future. Since the system is demand paged, OS.2 2.0 can run in a configuration with 3MB to 4MB of memory. The multiple DOS application support is a protected implementation so that DOS applications cannot breach the system's integrity and cause failures. Windows 3.0 application compatibility encourages users who run Windows 3.0 on an 80386 platform to upgrade to OS/2 2.0. Table 1.2 summarizes the evolution of the OS/2 system through the OS/2 2.0 release.

The 64KB barrier broken by OS/2 2.0 is one inherited from the original 8088 family of processors. Since a 16-bit processor can naturally address only 64KB of memory at a time, programmers had to manage memory in terms of segments that could be up to 64KB long. This made programs sensitive to the underlying addressing scheme of the processor, and nonportable to anything but Intel processors. The 64KB barrier was an even larger problem for 16-bit OS/2 applications than it was for DOS applications, since OS/2 runs applications in protected mode. In protected mode, the instruction for changing the segment to be addressed runs more than eight times slower than in real mode— so 16-bit OS/2 applications incur a large performance penalty to pay for their protection.

Date	Version	System Contents
1987	1.0 SE	Initial 16-bit system Multitasking Memory management Protection Dynamic linking 16-bit API DOS environment
1988	1.0 EE	Communications SNA X.25/APPC/LU 6.2 LAN Manager Database Query Manager SQL
1988	1.1 SE	Presentation Manager (PM)
1989	1.1 EE	Remote Database
1989	1.2 SE	High Performance File System (HPFS) Installable File System Better DOS environment
1990	1.2 EE	Exploit PM TCP/IP and Ethernet support
1990	1.3 SE	Faster/smaller Intelligent fonts
1991	1.3 EE	
1991	2.0 SE	Initial 32-bit system Demand paging Portable 32-bit API Multiple DOS sessions Windows 3.X compatibility Workplace shell

Table 1.2   OS/2 evolution.

Furthermore, the 64KB barrier requires both DOS and 16-bit OS/2 applications to have code to deal with segmented memory addressing, which makes them highly nonportable to a processor architecture where their required type of segmentation is not available in the hardware.

1.10 THE 1990s

Where does this evolution of operating systems leave the user? What choices are there? The answers depend on available hardware platforms and on the user's requirements. IBM and Microsoft have stated that systems with less than 4MB of memory are DOS/Windows systems, and that the remainder are OS/2 systems. But this distinction fails to clarify what users should do, especially since OS/2 2.0 can also run in the same environment and perform more functions reliably.

Hardware generally has been made available before the software that could exploit it. How to ensure the migration of software to newer hardware platforms where better price/performance is achieved is one of the most difficult problems facing the computer industry. Thus far, the solution for the DOS world has been for each microprocessor to provide binary compatibility for the processor of the previous generation. However, this solution prevents software from truly becoming open enough to migrate to any platform.

The creation of standards for source-code portability for a given operating system across different platforms is an initial requirement if the operating system and its applications are to migrate across different hardware architectures. The OS/2 2.0 32-bit programming model, like UNIX, is designed to be portable across almost any platform, whether uniprocessor or multiprocessor. This portability will enable 32-bit OS/2 programs to penetrate platforms other than Intel-based systems when the underlying operating system is enabled on other processor platforms, such as RISC-based systems.

The trend in hardware systems toward workstation configurations that contain a generic workhorse processor attached to large amounts of memory and DASD illustrates that hardware is quickly becoming a commodity rather than a technology. This distinction is evident every time one company puts out a system that achieves a certain performance level, and another company quickly assembles a system offering the same components, but with a slightly higher clock rate and at a slightly lower price. Portable software will hasten recognition of the trend to turn hardware into a commodity and will demonstrate that the true technology of the future lies in software. This core issue is addressed by architectures such as SAA and open systems. In Chapter 12, these issues and others are explored with respect to the future of OS/2, and with respect to the PC/workstation operating system market.

SUMMARY

This chapter described the history of personal computers and of personal computer operating systems. DOS is the most popular single-user, single-tasking personal computer operating system. OS/2 is an advanced single-user, multitasking personal computer operating system that exploits advanced hardware platforms and meets the needs of the future.

TERMINOLOGY

bank switching
Basic Input Output System (BIOS)
binary compatibility
build group
build process
demand paging
device driver
disabling interrupt
DOS
DOS 1.0
DOS 2.0
DOS 3.0
DOS 3.1
DOS 3.2
DOS 3.3
DOS 4.0
DOS evolution
DOS Protected Mode Interface (DPMI)
DOS system service
dynamic linking
expanded memory
extended memory
Extended Memory Specification (XMS)
external device interrupt
family API (FAPI)
FAT file system
file allocation table (FAT)
graphical user interface (GUI)
hardware interrupt
High-Performance File System (HPFS)
hot-key pop-up application
IBM PC/XT
IBM Personal Computer
IBM PS/2
independent software vendor (ISV)
INT instruction
INT 21
Intel 80286
Intel 8086/8088 processors
interrupt-vector table (IVT)
IRET
Lotus/Intel/Microsoft

Expanded Memory
  Specification (LIM EMS)
Micro Channel Architecture
Microsoft
Microsoft Windows
migration
mode switching
MT-DOS
multiprogramming
multitasking
open systems
OS/2
OS/2 1.2
OS/2 Extended Edition
OS/2 Standard Edition
overlay
paged memory management unit (PMMU)
PC/AT
polling
Presentation Manager (PM)
protected mode
protection
real mode
real-mode multitasking
ROM BIOS
segmentation
segmented memory addressing
single-task environment
single-thread environment
16-bit OS/2
640KB barrier
64KB barrier
software interrupt
source-code portability
statically linked interface
synchronous execution
terminate-and-stay-resident (TSR) module
32-bit API
32-bit OS/2
Virtual Control Program Interface (VCPI)
virtual 8086 mode
Windows 3.0

EXERCISES

1.1 Describe the strategy IBM used to bring its PC to market quickly.

1.2 Discuss the layered architecture of the DOS system as shown in Fig. 1.1. Such layered architectures have become popular and effective designs for today's increasingly complex systems.
Give several pros and cons for using the layered approach to designing operating systems. As you
read this text, watch for the use of layering in OS/2.

1.3 What first motivated designers to include a UNIX-like hierarchical file system in an early
version of DOS?

1.4 Discuss the problems inherent in real-mode multitasking systems.

1.5 What capabilities were provided in the Intel 80286 to support a protected multiprogramming
environment? Given these capabilities, why were most 80286s initially used as fast 8088/8086s?

1.6 Describe the limitations of DOS that motivated IBM and Microsoft to begin development of
OS/2.

1.7 What software technique did DOS application developers use to relieve the 640KB memory
constraint? Give several disadvantages of this scheme.

1.8 How do terminate-and-stay-resident modules (TSR) work? What is a hot-key pop-up application? What problems do TSRs present to the application developer?

1.9 DOS applications can disable interrupts with a single instruction. Describe a scenario using
this capability that might cause the system to hang (i.e., to deadlock).

1.10 Discuss several benefits of building multitasking into the operating system, rather than having applications do multitasking themselves.

1.11 Explain the operation of the software-interrupt mechanism.

1.12 What does it mean to hook an interrupt? Why is this possible in the DOS environment? Give
several examples of software that might hook interrupts. What serious problem might develop in a
system in which interrupt hooking is commonly used?

1.13 What is a statically linked interface?

1.14 What major requirements did the design of OS/2 have to address?

1.15 Given the numerous limitations of DOS that motivated the development of OS/2, why was
it considered so important to be able to run existing DOS applications under OS/2?

1.16 Why was the family API (FAPI) developed?

1.17 From the early stages in the development of OS/2, it was known that OS/2 on the 80286
would not be able to multitask DOS applications or to run them in the background. At the time,
this limitation was not viewed as a serious problem from a marketing standpoint. Give several reasons why marketing specialists believed that users would not be concerned about the lack of these
capabilities. Give several reasons why users would indeed like to multitask DOS applications and
to run them in the background.

1.18 What short-term hardware techniques were developed to relieve DOS's 640KB memory
barrier? From the applications developers' standpoint, what key problem did these techniques
have in common?

1.19 Discuss the factors that tended to inhibit the broader acceptance of early versions of OS/2.

1.20 What considerations motivated the development of the High-Performance File System (HPFS)?

1.21   One factor that tended to confuse the applications development marketplace in 1990 was that the Windows and Presentation Manager application programming interfaces (APIs) were different. Given the obvious advantages of a common interface, why do you suppose the APIs are indeed different?

1.22   What factors motivated the development of OS/2 1.3?

1.23   Compare and contrast Windows 3.0 and OS/2 1.3 with regard to memory requirements, processor requirements, and product capabilities.

1.24   What key capabilities was 32-bit OS/2 2.0 designed to provide?

1.25   What issues hinder the portability of 16-bit OS/2 programs?

1.26   Why do 16-bit OS/2 applications incur a large performance penalty to pay for their protection?

1.27   The OS/2 2.0 system, like UNIX, is designed to be portable across a wide variety of platforms. What kinds of standards facilitate such portability?

1.28   Argue that compatibility with widely used hardware and software is an important consideration for designers of new operating systems. Explain how the design of OS/2 reflects the importance of compatibility issues.

2

Microprocessor Architectures

"Now! Now!" cried the Queen. "Faster! Faster!"
Lewis Carroll

Our life is frittered away by detail . . . . Simplify, simplify.
Henry Thoreau

Addresses are given to us to conceal our whereabouts.
Saki (H. H. Munro)

Outline

2.1 INTRODUCTION

This chapter describes the processor architectures on which the DOS and OS/2 systems execute. The various microprocessors and their memory organizations are described and analyzed with respect to their capabilities for supporting systems and applications software.

2.2 INTEL 8088/8086

The Intel 8088 is a 16-bit general-purpose microprocessor used in early IBM PCs and compatibles. The 8088 and 8086 are architecturally identical chips, except that the 8088 has an 8-bit external data bus and the 8086 has a 16-bit external data bus. Throughout this book, references to the 8088 include the 8086. The 8088 is capable of developing 20-bit physical addresses for a maximum of 1MB of memory addressability.

2.2.1 Memory Architecture

The memory architecture of the 8088 is a *segmented model*. Since a 16-bit processor with 16-bit registers is capable of addressing only 64KB using a direct addressing scheme, the segmented model was designed to allow access to 1MB of memory. Each physical location of memory is addressed by two 16-bit values—a *segment* and an *offset*. The segment value denotes the start of a 64KB region, and the offset value is the number of bytes from the beginning of the 64KB segment to the byte being addressed. Memory locations are described by logical addresses in the *segment:offset* format or *16:16* format. Segment values are loaded into one of four *segment registers* that point to the beginning of the four currently addressable memory segments. Figure 2.1 illustrates the four segment registers.

When a memory location is accessed, the value in the segment register is used to determine the 20-bit base physical address of the segment, and the offset value is the distance in bytes from the segment base address to the desired memory location. The system calculates the base physical address by shifting the value in a segment register to the left 4 bits, effectively multiplying the segment value by 16. The offset is then added to the base segment address, resulting in a final physical address that is a 20-bit value

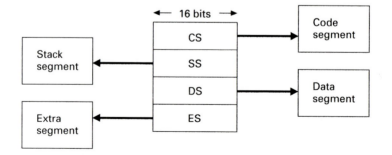

Fig. 2.1   8088 segment registers.

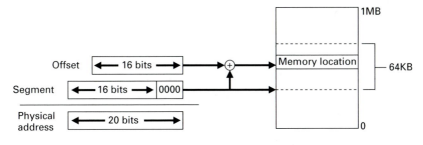

Fig. 2.2   8088 address calculation.

ranging from 0 to 1MB + 64KB. References to the memory between 1MB and 1MB + 64KB are wrapped by hardware to the lower 64KB of physical memory in 8088-based systems. Figure 2.2 illustrates the 8088 address calculation.

Due to the nature of the address computation, the segment values are 16-byte or *paragraph* granular. A paragraph on the 8088 is 16 bytes. Since addresses are calculated arithmetically, segments can overlap, and there can be more than one combination of *segment:offset* for each byte in the 1MB of storage. Figure 2.3 illustrates this aspect of 8088 addressing, called *aliasing*.

2.2.2 Register Set

The 8088 register set consists of general registers, special registers, and segment registers. Figure 2.4 illustrates the 8088 register set.

The AX, BX, CX, DX, SI, and DI registers are used to contain the operands of logical and arithmetic operations. These registers can be used in most simple instructions, and each one also has a specialized role in some of the more complex instructions available. The AX register is used as an accumulator by default in many instructions. The BX register is used as a base-addressing register, the CX register is used as a counter in loop operations, and the DX register is used in I/O operations. The SI and DI registers can be

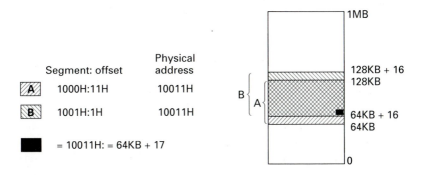

Fig. 2.3   8088 address aliasing.

General registers

← 16 bits →

AX	Accumulator
BX	Base*
CX	Count
DX	Data, I/O
SI	Source index*
DI	Destination index*
BP	Base pointer*
SP	Stack pointer

Special registers

← 16 bits →

IP	Instruction pointer

FLAGS	Status flags

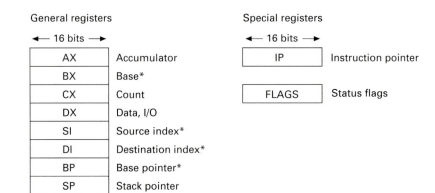

* can be used as an index (offset) register.

Fig. 2.4   8088 register set.

used as source and target offsets with special string instructions to perform memory-to-memory transfers of data. The BX, SI, DI, and BP registers are the only registers that can be used as index or offset operands of general address calculations.

As previously stated, the segment registers establish the four 64KB segments the 8088 currently addresses. Each segment register has a special usage. The CS segment register determines the base address of the segment containing the currently executing sequence of instructions, called a *code segment*. The 8088 fetches all instructions from this code segment using as an offset the contents of the IP register. The CS:IP register combination forms the *instruction counter* and is changed implicitly as the result of control-transfer instructions such as CALL, JMP, interrupts, and exceptions. When a transfer occurs without the CS register changing, the transfer is called "near," since the reference is to a location within the current code segment. When a transfer occurs and CS is reloaded, the transfer is called "far," since the transfer is to a location not in the current code segment.

The 8088 uses a *stack* to facilitate subroutine linkages, parameter passing, and the creation of local activation records. The SS register always contains the base address of the current stack, and the SP register points to the top of the stack. The stack is referenced implicitly by PUSH, POP, CALL, and other control-transfer operations. Unlike CS, the SS register can be loaded explicitly, allowing programmers to define stacks dynamically. The BP register is usually used as a stack-frame base pointer for accessing activation records and dynamically allocated local data on the stack. When BP is used as the index register in an address calculation, the current stack segment is used in the address calculation by default.

The DS and ES registers allow the specification of data segments. Typically, the DS register is used to reference an application's default data segment, and ES is used for other data references outside the scope of the default data segment. Most instructions that reference memory use the DS register by default to select the segment to be addressed, allowing the instructions to be encoded more efficiently.

The FLAGs register contains the status flags or condition codes. These flags allow the results of one instruction to influence later instructions by preserving the status of arithmetic and logical operations. The status flags are carry, parity, auxiliary, zero, sign, and trap.

2.2.3 Interrupts and Exceptions

Interrupts and exceptions are two mechanisms used to interrupt program execution. Exceptions are synchronous events that are the responses of the processor to conditions detected during the execution of an instruction, such as attempts to divide by 0 or to execute an invalid opcode. Interrupts are asynchronous events triggered by external devices requiring attention. Another class of interrupts, called *software interrupts,* facilitates intentional synchronous control transfers using the interrupt mechanism. Software interrupts are executed using the INT instruction.

The 8088 uses the stack and the *interrupt vector table (IVT)* to effect a control transfer when an exception, interrupt, or software interrupt occurs. The IVT table begins at physical address zero; it consists of an array of addresses in the segment:offset format. When an exception, interrupt, or software interrupt occurs, the 8088 saves the current instruction pointer (CS:IP) and the contents of the FLAGs register on top of the current stack, then indexes into the IVT based on the interrupt or exception number to find the new address from which to continue execution. An *interrupt handler* is called when an interrupt or an exception occurs. When the interrupt or exception has been completed, the IRET instruction is used by the handler to return control to the original point of the interrupt.

2.2.4 Input/Output

The 8088 allows I/O to be performed using one of two techniques: a separate *I/O-address space* with specific I/O instructions, or *memory-mapped I/O* using general-purpose instructions. The 8088 I/O address space is divided into *ports* that can be 8, 16, 32, or 64 bits wide. That is, each port can map an I/O device internal register that can range in size from 8 to 64 bits. Using the IN and OUT instructions, 8088 programs read and write ports in the I/O address space. Memory-mapped I/O is used by connecting the peripheral devices to respond like normal memory components. Memory-mapped devices can then be accessed using regular instructions such as MOV. An example of a memory-mapped device is the video RAM associated with the display.

2.2.5 Analysis

Since the 8088 does not provide memory protection or I/O protection, it is not appropriate as a multitasking platform. Due to the segmented memory addressing scheme, source code written for the 8088 is portable only to systems with exactly the same segment semantics and addressing scheme. The segmented memory model and small register set add a level of complexity to the development of programs and programming tools to support the 8088.

2.3 INTEL 80286

The 80286 microprocessor is used in the IBM PC/AT and compatible systems. The 80286 has two modes of operation, called *real mode* and *protected mode*. In real mode, the 80286 behaves like a fast 8088, and is compatible with all systems and applications that run on the 8088.

When protected mode is enabled, the 80286 provides an architecture that supports virtual addressing, memory protection, I/O protection, and access to 16MB of physical memory. As in the 8088, the maximum segment size is 64KB, so the 16MB of physical memory must still be accessed in 64KB chunks. The instructions and register set used by applications running in protected mode are identical to those used in real mode; various system registers not available to applications are used by the operating system to implement the operating system's functions and policies.

2.3.1 Memory Architecture

The 80286 is put into protected mode by setting the protected mode bit in the *Machine Status Word (MSW)*, a system register of the 80286. Once put into protected mode, the 80286 cannot be reset to real-mode operation without special external circuitry on the system board. Mode switching an 80286 from protected mode to real mode is described in more detail in Chapter 10.

2.3.2 Descriptors

When the 80286 runs in protected mode, the memory model is different from the real mode 8088 memory model. On the 8088, the segment values are directly related to the real storage address that the segment occupies. The virtual addressing of the 80286 disassociates the addresses referenced by a program from the actual addresses available in primary storage. The addresses used in protected mode are called *virtual addresses.* The addresses available in primary storage are called *real addresses* or *physical addresses.* To map virtual addresses to physical addresses as a program executes, the 80286 uses a construct called a *descriptor* to implement direct segment translation.

A descriptor is 8 bytes and contains what the base physical address of the segment is, what the segment size or limit is, how the segment can be accessed, and what privilege is required to access the segment. Figure 2.5 shows the information in an 80286 data segment descriptor.

The *segment base address* is the 24-bit physical address where the segment begins. Since this base address is not visible to the running program, an operating system may relocate segments dynamically in physical memory. This relocation is transparent to a program using virtual addresses.

The *segment limit* field in the descriptor denotes the size of the segment. An important feature of the Intel segmentation scheme is that segments are variable in size and can be grown and shrunk dynamically. This feature allows an operating system to provide a segmented memory model in which memory objects can be dynamically resized.

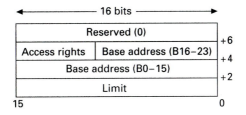

Fig. 2.5 80286 segment descriptor. (Reprinted by permission of Intel Corporation, Copyright/Intel Corporation 1983.)

The remaining information in the descriptor is called *access rights* information, and describes how the segment can be referenced. Both of these fields are discussed further in Section 2.3.6.

2.3.3 Descriptor Tables

The 80286 architecture groups descriptors into *descriptor tables,* which are arrays of descriptor entries. A descriptor table is a special variable-length segment that can contain up to 8192 entries for a maximum size of 64KB. There are two primary descriptor tables in the 80286 architecture, the *global descriptor table (GDT)* and the *local descriptor table (LDT).* There can only be one GDT in an 80286 system, whereas there may be multiple LDTs. Although the 80286 does not prohibit a system with multiple GDTs, switching and managing multiple GDTs under system software control is not realistic. Furthermore, the 80286 has a multitasking model that uses a single descriptor table (GDT) for the system resources, and a descriptor table (LDT) for each 80286 task's resources. An 80286 task is not the same as an OS/2 process, since OS/2 does not use the 80286 multitasking model. Chapter 5 describes the differences in the 80X86 and OS/2 multitasking models with respect to context switching and process management. The 80286 version of OS/2 puts in the GDT descriptors for segments that are global to all processes.

Descriptors for segments that are owned or accessed on a per-process basis are put into an LDT associated with each process. The GDT and LDT segments are located by the 80286 using two special registers called the GDTR and LDTR. These registers store the base address and limits of the descriptor tables.

2.3.4 Selectors

Unlike addressing on the 8088, the segment values on the 80286 no longer represent actual locations in physical storage; rather, they are indices into a descriptor table, and are called *selectors.* On the 80286, 16:16 addresses in protected mode are virtual addresses in *selector:offset* format. Figure 2.6 illustrates the format of a selector.

Selectors are 16-bit values, but not all 16 bits are used as an index into a descriptor table. The table-indicator bit designates whether the index should reference the GDT or LDT. The remaining bits are used for protection information, as discussed in Section 2.3.6.

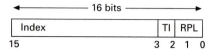

Index = descriptor-table index
TI = descriptor-table indicator
RPL = requestor privilege level

Fig. 2.6 80286 selector format. (Reprinted by permission of Intel Corporation, Copyright/Intel Corporation 1983.)

2.3.5 Address Translation

When a 16:16 memory reference occurs, the descriptor table is used in the address calculation to determine a 24-bit base segment address that is added to the offset of the target address. Figure 2.7 illustrates the address translation through a descriptor table in protected mode.

If a selector that references an invalid segment descriptor is loaded into a segment register, the 80286 raises a *general protection fault* that the operating system handles. Illegal memory accesses after the loading of a valid selector can also trigger a general protection fault. Although applications are aware of selectors, they do not have direct

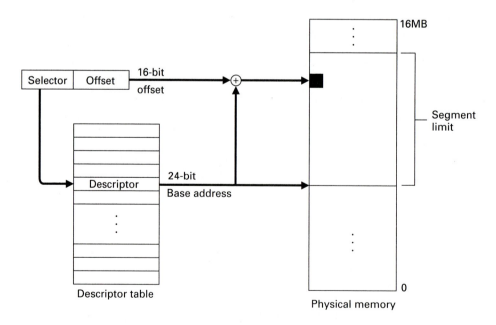

Fig. 2.7 80286 protected-mode address translation. (Reprinted by permission of Intel Corporation, Copyright/Intel Corporation 1983.)

access to the descriptor tables. The descriptor tables are maintained by the operating system on behalf of executing programs.

Since the descriptor tables of the 80286 are maintained in memory, it would seem that memory access would be a slow operation, since the contents of a descriptor would have to be examined on each memory access. To provide fast address translation, the 80286 maintains a hidden descriptor cache for each segment register. When a segment register is loaded with a valid selector, the descriptor is read into the on-chip segment-register cache automatically. Subsequent memory access operations within the segment proceed without the descriptor table needing to be referenced. To maintain the integrity of the descriptor cache, the operating system must be careful not to change the contents of a descriptor that is in use, since the 80286 will not reload the cache until the segment register is reloaded.

2.3.6 Protection

The concept of protection is key in multiprogrammed virtual-addressing systems. The operating system must be protected from errant applications, and applications must be protected from one another. The 80286 provides a protection model that allows an operating system to isolate itself from user applications, to isolate user applications from one another, and to validate memory accesses. Whenever memory is referenced, the memory management unit (MMU) hardware on the 80286 checks the reference to verify that it satisfies the protection criteria. Since these checks are made before an instruction that references memory completes, any protection violation occurring during the checks will cause the 80286 to raise an exception.

The 80286 privilege levels are used to protect critical system code and data from less trusted code. When applied to procedures, privilege is the degree to which the procedure can be trusted not to make a mistake that might affect other procedures. When applied to data, privilege is the degree of protection that the data should have from less trusted procedures. The system uses LDTs to isolate each task or process segment by allocating an LDT for each one and by switching LDTs when tasks or processes are switched.

Since the segment is the unit of protection, the natural place in which to store the protection information is the segment descriptor. The access-rights information in the segment descriptor contains the protection information for each segment. When a selector referencing a segment is loaded into a segment register, the processor loads not only the base physical address and limit of the segment into the descriptor cache, but also the protection information. Figure 2.8 illustrates the access rights portion of a segment descriptor.

The accessed bit is reset each time that a selector is loaded into a segment register. It is set whenever the segment is read or written, and can be used by an operating system to monitor segment usage.

The present bit in the descriptor tells whether the segment is in memory. If a program loads a selector to a segment that is marked not present, then a *segment not-present fault* is raised. The present bit and a segment-not-present fault are used by

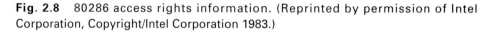

P = present bit
DPL = descriptor privilege level
Type = descriptor/segment type
W = writable bit
A = accessed bit

Fig. 2.8   80286 access rights information. (Reprinted by permission of Intel Corporation, Copyright/Intel Corporation 1983.)

operating systems to manage virtual memory. Chapter 6 describes how 16-bit OS/2 uses the segment-not-present fault mechanism to extend the physical memory resource.

2.3.7 Type Checking

The type field of a descriptor distinguishes among different descriptor formats, and specifies the intended use of a segment. For instance, the type field indicates whether the descriptor is for a code segment, a data segment, or a special segment used by the system. The segment type checking occurs both when a selector is loaded into a segment register and during memory references. The type checking ensures that the CS register can be loaded only with the selector of a code segment, and that only selectors of writable data segments are loaded into SS.

The writable bit in the access rights information indicates whether a data segment is read-only. For code segments, this bit means execute-only, which prevents the contents of a code segment from being read.

2.3.8 Limit Checking

The segment-limit field in the descriptor denotes the size of the segment. Since 80286 segments are variable sized, they support byte-granular protection checks. If a program attempts to access an offset beyond the limit of a segment, a general protection fault is raised. When a general protection fault occurs, the invalid memory access is reported with byte-level accuracy. Limit checking is useful for detecting programming errors such as array subscripts that are out of the boundary of the array and invalid pointer calculations.

2.3.9 Privilege Levels

The 80286 has a four-level protection scheme that an operating system can use to define how the system and programs are protected from one another. Privilege value 0 represents the greatest privilege and the most trust; privilege value 3 represents the least trust. The privilege model can also be thought of as comprising *rings of protection,* in which the center ring is for segments containing the system software, and the outer rings are for segments of less trusted user software. An operating system may use as many or as few of the protection levels as needed in the system architecture. Figure 2.9 illustrates the ring protection model.

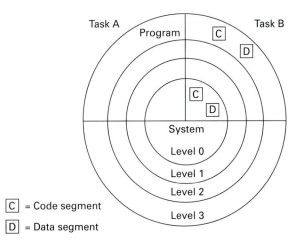

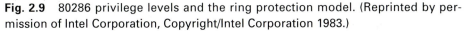

Fig. 2.9 80286 privilege levels and the ring protection model. (Reprinted by permission of Intel Corporation, Copyright/Intel Corporation 1983.)

Privilege levels are found in three areas of 80286 architecture. Descriptors contain a field, called the *descriptor privilege level (DPL)*, that indicates the privilege level required to access the segment. Selectors contain a field called the *requestor privilege level (RPL)*. The RPL represents the privilege level of a procedure that supplies a selector as a parameter. The 80286 also internally tracks the *current privilege level (CPL)*. The CPL is usually equal to the DPL of the currently executing code segment. The CPL value changes when control is transferred to code segments with different DPLs.

The 80286 determines the right of a procedure to access segments by comparing the CPL with the privilege levels (DPL and RPL) of the segments to be accessed. The privilege level access checks occur when a selector is loaded into a segment register. If the checks fail, the instruction loading the selector into a segment register does not complete and a general protection fault is raised.

2.3.10 Protected Data Access

When a program loads the selector of a data segment into a segment register, the 80286 checks to see whether the program has access to the desired segment by comparing privilege levels. The privilege check is successful if the CPL is numerically less than or equal to the DPL of the segment (CPL_DPL). That is, if the processor is currently running at a privilege level (CPL) that is the same or more trusted than that of the data being accessed (DPL), the access is valid. Therefore, a procedure can access only data that are at the same or a less trusted privilege level.

The segments addressable by a program or task change when the CPL changes by executing a protected control transfer. When executing at ring 0 (CPL = 0), data segments at all privilege levels are accessible; when executing at ring 1 (CPL = 1), data segments with DPL = 1 and higher are accessible; and so forth.

2.3.11 Protected Control Transfers

The 80286 accomplishes control transfers using the JMP, CALL, and RET instructions (interrupts and exceptions are discussed separately). There are three flavors of control transfer that differ based on the "distance" of the transfer.

Control transfers within a single segment require no change in privilege level and are called *near transfers* since the transfer is within the current code segment. The near variant of the CALL or JMP instruction is used with an offset in the current code segment as an operand.

Transfers between code segments are called *far transfers* and require the CS register to be reloaded with the selector of the transfer target. If a far transfer is to another code segment at the same privilege level as the source code segment, the far variant of the CALL or JMP instruction is used, specifying the selector of the target code segment and the offset in the target code segment to which control should be transferred. When the CALL or JUMP instruction is issued, the 80286 checks to see whether the DPL of the target code segment is equal to the CPL (the DPL of the current code segment). The 80286 also performs a type check on the target descriptor to make sure the latter is a code descriptor, and a limit check to ensure that the target offset is actually within the target code segment.

If a control transfer is between segments at different privilege levels, a special 80286 protection construct called a *gate* must be used as the operand of the CALL instruction to execute a far call across privilege levels. A gate is represented by a special descriptor, called a *gate descriptor*. There are four types of gate descriptors, called *call gates*, *trap gates*, *interrupt gates*, and *task gates*. This section describes the general gate mechanism using call gates. The call gate's two main functions are to define an entry point to a procedure and to specify the privilege level of the entry point.

To understand why a construct such as a gate is necessary, we can imagine an 80286 operating system implemented at ring 0 with an application running at ring 3. According to the rules of protection, the application at ring 3 has no way to call the operating system for trusted system services such as system calls, since the target code descriptor has a DPL that is numerically less (more trusted) than that of the requestor. We need a construct allowing the operating system to make a protected entry point available to the less trusted code of the application.

Call gate descriptors are used in CALL instructions the same way as are code segment descriptors, except the selector operand references a gate descriptor, and the offset operand is ignored. When the 80286 executes the CALL instruction and recognizes that the target descriptor is a gate instead of a code segment, the call is executed according to gate semantics. Figure 2.10 illustrates the contents of a call gate.

The call gate contains a unique identifier in the type field of the access rights byte to identify to the 80286 that it is a gate descriptor. The gate contains the *selector:offset* of the entry point to the desired procedure and a DPL that is the privilege level of the gate, not of the target code segment. The gate DPL determines what privilege levels can use the gate for a control transfer. For instance, in the example of an operating system at ring 0 attempting to provide a protected entry point for ring 3 applications, a call gate of

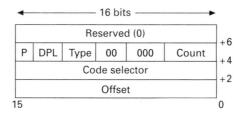

Fig. 2.10 80286 call gate descriptor. (Reprinted by permission of Intel Corporation, Copyright/Intel Corporation 1983.)

DPL = 3 is inserted into one of the descriptor tables and contains the *selector:offset* of the protected ring 0 entry point. Figure 2.11 illustrates the indirect control transfer through a call gate.

To guarantee system integrity, the 80286 architecture provides for a different stack at each privilege level. This provision is necessary so that a trusted procedure does not have to rely on the caller to provide sufficient stack space. Also, the trusted system code should not run on a stack that can be accessed by less-trusted code. The 80286 maintains pointers to the privilege-level stacks in a structure called a *task state segment (TSS)*. The TSS is the 80286 data structure used for maintaining a task and the data associated with that task. The TSS contains an entire register set for the currently executing task, including the stack pointers for privilege levels 0, 1, and 2, it is located by the tasking register (TR). Although OS/2 does not use the TSS for representing OS/2 processes, a TSS must

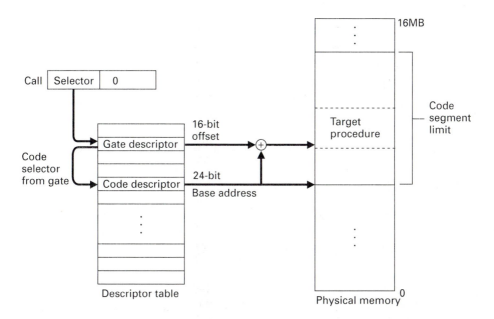

Fig. 2.11 80286 call gate control transfer.

be used to facilitate ring transitions. Chapter 5 describes the OS/2 system's minimal dependency on the TSS construct with respect to process management and context switching.

When a control transfer between privilege levels occurs using a call gate, the 80286 automatically switches from the current stack to the more privileged stack by accessing the TSS. However, there is a requirement to copy the parameters from the original stack to the more privileged stack, so the trusted code can validate them and perform its trusted service. It is here that the count field in the call gate descriptor comes into play. The 80286 automatically copies the parameters from the target stack to the new stack based on the count field in the gate descriptor. During the transfer, all protection checks are active when the new stack selector is loaded and when the parameters are copied. This capability allows the operating system to make transparent to the caller whether the call instruction goes through a gate to more privileged code or directly to a code segment at the same privilege level.

2.3.12 Parameter Validation

An important part of the implementation of operating system calls is the validation of pointer parameters passed into the system by application programs. The operating system must verify that each pointer parameter is to valid application memory, not to system memory, to prevent application programs from inadvertently or maliciously destroying system integrity. If an application attempts to access a system address by passing a pointer to system addresses as a parameter to a system call, the pointer is called a *Trojan horse*. The pointer's action parallels that of the soldiers during the Trojan war who concealed themselves in a wooden horse that they presented as a gift to the enemy. The enemy soldiers took the horse into their camp, allowing the concealed soldiers to attack them. Any protection system must account for Trojan horses, preventing less trusted code from passing a parameter to a trusted data object. To assist trusted code in validating pointers and avoiding Trojan horses the 80286 provides the requestor privilege level (RPL) and an instruction called ARPL.

The RPL field of a selector indicates to the 80286 the privilege level of the original supplier of the pointer. For an access to be valid, the RPL must be numerically less than or equal to the DPL of the selected segment, indicating greater or equal privilege of the originator (RPL_DPL). In other words, the original caller had to be able to access the selected segment. The privilege-level check verifies that the maximum of the RPL and the CPL is less than or equal to the DPL.

An example of a Trojan horse scenario on an 80286 is a ring 3 procedure calling a ring 2 procedure using a call gate, which passes a selector to a ring 2 segment with RPL = 2 as a parameter. The ring 2 procedure must have some way of determining the validity of the data selector with respect to the originator's privilege level. The ring 2 procedure could simply insert the caller's privilege level into the RPL portion of the selector, but this policy would cause the originating caller's RPL to be lost if the selector was passed subsequently to a ring 0 procedure. Therefore, the 80286 provides the ARPL instruction to allow more trusted code to adjust the RPL field of a data selector before that field is used to be the maximum of the selector's RPL and the caller's CPL. This adjustment stamps the selector with the minimum privilege, and assures the trusted code that a Trojan horse cannot be passed in.

In this example, a ring 2 procedure is passed a selector that has RPL = 2. When the ring 2 procedure stamps the selector with the ARPL instruction, it alters the RPL of the selector to RPL = 3, the minimum privilege (numerically greater) of the CPL and RPL. If the ring 2 procedure then passes the selector as a parameter to a ring 0 procedure, the ARPL instruction will result in restamping of the selector with RPL = 3, since the original RPL = 3 and the caller's CPL = 2. If the ring 0 procedure executing with CPL = 0 attempts to access the ring 2 segment using the passed selector, the access will cause a general protection fault, since the maximum of the RPL and CPL (3) is greater than the DPL (2) of the selected segment.

2.3.13 Protected Instructions

Since some instructions have the capability of affecting the entire protected system, the 80286 provides protection to ensure that only trusted procedures with appropriate privileges execute these instructions. Two classes of protected instructions exist: privileged instructions used by an operating system, and sensitive instructions used for I/O operations. Privileged instructions can be executed at only privilege level 0. Sensitive instructions are categorized in Section 2.3.15.

2.3.14 Interrupts, Exceptions, and Faults

Interrupts and exceptions in protected mode on the 80286 are similar to those found in real mode on the 80286, except that the IVT is replaced by a descriptor table called the *interrupt descriptor table (IDT)*. Unlike the IVT, the IDT can reside anywhere in physical memory and is located by the IDTR register. The IDT may consist of trap, interrupt, and task gates. When an interrupt or exception occurs, the number of the interrupt is used as an index into the IDT to select a gate that determines the target of the control transfer.

Trap and interrupt gates are similar to call gates, except that they contain no count field. The difference between interrupt and trap gates is that interrupt gates transfer control to the target code with external interrupts disabled, whereas trap gates transfer control with external interrupts enabled. Interrupt and trap gates also have a privilege level field associated with them that allows the system to control access to the interrupt and exception routines.

For example, assume an operating system with applications at privilege level 3 and the system at privilege level 0. All interrupt and fault handling is performed by the system at privilege level 0. If an interrupt occurs while CPL = 3 and the interrupt gate descriptor has DPL = 0 and a selector to a ring 0 interrupt handling procedure, a general protection fault will occur, since the caller (the interrupted code) does not have sufficient privilege to access the gate. Therefore, interrupts and traps that may occur at less trusted privilege levels need to have the DPLs in their gate descriptors set to the minimum trusted (numerically greatest) privilege level to support potentially less trusted clients.

A fault uses the same mechanism as an exception or interrupt, except that a fault is caused by synchronous execution of an instruction and the instruction is restartable. A fault is a special case of an interrupt or exception. The segment-not-present fault is usually used by operating systems that swap segments to secondary storage. The general protection fault occurs when a protection violation occurs. The operating system determines whether faults result in program termination.

2.3.15 Input/Output

The 80286 has the same I/O capabilities in protected mode as exist in real mode or on an 8088. However, the I/O instructions used for accessing the ports in the 80286 I/O address space are protected; they are called *sensitive instructions*. The 80286 has a field in the FLAGs register called the *input/output protection level (IOPL)* field. The IOPL field defines the privilege necessary to execute the sensitive I/O instructions, and other instructions that manipulate the processor's interrupt flag, such as CLI and STI. If a task attempts to use sensitive instructions and is running at a privilege level numerically greater (less trusted) than the system's IOPL, its behavior is considered a protection violation, and a general protection fault occurs.

2.3.16 Analysis

The 80286 protected model provides the functions necessary to implement a multitasking virtual memory operating system. Due to the 64KB limitations in the addressing architecture, programming the 80286 is nontrivial, and source code is relatively nonportable. Since large 80286 programs must change segment registers often, and since this operation is slow due to the protection checks (compared to loading a segment register in real mode), performance of a protected 80286 system is usually not as good as is that of an equivalent nonprotected real-mode or 8088 system. However, the 80286 can be used to break the 1MB barrier associated with the 8088 and to provide rudimentary segmented virtual memory management. Although 80286 protected mode applications use the same instructions as do 8088 applications, due to the difference in segment semantics and to errata on most 80286 chips in the field, it is not feasible to run 8088 real-mode programs in protected mode on the 80286 to take advantage of more than 1MB of memory.

2.4 INTEL 80386

The 80386 microprocessor is used in some IBM PS/2 and AT-compatible systems. Like the 80286, the 80386 has a real mode and a protected mode; it also has another mode called *virtual 8086 mode*. In real mode, the 80386 behaves like a fast 8088. Therefore, in real mode, the 80386 is compatible with all systems and applications that run on the 8088. In protected mode, the 80386 is compatible with protected mode software written for the 80286. Virtual 8086 mode is designed to allow 8086/8088 programs and, systems to run in a protected-mode environment.

The 80386 register set and protected mode addressing architecture have stretched the 80286 to 32 bits to support 32-bit arithmetic, segments up to 4GB in size, and physical memory configurations of up to 4GB. The 80386 provides a *paged architecture* underneath the segmented model to enable more efficient usage of physical memory in systems with large memories.

There are two versions of the 80386 processor; the 80386DX and the 80386SX. From the software perspective, the two versions are architecturally equivalent. In the remainder of this book, we shall specify the type of 80386 only where it is significant to the discussion. The difference between the two 80386 chips lies in the external connections: The 80386DX has 32-bit external data and addressing paths, whereas the 80386SX has a 16-bit external data path and 24-bit external addressing path. Therefore, the 80386SX can be used to provide 80386 function and performance in a 16-bit bus architecture, such as those found in 80286-based computers, whereas the 80386DX requires a 32-bit bus architecture. Although the 80386 32-bit memory architecture supports up to 4GB of physical memory addressing, 80386SX systems are limited to 16MB of physical memory because of the smaller external bus architecture.

2.4.1 Register Set

The general register set of the 80286 has been extended to 32 bits to support 32-bit arithmetic and addressing operations. This extension allows software to provide significantly higher performance than is possible on 16-bit architectures. Figure 2.12 illustrates the 80386 register set.

Unlike in the 80286, any of the general registers can be used as the offset portion of a memory address calculation. Although the registers are each 32 bits, the 16-bit portions of the registers used by 8088/8086 and 80286 programs can be accessed in real mode, protected mode, and virtual 8086 mode. The segment registers are the same as the 80286, except for the addition of two more segment registers, FS and GS. The FLAGs register has been extended to provide a flag bit to indicate virtual 8086 mode operation.

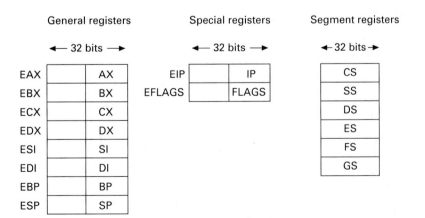

Fig. 2.12 80386 register set. (Reprinted by permission of Intel Corporation, Copyright/Intel Corporation 1986.)

In the past, breakpoint debugging had to be implemented by software, but the 80386 contains debugging registers that facilitate the implementation of hardware debugging breakpoints. The 80386 retains the same memory management system registers as found on the 80286: the GDTR, LDTR, IDTR, and TR.

The 80386 contains a new set of system registers called *control registers*. Figure 2.13 illustrates the 80386 CR0, CR1, CR2, and CR3 control registers.

Like the MSW on the 80286, CR0 contains the system control flags; it also contains a new flag for indicating whether paging is enabled in the system. CR3 is used to locate the paging directory structure and is also called the *page directory base register (PDBR)*. CR2 is used when paging is enabled to indicate the linear address of a page fault. The control registers and paging are discussed in Section 2.4.4.

The 80386 also contains a set of test registers used for testing the *translation looka-side buffer (TLB)*, a cache used for storing paging information. The TLB is discussed in Section 2.4.4.

2.4.2 Memory Architecture

The 80386 provides segmented and paged virtual address translation. When protected mode is enabled, 32-bit segmented address translation occurs by default. Addresses resulting from segmented address translation are physical addresses, as on the 80286, unless paging is enabled. If paging is enabled, the addresses generated by segmented address translation are called *linear addresses*. The linear addresses are then further translated by the paging unit to create physical addresses. Neither of these translations is visible to applications programmers, but both allow system programmers great flexibility in designing different memory models.

2.4.3 Segmentation

Segmented address translation occurs in the protected mode of the 80386, whether or not paging is enabled, so we shall discuss segmentation without regard for paging and its associated address translation and structures. The segmented memory architecture of the 80386 uses exactly the same constructs as are used on the 80286 to facilitate virtual

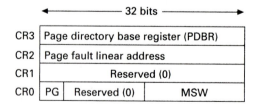

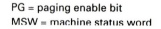

PG = paging enable bit
MSW = machine status word

Fig. 2.13   80386 control registers. (Reprinted by permission of Intel Corporation, Copyright/Intel Corporation 1986.)

memory addressing and protection. The 80386 uses the same descriptors, descriptor tables, associated system registers, and protection mechanism as does the 80286. *All the "32-bitness" of the segmentation on the 80386 results from the redefinition of reserved fields in the descriptors to support 32-bit addressing.* Since the 80286 required these fields to be 0, all 80286 system and application code that correctly zeros the reserved fields in descriptors runs on the 80386 without any changes. As we shall see, 32-bit addressing does occur, but the high-order 8 bits of physical addresses generated by the 80386 will always be 0. Therefore, when 80286 code is being run, physical addresses larger than 16MB are not generated by the 80386, and the system effectively is a fast 80286 running in protected mode.

As in the 80286, a segment descriptor is 8 bytes and contains the base address of the segment, the segment size or limit, and access information that describes what the segment type is and how it can be used. Figure 2.14 illustrates the contents of an 80386 segment descriptor.

The high 2 bytes of the segment descriptor that were reserved on the 80286 are used to extend the basic descriptor definition on the 80386. There is a 32-bit segment base address, a 24-bit segment limit field, and several new access bits. A segment's base address can be anywhere in the 4GB range.

The 24-bit segment limit specifies the size of the segment using one of two methods, depending on the setting of the *granularity bit*. If the granularity bit is clear, the limit is defined in units of 1 byte up to a maximum of 1MB. If the granularity bit is set, the limit is defined in units of 4KB up to a maximum of 4GB. Notice that an 80286 system running on the 80386 will always have this bit clear, so limits are interpreted as 16-bit and byte granular.

The interpretation of the bit labeled "default/big" (D/B) in Fig. 2.14 depends on whether the descriptor type indicates a code or a data segment. If the descriptor is for a code segment, then the bit is called the *default bit* or *D-bit*. If the descriptor is for a data segment, the bit is called *big bit* or *B-bit*. To understand the purpose of these bits, we must examine how the 80386 deals with providing 16-bit and 32-bit semantics with essentially the same instruction set as is used on the 80286.

When running on the 80286, operands such as registers and address offsets are 16 bits. On an 80386, however, each of these entities can be 32 bits as well. So that it can

Base address (B24–31)	G	D/B	O	AVL	Limit (B16–23)
Access rights			Base address (B16–23)		
Base address (B0–15)					
Limit (B0–15)					

G = granularity bit
D/B = default/big bit
AVL = available for system

Fig. 2.14 80386 segment descriptor. (Reprinted by permission of Intel Corporation, Copyright/Intel Corporation 1986.)

track in which mode the 80386 is running, the 80386 maintains internally a default operand and address state. When the 80386 runs in real mode or in virtual 8086 mode, this state is 16 bit by default, enabling 8088/8086 program execution. When the 80386 is in protected mode, the default operand and address size are determined by the D-bit in the descriptor of the segment that the processor is executing currently. Therefore, when the 80386 is running a code segment with the D-bit clear, 80286 semantics are applied when instructions are executing, resulting in the use of 16-bit registers, operands, and addresses. By "16-bit addresses" here, we mean 16-bit address offsets, instead of 32-bit address offsets, being the default during segmented address translation. If the D-bit is set, the 80386 defaults to using the 32-bit registers, operands, and address offsets when an instruction is executed. Special instruction prefixes, called *overrides,* are available in all processor modes when the default semantics of an instruction must be changed temporarily.

The B-bit also plays a large role in the interpretation of the instruction stream. When the selector of a data segment descriptor is used in the SS register to set up a stack, the B-bit in the descriptor is used to determine the default size of the stack pointer. If the B-bit is clear, the 80386 applies 80286 16-bit stack semantics—stacks are no larger than 64KB and have a 16-bit stack pointer, the SP register. If the B-bit is set, the 80386 supports 32-bit stacks larger than 64K and uses a 32-bit stack pointer, the ESP register. The B-bit also allows the 80386 to apply the correct stack semantics when executing an instruction that implicitly references the stack, such as PUSH, POP, and CALL.

The protection mechanisms of the 80386 are identical to those found on the 80286. The same four-privilege-level protected architecture and rules apply. However, the 80386 defines gate descriptors with a different type than 80286 gate descriptors, so that it can apply different semantics when executing gated control transfers. The difference between 80286 and 80386 gate descriptors is that 80386 descriptors contain a full *16:32* target address, and the count of stack parameters to transfer during the transition is interpreted as 4-byte words. Another difference during gated transfers is that the new stack pointer retrieved from the TSS needs to have 32 bits of offset, instead of the 16 bits found in the TSS on an 80286. To facilitate this, the 80386 defines an 80386 TSS that contains a 32-bit version of the task state information. However, note that a 32-bit TSS is not needed if the 80386 is running an 80286 operating system and applications, since no 32-bit gated transitions will occur.

2.4.4 Paging

Paging is a technique of managing virtual memory as fixed-length blocks (called *pages*), as opposed to variable-length segments in segmented systems. The 80386 uses a paged architecture to provide a mechanism for managing the allocation of physical memory in a system with large segments. Since the 80386 allows segments to be much larger than 64KB, managing the physical memory resource without paging can be difficult, since the segment must reside in physically contiguous memory. Also, swapping large variable-length segments to secondary storage can cause a virtual memory system to perform poorly. Therefore, the paging mechanism of the 80386 allows segments to reside in physically discontiguous memory, and allows virtual memory to be managed in terms of small, fixed-length blocks.

In previous sections, we referred to the 32-bit address that is the result of a segmented address translation as a physical address. On the 80386, however, this address is called a *linear address*. If the 80386 does not have paging enabled, the linear address is the same as the physical address. However, if the paging mechanism is enabled by the paging bit in CR0 being set, then the linear address is not equal to the physical address. Rather, the 32-bit linear address is translated by the paging unit on the 80386 into a final 32-bit physical address.

With paging enabled, the 80386 divides physical memory into 4KB units of contiguous addresses called *page frames*. A linear address is actually an ordered tuplet that specifies a *page table,* a page frame within that page table, and an offset within the page frame. Figure 2.15 illustrates the format of a linear address.

The 80386 paging unit performs dynamic address translation using a two-level *direct mapping*. The structure used by the paging unit to map addresses is called the page table. A page table is itself a page and contains 1K 32-bit entries that are page specifiers. Two levels of page tables are used to address a page of memory. The first level is a page table, called a *page directory,* that is located by the CR3 register. The page directory addresses up to 1K page tables of the second level. A page table of the second level addresses up to 1K page frames. Therefore, each page table can map 4MB of physical memory, and a page directory can map 1K * 4MB = 4GB of physical memory. Figure 2.16 shows how the 80386 converts a linear address into a physical address.

Page table entries have the same format regardless of whether they are in the first or second level. Since each page in the system is on a 4KB boundary, each *page table entry (PTE)* uses only the high-order 20 bits to designate a page. The remaining 12 bits of a page specifier are used to signify the page attributes. Figure 2.17 illustrates the format of a page table entry.

The *present bit* indicates whether a PTE can be used in address translation. If the present bit is not on in either set of page tables for an entry when an address translation occurs, the 80386 raises a *page fault*. The fault handler can bring the required page into

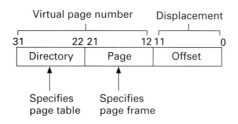

Fig. 2.15 80386 linear address.

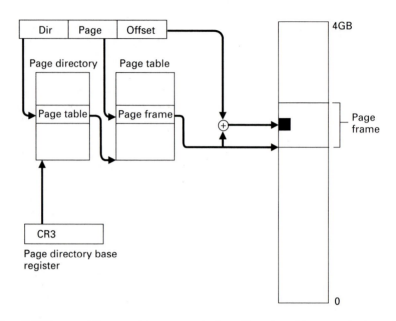

Fig. 2.16   80386 paged linear address translation. (Reprinted by permission of Intel Corporation, Copyright/Intel Corporation 1986.)

physical memory and restart the faulting instruction. This can occur twice for a given memory access if the page table is also not present.

The *accessed bit* and the *dirty bit* are used to profile the usage of a page frame. The 80386 sets the accessed bit whenever a memory reference attempts to read or write to an address mapped by a PTE. The dirty bit is set only when the write is to an address mapped by a PTE. The 80386 does not clear either of these bits. Typically, an operating system uses these bits and resets them to age the pages in the system and to determine which pages should be swapped out of physical memory when the demand for physical memory exceeds the available resources. In Chapter 6, we explain how 32-bit OS/2 uses these bits to age pages.

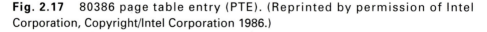

P = present bit
R/W = read/write bit
U/S = user/supervisor bit
A = accessed bit
D = dirty bit
AV = available for system
Page frame address = virtual page number

Fig. 2.17   80386 page table entry (PTE). (Reprinted by permission of Intel Corporation, Copyright/Intel Corporation 1986.)

2.4.5 Page Protection

The *read/write bit* and the *user/supervisor bit* are used for page-level protection. The user/supervisor bit specifies which privilege levels are allowed access to a page. If the user/supervisor bit is clear, the page is a *supervisor page;* if it is set, the page is a *user page*. The current privilege level (CPL) is used to determine whether the 80386 is currently running at the user or supervisor privilege level. If the CPL is 0, 1, or 2, the 80386 is executing at supervisor privilege level. If the CPL is 3, the CPU is executing at user privilege level. When the 80386 is executing at supervisor privilege level, all pages are addressable; when it is executing at user privilege level, only user pages are addressable.

The read/write bit determines the access type of a given page. If the read/write bit is clear, the page may only be read; if it is set, the page can be read or written. When the 80386 is executing at supervisor level, all pages are both readable and writable. When it is executing at user level, attempts to access a supervisor page or to write a read-only page result in a page fault. Since read-only supervisor pages can be written when running at privilege levels 0, 1, or 2, operating systems that use privilege level 1 or 2 for user pages cannot implement *copy-on-write* algorithms to optimize performance. Chapter 6 examines copy-on-write pages in more detail.

Since the page tables are in physical memory, a reference to a memory location requires memory cycles to bring the address information from the paging data structures to the 80386 processor for address translation. To increase the performance of this critical operation, the 80386 uses a four-way associative cache called the *translation lookaside buffer (TLB)* to store the most recently used page table data on-chip. The existence of this cache implies that system programmers must include instructions that flush the cache whenever the contents of page tables are changed. They can flush the cache by reloading CR3, the *page directory base register (PDBR = CR3)*. The TLB is similar in concept to the segment descriptor cache for increasing descriptor lookup performance during segmented address translation. Figure 2.18 illustrates 80386 memory addressing with segmentation and paging.

Since the 80386 provides both segmentation and paging, two methods of combining them are used to construct system memory models. The *flat architecture* is used to execute software that does not use segments, but rather relies on a large *flat address space* that can be addressed using 32-bit pointers. Although this effectively disables segmentation, the segment translation of protected mode cannot physically be disabled. However, we can achieve the same effect by loading the segment registers with selectors for descriptors that map the entire 32-bit linear address space. Once loaded, the segment registers do not need to be changed, and the 32-bit offsets are used to address the entire address space. Because each task is provided with its own page tables, each task gets a unique protected 32-bit linear address space.

Contrasted with the flat architecture is a memory model that utilizes the full segmented capabilities of the 80386. The 80386 supports segments smaller than a page, segments that span pages, and packing of small segments on a single page. A segmented system can be constructed using several combinations of the descriptor tables and page tables to provide address isolation for individual tasks. Since access to memory is

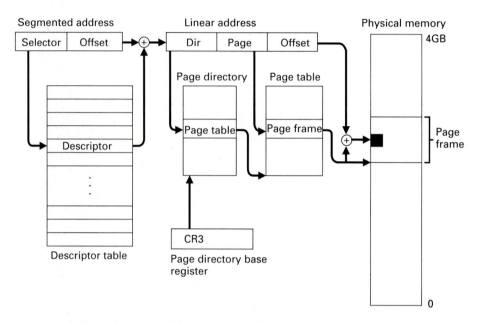

Fig. 2.18   80386 address translation.

through segments, the system could conceivably have a single linear address space shared among tasks that have their own LDT, or a linear address space for each task.

2.4.6 Virtual 8086 Mode

The 80386 virtual 8086 mode supports execution of 8086 or 8088 programs in a protected-mode environment. Virtual 8086 mode enables system software to emulate an 8086 environment with a *virtual machine*. The 80386 hardware provides an encapsulated virtual 8086 environment, while system software controls the external interfaces of the virtual machine, such as I/O devices, interrupts, and exceptions.

The 80386 executes in virtual 8086 mode (called *v86 mode*) when the virtual machine (VM) bit in the EFLAGS register is set. Paging does not have to be enabled for v86 mode to be entered, but the 80386 must be in protected mode. The 80386 leaves v86 mode and returns to protected mode when an interrupt or exception occurs. When the 80386 is in v86 mode, loading the segment registers causes the 80386 to use 8088-style address formation, resulting in addresses in the range of 0 to 1MB. In addition, the 80386 allows a system to trap the execution of sensitive instructions in order to allow system software to virtualize I/O devices and interrupts.

When the 80386 is in v86 mode, the 8088 address calculation generates 20-bits of significant address information. However, 32 bits of address are actually generated with the unused bits set to 0. Therefore, the *linear addresses* calculated during v86 mode execution (which are always in the range of 0 to 1MB) can be mapped using page tables to any 32-bit physical address. Without paging enabled, only one v86 mode task can run effectively, since there is only one unique range of addresses from 0 to 1MB that the v86 mode task can use. If paging is enabled, however, the system software can provide a separate linear address space for each v86 mode task, supporting an environment in which multiple encapsulated v86 mode tasks can run concurrently. Figure 2.19 illustrates multiple v86 address spaces.

Paging has several other uses when a v86 mode environment is being provided. Paging can allow to exist multiple v86 mode environments that are larger than the size of the available physical address space. Another use is to map a single copy of the 8086 system code or the ROM BIOS code that is common to all v86 tasks into the address space of the virtual machines. Paging also can be used to redirect or trap references to memory-mapped I/O devices using the page protection attributes and page faults. Emulation of expanded memory using extended memory also can be provided by utilization of the paging feature.

Since the 80386 does not use descriptors for address calculations when executing in v86 mode, it also does not use the segment protection mechanisms while executing in v86 mode. A v86 virtual machine can be encapsulated and protected by use of an independent address space for each virtual machine, and use of the user/supervisor bit of PTEs to protect the system software that is located in each v86 task's address space. When the 80386 executes in v86 mode, CPL is set to 3, so an executing v86 mode task receives user-level page privileges.

When the system is in v86 mode, instructions that alter the state of the EFLAGS register (such as INT, IRET, CLI, and STI) are sensitive to the system's I/O privilege

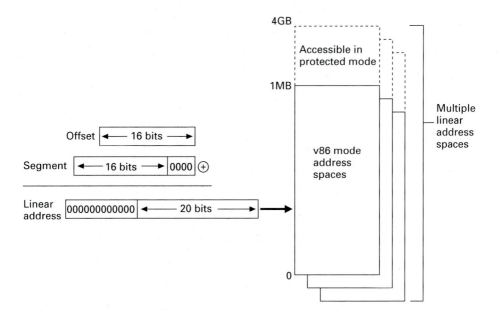

Fig. 2.19   Multiple v86 mode address spaces.

level (IOPL). The I/O address-space instructions IN and OUT, which are normally sensitive to IOPL are not sensitive to IOPL in v86 mode. Since the CPL is always 3 in v86 mode, setting IOPL to less than 3 causes the execution of sensitive instructions to generate general protection faults. It is up to the v86 mode emulation software to determine a policy for handling sensitive instructions when emulating DOS INT-style system calls or virtualizing the state of the v86 task's interrupt flag.

2.4.7 Virtual I/O

Most 8086 programs and systems were designed to execute on single-task 8086 systems and to use the hardware devices directly. However, when a user attempts to run these programs concurrently, this use of the actual devices can disrupt system operation. Therefore the 80386 provides mechanisms that allow the system software to control the I/O occurring in v86 tasks in a transparent manner. *Virtual I/O* refers to the capability of providing to each virtual machine virtual devices that respond transparently like the real devices that the v86 task believes it is using. The system software can emulate or virtualize the hardware devices for the v86 mode tasks.

We have already seen how the paging mechanism can be used to virtualize memory-mapped I/O devices. There also exists a mechanism for trapping accesses to the I/O address space. Port-based I/O in v86 mode differs from protected mode only in that the protection mechanism does not consult IOPL when executing the IN and OUT I/O instructions. Instead, a special map contained in a v86 task's TSS, called an *I/O-permission bitmap,* specifies which I/O port addresses are valid for that v86 task. Each v86 task may have its own bitmap or may share a global map describing the I/O address space for v86 tasks. When a v86 program executes an IN or OUT instruction, the bitmap is consulted to see if the port is valid for the v86 task. If the port address is not valid in the bitmap, a general protection fault is raised by the 80386. Using this type of protection, system software can provide virtual I/O services for v86 tasks, or can permit a v86 task to have direct access to a particular piece of hardware.

2.4.8 Analysis

The 80386 contains the functions necessary to provide a 32-bit protected multitasking environment. Just as important is the virtual 8086 mode feature that allows an 80386 operating system to provide a protected environment for the concurrent execution of 8086 systems and programs. The 32-bit programming model allows systems to break the 64KB barrier associated with 80286 systems and defines the 32-bit programming platform for the future.

2.5 INTEL 80486

The 80486 is an 80386-compatible 32-bit processor. Functionally, both the 80386 and 80486 are identical, except for several changes in the latter to enhance performance. Throughout this book, references to the 80386 include the 80486 unless specified otherwise. The 80486 has an 8KB on-chip cache for storing frequently used instructions and data. The 80486 also integrates the 80387 numeric coprocessor onto the 80486 chip. From the perspective of system software, the 80486 is a fast 80386 with an on-chip cache and 80387. The 80486 allows the page-level protection to be configured in a way different from on an 80386. Recall that read-only pages may be written by code running in supervisor mode. This prohibits system software from using lazy page allocation strategies such as *copy-on-write* pages (see Chapter 6). The 80486 has a *write-protect (WP) bit* defined in the CR0 control register that allows a system to protect read-only pages from supervisor mode access. The 80486 also achieves pipelined instruction execution; this allows the processor to process instructions in parallel, and in most cases, it increases processor performance.

2.6 RISC PROCESSORS

The fundamental goal of *reduced-instruction-set computing (RISC)* architectural designs is to maximize the effective speed of a processor design. RISC does this by performing most functions in software. The only functions remaining in hardware are those whose inclusion in the instruction set yields a net gain in performance when used by programs written in a high-level language (HLL). The 80286, 80386, and 80486 processors are *complex-instruction-set computing (CISC)* architectures. RISC processors have simple hardwired instruction sets with little microcode, single-cycle instruction execution, fixed instruction length, simple addressing modes, and deep pipelined architectures. Although not all RISC processors adhere to these guidelines, most on the market do. For the purpose of studying RISC as a hardware platform, a RISC processor is treated as a generic 32-bit or 64-bit processor with a large number of registers and a high-performance virtual memory system (usually paged). RISC programming is always done in high-level languages, and the compilers and linkers are responsible for optimizing the use of the hardware.

There are many popular RISC chips on the market today, including SPARC, MIPS, AMD 29000, the Intel 80860 and 80960, and the IBM POWER architecture used in the RISC System/6000. Most of these architectures conform to most of the tenets of RISC design. However, the major drawback of these chips is their lack of support for 8088 compatibility. Although it is feasible to simulate the entire 8088 instruction set with a RISC engine, protected concurrent execution of DOS applications and of extended DOS applications such as those found in the Windows 3.0 environment is difficult without extra hardware support.

SUMMARY

The Intel family of microprocessors includes the segmented 8086/8088, 80286, 80386, and 80486. Each of these processors includes a common mode, called real mode, that is used by the DOS operating system. Real mode supports 16-bit execution and a 1MB address space that is divided into 64KB segments. Real mode provides no virtual memory capability or protection mechanisms; it is suitable for small single-user, single-task operating systems such as DOS.

The 80286, 80386, and 80486 provide another mode, called protected mode, which provides support for virtual memory, program, and system isolation. These features enable these processors to access up to 16MB (80286) or 4GB (80386 and 80486) of physical memory while providing protection mechanisms that meet the needs of multitasking virtual-memory operating systems, such as OS/2 and UNIX.

The 80386 and 80486 provide a virtual 8086 mode, which allows multiple 8086 programs to be run within a protected environment.

RISC processors provide generic 32-bit and 64-bit platforms that can address large amounts of memory using reduced-instruction-set technology.

TERMINOLOGY

accessed bit
access right
aliasing
ARPL instruction
associative mapping
asynchronous events
AX register
B-bit
big bit
BX register
call gate
call gate descriptor
CALL instruction
code segment
complex-instruction-set
  computing (CISC)
control registers
copy-on-write pages
current privilege level (CPL)
CX register
D-bit
default bit
descriptor privilege level (DPL)
descriptor table
DI register
direct mapping
dirty bit
DX register
exception
far transfer
fault
flat address space

flat architecture
gate
gate descriptor
general protection fault
general register
global descriptor table (GDT)
global-descriptor-table register (GDTR)
granularity bit
input/output protection level (IOPL)
Intel 8088
Intel 80386
Intel 80486
interrupt
interrupt descriptor table (IDT)
interrupt handler
interrupt gates
interrupt vector table (IVT)
I/O address space
I/O-permission bitmap
I/O protection
IRET instruction
JMP instruction
linear addresses
local descriptor table (LDT)
local-descriptor-table register (LDTR)
machine status word (MSW)
memory management unit (MMU)
memory-mapped I/O
memory protection
near transfer
offset
page directory

page directory base register (PDBR)
page frame
page-not-present exception
page table
page table entry (PTE)
paging
paragraph granular
physical address
ports
privilege value fault
privileged instructions
protected mode
protection
read/write bit
real address
real mode
reduced-instruction-set computing (RISC)
requestor privilege level (RPL)
RET instruction
rings of protection
segment
segment base address
segment descriptor
segment limit field
segment-not-present fault
segment:offset format
segment register

segmented model
selector:offset format
sensitive instruction
SI register
16:16 format
software interrupt
special register
stack
supervisor page
synchronous event
task gate
task state segment (TSS)
tasking register (TR)
32-bit linear address space
translation lookaside buffer (TLB)
trap gate
Trojan horse
user page
user/supervisor bit
virtual address
virtual addressing
virtual 8086 mode
virtual I/O
virtual machine (VM)
virtual memory
write-protect bit

EXERCISES

Questions pertaining to the 8088:

2.1   Describe the 16:16 segment:offset logical addressing scheme of the 8088 microprocessor. Show precisely how a typical physical memory address is calculated from a logical memory address.

2.2   What does it mean for 8088 segment values to be 16-byte or paragraph granular? Explain the concept of 8088 address aliasing.

2.3   Distinguish between near transfers and far transfers.

2.4   Discuss the usage of each of the registers (including segment registers) in the 8088's register set.

2.5   Distinguish among the 8088's notions of interrupts, exceptions, and software interrupts. Which are synchronous events and which are asynchronous? Explain how the 8088 uses the interrupt vector table (IVT) to route interrupts, exceptions, and software interrupts to appropriate handler routines. How does the handler return control after handling an event?

2.6 Discuss each of the two ways the 8088 performs I/O—namely, the use of the I/O address space with specific I/O instructions, and the use of memory-mapped I/O with general-purpose instructions.

Questions pertaining to the 80286:

2.7 Explain the 80286's notions of real mode and protected mode.

2.8 How does the 80286 distinguish between segments that are global to all tasks and segments that are local to particular tasks?

2.9 Explain the following statement: "Unlike in the addressing scheme on the 8088, the segment values on the 80286 do not represent actual locations in physical storage." Specify what these segment values do represent.

2.10 Describe in detail how virtual address translation occurs in 80286 protected mode.

2.11 Why are descriptor tables in an 80286 system maintained by the operating system instead of being made directly accessible to executing programs?

2.12 The descriptor tables of the 80286 are maintained in memory, so we might expect memory access to be a slow operation, since the contents of a descriptor would have to be examined on each memory access. What special hardware does the 80286 use to speed up memory references? What assumption about a program's memory reference pattern makes the use of such hardware worthwhile?

2.13 Explain the importance of protection in the 80286. Describe how protection is implemented.

2.14 When applied to procedures, what does "privilege" mean? When applied to data, what does "privilege" mean?

2.15 When a program loads a selector to a segment that is marked as not present, then a segment-not-present fault is raised. A fault is not fatal; it merely indicates to the operating system that some action needs to be taken before a program can resume normal execution. What actions must the operating system take in response to a segment-not-present fault?

2.16 How is the segment limit field used in error checking? What error is explicitly tested for by examination of the segment limit field? What kinds of program errors might be detected with this check?

2.17 Explain the 80286's ring protection model.

2.18 Describe how the 80286 enables an indirect transfer through a call gate.

2.19 Distinguish between privileged instructions and sensitive instructions.

2.20 Discuss the differences between trap gates and interrupt gates.

2.21 How is the input/output protection level (IOPL) field of the FLAGs register used in conjunction with sensitive instructions?

2.22 What aspects of the 80286 addressing architecture make programming the 80286 nontrivial and hinder 80286 source-code portability?

Questions pertaining to the 80386 and the 80486:

2.23 Discuss each of the 80386 modes of operation: real mode, protected mode, and virtual 8086 mode.

2.24 The 80386 allows for segmented addressing either with or without paging enabled. Explain both addressing schemes.

2.25 Explain the use of the granularity bit in the 80386.

2.26 How does the 80386 provide both 16-bit and 32-bit semantics with essentially the same instruction set as is used by the 80286?

2.27 What problems of segmentation make the use of paging in addition to segmentation attractive?

2.28 Explain 80386 paged linear address translation.

2.29 Explain 80386 memory addressing with segmentation and paging.

2.30 Discuss the notions of virtual 8086 mode, virtual machines, virtual I/O, and virtual devices as they are used in the 80386.

2.31 How does the 80486 differ from the 80386?

2.32 Explain the fundamental differences between CISC architectures and RISC architectures.

3
Hardware Architectures

"The question is," said Humpty Dumpty, "which is to be master — that's all."

Lewis Carroll

What's going to happen in the next decade is that we'll figure out how to make parallelism work.

David Kuck
quoted in *TIME,* March 28, 1988

… In a new channel, fair and evenly.

William Shakespeare
Henery IV, Part 1

59

Outline

3.1 INTRODUCTION

This chapter explores the system configurations found in personal computers in order to lay a foundation for understanding how the OS/2 system is designed and implemented.

Most PC hardware architectures are *uniprocessor* systems that consist of a main processor, memory, and peripheral devices attached to a single shared *bus*. The bus connects the units in a system and defines the medium for data exchange in a computer. A bus typically is composed of *data lines* for sending data, *address lines* for sending addresses, and *control lines* for sending interrupts and for operating the bus.

The system is built on a system *planar* or *motherboard*. The motherboard contains slots or connectors for adding cards that extend the functionality of the system. There are various ways these components can be configured, as well as various bus technologies. This chapter surveys PC hardware architectures from the original IBM PC to the latest systems.

3.2 IBM PC

The original IBM PC, also called the PC-1, contains an 8088 microprocessor that is driven by a 4.7MHz clock. The 8088 and peripherals are configured on a bus that allows 20 bits of addressing and 8 bits of data to be transferred at about 2MB per second. Only a single transfer can occur on the bus at any one time, requiring software to pace and serialize access to the bus by the 8088 and the peripheral devices. The planar contains several bus-extension slots for adding peripheral attachment cards, such as serial and parallel ports, hard disk controllers, communications cards, and memory. The IBM PC supports 16 different *interrupt levels* for interrupt-driven I/O, and a *DMA controller* to allow devices to steal cycles from the 8088 during large I/O transfers. DMA is described further in Chapter 8. Figure 3.1 shows the layout of the IBM PC system.

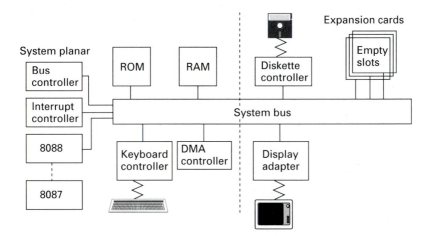

Fig. 3.1   IBM PC system architecture.

Since the 8088 does not support any floating-point arithmetic operations, the 8087 numeric *coprocessor* can be added optionally to the IBM PC to enhance performance of floating-point operations. The 8087 is closely tied to the 8088—the 8088 is called the *master,* and the 8087 is called the *slave* since it operates only on behalf of the 8088.

The system read-only memory (ROM), video buffer (VRAM), and other memory-mapped devices are mapped into the 8088 address space in the range from 640KB to 1MB. The system ROM contains the power-on self-test (POST) and BIOS. POST is executed each time the PC is started. The BIOS is a set of routines accessed by software interrupt in real mode that can be used by operating systems to provide a level of hardware device independence.

The first IBM PCs provided up to 256KB of RAM on the planar, which could be expanded to 640KB by attachment of memory cards. The IBM PC/XT planar was further enhanced to support up to 512KB. Access times for planar memory are generally shorter than are access times for memory that is attached to the bus via a memory card (bus-attached memory).

The IBM PC is configured using switches called *dip switches,* which are small toggles the size of a pencil tip. When the PC display is set up or memory is added, dip switches must be set to indicate the configuration on the planar and on the expansion card.

3.3 IBM PC/AT

The IBM PC/AT is similar to the IBM PC, but it contains an 80286 processor that is driven by a 6MHz clock. The 80286 uses the 80287 numeric coprocessor to perform floating-point operations. Since the PC/AT utilizes the 80286, it can be configured with up to 16MB of memory.

The system bus is wider than that on the PC-1 to allow 24 bits of addressing and 16 bits of data to be transferred on the bus at rates up to 4MB per second. The bus architecture is extended in an upward-compatible fashion so that 8-bit expansion cards that could be added to the IBM PC can still be used in an IBM PC/AT. This bus architecture is known as the *Industry Standard Architecture (ISA)* because it has become the standard bus of IBM compatibles and clones. Figure 3.2 illustrates an IBM PC/AT with an ISA bus configuration.

Whereas the original IBM PC/ATs came with 512KB on the planar, later models provided 640KB on the system board. Since the 80286 and the PC/AT system allow more than 1MB of memory to be attached, the AT system allows memory cards to be added to the system using the bus. As on the PC-1, bus-attached RAM is slower than the RAM on the planar.

Memory cards for the IBM PC/AT are configured with dip switches like expansion cards on a PC-1, but the PC/AT planar has no dip switches. Instead, the system configuration information is saved in a 64KB CMOS RAM that is powered by a small lithium battery.

Although the ISA bus allows expansion cards with intelligent processors that can access all of installable system memory, these cards must access system memory under

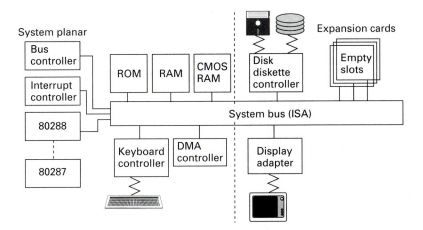

Fig. 3.2   IBM PC/AT system architecture.

direct control of the processor or the DMA controller. For example, the IBM PC LAN card contains an 80186 processor to perform NETBIOS-level network services. Although the 80186 on the LAN card contains its own memory, which is not visible to the main processor, it can transfer data between its memory and the system's memory only by using the system's DMA controller.

3.4 AT 80386

While IBM does not have any 80386 PCs based on the ISA bus, Compaq and many other vendors have produced a class of PCs called *AT 80386 machines*. These PCs use the 80386 as the main processor and the 80287 or the 80387 numeric coprocessor for floating-point operations. The bus in this class of machine is the same as the ISA bus, but special extended connectors for memory cards allow one or two 32-bit memory cards to be attached to the system. The 16-bit memory cards used in 80286 AT machines can usually be installed in most machines of the 80386 AT class. However, none of the 80386 AT-class machines provide 32-bit I/O capabilities.

3.5 MICRO CHANNEL ARCHITECTURE

When IBM staff began designing its first 80386-based PC, they realized that the 16-bit ISA architecture had several limitations that inhibited performance and decreased quality. These problems were in the areas of system configuration, interrupt sharing, bus sharing, and 32-bit I/O. To overcome these problems, IBM created the *Micro Channel Architecture*.

Since many hardware problems on PCs were directly related to incorrect dip-switch settings, IBM wanted to provide a self-configuring system. With the large number of expansion cards in the market, IBM could not provide such a system without changing the extension card and bus architecture. The Micro Channel requires extension cards to have special registers and identifiers that are used when configuring the system.

Interrupt sharing, which occurs when two different expansion cards have I/O devices that use the same interrupt level, is difficult to implement on the ISA bus since it uses *edge-triggered interrupts.* An edge-triggered interrupt is equivalent to a pulse sent down the bus on an interrupt line. If the processor or interrupt controller is not ready for the pulse, the interrupt can be lost and a system crash may result. The Micro Channel Architecture supports interrupt sharing with *level-triggered interrupts.* In a level-triggered system, an interrupt causes a specific interrupt line on the bus to be held at an interrupt level. Only when the software interrupt handlers clear the interrupting device is the interrupt line released. Therefore, the Micro Channel Architecture provides a much more reliable environment for interrupt sharing.

As previously described, the ISA bus does not support generic bus sharing. To allow intelligent devices attached to the bus to take over or master the bus, IBM had to make significant changes in the bus architecture. The Micro Channel Architecture provides a function called *bus arbitration* that regulates access to the bus by extension cards and by the main processor. Different arbitration levels are assigned to components on the bus. When a bus arbitration cycle occurs, the "winning" device is awarded exclusive access to the bus for a period of time. Devices that attach to the Micro Channel and arbitrate to take over the bus are called *bus masters.* Bus master support also allows multiprocessor configurations of the Micro Channel to be created by the addition of bus master adapters containing a processor and its support chips.

Since the Micro Channel Architecture is intended to support 16-bit and 32-bit systems, it comes in both 16-bit and 32-bit versions. Both versions of the Micro Channel Architecture have the same functions, but the 16-bit bus contains a 24-bit address path and 16-bit data path like the ISA bus, and the 32-bit bus provides a 32-bit address path and 32-bit data path. The Micro Channel is capable of transferring data at rates from 20MB to 40MB per second, which is much faster than the ISA bus transfer rate.

As a result of the improvements to the ISA to form the Micro Channel Architecture, it was necessary for IBM to alter the *form factor* of the system. The form factor describes the size of the extension cards and the shape of the connector used to attach the cards to the bus. As we shall see, since PS/2s include far more devices on the planar, there is not much reason to provide the capability to attach old ISA cards to the system, although many people thought that this capability was necessary to preserve their investment in extension cards.

3.6 IBM PS/2

The IBM PS/2 machines are available in various models based on the processor type, clock speed, and bus technology. There are both 16-bit 80286-based PS/2s, and 32-bit 80386-based and 80486-based PS/2s. Table 3.1 summarizes the PS/2 product line.

Figure 3.3 illustrates the PS/2 Model 80 system architecture. Unlike that of the PC-1 and PC/AT, the PS/2 planar includes a *Video Graphic Array (VGA)* display controller,

Model	Processor	Clock rate	Bus	Chassis	Notes
30	80286	10 MHz	ISA	Desk	
50/50Z	80286	10 MHz	MC	Desk	
55	80386 SX	16 MHz	MC	Desk	
57	80386SLC	25 MHz	MC	Desk	Multimedia system
60	80286	10 MHz	MC	Floor	
65	80386 SX	16-20 MHz	MC	Floor	
70	80386	16-20 MHz	MC	Desk	Processor card
70-A21	80386	25 MHz	MC	Desk	Processor card External cache
70-B21	80486	25 MHz	MC	Desk	Processor card External cache
80	80386	16–20 MHz	MC	Floor	
80-A21	80386	25 MHz	MC	Floor	Processor card External cache
80-B21	80486	25 MHz	MC	Floor	Processor card External cache
90	80486	25–50 MHz	MC	Desk	Processor bus External cache
95	80486	25–50 MHz	MC	Floor	Processor bus External cache

Table 3.1   PS/2 product line.

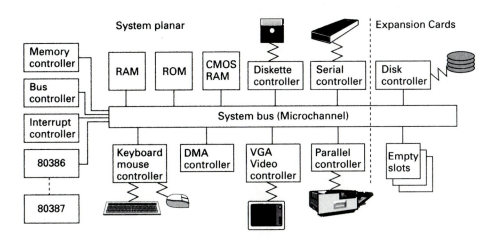

Fig. 3.3   IBM PS/2 system architecture.

diskette controller, serial controller, and parallel controller. Except for Models 90 and 95, PS/2s have nonuniform memory access speeds depending on whether memory is on the planar or is attached via the bus. The planar architecture of Models 90 and 95 is different from that of the other PS/2s. The processor, external cache, and DMA controller exist on a special hardware card called the *processor complex*. This reorganization of the planar allows the processor to be upgraded by changing the processor complex, and also provides an environment that facilitates consistent memory subsystem speeds. Models 90 and 95 also use a more advanced display controller called the *Extended Graphics Array (XGA)*, which provides video modes supporting 1024- by 768-pixel resolution and VGA compatibility.

3.7 EXTENDED INDUSTRY SYSTEM ARCHITECTURE

Since the Micro Channel Architecture was introduced by IBM, many other hardware vendors were reluctant to begin copying an IBM proprietary architecture in their products. Since these companies had mostly ISA-based products, they decided to create an extension of the ISA that would not be owned by a single company, and that would meet the same requirements met by the Micro Channel Architecture. The *new extended ISA architecture (EISA)*, describes a bus architecture similar to, but not compatible with, the Micro Channel Architecture.

EISA provides for optional self-configuring systems and shared interrupts, 32-bit I/O, and the capability of adding bus master devices to the system. EISA transfers data at rates up to 33MB per second. The main difference between EISA and the Micro Channel Architecture is the shape of the connectors of extension cards. The Micro Channel Architecture uses a connector that is totally different from that found on ISA systems, whereas EISA uses a connector similar to that used by ISA.

3.8 CACHE SYSTEMS

Several models of the 80386 and 80486 PS/2s, EISA systems, and 80386 ATs are driven by 20MHz to 33MHz clocks, resulting in a large mismatch between the speed of the processor and the mean memory access time. So that *wait states* do not have to be added to the bus cycles to match the processor and memory speeds, these systems make use of an external cache to allow the 80386 to sustain its high performance. A cache subsystem is usually composed of a small amount of fast memory in the form of *static RAM (SRAM)*, a large amount of slow memory in the form of *dynamic RAM (DRAM)*, and a cache controller. Static RAM is faster but more expensive than dynamic RAM. Figure 3.4 illustrates a cache subsystem.

In a cached system, main memory is used to store all the data, but some of the data is replicated in the cache. When the main processor accesses memory, the cache is checked for the data first. If the data is not in the cache, a *cache miss* occurs, and the cache controller fetches the data from main memory for the processor and retains the data in the cache. If the data is found in the cache, a *cache hit* occurs, and the processor receives the data quickly, since the data is in the static RAM cache. The *cache-hit ratio* is the percentage

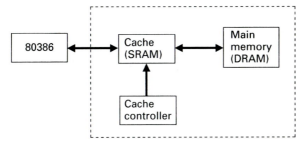

Fig. 3.4   Cache memory subsystem. (Reprinted by permission of Intel Corporation, Copyright/Intel Corporation 1987.)

of accesses that are cache hits; its value is affected by the size of the cache and the algorithm used to allocate cache blocks. Common cache algorithms are the fully associative, direct-mapped, and set-associative cache. Each has its own characteristic methods for attempting to provide a balance among hit rate, performance, and cost.

Since two copies of the same data can exist at once at the same address in cache systems, the cache controller must have a system for maintaining the integrity of the cache and of memory. To prevent stale data from being used, cache controllers use schemes called *write-through* and *write-back* to update the cache during memory write operations.

In a write-through cache, the cache controller copies the data to be written to main memory immediately after it is written to the cache. The result is that main memory always contains correct data. In a write-through cache, any block of data in the cache can be overwritten without loss of data.

In a write-back cache, information is retained by the cache controller in the cache that indicates whether the data has been written and is more recent than the data in main memory. Before any data in the cache is overwritten, this information is checked, and the controller writes the data to main memory before overwriting the block. Write-back caching is faster than write-through caching, since the number of times a changed memory block must be copied to main memory is usually less than the number of memory write operations. However, write-back caches are more complex and must write all altered data in the cache to main memory before any I/O device accesses main memory.

Although write-through caches and write-back caches eliminate stale data in main memory, if caches are used in a system where more than one device has access to main memory, a new stale data problem is introduced. For example, if a bus master device on the Micro Channel writes data to main memory, the 80386 cache may now contain stale data. A system that prevents the stale data problem in this situation is said to maintain *cache coherency*. Four methods of maintaining cache coherency are *bus watching, hardware transparency, noncacheable memory,* and *cache flushing.*

With bus watching, also called *snooping*, the cache controller watches the system address lines on the bus to see whether another bus master writes to main memory. If the main memory altered by the bus master also exists in the processor cache, then the controller invalidates the cache entry.

Hardware transparency ensures cache consistency by making sure that all accesses to memory mapped by a cache are routed through the cache, or by broadcasting all cache writes to all other caches that share the main memory.

Noncacheable memory allows certain accesses of selected memory addresses, such as those for memory-mapped I/O buffers, to bypass the cache. Cache flushing causes all data in a cache to be written to main memory. In this technique, the operating system must flush the cache before any device I/O occurs to main memory.

In most cached architectures on PCs and PS/2s, a combination of these four strategies is applied. Since the PS/2 uses direct memory access (DMA) to overlap disk and main processor cycles, the cache controller must also monitor DMA write operations to main memory in order to maintain cache coherency.

3.9 MULTIPROCESSOR SYSTEMS

As we saw in systems built around the Intel 80X86 series of processors, an auxiliary processor called a floating-point *coprocessor* was used to perform floating-point operations for the main processor. This configuration is not a multiprocessor; the floating-point processor is called a "coprocessor" since it is performing only functions needed by a single 80X86 processor, and since it does not run without the 80X86 processor to tell it what operations to perform.

Another type of configuration that appears to be a multiprocessor configuration is a general-purpose processor used on an extension card to drive an intelligent device. For example, a RISC processor on a graphics card might be used to perform graphics operations, instead of the main processor performing the operations. In this configuration, the RISC processor is called a *dedicated processor* or a *peripheral processor*.

Multiprocessor systems are characterized by having multiple processors used in parallel to achieve a greater system throughput than can be achieved by a uniprocessor configuration. Multiprocessor systems have the common traits of being able to execute multiple instruction streams and to manipulate multiple data streams in parallel. Some people recognize any system with multiple processors as being a multiprocessor machine; however, by "multiprocessor systems," we mean a configuration in which the multiple processors work to increase the general computing power of a system. Multiprocessor systems also usually have the capability of losing a processor and allowing the system to continue operation. The development of multiprocessing hardware requires a multithreaded, multitasking operating system that is designed to have minimum code and data serialization.

A multiprocessor system in which all of the processors are of the same type is called a *homogeneous system*. A system in which at least one processor is different is called a *heterogeneous system*. For example, a system composed of an Intel 80486 and an Intel 80860 is a heterogeneous system; a system composed of several 80486s is a homogeneous system.

Multiprocessor systems are also classified by the way they are treated by an operating system. There are two primary models for operating system distribution in a multiprocessor environment: master/slave and peer. In a *master/slave system,* one processor is the master and the rest are slaves. The master processor governs I/O and system resources while assigning computational jobs to the slave processors. In a peer processor system, each processor either runs a copy of the same operating system or actually runs the same operating system. In both cases, all processors are capable of I/O processing and job scheduling. Operating system distribution in a multiprocessor system is discussed in Chapter 6.

3.10 MULTIPROCESSOR SYSTEM INTERCONNECTION

A key issue in the architecture of multiprocessor systems is what processor interconnection scheme is used. How the processors are interconnected determines how memory is accessed, and how I/O is performed. The *coupling* of a system describes how closely associated the processors are connected. A *loosely coupled multiprocessor* system consists of several processors connected by an internal (bus) or external communications link. A loosely coupled multiprocessor is almost analogous to a network of processors, and communication between processors is usually done by *message passing* since none of the processors share memory. Another classification of loosely coupled systems is called *no-remote-memory-access (NORMA) multiprocessors* (Te87). NORMA configurations are distinguished by the characteristic that no processor can access another processor's memory. NORMA systems constitute the loosest coupling possible, and are the easiest to build in configurations with large numbers of processors. Figure 3.5 illustrates the interconnection scheme of a loosely coupled system.

A *tightly coupled* multiprocessor consists of several processors that share memory and I/O devices. Since all the processors can access main memory, interprocessor communication is done by shared memory. Typically, tightly coupled multiprocessor systems have some hardware support for locking shared memory, so that processor

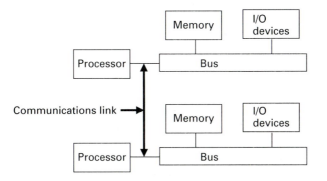

Fig. 3.5   Loosely coupled multiprocessor. (Reprinted from Harvey M. Deitel, *Operating Systems,* 2nd Edition, Copyright 1990, Addison-Wesley Publishing Co., Inc. Reading, MA. Reprinted by permission.)

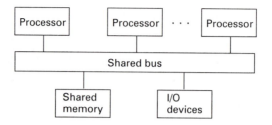

Fig. 3.6   Tightly coupled multiprocessor.

contention can be resolved. These systems are also called *symmetric multiprocessors*. In symmetric-multiprocessor systems, each processor runs the same operating system. Figure 3.6 illustrates the interconnection scheme of a tightly coupled system.

There are two types of tightly coupled systems, based on the memory access characteristics of the system. A system in which each processor has uniform access times to a shared memory is called a *uniform-memory-access (UMA) multiprocessor*. If each processor has a nonuniform memory access time—perhaps due to a local memory associated with each processor that is faster than the main shared memory—then the system is a *nonuniform-memory-access (NUMA) multiprocessor*. The UMA, NUMA, and NORMA designations were defined during research on the Mach operating system at Carnegie–Mellon University (Te87). Figure 3.7 illustrates how coupling relates to memory access.

The *shared bus* is an interconnection approach similar to the Micro Channel Architecture and EISA that is used on most UMA systems. Processors can be added to the system via attachment to the bus. If the processors have local memories on their extension cards but can also share main memory, the configuration is classified as falling between UMA and NUMA. If the processor extension cards can access only the local memory on their cards, the configuration is classified as NORMA, and the bus acts as an internal network.

In a typical UMA system, each processor has a cache. Caches cause problems in multiprocessor configurations since the hardware does not always guarantee cache coherency between processors. Furthermore, in a UMA composed of 80486s, each 80486 has its own translation lookaside buffer (TLB) for virtual address translation. Operating

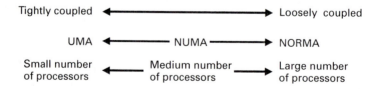

Fig. 3.7   Relationship between processor coupling and memory access. (Reprinted from A. Tevanian, Jr. "Architecture-Independent Virtual Memory Management for Parallel and Distributed Environments: The Mach Approach." Copyright 1987. PhD thesis at Carnegie-Mellon University. Reprinted by permission.)

systems supporting multiprocessing environments must take into account TLB and cache coherency between processors. Since the 80486 provides no capability to connect the processors such that TLB coherency is ensured by the hardware, this task must be performed by the operating system using a software-based interprocessor-communication scheme. As described in Section 3.8, cache coherency can be maintained in a UMA configuration if each processor snoops the bus for memory write transactions. Alternatively, a memory write to the shared memory can cause a cache invalidate signal to be sent to each processor, so that each processor can check for local stale data and can flush its cache if necessary. Figure 3.8 illustrates a UMA configuration.

UMA configurations work well for small numbers of processors; however, due to bus contention and cache flushing, nonuniform memory access times can result. Therefore we say that UMA architectures do not scale up to configurations with more processors. NUMA configurations typically attempt to avoid these problems by associating a local memory with each processor. The local memory can be accessed quickly by the local processor, but a performance penalty is incurred if the local memory is accessed by a nonlocal processor. In some NUMA systems, the local memory is addressable by only the local processor. Keeping cache contents consistent is more difficult in NUMA systems, leading most such systems to provide no cache consistency or to have no caches at all. In such cases, however, the local memory behaves in some ways like a cache. Figure 3.9 illustrates a NUMA configuration.

SUMMARY

The original IBM PC is based on the 8088 processor and is a single-bus uniprocessor system. The IBM PC/AT was the first PC to use the 80286 processor. The bus structure of the IBM PC/AT is known as the Industry Standard Architecture (ISA).

The IBM PS/2 line of systems uses a bus structure called the Micro Channel Architecture. The Micro Channel Architecture comprises a 32-bit bus that supports both

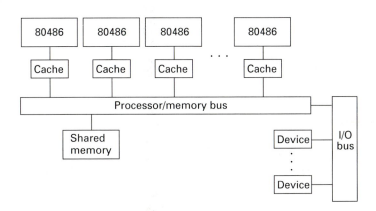

Fig. 3.8 Uniform-memory-access multiprocessor (UMA).

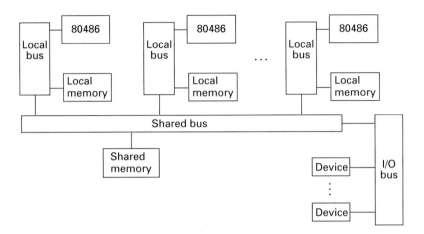

Fig. 3.9 Nonuniform-memory-access multiprocessor (NUMA).

uniprocessor and multiprocessor configurations, and a technique called bus mastering. The PS/2 line of computers includes systems based on the 8086, 80286, 80386, and 80486.

The Extended Industry Standard Architecture (EISA) is a bus architecture that competes with high-end Micro Channel systems and provides many of the same features. However, peripheral device adapter cards designed for the EISA and Micro Channel systems are not interchangeable.

Since systems with fast processors can run much faster than the memory they access, cache subsystems are used to improve performance of interactions between the processor and memory. A cache is a high-speed memory buffer between the processor and memory that is used to minimize the number of times a processor must access main memory. An algorithm is used to control the contents of the cache, and to ensure the integrity and coherency of the cache. Bus snooping, hardware transparency, cache flushing, and noncacheable memory are techniques used to maintain cache coherency. When a cache contains incorrect data or is not kept in a coherent state, we say that it contains stale data.

Multiprocessor systems use clusters of processors that run in parallel to increase throughput and performance. Multiprocessor systems are described by the coupling between the processors and by the way resources such as memory, I/O devices, and buses are shared.

TERMINOLOGY

address line	bus master
AT 80386 machines	bus master devices
BIOS	bus sharing
bus	bus snooping
bus arbitration	bus watching
bus-attached memory	cache coherency

cache controller
cache flushing
cache hit
cache-hit ratio
cache miss
contention
control line
coprocessor
coupling
cycle stealing
data line
dedicated processor
dip switch
direct memory access (DMA)
DMA controller
dynamic RAM (DRAM)
edge-triggered interrupt
Extended Graphics Array (XGA)
Extended Industry Standard
   Architecture (EISA)
floating-point coprocessor
form factor
fully associative
hardware transparency
heterogeneous multiprocessor
homogeneous multiprocessor
Industry Standard Architecture (ISA)
interrupt level
interrupt sharing
level-triggered interrupt
loosely coupled multiprocessor
master
master/slave multiprocessor

message massing
Micro Channel Architecture
motherboard
multiprocessor
noncachable memory
nonuniform-memory-access
   (NUMA) multiprocessor
nonuniform memory-access speed
no-remote-memory-access
   (NORMA) multiprocessor
parallel controller
peripheral processor
planar
power-on self-test (POST)
serial controller
set-associative cache
shared bus
shared memory
slave
snooping
static RAM (SRAM)
system ROM
tightly coupled multiprocessor
translation lookaside buffer (TLB)
uniform-memory-access
   (UMA) multiprocessor
uniprocessor
Video Graphic Array (VGA)
virtual address translation
wait state
write-back cache
write-through cache

EXERCISES

3.1 Discuss the functions of each of the lines typically included on a bus (data lines, address lines, and control lines).

3.2 Compare access times for planar memory to access times for bus-attached memory.

3.3 Describe the IBM PC system architecture.

3.4 Describe the IBM PC/AT system architecture.

3.5 What is the significance of the AT 80386 machines?

3.6 Discuss the limitations of the 16-bit ISA bus architecture that led IBM to introduce the Micro Channel Architecture.

3.7   Compare and contrast edge-triggered interrupts with level-triggered interrupts.

3.8   Why is interrupt sharing difficult on the ISA bus?

3.9   Explain the notions of bus arbitration and bus mastering associated with the Micro Channel Architecture.

3.10   Describe the IBM PS/2 system architecture.

3.11   Explain the notion of nonuniform memory access speeds in the context of the PS/2.

3.12   What was the primary motivation for the creation of the Extended Industry Standard Architecture (EISA) bus?

3.13   Describe the architecture of a typical cache memory subsystem used with an 80386.

3.14   Discuss the notions of cache miss, cache hit, and cache-hit ratio.

3.15   Explain the operation of write-through caches and write-back caches. Which is faster? Explain your answer.

3.16   Discuss each of the following methods of maintaining cache coherency: bus watching, hardware transparency, noncacheable memory, and cache flushing.

3.17   Why is a processor–coprocessor configuration fundamentally different in nature from a multiprocessor configuration?

3.18   Is using a RISC processor on a graphics card to perform graphics operations instead of having the main processor performing the operations, considered a multiprocessor configuration? Explain your answer.

3.19   What attributes characterize a multiprocessor system?

3.20   Distinguish between homogeneous multiprocessors and heterogeneous multiprocessors.

3.21   Distinguish between master/slave multiprocessing and peer multiprocessing.

3.22   Describe the architecture of a typical loosely coupled multiprocessor system. How is communication between the processors accomplished in such a system?

3.23   Describe the architecture of a typical tightly coupled multiprocessor system. How is communication between the processors accomplished in such a system?

3.24   What kind of hardware support is typically provided in a tightly coupled multiprocessor to resolve processor contention over shared memory?

3.25   Distinguish among UMA, NUMA, and NORMA multiprocessors.

3.26   How can cache coherency be maintained in a UMA multiprocessor?

4

Operating System Architectures

Within the Entry Systems Division, we really are dealing with systems software, the operating system, database management, communications. . . . We have no concept of a plan that would have our customers dependent on us for a very high percentage of the applications that they use.

William C. Lowe

Protection is not a principle, but an expedient.

Benjamin Disraeli

"If seven maids with seven mops
Swept it for half a year,
Do you suppose," the Walrus said,
"That they could get it clear?"

Lewis Carroll

The most general definition of beauty . . . Multeity in Unity.

Samuel Taylor Coleridge

Outline

4.1 INTRODUCTION

This chapter describes the overall architecture of the 16-bit and 32-bit OS/2 systems. To provide the reader with a background for the OS/2 content, we first review the overall architecture of the DOS system. Each system is described with respect to the structure and layering of the system, the architecture and content of the *application-program interface (API),* and the structure and tools used to construct programs and the system itself.

4.2 DOS SYSTEM

The DOS system is a single-user, single-task system: It is designed to allow one program at a time to use the processor and device resources. Therefore, DOS is the simplest type of operating system; it is a sequential one. Due to the lack of protection in the 8088 architecture, DOS does not provide any hardware enforced separation between the operating system and the running program. Both the DOS system and the programs can access all facilities in the machine, including special instructions, ROM BIOS routines, and the actual I/O ports that control the peripheral devices. Both the system and its programs execute using physical memory addresses and have the capability of altering each other.

As we saw in Chapter 1, the DOS system is composed of the DOS *kernel,* which provides all the system supervisor functions, and device drivers, which provide a layer of software between the system and the actual hardware. The system also requires a *shell* that allows users to start programs and to interact with the system. The shell provided with DOS Versions 1.0 through 3.3 is called COMMAND.COM, and it is a primitive command-line-oriented program. DOS 4.0 introduced a simple text-oriented user-interface shell to make the system easier for novice users not familiar with the command shell. Figure 4.1 illustrates the layering of the DOS system.

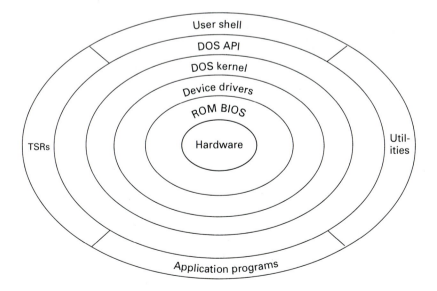

Fig. 4.1   DOS system structure.

DOS supports two types of devices—*block devices,* such as the disk and diskette drives, and *character devices,* such as the keyboard, printer, and serial devices. DOS maintains a data structure called the *device chain* that maps the logical device names onto the appropriate device driver that services each device. Block devices are designated by a letter in the alphabet followed by a colon—*A:, B:,* through *Z:.* Character devices are designated by names up to eight characters long, followed by a colon, such as *PRN:* and *LPT1:* for printer devices, and *COM1:* for serial devices. Figure 4.2 illustrates the DOS device chain.

The DOS device chain can be extended by the addition of a device driver to the system. Device drivers for devices that are not supported by the basic DOS system are installed when the system is started. Device drivers manipulate their respective devices by utilizing the ROM BIOS subroutines or by directly accessing the device hardware. ROM BIOS routines are accessed by the software interrupt mechanism.

4.3 DOS API

An executing program makes service requests of the DOS kernel by calling an *application program interface (API),* or by making a *system call.* The term "API" can refer to a collection of system call routines, or to a single system call routine. The API is also conceived as the boundary between applications and the operating system, providing a level of *information hiding.* The DOS kernel provides the DOS API to DOS programs. The DOS API contains functions for rudimentary memory management, file and device I/O, and program loading and termination.

Since the DOS API does not contain functions for graphics or mouse control, many DOS programs use a combination of ROM BIOS routines and direct hardware access for managing a graphic display or mouse. Therefore, the ROM BIOS routines should be considered part of the DOS API, since many DOS programs bypass the DOS I/O interfaces and use the lower-level code.

When a system call or a call to a subroutine in a library or program is used, a set of *calling conventions* describes how routines call each other. The conventions, also called *linkage conventions,* define rules for subroutine names, instructions for transferring control between routines, and conventions for register usage in the linkage between the routines. Calling conventions are usually invisible to a programmer using a high-level

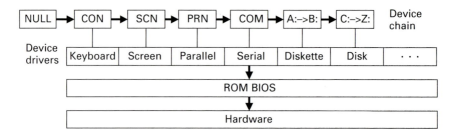

Fig. 4.2   DOS device chain.

language, but system programmers and designers pay attention to the required functions
and performance of the calling conventions because the latter have a significant effect
on the overall structure and performance of the system.

The calling conventions for the DOS API require the requestor to place the parameters in registers, including a special parameter that denotes by an *ordinal number* the
specific system call requested. The program then issues a software interrupt instruction
that causes the program's execution to transfer control to the DOS kernel. The DOS kernel dispatches the system call by looking up the system call number provided in the
parameters in a table and calling the appropriate routine. After the routine completes,
control returns to the requesting program with a *return code* that indicates the status of
the requested operation.

Most early DOS programs were written in BASIC and assembler. However, by
1984, high-level languages (HLLs) such as C were preferred by most programmers.
Since most HLLs use a *stack* for parameter passing and CALL instructions for control
transfers, they cannot directly invoke the DOS API, since the API uses registers for parameter passing and software interrupts for control transfer. Therefore, most HLLs provide *bindings* that move system call parameters from the stack to the registers and that
issue the software interrupt. This mismatch in calling convention models degrades application performance, since each system call takes slightly longer to execute. As we shall
see in Section 4.4, these bindings are packaged in a library and are linked into the program when it is created. Figure 4.3 illustrates a DOS system call with a binding layer.

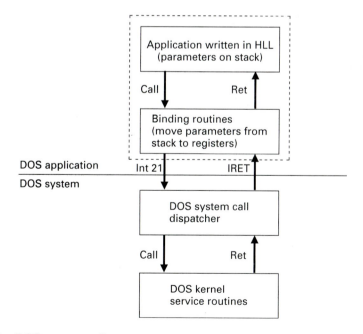

Fig. 4.3   DOS system call.

4.4 DOS PROGRAMS

A DOS program is a collection of code and data segments that is stored in an *executable (EXE) file* on a secondary storage medium. When a program is executed, its code and data objects are loaded into memory by the operating system *loader,* and the address of the initial routine within the code object is loaded into the instruction pointer of the processor. Most programs include a *stack,* a last-in-first-out (LIFO) data object used for temporary memory allocations. Due to the 8088 memory architecture, DOS memory objects are segments.

A program is specified in a source file using a programming language. Regardless of in what programming language a program is written, the program must be translated into machine instructions executable by the processor of the target system, and formatted into an executable file. Assembler language is used to specify programs using machine instructions, whereas a high-level language such as C or FORTRAN allows programmers to specify a program without having to understand the underlying machine language. High-level language programs are translated into machine instructions by compilers.

Due to the complex nature of programs, it is often useful to organize a program into separate *program modules*. Each program module contains a collection of code and data dedicated to a specific function of the program. By separating the components of a program in this fashion, programmers are better able to minimize errors and to make a program readable and maintainable. To enable programs to be developed in this fashion, the DOS and OS/2 development systems provide a two-step architecture that allows a program specified in multiple source files to be compiled separately, and then to be combined into an executable file by a tool called a *link editor*. The intermediate file created by a high-level language compiler or assembler is called an *object (OBJ) file*. Since all language translators use the same intermediate file format, the link editor is not programming-language specific, but rather is system specific. The link editor collects object files and combines them into a single system specific EXE file. Figure 4.4 illustrates the program development process.

So that tested subroutine modules can be reused, and so that programs can specify a minimum number of instructions for their tasks, *library (LIB) files* are supported by most development systems. A library is a collection of subroutines created using a *librarian,* a tool that collects single OBJ files into a library. When a reference to a subroutine in a library is made by a program, the compiler stores the external reference in the OBJ file. When the link editor is invoked, it resolves these external references to their locations either in another OBJ file or in a library.

There are two types of libraries that differ in the way they are linked or *bound* to programs. *Static link libraries* are linked into the final executable load module when the program is created. *Dynamic link libraries (DLLs)* are not linked into the final executable module, but instead are bound dynamically to the calling program when the program is loaded into memory or when they are loaded explicitly by an already executing program. When dynamic link libraries are used, the program load modules tend to be smaller and the delayed binding allows libraries and systems to be extended without

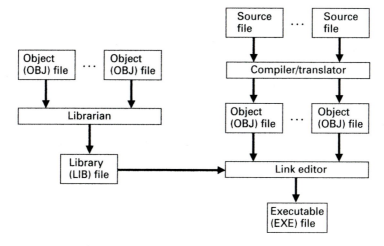

Fig. 4.4   Program development process.

requiring the programs to be recompiled and relinked. DOS supports only static link libraries, but both OS/2 and Windows 3.0 support dynamic link libraries. Like programs, libraries contain code and data—however, they do not contain an initial routine address, since they are called by programs. A library subroutine usually runs using the stack of the calling routine. Examples of libraries are the *run-time libraries* that come with programming languages and the *system libraries* or bindings that operating systems provide to allow programs to access their APIs.

The formats for intermediate object modules and for DOS executable modules were defined during the development of DOS. The Intel *Object Module Format (OMF)* describes the format of the object or OBJ files, and the *DOS Technical Reference* provided by IBM describes the DOS executable file format for executable or EXE files. The OMF is defined based on the characteristics of the 8086 processor, and supports multiple segments and all the addressing modes of the 8086. Therefore, the object module format exhibits the trait of *processor architectural dependence*. However, the EXE format is defined based on the characteristics both of the processor and of the DOS loader and memory environment. Therefore, the EXE format also exhibits the trait of *operating system architectural dependence*.

The OMF defines an object module to be a series of records that describe the memory objects of a source file in terms of *logical segments*. When a source file is compiled, the object module produced contains the logical code and data segments that represent the program. The object module also contains records that describe whether the symbols in the module are *public, external,* or *hidden*. A public definition of a symbol in an object module implies that the symbol can be referenced by other object modules when the modules are linked. Public definitions are used for global program data and routines that are used in multiple object modules of a program. An external symbol is used in an object module to denote a reference to a symbol in another object module. The *extern* keyword of the C programming language causes the compiler to generate external definitions in an object module. If a symbol is defined as hidden, it can be referenced only within the object module in which it is defined. The *static* keyword of the C programming language causes the compiler to place hidden definitions in an object module.

All address references within the logical segments are unknown at the time that the object module is created. Therefore, *fixup records,* which describe the locations that have unknown addresses and the types of those unknown addresses, are inserted into the object module. Addresses within a segment (near or short) are called *self-relative,* and addresses of other segments (far) are called *segment-relative.*

The DOS linker combines logical segments into *physical segments* and resolves self-relative fixups. The linker accepts as input object modules and library modules, and produces a DOS format executable file.

When the linker combines logical segments into physical segments, the addresses of the self-relative fixups can be resolved since they are relative to the base address of the segment. Since the base addresses of the physical segments are unknown when the object modules are linked, the segment-relative fixups are propagated into the executable file for relocation by the system loader. The ordering of the logical segments within physical segments is controlled using *group directives* in the object module.

The DOS system defines the format of executable modules loaded by the DOS loader. Figure 4.5 illustrates a simple DOS EXE file. Contained in an executable file are the segments of the program, the stack pointer (SS:SP), and the instruction pointer (CS:IP) of the starting point. The linker determines what to put in the starting point field of the EXE file from the input object modules. An object module may have a special main record indicating that it contains the starting point for code execution. Only a single OBJ can have this information when a program is linked, and the information is retained in

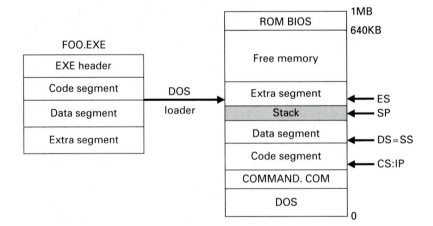

Fig. 4.5   DOS executable (EXE) file.

the executable file. Typically, the starting point is in the run-time library, since it must be initialized before the main entry point of the program defined by the programmer.

As previously mentioned, when a DOS program is linked, all references from the object modules that are input to the linker, except the references to segment addresses, are resolved. For the remaining segment-relative fixups, the linker inserts a relocation or fixup record into the EXE header that identifies (to the DOS loader) locations within the EXE file that contain addresses dependent on where the image is loaded into memory. For example, if a program executes the instructions in Fig. 4.6 to set the DS register to address the data segment DGROUP, the value of DGROUP to insert into the MOV instruction is not known until the program is loaded into memory.

Therefore, DOS programs are relocatable on a segment basis. Note that there are no references to other program or to library modules in a DOS EXE file. When the program is linked, all self-relative fixups in the OBJ files being linked that reference code or data within the program are resolved.

4.4.1 Memory Models

Since there are many ways to use multiple segments in a program, the programming languages for 8086 environments need a model for how a program's segments are specified. Assembler programs have complete control over which instructions and variety of segmentation are used in applications. Most high-level languages have no concept of segmentation, so they have to be extended to allow programmers to optimize segment usage in programs. Therefore, there are several program models available based on their segment usage: *small model, medium model, compact model, large model,* and *huge model.* Each programming model requires a unique version of the program-language run-time library for linking the application.

A small-model program is similar to a compact-model program, except that the code is contained in a separate segment. Therefore, a small-model program can contain at most 64KB of code and at most 64KB of data and stack. Figure 4.7 illustrates the segments of a small-model program.

```
                    Code segment

                    ⋮

                    MOV  AX, DGROUP      ; fixup here
                    MOV  DS, AX          ; load segment register

                    ⋮

                    Code ends
```

Fig. 4.6   Example of segment-relative fixup.

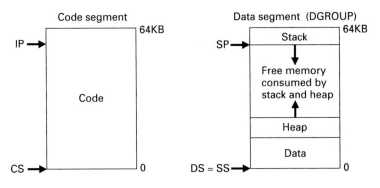

Fig. 4.7   Small-model program.

A program written in the C language must have an initial routine called *main*. When the program is loaded, a routine within the C run-time system called *startup* is called by the DOS loader after the program is loaded into memory. This routine initializes the C run-time library, loads the DS and SS segment registers to point to the data and stack segments, and then calls the program's main routine. The data segment is also called the *automatic data segment* or *DGROUP*. Since a small-model program contains only a single code segment and a single data segment, it does not make any intersegment (far) references.

Let us consider how a DOS program written in C is constructed using the programming tools. The example in Fig 4.8 shows a program composed of two separate C source modules that are compiled and then are linked together statically by the DOS link editor.

Assume that the program to be constructed is called MAIN.EXE and consists of a main routine that calls a subroutine named *foo*. The program uses the small memory model since less than 64KB of code and less than 64KB of data are necessary. However, the program is divided into two source files, MAIN.C and FOO.C. MAIN.C contains the main routine and FOO.C contains the *foo* subroutine. Since these routines are in different modules, the C source code in the file MAIN.C has an extern statement to tell the compiler that the address of subroutine *foo* will be resolved later by the link editor. Figure 4.8 illustrates the example program.

Compiling MAIN.C produces an object module called MAIN.OBJ, which contains an intermediate representation of the logical segments that represent the contents of MAIN.C. So that the linker can later process the CALL instruction generated by the C compiler to execute subroutine *foo*, a fixup record is inserted into MAIN.OBJ referencing the call instruction. Since the call instruction is to a target within the code segment, the type of the fixup is self-relative. The MAIN.OBJ object file also contains an *external definition record* for the reference to the name of subroutine *foo*.

When FOO.C is compiled, file FOO.OBJ is created. Besides the contents of the logical segments, FOO.OBJ has a *public definitions record* with the name of the subroutine *foo*. Without the public definitions record, the linker would treat subroutine *foo* as *hidden,* and would abort any attempted fixup resolution to subroutine *foo*. When the link editor links the two object files and the C run-time library into an executable image, it combines the contents of the logical segments in the two object files and matches the

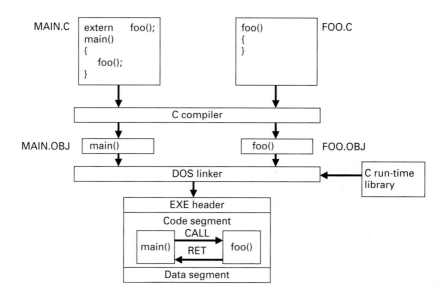

Fig. 4.8   DOS example program (static linking).

external definitions in MAIN.OBJ with the public definitions in FOO.OBJ. Then, the fixup for the call instruction to subroutine *foo* is replaced by the correct offset within the physical code segment created by the linker.

The other programming models—medium, large, and huge—allow more than 64KB of code and/or data to be used in different combinations. The medium model allows for more than a single code segment. Therefore, all code pointers in the medium model are of the far type and use segment-relative fixups, since they must contain both segment and offset values (a 16:16 or far pointer). The compiler generates the code from each C source file into a unique code segment, and uses the CALL FAR instruction when referencing a routine in another segment. Since the address of a segment is not known until the program is loaded into memory, only the offset portion of the CALL FAR instruction can be fixed up by the linker. The linker leaves a segment-relative fixup record in the final EXE file, to tell the DOS loader that there is a reference to a segment address that needs to be fixed up before the starting point is called. The compact model allows a program to have a single code segment and multiple data segments.

The large model allows data items as well as code items to be in separate segments, and all data pointers become far pointers by default. However, none of these programming models can minimize, as well as can an assembler program, the number of times that segment registers must be reloaded. This inefficiency occurs because programs code in languages that allow freeform pointer arithmetic and casting (like C) can have multiple levels of pointer aliases. This makes sophisticated flow analysis during program optimization difficult and, in many cases, infeasible. Therefore, languages for the Intel segmented architecture usually provide limited optimization of segment loading for far pointers.

4.5 OS/2 1.X SYSTEM

"OS/2 1.X" is used in this book to indicate the 16-bit versions of the OS/2 system. OS/2 is a single-user, multitasking operating system. It performs centralized resource management for sharing the processor, main and secondary memory, mass-storage devices, I/O devices such as the keyboard, display, and mouse, and communications interfaces. OS/2 provides architectural relief for the 640KB memory limitation of the DOS/8088 environment. OS/2 1.X also provides support for running a DOS application in order to provide backward compatibility for users migrating to OS/2 from DOS. The Sections 4.5.1 through 4.5.7 give an overview of the structure and major functions of the system.

4.5.1 System Structure

The OS/2 system is composed of the *kernel, device drivers, dynamic link libraries,* and application programs. Figure 4.9 illustrates the structure of the OS/2 system.

The kernel is the heart of the system; it contains the control program that runs with supervisor privileges. As in DOS, the kernel uses device drivers to access the system's hardware resources. The most critical portions of the system—such as multitasking, memory management, interprocess communication, DOS compatibility, and I/O—reside in the kernel. The architecture and content of the kernel are analyzed throughout this book as the system is exposed component by component.

Many of the system's APIs are located in the kernel, but some APIs are located in dynamic link libraries—shared libraries that can be used to extend the functionality of the system. As we shall see in Section 4.5.4, the location of APIs is transparent to applications, so designers can move and extend functions as requirements dictate.

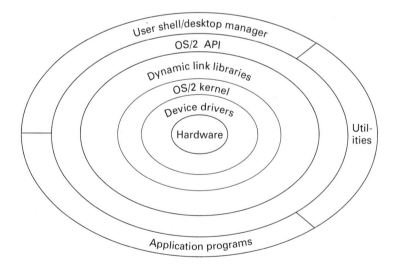

Fig. 4.9   OS/2 system structure.

4.5.2 Multitasking

The OS/2 multitasking architecture provides the capability to execute programs concurrently in a protected environment. It defines the model used for sharing the system's resources. The model consists of a hierarchy of multitasking objects called *sessions, processes,* and *threads.* The session is at the top of the hierarchy, and the thread is at the bottom. The session is the unit of user I/O device sharing. Processes are analogous to programs, and are the unit of sharing for such resources as memory, files, semaphores, queues, and threads. A thread is the basic unit of execution, and a single process may have multiple threads that execute concurrently within it.

Each session contains a *logical video buffer, logical keyboard, logical mouse,* and one or more processes that are said to be *running in* or *attached to* the session. The *logical devices* are per-session representations of the actual devices. Processes running in the session perform their user I/O on the session's logical devices. Only one session at a time has its logical devices mapped onto the actual devices; this session is called the *foreground session.* The other sessions are in the *background.* Users can change the current foreground session by issuing the commands to switch between sessions with the keyboard or mouse. Sessions are used to provide an infrastructure for program management and user I/O device sharing.

A process is the basic unit of resource management in OS/2. A process is created by the invocation of a particular program. Programs are invoked by issuance of a *DosExecPgm* system call with the name of an executable program file as a parameter. Each process has its own memory, threads, and file system and *interprocess communication (IPC)* data structures. When a process is created, it contains one thread, or sequential execution path. The thread is the unit of processor dispatching, and each thread has its own scheduling priority. A thread can create a new thread within a process by calling *DosCreateThread.* All threads within a process share all the process's resources, including the address space. The multithread process model helps the system to achieve a high degree of parallelism, concurrent execution, and interactivity. Since threads are less expensive to create and maintain than are processes, the cost of achieving concurrency is significantly lower than is possible in a single-thread process system such as UNIX.

OS/2 is a preemptive, priority-based, multitasking system. The scheduler determines what is the highest-priority thread in the system and runs that thread for a *timeslice.* At the expiration of a timeslice, the thread is preempted by the system, and the scheduler determines whether another thread is ready to run. The scheduler implements a multilevel priority scheme with *dynamic priority variation* and *round-robin scheduling* within a priority level. Dynamic priority variation changes the priority of threads based on their activity to improve overall performance and responsiveness. Round-robin dispatching within a priority level ensures that all threads at a common priority level have an equal chance to execute.

OS/2 is interrupt driven to allow the processor to be used while I/O is occurring. If an interrupt occurs while a thread is executing, and another thread of higher priority becomes ready to run, the original thread will be preempted to allow the higher priority thread to run. However, OS/2 does not provide complete preemption. A thread can be preempted only when it is running in user code. If the thread has issued a system call and is running OS/2 kernel code, the thread will not be preempted until it exits the kernel, unless it is running in the highest priority class.

4.5.3 Memory Management

OS/2 1.X presents a segmented memory model that takes advantage of the 80286 processor's virtual memory capabilities. Since the system runs in 80286 protected mode (except for the DOS environment), the system and applications can use up to 16MB of physical memory, a significant breakthrough of the 640KB barrier associated with DOS/8088 systems. However, each segment is limited to 64KB due to the 16-bit architecture of the 80286. The OS/2 1.X segmented memory model is also known as the *16:16 memory model* since a 16-bit selector to a segment must be specified, as well as a 16-bit offset into that segment, to address a single byte of memory.

The memory protection features of the 80286 described in Chapter 2 are used to isolate the system memory from user memory, and to protect individual processes from one another. The memory segments that make up the system are mapped into privilege level 0 of the 80286's ring architecture, the highest privilege level. Executing at ring 0 is also known as executing in *supervisor mode*. The system is mapped by the 80286 GDT to make it accessible from every process. Since the system is mapped at ring 0 and processes are mapped at rings 2 and 3, the system is protected from the processes.

Each process is allocated its own LDT for mapping the process's address space into physical memory. Memory allocated by the process is mapped into the LDT at privilege level 2 or 3. When a thread context switch occurs between threads in different processes, the OS/2 kernel switches process address spaces by switching LDTs. Since each process has its own LDT, processes are protected from one another.

The OS/2 memory manager supports sharing of memory among processes. Shared memory is a powerful form of interprocess communication, and plays a large role in the architecture of shared libraries and subsystems. There are two varieties of shared memory: named and anonymous. *Named shared memory* is accessed by a name, whereas in *anonymous shared memory,* access is controlled directly by processes. Both named and anonymous shared memory are implemented by a common virtual address in the address space of different processes that maps a single physical memory segment. *Instance memory* is used to provide to each process a unique copy of a data segment. Like shared memory, instance memory is mapped at the same virtual address in each process's address space.

OS/2 also manages memory such that more memory can be allocated than the machine actually has. This service, called *memory overcommit,* allows the user to continue running programs in a memory-constrained environment. Segments that are not actively being used can be swapped out to the *swap file* on a secondary storage medium to make room in physical memory for more segments. When a segment that is swapped out is referenced, the system *swapper* brings the segment into memory and restarts the operation that referenced the segment. Since all the memory used by a segment must be physically contiguous, OS/2 also moves segments in physical memory to maximize the amount of free space available. This segment motion is called *compaction*. Code segments and read-only segments can be discarded rather than swapped, since they can be reloaded on demand from their original disk images. This type of memory management is called *demand segment swapping*. Since segments are of variable length and the performance of personal computer secondary storage media is relatively poor, the system swapping policy is to allow applications to continue running when physical memory is overcommitted, rather than to attempt to provide large amounts of virtual memory on the secondary storage media.

4.5.4 Dynamic Linking

Dynamic linking allows the binding of code and data references to be delayed until the program is actually loaded or until the program specifically requests the operating system to link dynamically to a *dynamic link library (DLL)*. The former type of dynamic linking is called *load-time dynamic linking,* whereas the latter is called *run-time dynamic linking*. There are two types of executable modules in the OS/2 environment: EXE modules for programs and DLL modules containing shared libraries. Both module types use the OS/2 segmented executable file format, but they are distinguished by a special bit in the executable file header.

Dynamic linking requires *imports* and *exports* of code and data objects across EXE or DLL modules. The OS/2 linker allows the programmer to specify that an external reference is in another executable module; this causes the linker to create an *import record* in the *import table* of the EXE header that describes the external reference by *module name* and *object name,* or *ordinal number*. When the OS/2 loader attempts to load an EXE into memory following a *DosExecPgm* request, or to load a DLL as the result of a reference in an EXE or a *DosLoadModule* request, it attempts to resolve a module's imports. It attempts resolution by loading the module(s) that export the desired import references, and performing fixups on the dynamic link references in the module being loaded. The program loading process continues until the program or library is ready to execute. If the system loader is unable to resolve a load-time dynamic link request, the program or library load is aborted. If necessary, one or more DLL may be loaded and fixed up so that loading of an EXE or a DLL can be completed. Figure 4.10 illustrates how dynamic linking could be used for linkage between the main and *foo* routines in the example cited earlier.

Whereas an EXE file typically only imports dynamic links, a DLL file usually imports and exports dynamic links. If an EXE attempts to import a dynamic link and there is no corresponding exported dynamic link, the program load fails. In general, the dynamic link mechanism can be likened to an external reference that exists in a different program module. All dynamic links use 16:16 far addresses, since they resolve linkages across segments in different program modules.

Dynamic linking is also a powerful mechanism for providing linkages to shared code and data objects in a multitasking virtual memory environment. It provides an extendible and flexible foundation for meeting the criteria of API abstraction and information hiding.

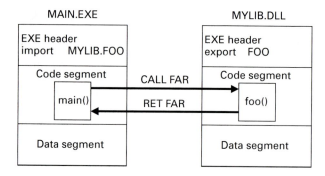

Fig. 4.10   Dynamic linking.

Another benefit of dynamic linking is that EXE files are not as large, since commonly used routines can be placed in a DLL instead of being replicated in each EXE that uses them. This results in saved disk space and potentially faster program loading. Dynamic linking is described further in Chapter 6 with respect to memory management, and in Chapter 7 with respect to interprocess communication and resource sharing.

4.5.5 I/O

As in DOS, devices in OS/2 are categorized as either block devices or character devices, and the same naming conventions are used. In fact, the system uses a similar device chain for managing the devices and their names. However, the user I/O devices—such as the display, keyboard, and mouse—are accessed differently from in DOS. Reentrant subsystems with well-defined APIs allow concurrently executing processes to share the user I/O devices. The block devices are accessed using the file system API as in DOS, and the other character devices are accessed by APIs.

OS/2 supports the FAT file system used by DOS, and consequently can read and write DOS files. Although this capability is desirable from compatibility and migration standpoints, the FAT file system was not originally designed to support many concurrent I/O requests from different processes on large block devices. Therefore, OS/2 provides an alternative file system, called the *High Performance File System (HPFS)*. To provide an architecture in which programs are transparent to the type of file system, OS/2 has an *installable file system (IFS)*. The system has facilities for installing multiple file systems, and a standard file system API to which all installable file systems adhere to. Figure 4.11 illustrates the OS/2 file system architecture.

OS/2 device drivers are significantly different from DOS device drivers. Like the kernel, they run in the most privileged execution state, privilege level 0. Device drivers have two main entry points: a *strategy routine* that receives requests from the kernel, and an *interrupt routine* that is called when a hardware interrupt occurs. Since the strategy routine and interrupt routine may both need access to the same structures, the device driver must carefully serialize access to shared structures and manage race conditions between the strategy and interrupt routines. Strategy routine requests are made in the

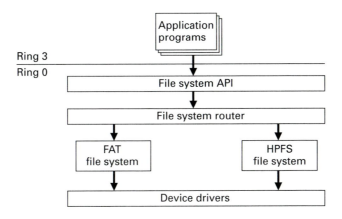

Fig. 4.11 OS/2 file system architecture.

form of *request packets* that describe the operation. Device drivers perform the requested operation using a combination of the hardware and a set of system services created
specially for device drivers called *device-help (DevHelp)* routines. Figure 4.12 illustrates
the interfaces of device drivers.

When a request to a device driver's strategy routine occurs, it is made within the
context of the currently running thread. The strategy routine either satisfies the request
immediately and returns, or initiates an I/O request that will complete on a hardware interrupt notification and blocks the requesting thread. When the strategy routine blocks
the requesting thread, the system dispatches another thread to run. When the original
thread's interrupt occurs, notifying the device driver that the I/O is complete, the interrupt routine is not able to assume that it is running in the context of the requesting
thread. Thus, the system must provide services that allow device drivers to maintain
global data that can be accessed in any context. This facility also allows device drivers
to service multiple requests concurrently and to perform overlapping I/O operations.
Chapter 8 provides a more detailed description of the OS/2 I/O architecture.

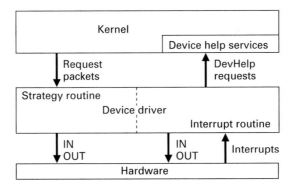

Fig. 4.12 Device driver interfaces.

4.5.6 Presentation Manager

The Presentation Manager (PM) is the graphical user interface for OS/2. It provides an environment for graphical applications to share the video display in a windowed environment. PM programs have a common user interface composed of windows, scroll bars, dialog boxes, pull-down menus, and other desktop controls that are accessed through the keyboard, mouse, or other user input devices. The user interface of PM applications is easier to learn and more consistent than are traditional user interfaces such as command lines or application-specific interfaces.

The PM consists of a large API that contains functions for managing windows and performing graphic operations on a *device-independent presentation space*. The PM maps the applications' requests to alter the presentation space into device-dependent operations on the actual output device, whether that device is a video display or high-resolution printer. This strategy allows all PM programs to be transparent to the specific characteristics and nuances of the actual output device. The PM accomplishes this task with the assistance of special PM device drivers that are different from the base system's device drivers.

When OS/2 is started, the system executes the user shell, a PM program called the *desktop manager*. The desktop manager provides an icon-oriented interface that allows users to start programs, to switch between programs, and to manage programs as groups. The desktop manager represents each program in the system with a name or icon. The desktop manager and all other PM programs share a single session called the PM session. Programs that do not use the PM API for their user I/O are called full-screen programs, and they each run in their own session. Chapter 9 gives a complete treatment of session management and the PM architecture.

4.5.7 DOS Compatibility

One of the most critical features of OS/2 is the capability to run DOS programs. This facility allows users migrating to OS/2 from DOS to continue running their current programs. It helps customers to preserve their investments in DOS software while migrating to OS/2. DOS compatibility also permits OS/2 users to draw on the large applications base of DOS programs, until there are comparable OS/2 programs available. However, capturing the unprotected DOS environment in a system such as OS/2 that provides traditional resource management is a difficult problem. This task is even more difficult since the 80286 architecture does not provide the ability to run 8088 real-mode programs in the protected-mode environment.

The goal of OS/2's DOS environment for 80286-based systems is to allow a single DOS application to run in the foreground while OS/2 programs continue to run in the background. Thus, DOS programs do not benefit from the multitasking features of OS/2. When the DOS environment is moved to the background by the user, its execution is frozen. The DOS environment exists in a special session called the *DOS session*.

OS/2 uses a technique known as *mode switching* to support the concurrent execution of the DOS environment in real mode, and OS/2 programs in protected mode. Because the 80286 was designed to switch easily into protected mode from real mode, but not from protected mode to real mode, this mode switch back to real mode from protected mode is accomplished with the assistance of extra circuitry provided on 80286-class machines.

Due to the presence of mode switching, certain critical parts of the OS/2 kernel and device drivers must be accessible in both real mode and protected mode. These include device and interrupt management, mode and context switching, and anything that must be accessed at interrupt time. Code that can run in either real or protected mode is called *bimodal code*. Bimodal code enables OS/2 to minimize the amount of mode switching that is done on performance-critical paths, such as device and interrupt handling. However, bimodal code must reside in the physical memory addresses below 640KB to be addressable in both real and protected modes. The challenge of partitioning the system into bimodal and protected-mode code so that as much of the lower 640KB would be available to DOS applications was one of the most difficult in the design of the system. For instance, although the file system is used by DOS applications, it resides in memory above 1MB, and the system mode switches to protected mode to service DOS application file system requests. Chapter 10 describes the architecture for DOS compatibility in much greater detail.

4.6 OS/2 1.X API

Dynamic linking is at the center of the OS/2 API architecture. Because it uses dynamic linking as the linkage for system calls, OS/2 has the flexibility to extend and relocate system functions without requiring programs to be recompiled and relinked. Also, the location of an API is transparent to the requestor, so API routines can be in the OS/2 kernel or in a DLL module. This capability has allowed OS/2 to be extended by communications and database products.

The OS/2 API calling conventions specify that all API parameters are placed on the stack, and the CALL FAR instruction is used to transfer control to an API service routine. Since this model parallels the linkage architecture found in most high-level languages, APIs can be invoked directly instead of requiring a library of bindings. Each API preserves the state of the registers except AX, which is used for return codes. Also, it is the API routine's responsibility to remove the requestor's parameters from the stack on completion of service.

The OS/2 API is composed of several APIs that are grouped according to the services they provide. The prefixes of the names of the functions within an API indicate the portion of the OS/2 API to which the functions belong. The base system API is called the *Dos API*. The keyboard, mouse, and video subsystem APIs used by full-screen programs are called the *Kbd, Mou,* and *Vio APIs,* respectively. The PM API is distinguished from the base system API by the prefixes *Win* for window management, and *Gpi* for graphics management. Table 4.1 summarizes the names of the OS/2 APIs and the type of functionality contained in each API.

Category	API name	Functions
DOS (base)	*DosXXX*	Multitasking, interprocess communication, memory management, dynamic linking, file system, exceptions, signals, session management
KBD (base)	*KbdXXX*	Logical keyboard management
VIO (base)	*VioXXX*	Logical video management
MOU (base)	*MouXXX*	Logical mouse management
WIN (PM)	*WinXXX*	Window management and I/O
GPI (PM)	*GpiXXX*	Presentation graphics

Table 4.1   OS/2 API content.

4.7 OS/2 1.X Programs

Similar to the DOS programs, 16-bit OS/2 programs are collections of relocatable segments containing code and data. Also, the same variety of language memory models found in DOS applications are available to support the different flavors of segmentation in OS/2. The major difference between DOS and OS/2 with regard to program structure and development is the usage of selectors for segment fixups, dynamic linking, and the different API functions in OS/2. The OMF used by the OS/2 development tools is the same as that on the 8086, since the instruction sets and addressing modes are virtually identical. OS/2 uses an enhanced executable file format that provides support for dynamic linking and demand loading of segments from EXE and DLL modules.

4.8 OS/2 2.X SYSTEM

"OS/2 2.X" is the general moniker used in this book to reference the 32-bit versions of the OS/2 system. At the time this book was published, OS/2 2.0 was the first and only 32-bit version of the OS/2 system. OS/2 2.0 is targeted for the Intel 80386 and 80486 computer systems. It uses the paging feature of the 80386 to provide a demand-paged, virtual memory environment that supports a new 32-bit portable programming model. OS/2 2.0 provides binary compatibility for OS/2 1.X applications and dynamic link libraries. The DOS compatibility environment is enhanced to take advantage of the virtual 8086 mode of the 80386, enabling multiple DOS sessions to run concurrently and in the background. In general, the system has the same content as do the OS/2 1.X systems, but it is scaled up to 32 bits and has an architecture designed to allow applications, dynamic link libraries, and ultimately the system itself to be portable to other processor platforms.

OS/2 2.0 also provides greater ease of use in the areas of installation and the user shell. It features a PM-based installation program, and the capability of performing installations across a local area network. A new user shell called the *workplace shell* provides an object-oriented environment that seamlessly integrates programs and data so that the system is intuitively easy to use. Sections 4.8.1 through 4.8.6 describe the major enhancements compared to the 16-bit version of the system.

4.8.1 Memory Management

The overriding goal in the design of the 32-bit programming environment is to provide an architecture that allows applications, subsystems, and the system itself to be portable to processing platforms other than the uniprocessor Intel 80X86-based machines. This requirement led to the development of a new memory model called the *flat model,* which enables processes to view memory as a large linear address space addressable by 32-bit offsets, rather than as a collection of segments, as in OS/2 1.X systems. The flat model is an architecture that is easily portable to most processor architectures, since all that the hardware must provide is a base register capable of addressing a large, paged linear address space and an offset register for indexing into the address space. The flat model effectively hides all segmentation from the programmer, resulting in a portable programming model with much higher performance than a segmented system could provide. The flat memory model is also known as the *0:32 memory model,* since only the 32-bit offset into the process's address space is used to develop the address of a single byte of memory. OS/2 2.0 was not designed to be a 386-specific OS/2, but 32-bit OS/2 is implemented on the 80386 and 80486 platform.

In the flat model, the basic unit of allocation and sharing is a 4KB page, and memory is divided not into segments, but rather into *memory objects* that consist of one or more 4KB pages. Memory objects are not relocatable (as segments are in OS/2 1.X), are allocated in units of 4KB, can be larger than 64KB, and are aligned on page boundaries in the process address space. A major difference between memory objects in the flat model and segments in the 16-bit segmented model is memory protection. In the 16-bit segmented model, protection exists on a per-segment basis. However, in the flat model all an application's memory objects exist within a single large segment, so the Intel segment protection semantics are bypassed and 80386 page-level protection is used to manage the memory in the process's address space. To provide each process with a unique address space, OS/2 2.0 allocates a different set of page tables for each address space, instead of allocating an LDT per process like OS/2 1.X.

The high performance of applications, subsystems, and the system using the flat model is derived from several areas. In the segmented or 16-bit model, segment registers had to be reloaded with selectors every time a different 64KB block of memory needed to be accessed. These selector load operations are expensive in protected mode on 80X86 processors due to the checking that must occur to provide segment protection. In the flat model, a 32-bit offset relative to the base of the process address space is used to address any byte of memory without reloading any selectors. In fact, 32-bit programs and subsystems do not use or know about the segment registers. Performance is also increased by the use of the 32-bit registers and arithmetic that the 32-bit Intel architecture provides.

4.8.2 Paging

The paging feature of the 80386 is used not only to support the flat model and multiple DOS address spaces, but also to allow OS/2 to provide memory overcommitment different from that offered by OS/2 1.X. In OS/2 1.X, segment swapping is used to keep the system running in memory-stressed conditions; due to the I/O performance of most fixed disks, however, segment swapping does not perform well enough to provide general-purpose virtual memory on demand. However, since the 80386 provides paging, storage can be virtualized on fixed disk media at a much lower I/O cost, because the size of a page is not variable. Also, the system can do a better job of tracking memory usage, since memory aging algorithms operate on a page granularity, instead of a segment granularity, resulting in better memory utilization. Therefore, OS/2 2.0 is a demand-paged, virtual memory system and is designed so that the system will run acceptably in nominally overcommitted situations.

4.8.3 Multitasking

The multitasking architecture of 32-bit OS/2 is essentially the same as that of 16-bit OS/2, except for increased limits on the number of threads and processes supported, and enhancements to the multitasking API. The 32-bit system supports up to 4095 processes instead of 255, and 4095 threads instead of 512. The multitasking API is enhanced to allow better control of thread creation and termination. Also, the system's timeslice management uses *dynamic timeslicing* to maximize processor utilization for applications.

4.8.4 Dynamic Linking

OS/2 2.0 provides dynamic linking, but the elimination of segmentation in the flat model is propagated to the dynamic link model of the system. Instead of all dynamic links being far, all objects are near, and objects do not require segment register reloading when an API or dynamically linked object is referenced. Therefore, the cost of making dynamic links and API calls is significantly less than the cost of making the comparable calls in OS/2 1.X.

4.8.5 OS/2 1.X Compatibility

OS/2 2.0 runs all OS/2 1.X application and dynamic link library executable files without change. To provide this portability, the OS/2 designers had to come up with an architecture in which 16-bit and 32-bit modules could coexist. The difficulty of this task lies in the differences in the segmented and flat memory models. The major requirement for laying a foundation in which both models can coexist is a high-performance mechanism for converting 16-bit addresses to 32-bit addresses, and vice versa. Once this problem is solved, the task of servicing a 16-bit API call with a 32-bit routine, or vice versa, becomes a feasible task. The technique used to deal with address conversions between the segmented and flat models is called *LDT tiling*.

The rest of the 16-bit compatibility requires a layer of procedures that takes 16-bit API requests, converts them into 32-bit API requests, issues the requests, and completes the API return conditions with 16-bit semantics. The name of a routine that does this function for a single API is called a *thunk* or, more specifically, a *16-to-32 thunk*. Thunks can also be created to go in the opposite direction, from 32-bit semantics to 16-bit semantics—these thunks are called *32-to-16 thunks*. Thunks are merely tools that allow us to build one type of API (16 or 32) from the other when both APIs are needed in one system. Thunks are not APIs. Chapter 10 describes LDT tiling and thunks in more detail, and discusses other compatibility issues.

4.8.6 DOS Compatibility

OS/2 2.0 provides DOS 5.0 compatibility using the virtual 8086 mode of the 80386 processor, and uses paging to provide more than one DOS compatibility environment. The DOS environment is more DOS compatible than is the environment offered with OS/2 1.X, due to the ability to encapsulate the entire DOS environment in a *virtual DOS machine (VDM)*. This virtual DOS machine gives the system far better protection than is offered by the OS/2 1.X DOS compatibility environment. In OS/2 1.X, an errant DOS application could conceivably hang the entire system. In OS/2 2.0, an errant DOS application can hang only its own DOS session, and the hung DOS session can be terminated from the desktop manager.

DOS applications can be run full screen, windowed, or iconized in the background. In addition to being better protected, providing better compatibility, and allowing more DOS sessions, the OS/2 2.0 DOS environment leaves applications approximately 620KB in which to execute—more space than is available in DOS. Both EMS and XMS expanded memory support are provided using the paging feature of the 80386 for emulation. Since the DOS environments are swappable, starting many DOS sessions does not drive up system memory requirements.

The DOS environment in OS/2 2.0 allows specific versions of DOS to be booted into VDMs, enabling DOS version-dependent applications to run. It also provides DPMI server functions, enabling DPMI-based DOS extenders and their applications to run, including Windows 3.0 and its applications.

The OS/2 2.0 DOS support provides an extendible OEM architecture that allows the environment to be tailored to emulate any DOS environment. At the heart of this extendibility is an architecture that uses a *virtual device driver (VDD)*. The OS/2 1.X bimodal device-driver architecture is changed to move all low-level DOS support into virtual device drivers and out of the physical device drivers. Due to the 80386 virtual 8086 mode, all interrupt processing is done in protected mode, so the need for bimodal device drivers no longer exists. The OS/2 2.X device driver architecture distinguishes between *physical device drivers (PDDs)* for basic device support, and VDDs for virtual devices in the DOS environments.

4.9 OS/2 2.X API

OS/2 2.0 provides the dynamically linked 32-bit API to allow flat-model applications to use the OS/2 system services. The 32-bit API has been designed so that applications and subsystems that use and provide 32-bit APIs will be portable to any future OS/2 2.X platform.

The major differences in the API architecture between OS/2 1.X and OS/2 2.0 are that there are no 64KB restrictions, and API pointers are of the 0:32 format. The API calling conventions are different to allow support of the dynamic linking in the flat model environment and the 32-bit register set. Also, the basic word size exploited by the API is the 4-byte double word, instead of the 2-byte word found in OS/2 1.X. Many of the API names are changed to be more consistent than they are in the OS/2 1.X API.

Several areas of the API have been enhanced to provide greater functionality and portability. The multitasking API provides better thread management in the areas of creation and termination, and the system supports up to 4095 processes and 4095 threads. The memory management API has functions similar to those of its 16-bit counterpart, but it manages memory objects composed of pages instead of segments. The semaphores portion of the interprocess communications API are portable and are more reliable than their 16-bit counterparts. The exception management API provides the capability of handling exceptions on a per-thread, instead of a per-process, basis, and is also machine independent. The keyboard, mouse, and video APIs from the 16-bit API have no counterparts in the 32-bit API, since they are extremely device dependent. Instead, 32-bit programs use the PM for managing their user I/O.

4.10 OS/2 2.X PROGRAMS

The overall program-development process and architecture for 80386/80486 32-bit OS/2 systems are similar to those for 16-bit OS/2 and DOS, but the definition of memory objects and the addressing capabilities of the 32-bit architecture are different. This difference leads to enhancements in the programming languages and OMF to support fixups with 32-bit offsets, and to the definition of an EXE format that supports a demand-paged, dynamically linked environment.

The OMF in the 32-bit environment is extended to support 32-bit offset fixups called 0:32 fixups, and to allow memory objects larger than 64KB. Since the OMF is different from the one used in 16-bit OS/2 or DOS, the compilers that generate the OMF are significantly different from their 16-bit counterparts.

The proliferation of memory models to allow various flavors of segmentation in 16-bit OS/2 does not occur in the 32-bit flat addressing environment. Instead, all the memory models are replaced by the flat model. The flat model is the equivalent of a small-model program that can have up to 4GB of code and data simultaneously addressable using 32-bit offsets.

The link editor for 32-bit OS/2 is significantly different from that for 16-bit OS/2 or DOS. The 32-bit OS/2 link editor deals in memory objects and creates executable files suitable for the demand-paged environment. The link editor combines objects in different object files, and relocates all objects relative to a fixed absolute base in the EXE file emitted. The EXE image is the equivalent of a single large segment that contains the memory objects of the program, so there are no fixups remaining in a 32-bit EXE file except those for dynamic links external to the EXE. Since dynamic links in 32-bit OS/2 provide linkage to memory objects instead of to segments, each dynamic link is represented by a self-relative fixup rather than by a segment-relative fixup, as in 16-bit OS/2 dynamic linking.

Since EXE files are guaranteed to load at the same base address in the linear address space, the linker performs the internal self-relative fixups and then discards them. However, since DLLs must remain relocatable, the link editor retains the fixup information for relocating the DLL's memory objects.

The EXE format used in 32-bit OS/2 reflects the requirements of the demand-paged environment. In a demand-paged system, pages are loaded and reloaded into memory directly from executable files. For this mechanism to be efficient, the EXE files are organized into pages instead of segments, and all the fixup information within the EXE files is organized on a page basis instead of a segment basis. Another important property of EXE formats for demand-paged systems is the reduction of the number of fixups in the pages of an EXE file; a page with no fixups is called a *pure page,* since it can be loaded directly into memory without processing by the system's loader.

SUMMARY

This chapter described the overall architecture of the DOS, OS/2 1.X, and OS/2 2.X systems. The structure of the systems and their content were elaborated, and their API and program functionality explained.

TERMINOLOGY

anonymous shared memory
application programming
   interface (API)
automatic data segment
background session
bimodal code
binding
block device
calling convention
character device
code segment
COMMAND.COM
COM:1
compaction
compact model
context switch

data segment
demand paged virtual memory
demand segment swapping
desktop manager
device chain
device drivers
device help (DevHelp)
device independent presentation space
dispatching
Dos API
DOS box
DOS compatibility
DOS device chain
DOS session
dynamic link library (DLL)
dynamic linking

static link libraries
strategy routine
supervisor mode
swap file
swapper
system call
system library
32-bit flat addressing
   environment
32-bit OS/2

32-to-16 thunk
thread
thunk
timeslice
user shell
virtual device driver (VDD)
virtual DOS machine
virtual 8086 mode
0:32 memory model

EXERCISES

Questions pertaining to the DOS system:

4.1   Discuss the layered architecture of the DOS system as presented in Fig. 4.1.

4.2   Distinguish between block devices and character devices.

4.3   Describe the organization of the DOS device chain.

4.4   How do DOS programs typically manage a graphic display or a mouse, given that the DOS API does not contain functions for these purposes?

4.5   Why is it that most high-level languages cannot directly invoke DOS API calls?

4.6   List several advantages of using dynamic linking instead of static linking.

4.7   What do we mean when we say that the OMF exhibits the trait of processor architectural dependence and the EXE format exhibits the trait of operating system architectural dependence?

4.8   Distinguish between self-relative addresses and segment-relative addresses.

4.9   Briefly describe each of the following program models: compact model, small model, medium model, large model, and huge model.

Questions pertaining to the OS/2 1.X system:

4.10   Indicate the new capabilities OS/2 offers compared to DOS.

4.11   Many of the APIs are located in the kernel, but some APIs are located in dynamic link shared libraries. Why are both locations used?

4.12   Define the OS/2 notions of sessions, processes, and threads.

4.13   What are logical devices? What logical devices are available?

4.14   Distinguish between foreground and background sessions.

4.15   How are processes and threads related? How do threads provide a lower-overhead form of parallelism than is possible with processes?

4.16   Describe briefly how OS/2's preemptive, priority-based multitasking operates.

4.17   Under what circumstances will OS/2 not preempt a running thread?

4.18   Compare and contrast OS/2 1.X memory management with DOS memory management.

4.19   When a thread context switch occurs between threads in different processes, how does OS/2 switch process address spaces? How is protection between address spaces ensured?

4.20   Distinguish among named shared memory, anonymous shared memory, global shared memory, and instance shared memory.

4.21   Describe OS/2 notion of memory overcommit. How does OS/2 enable processes to run even though not all their segments are in physical memory at once?

4.22   Explain how dynamic linking operates. Discuss the advantages that dynamic linking provides.

4.23   Why are I/O devices—such as the display, keyboard, and mouse—accessed in OS/2 differently from in DOS?

4.24   Why does OS/2 have an installable file-system (IFS) architecture?

4.25   Discuss the architecture of OS/2 device drivers. In particular, explain the functions performed by the various device-driver routines.

4.26   Why does the presentation manager use device drivers different from the base system's device drivers?

4.27   Why is DOS compatibility such an important feature of OS/2?

4.28   Why is it that DOS programs do not benefit from the multitasking environment of OS/2?

4.29   Discuss the OS/2 technique of mode switching. What limitation of the 80286 with regard to mode switching was corrected with the use of additional hardware on PC/AT-class machines?

4.30   What is bimodal code? What performance advantage does it offer? In what physical memory addresses must bimodal code reside? Explain your answer.

Questions pertaining to the OS/2 2.X system:

4.31   Describe the key new capabilities offered by OS/2 2.X systems over OS/2 1.X systems.

4.32   What capability of the 80386 processor enables OS/2 2.X to run multiple DOS sessions concurrently and in the background?

4.33   Comment on the following statement and indicate its importance in defining OS/2 as a UNIX competitor: "The overriding goal in the design of the 32-bit programming environment is to provide an architecture that allows applications, subsystems, and the system itself to be portable to processing platforms other than the single-processor, Intel 80X86 machines."

4.34   What is the significance of the flat model? Why is it appropriate to call the flat model the 0:32 memory model?

4.35   How does OS/2 2.X provide each process with a unique address space?

4.36   Discuss several reasons for the high performance of OS/2 2.X applications, subsystems, and the system using the flat model compared to the memory model used in OS/2 1.X systems.

4.37   How does OS/2 2.X support memory overcommit?

4.38   Why is the cost of making dynamic links and API calls in OS/2 2.X systems significantly lower than the costs in OS/2 1.X systems?

4.39   What challenges did the designers of OS/2 2.X face in enabling OS/2 1.X applications and dynamic link library executable files to run without change? What are LDT tiling and thunks?

4.40   Distinguish between OS/2 2.X's physical device drivers and virtual device drivers.

4.41 What are the major differences between the API architectures of OS/2 2.X and OS/2 1.X?

4.42 Compare the 32-bit flat model to the 16-bit compact model.

4.43 How does an API encapsulate the hardware and the operating system? Could two different operating systems offer identical APIs? What would be advantages and disadvantages of such an approach?

5
Multitasking

It was surprising that Nature had gone tranquilly on with her golden process in the midst of so much devilment.

The Red Badge of Courage
Stephen Crane

I claim not to have controlled events, but confess plainly that events have controlled me.

Abraham Lincoln

Learn to labor and to wait.

Henry Wadsworth Longfellow

Outline

5.1 INTRODUCTION

This chapter describes the multitasking aspects of the OS/2 system. In any multitasking operating system, the hardware is managed as a shared resource to be distributed among concurrently executing entities. The architecture that describes how these concurrent entities are created, terminated, and managed is called the tasking or multitasking model. The multitasking model describes how resources—such as the processor, memory, files, devices, and interprocess communications structures—are shared in the OS/2 system.

Perhaps the most important resource that is shared in a multitasking environment is the processor. The operating system shares the processor among concurrently executing entities using a technique known as *timeslicing*. An operating system that provides timeslicing switches between programs, enabling each program to run for a short period of time called a *timeslice* or *quantum*. This technique results in the processor resource being shared among the programs.

The DOS operating system is not a multitasking system; it runs only one application at a time. However, DOS applications can do their own timeslicing by taking over the *system timer* and dividing up the processor time among different programs that are specifically known to them. In an unprotected environment such as DOS, it is difficult for multiple applications that do their own timeslicing to coexist without resource conflicts occurring.

In the OS/2 system, multitasking services are built into the system. This centralized tasking scheme allows all applications to take advantage of the multitasking functions of the operating system. Figure 5.1 illustrates the difference between multitasking in DOS and OS/2.

As we saw in Chapter 4, the multitasking hierarchy of OS/2 consists of sessions, processes, and threads. Sessions are described more completely in Chapter 9. This chapter concentrates on the description of processes, threads, and scheduling, and examines the kernel architecture that supports the multitasking of processes and threads. This chapter deals with both the 16-bit and 32-bit versions of OS/2. For the most part, the

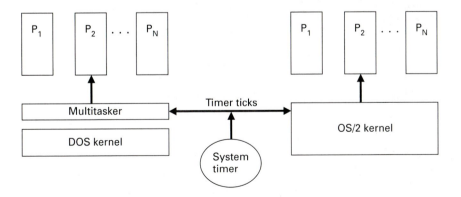

Fig. 5.1   DOS versus OS/2 multitasking.

multitasking architectures of both 16-bit and 32-bit OS/2, of OS/2 1.X, and of OS/2 2.X are identical. Where they differ significantly, the differences are explained.

5.2 PROCESSES

A process is the basic unit of programming and resource sharing in OS/2. A process corresponds to a program and is created when a program is loaded. A process is the central abstraction for the sharing of resources, such as processors, memory, files, and interprocess communication data structures. Each process is assigned a unique *process identifier (PID)* by the kernel. The 16-bit version of OS/2 provides support for up to 255 processes; the 32-bit version provides support for up to 4095 processes. Figure 5.2 illustrates the structure of an OS/2 process.

The system maintains many resources on a per-process basis. The primary resources contained in a process are the memory domain and the threads of execution. A thread provides a sequence of instructions with an instance of execution. All processes are created with one thread and have the capability of creating more threads. The threads within a process all share the process's resources and have access to one another. Although memory and threads are the main features within a process, the system also tracks many other resources on a process basis, such as signal handlers, open files, and interprocess communication features such as semaphores, queues, and pipes.

5.2.1 Process Virtual Address Space

The per-process memory domain is called the *process virtual address space*. Since each process receives its own unique process virtual address space, the memory accessible by each process is protected from other processes. Also, the system is protected from application processes, since it is not accessible by user-level code within the process virtual address space. In other words, a process cannot access memory in another process, and a

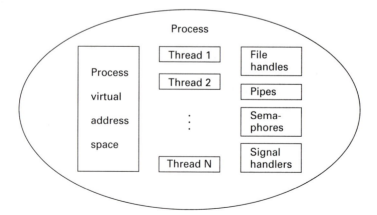

Fig. 5.2   Process layout.

process cannot access the system's memory. This scheme is known as *memory protec-tion* and is a key feature in any multitasking virtual memory operating system. Memory protection allows the OS/2 system to provide an architecture with much more integrity than is found in DOS or any of the extended DOS environments.

The process virtual address space is implemented differently in the 16-bit and 32-bit versions of OS/2 because of their different memory models. The process virtual address space in 16-bit OS/2 is represented as a collection of segments mapped by a local de-scriptor table (LDT). The system switches LDTs when switching between processes. A process can access only memory that is mapped by its own LDT. In 32-bit OS/2, the process virtual address space is a single large segment (on the order of 512MB) that rep-resents a flat linear address space. Each process virtual address space is mapped by a per-process set of page tables. When processes are switched, the page tables that map the process virtual address space are switched, effectively changing process virtual address spaces. In either case, each process has a unique protected virtual address space that maps all the memory it can access.

Chapter 6 discusses the management of the process virtual address space, such as the switching of address spaces, the allocation and deallocation of memory objects with-in address spaces, and the sharing of memory objects across address spaces. Memory management is described there in detail.

5.2.2 Process Creation

Processes are created using *DosExecPgm*. *DosExecPgm* services requests by creating a process, loading an executable program file into the process virtual address space, and calling the entry point specified in the program file. The name of the executable file and a set of execution flags are the parameters required by *DosExecPgm*. For example, call-ing *DosExecPgm* with the parameter FOO.EXE causes the program in the executable file FOO.EXE to be loaded into a new process virtual address space and starts that pro-gram running. All processes are initially created with a single thread. However, the ini-tial thread may create other threads within the process and also may create other processes. *DosExecPgm* returns to its caller the PID for the created process.

The loading of an executable program file into a process's virtual address space is performed by the *program loader* component of the OS/2 kernel. To load an executable file into the process's memory, the program loader must resolve any dynamic link imports that the program contains. As we saw in Chapter 4 when we described dynamic linking, these imports are references to routines and data items outside the program module itself. These references are either to the kernel or to dynamic link libraries that provide APIs.

When the program loader detects an external reference in a program (EXE) module or dynamic link library (DLL) module to an API in the kernel, the reference can be resolved immediately. However, if an external reference is to code or data in a DLL, that DLL must be loaded into the process's virtual address space before the original external reference can be resolved. Therefore, program loading is a recursive mechanism that usually ends up loading several DLLs to load just one executable (EXE) file. After all the necessary DLLs have been loaded, then the optional initialization entry point in each

DLL is called so that it can initialize any structures necessary for the operation of that DLL. Once all the external references within the original executable program file and its imported DLLs are resolved, the new process and its first thread are ready to be dispatched according to the execution flags passed into the *DosExecPgm* request. Chapter 6 further explains the role of the program loader with respect to memory management, and describes the sharing of DLLs among processes.

OS/2 processes have a hierarchical structure. The process that calls *DosExecPgm* to create another process is called the *parent process*, and the created or spawned process is called the *child process*. Processes that share the same parent are called *sibling processes*. Therefore, as processes are created, they form a *process tree*. Figure 5.3 illustrates the hierarchical nature of processes.

In Fig. 5.3, process A is at the *root* of the process tree. Processes B, C, and D are children of the parent process A and have a sibling relationship with one another. Processes E and F are children of process B, and grandchildren of process A. The process hierarchy enables processes to control their children and descendants.

The execution flags provided as a parameter to *DosExecPgm* allow the parent process to control the execution of each child process. They specify whether a new child process should be run *synchronously* or *asynchronously* relative to the parent, and whether a child is being traced by a debugger. When a child process is executed synchronously, the parent process is suspended during the *DosExecPgm* request until the child process terminates. In the case of a child being executed asynchronously, both the parent process and the child process execute concurrently.

5.2.3 Process Termination

A process is terminated when its last thread dies. Termination is accomplished by a call to *DosExit*. *DosExit* can be called to terminate a single thread or to terminate all the threads in the process.

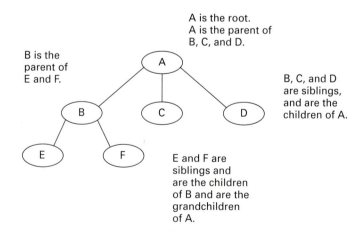

Fig. 5.3   Process hierarchy.

When a process dies, it may be necessary to notify the process itself or the DLLs referenced by this process that the process is ending. An EXE or DLL needing process termination notification can call *DosExitList* to register a *process-termination (exitlist) handler*. The kernel maintains a list of exitlist procedures that have been registered for notification when the process is being terminated. During process termination, the kernel calls each of the exitlist handlers for the terminating process using the context of thread 1 in the process. After the exitlist handlers have been called, the system reclaims any other process resources managed by the kernel, such as memory and semaphores.

The 32-bit version of OS/2 provides alternatives for process termination notification. A thread executing in an EXE or a DLL can register a process termination exception handler. Also, 32-bit DLLs can have a termination routine, as well as an initialization routine, that is called when a process releases a DLL. Exception handling is discussed in more detail in Section 5.5.8 and in Chapter 7.

Another way for a process to be terminated is via the *DosKillProcess* call. *DosKillProcess* can be used to send a notification indicating process termination to a single process or to a process and its descendants. In 16-bit OS/2 system, *signals* are used to send asynchronous events between processes. In 32-bit OS/2, the signals have been integrated into the exception management architecture as *asynchronous exceptions*. In both systems, signals and asynchronous exceptions are used to notify a process of the Ctrl-C and Ctrl-BREAK keyboard sequences (SIGINTR and SIGBREAK), process termination requests (SIGTERM), or application-defined events sent using the signals or exceptions API. When a signal is received by a process in the 16-bit system, one of three alternatives occurs: The process can choose to ignore a signal, to take the default action, or to handle a signal by providing a *signal handler*. In the case of the termination signal, SIGTERM, the default action is to terminate the process. For example, in Fig. 5.3, process A can kill process B and B's children (processes E and F) by invoking *DosKillProcess* with the PID of process B. The handling of exceptions and signals is discussed in more detail in Chapter 7.

5.2.4 Process Control

Process identifiers (PIDs) are used to indicate which process is to be controlled. In the 16-bit system, the *DosGetPID* call is used to get the PID of the current process. In 32-bit OS/2, the priority is stored in the *thread information block (TIB)*, a system-provided per-thread data area in the process address space. Chapters 6 and 7 explain the role of the TIB and the way it is accessed. In both versions of the system, *DosGetPPID* is used to get the PID of the current process's parent.

Process execution can be synchronized using a function called *DosWaitChild* in OS/2 2.X, and one called *DosCWait* in OS/2 1.X. *DosWaitChild* allows a parent process to wait for the termination of a specific child process or for the termination of all its descendants (the entire process subtree). For example, in Fig. 5.3, process A executes child processes B, C, and D asynchronously. At some later time, process A may wish to wait until one of the child processes has terminated and also to acquire the exit status of the child's termination. Alternatively, process A could wait until all its descendants have terminated before resuming execution.

For debugging a process, a special function—called *DosDebug* in OS/2 2.X and *DosPTrace* in OS/2 1.X—is provided to permit a parent to trace the execution of a child process. The parent process is usually a debugger program that creates the child process being debugged by calling *DosExecPgm* with the execution control flags that indicate the process is to be traced. The debugger program then issues *DosDebug* or *DosPTrace* requests to access and modify the child process's context.

5.3 THREADS

Threads are the dispatchable units within an OS/2 process. In other words, processes do not really run, but threads do. A thread provides within a process a piece of code with an execution instance. Each process in the system has a least one thread. From the user's perspective, a thread's context consists of a register set, a stack, and an execution priority. Figure 5.4 illustrates the context of a thread.

Threads share all the resources owned by the process that creates them. All the threads within a process share the same virtual address space, open file handles, semaphores, and queues. Each thread is in one of three states: *running, ready to run,* or *blocked.* Only a single thread in the system is actually in the running state on uniprocessor hardware platforms. The running thread is the ready-to-run thread that is currently selected to run according to the OS/2 priority scheme. Threads that are in the blocked state are awaiting the completion of an event.

When OS/2 switches between threads, it automatically saves the context of the current running thread and restores the context of another thread that is ready to run. The 16-bit version of OS/2 supports up to 512 threads; the 32-bit version supports up to 4095 threads. The 16-bit system has limitations on the number of threads that can run within a process (on the order of 50 threads per process) due to the segmented nature of the 16-bit kernel. The 32-bit system allows as many threads as the user desires within a process, up to the limit of the number of threads available in the system.

There are several advantages to a multithread process model over the traditional single-thread process model found in systems such as UNIX. Since threads share the process's resources, thread creation is far less expensive than process creation, and threads within a process enjoy a tightly coupled environment. When a thread is created, the

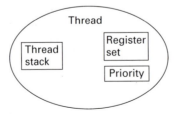

Fig. 5.4   Thread layout.

system does not have to create a new virtual address space or to load a program file, resulting in an inexpensive additional concurrent execution path. If a system with a single-thread process model requires two concurrent execution paths, two processes must be created, their execution must be synchronized, and any resource sharing between the processes must be managed. In contrast, in the OS/2 multithreaded process model, a single process with two threads is used, and the threads naturally share the process address space and resources. In addition to the lower cost for creation and termination of threads compared to that for processes, any synchronization needed between the execution of the threads is less expensive than that between processes, since the threads already share the process virtual address space. Chapter 7 discusses the different approaches used in OS/2 for interthread communication, regardless of whether or not the threads are in the same process.

Another benefit of a multithread process model is that multiple threads promote a greater overlapping of I/O requests. A multithreaded system is able to be more interactive than is a single-threaded one, due to the greater level of concurrency achieved. For instance, programs usually dedicate a single thread to servicing requests from the user interface while other threads actually perform the work requested by the user. Multiple threads better support an environment where parallel applications can execute with a far better performance than is possible in a single-thread process model.

All these benefits accrue on both uniprocessor and multiprocessor hardware architectures. In a multiprocessor environment, the multithreaded architecture also promotes parallelism, in which many portions of a program can execute concurrently on different processors. Chapter 12 discusses issues relevant to implementing the multithread process model on different multiprocessor architectures.

5.3.1 Thread Creation

Threads are created by a call to *DosCreateThread*. In 16-bit OS/2, the requestor must allocate a stack for the thread, and must pass to *DosCreateThread* the address of the stack and the address of the code the thread is to execute. In 32-bit OS/2, the system allocates the stack and dynamically resizes it as necessary during the thread's life. *DosCreateThread* returns a *thread ID (TID)* that is similar to a PID. Each thread in the system can be uniquely identified by a *PID:TID* pair. Unlike processes, threads are not hierarchical. All threads in a process have a sibling relationship with one another and remain part of that process until they terminate.

The thread that is created when a process is created with *DosExecPgm* is called *thread 1,* and it has some special properties that other threads within the process do not have. Thread 1 receives all signals sent to the process, is used for exitlist processing when the process dies, and also is used for per-process DLL initialization during program and library loading. In other words, each of these special per-process entry points executes using the context of thread 1. As a result, if thread 1 terminates, then all other threads in the process are terminated. Otherwise, another thread could potentially hang the process, since the process would be unable to receive the SIGTERM signals or to perform existlist handling during termination.

5.3.2 Thread Termination

A thread is terminated by a call to *DosExit*. *DosExit* can be used to terminate the current thread or all threads in a process. Whereas there is no function in the multitasking API of the 16-bit system for killing another thread that is analogous to *DosKillProcess,* the 32-bit system provides *DosKillThread* for terminating another thread in the current process. Neither is there a mechanism for handling thread termination in the 16-bit system that is analogous to the exitlist mechanism for process termination. However, the 32-bit system does provide a *process termination exception* that is sent to all threads of a process during process termination. Per-thread process termination exception handlers can be registered using the 32-bit exception management API discussed further in Chapter 7.

The 32-bit system also provides the *DosWaitThread* call, which allows a thread to wait explicitly on the termination of a specific or nonspecific thread within the process. *DosWaitThread* is useful when the threads within a process have a master/slave relationship with each other, in which the master dispatches slave threads to perform tasks.

5.3.3 Thread Control

There are several functions in the multitasking API for controlling thread operation. The *DosEnterCritSec* and *DosExitCritSec* calls allow threads within a process to disable thread switching within that process. This facility is useful when threads in a process need to execute concurrently code that accesses data shared by the threads. The region of code that must be managed carefully is called a *critical section*. Critical sections require that each thread executing the code has mutually exclusive access to that code. Using the critical section functions around the critical section guarantees mutual exclusion for threads within a process. However, since the critical section calls totally disable thread switching within the process, they may negatively affect interactive response if the critical section is too long. There are other mechanisms better suited to synchronizing thread execution, such as the semaphores discussed in Chapter 7.

Another method of controlling threads within a process is to allow one thread to *suspend* the execution of another thread, and to *resume* execution at a later time. Suspension and resumption can be accomplished using the *DosSuspendThread* and *DosResumeThread* calls, respectively. Both calls take a TID as a parameter to indicate which thread should be suspended or resumed. A thread can suspend or resume only a thread that is within the same process.

5.3.4 Process and Thread Information

The 16-bit system provides several special memory objects called *information segments,* or *infosegs*. The system contains two infosegs: a *global infoseg* shared by all processes, and a *local infoseg* for each process. The global infoseg contains system-wide information that is used by all processes, such as the date, time, and other system configuration parameters. The local infosegs contain per-process information such as the process's priority, current thread ID, and current thread priority, as well as the address of the process's environment information. A process requests the system to map the infosegs into its address space by calling *DosGetInfoSeg*.

The 32-bit system does not use the infoseg architecture of the 16-bit system, except that it provides compatibility to 16-bit OS/2 applications. Chapter 10 discusses in more detail the 16-bit OS/2 compatibility issues. Since most of the information from the infosegs is already available via existing API functions, and the infoseg architecture is machine dependent, the infosegs are not continued in the 32-bit architecture. However, there exists a requirement for per-process and per-thread data structures that contain critical data that processes and their threads need to access quickly. The *process information block (PIB)* is a per-process memory object allocated within each process's virtual address space that contains per-process data, such as the process ID, process default priority, and module information. The thread information block (TIB) is allocated on a per-thread basis within the process virtual address space. It contains all the information pertaining to a thread in a process, such as the thread stack base and stack limit, the thread priority, and the thread ID. A thread can access its information blocks by calling *DosGetInfoBlocks*.

5.4 SCHEDULING

All threads in the system compete for processor time. To determine which threads should run, OS/2 implements a multilevel priority architecture with *dynamic priority variation* and *round-robin scheduling* within a priority level. Each thread has its own execution priority, and high-priority threads that are ready to run are dispatched before low-priority threads that are ready to run. Processes also have a priority; however, this priority does not enter into the calculations of which threads should run next. The process priority is merely the default priority for threads that are created by that process. A thread may change the priority of any or all threads within the current process using *DosSetPrty*. A thread can also change the default priority of threads in other processes, regardless of whether they are related in the process hierarchy.

In the 16-bit system, *DosGetPrty* is used to query the priority of a thread or process. In OS/2 2.X, however, *DosGetPrty* does not exist, since the priority information has been moved into the thread information block. Chapter 6 provides more information on accessing the thread information block.

There are four *priority classes* in the OS/2 system: *time critical, server, regular,* and *idle*. The server class is also called the *fixed-high* priority class. Each priority class is further divided into 31 *priority levels*. Figure 5.5 illustrates the priority classes and levels.

Threads in the highest, or time-critical, priority class, have timing restraints. An example of a time-critical thread is a thread that waits for data to come from a device driver monitoring a high-speed communications device. The system guarantees that there is a maximum interrupt disable time of 400 microseconds, and that time-critical threads are dispatched within 6 milliseconds of becoming ready to run. These timing criteria ensure that the system can respond rapidly to the needs of time-critical threads, and also be flexible enough to allow a user to switch between programs quickly. Most threads in the system are in the regular priority class.

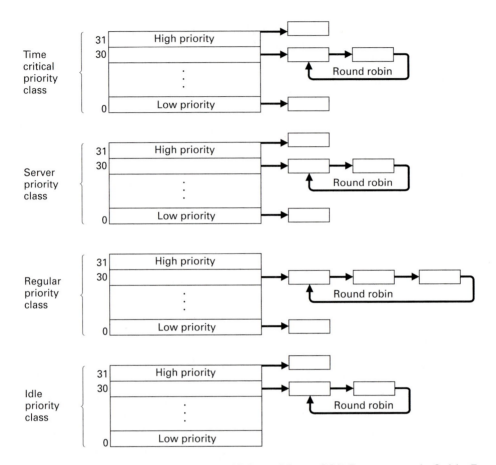

Fig. 5.5   Multilevel priority structure. (Adapted from *OS/2 Programmer's Guide,* E. Iacobucci, Copyright 1988, McGraw-Hill Publishing Company. Reprinted by permission.)

The server priority class is used for programs that run on a server environment that need to execute before regular-priority-class programs on the server. The server class ensures that client programs relying on the server processor do not suffer performance degradation due to a regular-class program running locally on the server itself.

Threads in the idle priority class will run only when there is nothing to run in time-critical, server, or regular priority class. Typically, idle-class threads are daemon threads that run in the background. A *daemon thread* is one that intermittently awakens to perform some chores, and then goes back to being blocked.

The scheduling algorithm is round-robin within the same priority level. For example, if five threads have the same priority, the system will run each of the five, one after another, by giving each one a timeslice. The timeslicing is driven by a system clock, and the user can configure the timeslices from 32 to 248 milliseconds by using the

TIMESLICE keyword in the CONFIG.SYS file. A thread runs for its entire timeslice unless an interrupt occurs that results in making another thread of a higher priority class ready to run. In such cases, the running thread is preempted. Otherwise, a thread runs for the length of its timeslice, unless it calls the kernel and blocks.

The 32-bit version of OS/2 implements optional *dynamic timeslicing* that maximizes utilization of the processor for threads running in user mode. Dynamic timeslicing reduces the number of interrupts the system processes to implement timeslicing by using the number of ready-to-run threads as a heuristic in the scheduling algorithm.

Since a thread can be preempted at any time due to an interrupt or timeslice end, threads that are sharing resources with threads in the same process or with threads in other processes must protect critical sections where these shared resources are manipulated. They can implement protection by using one of the interprocess communication constructs, such as semaphores. Chapter 7 explores several mechanisms for providing interprocess communication and critical section management.

Dynamic priority variation is the scheduler's ability to adjust the priorities of threads in the regular class to ensure that all threads get a chance to run, and that the system provides as interactive a response as possible. These priority adjustments are called *priority boosts*. Dynamic priority variation can be enabled or disabled by the user when the system is started.

The process that is running in the *foreground* has the locus of control of the user input devices (mouse and keyboard). This is also called the *input focus*, and only one process in the system can be in the foreground at a time. Processes that are not in the foreground are said to be in the *background*. So that the system will be responsive to the user's requests, all the threads of the foreground process receive a boost in priority. Then, the actual thread in the foreground process that performs the user I/O receives an additional priority boost. This priority adjustment is called the *foreground boost*.

When a thread becomes ready to run as the result of an I/O operation completing, the thread receives an *I/O boost* from the scheduler. Since the thread went from the running to the blocked state when it issued its I/O request, this boost assists the thread in getting rescheduled quickly so that it can continue execution. An I/O boost changes a thread's priority to be the highest level within that thread's priority class.

The third boost is called the *starvation boost;* it is applied to threads in the regular priority class that are in the ready-to-run state and that have not run recently. The amount of time a thread waits until the scheduler considers it starved can be configured by the user using the MAXWAIT keyword in the CONFIG.SYS file. The starvation boost causes the priority of a thread to be boosted out of its current class to a level just below the time-critical priority class.

When a thread receives either an I/O boost or a starvation boost, the thread's priority is adjusted, and the timeslice also is adjusted to a minimum timeslice quantum that can be configured using the TIMESLICE keyword in the CONFIG.SYS file. The minimum timeslice value can be set from 32 to 248 milliseconds, and must be less than or equal to the regular timeslice configuration parameter. A boosted thread retains its boost priority until it runs for a single timeslice; then, the priority and timeslice are reset to their original values.

5.5 KERNEL ARCHITECTURE

The kernel is the OS/2 control program, or supervisor. It contains the nucleus of functions for multitasking, interprocess communications, memory management, interrupt management, device I/O, and DOS compatibility. In this section, we focus on the general architecture of the kernel in the 16-bit and 32-bit versions of OS/2, and on the multitasking portion of the kernel.

The 16-bit and 32-bit OS/2 systems have different kernels that reflect their architectural differences. Since the 16-bit system is targeted for the 80286 processor, the 16-bit kernel is segmented and is highly sensitive to 64KB restrictions in the management of its data structures. It is written in assembler to be fast as possible, while using a minimal amount of memory. Since the 16-bit kernel is written in assembler, all subroutine linkages in the kernel use registers for passing parameters. Because applications pass parameters on API requests using the stack, the kernel must take the parameters off the stack and put them in registers before calling the kernel functions for implementing the APIs. A component called the *system call interpreter* is used to move the API parameters from stacks to registers and to call the kernel routine for implementing the API, so that there is no need for a separate piece of code for dispatching each API request.

Reflecting the segmented nature of the system, the routines in the 16-bit kernel are grouped into segments that are mapped by the global descriptor table (GDT). Mapping the kernel and its segments using the GDT ensures that the kernel is accessible at all times because the GDT is present in the context of all processes. However, the kernel segments are protected from applications since they are mapped at privilege level 0, the most trusted privilege level in the protected ring architecture of the 80286. Like 16-bit applications, the kernel must reload segment registers when establishing addressability to different segments. Most of the segments that compose the 16-bit kernel reside permanently in memory.

The 32-bit kernel reflects the linear nature of the 32-bit flat memory model. The 32-bit kernel is written in C for portability, although it contains portions that must be written in assembler on any architecture. Since it uses C, the 32-bit kernel routines use stack-based linkages for passing parameters within the kernel. Thus, no system call interpreter is necessary for moving the users' parameters to the registers during a kernel API request. Since the 32-bit kernel is flat, segment registers do not have to be loaded to establish addressability to different memory objects, resulting in better performance since segment register loading is a relatively slow operation.

Like the 16-bit kernel, the 32-bit kernel also is mapped into the GDT at privilege level 0. However, since the 32-bit system is paged instead of segmented, portions of the kernel that are not used frequently are swappable instead of resident. Frequently executed portions of the 32-bit kernel reside permanently in memory.

Logically, the kernel can be viewed as a *top half* and a *bottom half*. The API interfaces, worker routines, and most of their associated components compose the top half. When a thread is executing in the top half of the kernel, it has access to the kernel data structures and to the context of the current process and thread executing. When a thread in the top half of the kernel blocks, it usually waits on the bottom half to be unblocked.

The bottom half of the kernel is the collection of routines for handling hardware interrupts and faults that are unrelated to the current process and thread executing. Also in the bottom half are routines provided by the kernel needed to assist the interrupt and fault handlers in completing their services. Since the activities serviced by the bottom half of the kernel occur asynchronously, the bottom half cannot rely on a specific process or thread context to be mapped. Routines that access data shared by the top and bottom halves must serialize their access to the shared data in a mutually exclusive fashion to guarantee the data's integrity.

Both the 16-bit and 32-bit kernels are organized into components. Each component has a set of routines for system call service, called *worker routines*. When a system call is dispatched, the worker routine from the appropriate component is called to service the request. The worker routine uses the kernel interfaces provided by the kernel components to validate parameters; it then performs the system call request. During a system call, the kernel either completes the request immediately or blocks the requesting thread awaiting an event, such as completion of I/O or the availability of a required resource.

The kernel components involved in the management of multitasking are the *tasking manager, the dispatcher, the scheduler, the interrupt manager,* and the *trap manager.* The tasking manager provides the process and thread API routines, and manages the kernel data structures that represent processes and threads. The dispatcher manages the operational loop that drives the system, context switching, and blocking and unblocking of threads. The scheduler manages thread priorities, thread states, and processor usage, and also chooses the next thread to run when the dispatcher switches contexts. The dispatcher and the scheduler work together in determining when to context switch and which thread to run. The interrupt and trap managers are responsible for routing and for handling hardware interrupts and exceptions. Figure 5.6 illustrates the multitasking components.

5.5.1 User Mode

Since the OS/2 system is protected, a distinction is made between the state of a thread running in the kernel and that of one running in an application. When a thread is running code from a program or dynamic link library, the thread is said to be in *user mode.* A thread that is running in user mode runs at privilege level 2 or 3, executes within the domain of the process's virtual address space, and can be preempted. The process's virtual address space is also called its *user space.*

While running in user mode or user space, a thread can access memory only within its own process's virtual address space. It is unable to access memory in another process's virtual address space, unless memory sharing has been set up by the memory

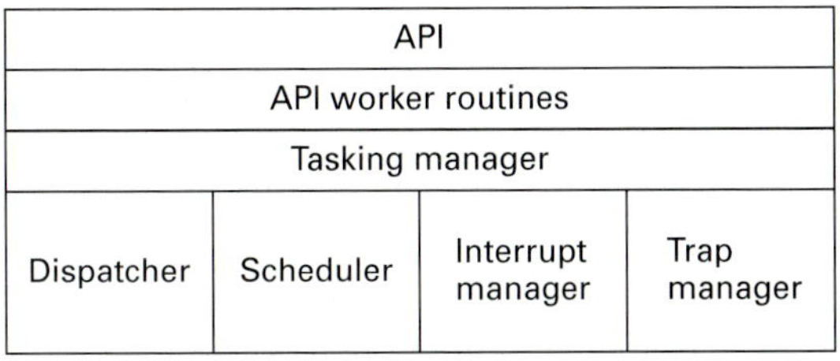

API			
API worker routines			
Tasking manager			
Dispatcher	Scheduler	Interrupt manager	Trap manager

Fig. 5.6   Multitasking kernel components.

manager. A thread in user mode is also unable to access memory belonging to the system. If a thread attempts to access memory addresses within its address space that have not been mapped by the memory manager, a *general protection fault* is raised, and the errant thread and process are terminated. In the 32-bit version of OS/2, general protection faults can be handled in user mode by setting of an exception handler. Protection is implemented using the protection and memory mapping hardware of the processor. The implementation of the process virtual address space in both the 16-bit and 32-bit systems is explained in Chapter 6.

5.5.2 Kernel Mode

A thread that is running code in the top half of the OS/2 kernel is in *kernel mode*. A thread makes the transition from user mode to kernel mode during API requests to the kernel and potentially during interrupt processing. A thread that enters the kernel has two options: it either completes the operation and attempts to exit the kernel, or blocks awaiting some resource's availability or event to complete an operation (e.g., I/O). When running in kernel mode, a thread executes at privilege level 0, and is *not* preemptible. An interrupt may cause control to transfer temporarily for interrupt service, but control is always returned to the thread in kernel mode. A thread running in kernel mode has access to all the memory in the system—all of the process virtual address spaces, as well as the kernel's code and data areas. The aggregate of these memory areas is called the *system virtual address space,* or *kernel space.*

The OS/2 kernel architecture makes further distinctions among user mode, kernel mode, and the privilege level architecture. It is possible for a thread to be executing at privilege level 0 but not be in kernel mode. A thread officially enters kernel mode when a special entry point in the dispatcher named *EnterKMode* is called. *EnterKMode* saves the state of the thread and sets a global flag in the kernel named *InDOS*. Actually, a thread is not preemptible if it is executing at privilege level 0 or if *InDOS* is set indicating that the thread is in kernel mode. An example of a thread executing at privilege level 0 that is not in kernel mode arises when an interrupt occurs while a thread is in user mode—the interrupt handling occurs in interrupt mode. A thread that is in kernel mode returns to whatever mode it was in previously by calling the dispatcher routine *ExitKMode.* The only time that a context switch can occur is when a thread exits kernel mode. The logic of this constraint is described later in this chapter, where the operational loop of the system is discussed.

5.5.3 Kernel Process Context

The data structure used by the kernel to track each process in the system is called the *per-task data area (PTDA).* Each PTDA is allocated, when a process is created, by a call to *DosExecPgm;* each PTDA uses fixed memory within the kernel space. Figure 5.7 illustrates some of the major fields of a PTDA.

The PTDA contains the PID of the process and links to the parent, sibling, and first child processes, a pointer to the process virtual address space, a list of open file handles and semaphores, a pointer to the chain of threads within the process, and a pointer to the current thread within the process that is running. Also in the PTDA are the default process

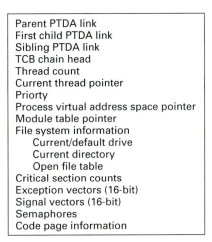

```
Parent PTDA link
First child PTDA link
Sibling PTDA link
TCB chain head
Thread count
Current thread pointer
Priorty
Process virtual address space pointer
Module table pointer
File system information
      Current/default drive
      Current directory
      Open file table
Critical section counts
Exception vectors (16-bit)
Signal vectors (16-bit)
Semaphores
Code page information
```

Fig. 5.7   Per-task data area (PTDA).

priority, signal and exception handling information, and a link to the *module table entry (MTE)* that describes the executable file loaded into the process virtual address space. MTEs are described in more detail in Chapter 7, in the discussion of the program loader.

When a thread is in kernel mode, the PTDA for the current process is always mapped by a global kernel variable so that kernel routines always have access to the PTDA of the current process. In the 16-bit system each PTDA is a segment, and the current PTDA is always mapped by having the SS register loaded with the selector of the PTDA. In the 32-bit system, each PTDA is a flat memory object accessible by a 32-bit offset relative to the kernel's system virtual address space—the current PTDA is accessible through a global kernel variable that contains the offset of the current PTDA.

5.5.4 Kernel Thread Context

The data structure used by the kernel to track each thread in the system is called the thread control block (TCB). Each TCB is allocated either by a call to *DosCreateThread* when a thread is created, or by a call to *DosExecPgm* when the initial thread is created during process creation. Like the PTDAs, TCBs use fixed memory and reside within the kernel space. The TCBs for each process are linked in a chain, with the head of the chain in the PTDA. Figure 5.8 illustrates the layout of a TCB.

The primary structure in each TCB is the *kernel stack,* which is used when the thread is running at privilege level 0 or in kernel mode. Each thread in the system must have its own kernel stack for two reasons. First, since a thread may block while in the kernel, a place is needed for saving the blocked state information, as well as the local data already allocated as the thread made its way to the point where it had to block. Second, since there are special cases where a thread voluntarily yields the processor while in kernel mode, the top half of the kernel must be reusable. Voluntary preemption and yielding are discussed later in this chapter.

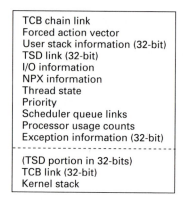

Fig. 5.8   Thread control block (TCB).

When a thread makes the transition from user mode to kernel mode through a gate, the 80X86 gate hardware automatically switches from the user stack to the kernel stack. Therefore, the gated architecture of the 80X86 processors supports a natural, stack-based implementation of dynamic linking. The pointer to the kernel stack for the current thread is maintained in the *task state segment (TSS)*, which is accessed by the processor when privilege level transitions occur. The kernel stack is used to preserve the state of the user's context when *EnterKMode* is called, and to provide local storage during kernel processing. Also contained in each TCB is information for controlling I/O; scheduling information, such as priorities and processor usage fields; and forced-action flags that indicate pending actions that the thread must perform when exiting the kernel.

In the 16-bit version of the system, the TCBs belonging to a process are allocated in the same segment as the PTDA. When a new thread is created, the PTDA segment is re-sized and the new TCB is allocated. Figure 5.9 illustrates the layout of PTDAs and TCBs in the 16-bit system.

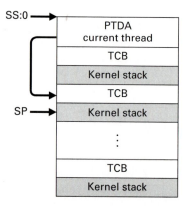

Fig. 5.9   Layout of 16-bit PTDA and TCB.

Allocating the TCBs in the same segment as the PTDA has several interesting ramifications. Since the current PTDA segment is always addressable by the SS segment register, the current thread's TCB is always addressable by loading of an offset register—typically, the current running thread is always addressable by SS:BP. Also, the links in the chain of TCBs need to be only 16-bit fields, since they are relative to the base of the PTDA segment. However, there is a cost for this quick access to the current thread's TCB: Since the maximum segment size on an 80286 is 64KB, there is a limitation of approximately 50 threads per process. Also, in potential future versions of the 16-bit system, any growth in the TCB or kernel stack will decrease the number of threads available per process.

The 32-bit version of the system does not have this limitation, since the TCBs are allocated out of the kernel space as flat memory objects addressable using a 32-bit offset relative to the base of the system virtual address space (like PTDAs in the 32-bit system). Therefore, the links in the chain of TCBs within a process are 32-bit offset fields. Since the 32-bit kernel is written in 32-bit C, the kernel stacks are larger than in the 16-bit version, since the code is 32-bit granular instead of 16-bit granular, and high-level languages such as C use the stack for local storage. Therefore, the 32-bit system divides the TCB into a fixed portion called the TCB and a swappable portion called the *thread swappable data (TSD)*. The TSDs primarily contain the kernel stacks, and can be swapped out when a thread is in the blocked state. Figure 5.10 illustrates the layout of PTDAs, TCBs, and TSDs in the 32-bit system.

5.5.5 Context Switching

Context switching refers to the mechanism used by the kernel to stop running one thread and to start running another. The OS/2 dispatcher implements a policy of context switching only when a thread attempts to exit the kernel (*ExitKMode*) or when a thread in the kernel blocks waiting on an event or resource. Therefore, the *ExitKMode* routine

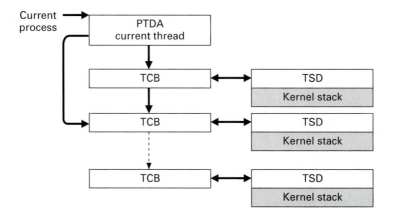

Fig. 5.10   Layout of 32-bit PTDA, TCB, and TSD.

becomes the single locus of control for forced actions that a thread must perform, such as context switching, signal dispatching, and termination.

A global flag variable called *ReSched* is shared between the dispatcher and the scheduler. *ReSched* indicates whether there is potentially a thread of priority higher than that of the current thread that has been made ready to run. Part of the *ExitKMode* routine called whenever a thread attempts to exit kernel mode checks the *ReSched* flag. If the *ReSched* flag is set, the *SchedNext* routine of the dispatcher is called to switch out the current running thread in order to run the highest-priority ready thread in the system. *SchedNext* is the actual context switch routine of the system, and is the only place that a thread switch occurs in the kernel. It is called only from *ExitKMode* and from *ProcBlock;* the latter routine is used when a thread in the kernel blocks and gives up the processor.

The thread that is currently running when *SchedNext* is invoked is called the *outgoing thread,* and the thread to which *SchedNext* ultimately switches is called the *incoming thread.* Only outgoing threads call *SchedNext,* and only incoming threads return from *SchedNext.* We now look in more detail at how the *SchedNext* routine performs the context switch.

SchedNext begins execution by calling the *GetNextRunner* routine in the scheduler component to determine the highest-priority thread that should be the new running (incoming) thread. If the outgoing thread is the same as the incoming thread, *SchedNext* merely returns, and the current thread continues executing. If the outgoing thread is different from the incoming thread, *SchedNext* performs a context switch.

If *GetNextRunner* indicates that there are no threads in the system that are ready to run, it executes a loop known as the *idle loop.* The idle loop is executed when all threads in the system are blocked on some external event. This implies that there is no background activity and that there are no user requests occurring via keyboard or mouse—the entire system is waiting. The idle loop exists within *SchedNext,* and consists of polling the *ReSched* flag with interrupts enabled. When an interrupt occurs that makes a blocked thread ready to run, the thread running in the idle loop will exit, will call *GetNextRunner* again, and will continue executing *SchedNext* to switch in the ready-to-run thread.

Once a new thread to run has been selected, *SchedNext* determines whether the outgoing thread is within the same process as the incoming thread, or is within a different process. If the incoming and outgoing threads are in different processes, *SchedNext* must switch the process context (PTDAs, process virtual address spaces, etc.) and the thread context. If both threads are within the same process, only the thread context must be switched.

The actual switching of the process context entails changing the current PTDA, and calling the memory manager to switch process virtual address spaces. Switching a thread context entails setting the current thread variable in the current PTDA, changing kernel stacks, and resuming execution at a known place in *SchedNext* at which all threads resume running when they are outgoing. Since the task-state segment (TSS) of the system contains the address of the current thread's kernel stack, it also must be edited during a context switch to ensure that future privilege level transitions by the running thread use the proper kernel stack.

An interesting caveat in the OS/2 context switching model is that there is no explicit "save/restore" instruction or routine used to save all the registers from one thread and restore the registers for another. Although the TSS construct of the 80X86 tasking architecture provides this function, OS/2 does not utilize it except for the minimum of having a single TSS for supporting privilege level transitions. The TSS switching feature of 80X86 processors provides a mechanism for performing a save/restore for the entire register set in a single instruction. Since this set includes all segment registers on 80286 architectures, and also the paging registers on the 80386 and 80486, the TSS switch is slow due to flushing of the segment register caches, flushing of the translation lookaside buffer used for page translation, and the protection checks that occur as the segment registers are reloaded.

When contrasted with the OS/2 context switch model, this overhead is not required for several reasons. The thread's user mode register set is saved on the kernel stack when the thread enters kernel mode, and is restored when a thread exits kernel mode. Within *SchedNext,* only the process virtual address space needs to be switched (and only in the process switch case), since both the outgoing and incoming threads are executing in the system virtual address space. Also, all threads resume execution in *SchedNext* at a fixed point where known values are loaded into the registers—the threads do not rely on any saved state to resume their execution in the kernel, since they are on the kernel stack already. This results in much faster context switching compared to the TSS switching model. It also uses less memory, since the TSS model requires a TSS to be allocated and managed for each thread in the system.

5.5.6 System Calls

System calls, or API function requests, are used by threads running in user mode to access services provided by the operating system. Traditionally, most operating systems place all the system calls in the kernel. This implementation makes the system—and, consequently, its API—difficult to change without changing the kernel. So that the system and its API are more flexible and extendible, OS/2 system calls are implemented using dynamic linking. This implementation allows OS/2 APIs functions to reside in either a dynamic link library or the kernel transparently to the requesting thread.

All 16-bit and 32-bit OS/2 API requests are made by pushing the parameters on the user mode thread stack, then issuing a CALL instruction to transfer control to the target API routine. The address of the target API routine is a dynamic link that is resolved either when a process is created and loaded into the process virtual address space, or at run time using the dynamic linking API functions. In the 16-bit system, all addresses and dynamic links are segmented 16:16 virtual addresses, and the control transfer occurs using the far variety of the CALL instruction. In the 32-bit system, all addresses and dynamic links are flat 0:32 virtual addresses, and the control transfer utilizes the near variety of the CALL instruction.

5.5.6.1 DLL APIs

OS/2 DLLs are loaded into the process virtual address space when the process is created, and potentially while the process's threads are executing in user mode (at run time). Therefore, DLLs are effectively attached to the process, and the threads within the process can make use of the DLLs API functions. Since DLLs are mapped into user space, their code and data are swappable, instead of being fixed in the kernel. Also, a DLL can easily access the API parameters on the thread's user stack, since it is running in the requestor's context. Since a thread that has called an API in a DLL runs in user mode, a thread executing in a DLL can be preempted. For DLLs to be shared among processes, they must be reentrant. DLLs make use of interprocess communication constructs, such as semaphores and shared memory, to ensure their integrity. A DLL with integrity is one that can be shared by processes, yet not allow any process to hinder any other process. In this environment, an errant or malicious process can cause only its own termination. Chapter 7 discusses issues related to interprocess communication, memory sharing, and parameter validation that must be considered to guarantee this level of integrity.

An example of an API that is implemented in a DLL instead of in the OS/2 kernel is the queueing API, which provides functions for managing queues between processes. Since the queueing API can be implemented without requiring the protection or nonpre-emptive execution state of the kernel, it is a DLL that uses other functions in the API to provide services. The queueing code and data are swappable and can be preempted, resulting in more efficient memory and processor utilization. Since the dynamic linkage to the queueing API is transparent, the queueing API can be freely migrated to the ker-nel, or perhaps to another DLL module, without requestors having to change. However, some APIs require functions that exist only in the kernel, or have special performance or protection requirements. We now discuss the implementation of kernel system calls and APIs.

5.5.6.2 Kernel APIs

In both 16-bit and 32-bit OS/2 systems, the kernel's code and data are mapped into the system virtual address space at privilege level 0 using global descriptor table (GDT) se-lectors. This mapping makes the kernel and its API automatically accessible to all pro-cesses, since there is only one GDT in the system. However, since it is mapped at privilege level 0, it cannot be accessed directly by a thread running in user mode (privi-lege level 3) without a general protection fault occurring.

OS/2 uses the call gate mechanism employed on the 80X86 processors for transfer-ring control from threads running in user mode to an API implemented in the kernel. For each API implemented by the OS/2 kernel, a call gate is allocated in the GDT. Recall from Chapter 2 that a call gate has a privilege level, and has a target address field within its descriptor. The call gates for the OS/2 kernel APIs have privilege level 3, so that they are accessible to threads running in user mode executing CALL FAR instructions. The target address within the gate descriptor points to the entry point at privilege level 0 for the API.

Other traditional operating systems that employ static linking in their API calling conventions typically vector all API requests through a single call gate, along with an extra parameter called the *system call number*. Although, at first glance, this mechanism seems simpler than the call gate-per-API model, it implies that the requestor must have a layer of bindings statically linked into its code to put in place the static link or system call number. It also implies that the kernel must have a dispatch mechanism to fan out the API calls to the worker routines, rather than having them called directly from the call gate entry point. This prohibits API functions from being called directly from application code, slows performance, and restricts API extendibility and flexibility.

In any operating system, several events occur during the processing of a system call in the kernel. The application initiates transfer of control to the kernel using a trap or service call instruction. The kernel copies the user parameters from the user space to the kernel space to prevent them from being altered while the system call executes. The kernel then saves the user mode context and dispatches the system call to the proper kernel routine. The kernel routine responsible for the API validates the parameters, performs its service, and then exits with the return status. When the system call service routine completes, the kernel restores the user mode context, and transfers control back to the requestor with the return status.

In OS/2, the call gate mechanism is used for most of these steps. When the thread in user mode issues the CALL FAR instruction to a call gate in the GDT, the processor switches automatically from the thread's user stack to the kernel stack, and copies the parameters from the user stack to the kernel stack using the count parameter in the gate descriptor. Several necessary steps are thus accomplished—control has been transferred to an entry point in the system virtual address space, the processor is executing at the most trusted privilege level, and the requestor's parameters have been copied from user space to kernel space.

EnterKMode is then called to save the user context on the thread stack, and officially to stamp the thread as being in kernel mode. Note that there is a state where a thread is running at privilege level 0 but is not yet in kernel mode. The entry point then branches to the worker routine that validates the API parameters and performs the API function. After the worker routine completes, the thread then calls *ExitKMode* to restore the user-mode context and subsequently to return to user mode with the RET FAR instruction. Figure 5.11 illustrates the sequence of operations for a kernel system call.

When a system call is serviced in the kernel, the thread may either block awaiting some resource or event, or complete service without waiting. If the thread must stop to wait on some resource, it calls the *ProcBlock* routine of the dispatcher. *ProcBlock* moves a thread from the running state to the blocked state, and calls *SchedNext* to force a context switch. The *ProcRun* routine is used to wake up a blocked thread. *ProcRun* moves one or more threads to the ready-to-run state and sets the *ReSched* flag to force a dispatch cycle when the current thread exits the kernel. *ProcBlock* and *ProcRun* are discussed in more detail later in this chapter.

When the system call worker routine completes its service, the thread attempts to return to the calling code. The thread calls *ExitKMode* to exit kernel mode and to restore the user mode context. However, *ExitKMode* is the focal point of context switching policy; before restoring the user mode context and returning, it checks to see whether there are any per-process forced actions. Examples of forced actions are pending signals and exceptions, critical sections, and trace events used for debugging programs. After the process's forced actions have been serviced, the *ReSched* flag is tested to see whether a reschedule cycle is pending, indicating that another thread may be a better candidate to run. Note that interrupts must be disabled while the *ReSched* flag is tested, since it can

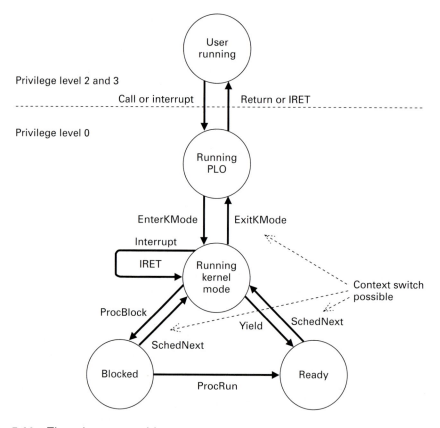

Fig. 5.11   Thread state transitions.

be set during an interrupt. If *ReSched* is set, *SchedNext* is called to perform a context switch. When a thread is ultimately scheduled and exits the kernel, the user mode context is restored from the kernel stack, and control is transferred back to the requestor using the RET FAR instruction.

You might wonder, if a thread executing in kernel mode is nonpreemptible, how can there be another thread that is a better candidate to run? Although the kernel is nonpreemptible, it is interruptible. Interrupts from external devices such as clocks, disk drives, and communications controllers can occur, and these interrupts usually result in completion of I/O service for another thread that is not in the current context. An interrupt occurring while a thread is in kernel mode causes a control transfer to a device interrupt handler. The handler often calls *ProcRun* to notify a blocked thread that the thread's request is complete and to make it ready to run. Since the interrupted code was executing in privilege level 0, and privilege level 0 and kernel mode are nonpreemptible, control reverts to the thread originally executing in kernel mode. When the thread exits the kernel, *ExitKMode* detects the set *ReSched* flag to indicate that a reschedule cycle is necessary.

Another interesting aspect of the system call mechanism is how threads executing 32-bit API requests within the flat model move to privilege level 0 from user mode. Since the 32-bit dynamic link is implemented with a CALL NEAR using a 0:32 pointer, and the 80X86 architecture requires a CALL FAR to use a call gate, a layer of *stub routines* is provided for each API function. The stub routines are near entry points that make a CALL FAR to a call gate in the GDT on behalf of the requestor. There is a two-line stub routine for each 32-bit API serviced by the kernel. The stub routines are invisible to users of the API, and are mapped into the process virtual address space within one of the system's DLLs.

5.5.7 Interrupts

Interrupts are special kinds of control transfers that are used to handle asynchronous events external to the processor. The 80X86 processor architectures provide both maskable and nonmaskable interrupts. Maskable interrupts can be inhibited by software that controls the interrupt flag of the processor flags. The CLI and STI instructions are used for enabling and disabling maskable interrupts. The interrupt controller used in all PC architectures is the Intel 8259 chip. The 8259 receives eight levels of interrupts. It assigns priorities to them, and dispatches them to the host processor according to how it is programmed. Most PCs have two of these chips, providing 15 levels of external interrupts. When a hardware interrupt occurs, the 8259 begins an interrupt cycle with the host 80X86 processor, and holds further interrupts on the active interrupt level and levels of lower priority until the processor sends an *end-of-interrupt (EOI)* command to the 8259.

In OS/2, interrupts refer specifically to external hardware interrupt service requests from devices. The *interrupt manager,* a component of the kernel, is responsible for handling the interrupt controller, managing interrupt handlers, and dispatching interrupt requests. The addresses of interrupt handlers registered by the kernel and device drivers are saved by the interrupt manager in an *interrupt table.* Since the PS/2 and EISA computer architectures allow multiple devices to have a single interrupt level, the table may have multiple handlers for each interrupt level. Figure 5.12 illustrates the interrupt table.

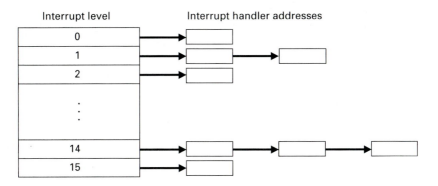

Fig. 5.12   Interrupt table.

Like system calls, the protected-mode interrupt mechanism of the 80X86 processors uses gates to facilitate privilege level transitions during interrupt service. The *interrupt descriptor table (IDT)* contains interrupt or trap gates for each interrupt and exception serviced by the system. Since hardware interrupts can occur while the system is in both user mode and kernel mode, the privilege level of the hardware interrupt gate descriptors is 3. Each gate descriptor points to a stub of code that saves the interrupt number and vectors to the interrupt manager's dispatch routine.

When an interrupt occurs, control is transferred through the IDT to the interrupt manager's dispatch routine with interrupts disabled. The registers of the interrupted context are saved, and the system switches into *interrupt mode* by switching from the current thread kernel stack to a global *system interrupt stack*. Interrupt mode is the bottom half of the kernel; it runs using a systemwide interrupt stack, since the bottom half should not alter the top half's current kernel stack, and it cannot rely on any specific process or thread to be currently running.

Once the system has entered interrupt mode, the interrupt manager's dispatch routine then uses the number of the interrupt as an index into the interrupt table, and calls all the interrupt handlers chained together for that interrupt level. The dispatch cycle finishes when an interrupt handler indicates that it has serviced the interrupt.

Before the dispatch routine prepares to return to the interrupted context, a critical part of the code for enforcing the system's preemption policy is executed. If the interrupted context was executing code at privilege level 0, then the interrupted thread was running in kernel mode or at privilege level 0. In this case, since kernel mode and privilege level 0 are nonpreemptible, the interrupted context is resumed directly by restoration of the registers and return of control to the interrupted point.

If the interrupted context was executing at privilege level 2 or 3, however, then the interrupted thread was executing in user mode. Since user mode is preemptible, the dispatcher checks the *ReSched* flag to see whether another thread is potentially ready to run. If the *ReSched* flag is set and the interrupted context indicates user mode, the interrupt dispatch routine calls *EnterKMode* immediately, followed by *ExitKMode*, to force a preemptive rescheduling cycle. The interrupt manager does not perform the context switch itself. The *ReSched* flag gets set when an interrupt handler issues a *ProcRun* for a blocked thread awaiting an interrupt.

Having a single global interrupt stack also allows the interrupt manager to identify and manage *nested interrupts*. A nested interrupt can occur after an interrupt handler sends an EOI command to the 8259 after clearing the interrupt at the original device. At this point, the interrupt handler can enable maskable interrupts, and the interrupt dispatch routine can be reentered before the current interrupt dispatch cycle completes. The code that performs preemption control at the end of the dispatch cycle also recognizes a nested interrupt when examining the interrupted context, and returns to the previous interrupt mode context even though the *ReSched* flag is set. Nested interrupts are an important feature that allows an operating system to be more responsive to interrupts and reduces *interrupt dispatch latency*. So that the requirements for interrupt dispatch latency are met, the maximum time that interrupts can be disabled in any portion of the system is 400 microseconds.

5.5.8 Exceptions

Exceptions are internal processor events that cause a special type of control transfer. On 80X86 processors, exceptions are dispatched the same way as interrupts, but there is no involvement with an external interrupt controller. Exceptions are assigned reserved interrupt numbers by the processor, and are delivered using trap or interrupt gates in the system's IDT.

Exceptions are further classified in the 80X86 architecture into faults, traps, and aborts. A *fault* is an exception that is reported before or during the instruction that will cause the exception. The state saved during the control transfer references the instruction that causes the fault, allowing instruction to be potentially restarted. Examples of faults include page faults, segment-not-present faults, and divide-by-zero or invalid-opcode exceptions. *Traps* are reported immediately after the instruction that causes them. A typical trap would be the use of the INT 3 breakpoint instruction for debugging a program. An *abort* is an exception that does not permit the precise location of the error to be reported; it is used to report nonrecoverable system errors.

The OS/2 *trap manager,* a component of the kernel, provides exception handlers for the 80X86 exceptions, and services for routing exceptions to the appropriate kernel or user exception handlers. The trap manager registers its exception handlers by initializing the appropriate IDT gate descriptors to point directly to the trap manager's low-level trap handlers. These trap handlers save the exception context and call an exception dispatching routine in the trap manager.

OS/2 divides the exceptions into those that can be handled by threads in user mode, called *user exceptions,* and those handled by the system. System exceptions are handled by the kernel and are routed directly to their components by the trap manager. Note that it is possible for the current thread to block during the handling of a system exception such as a page fault when swap I/O must be done before the thread can continue execution. User exceptions such as divide by zero, invalid opcode, and boundary check have *default actions* that are taken by the system if the user thread does not handle them. Typically, the default action in user exceptions is to terminate the process.

A difference between 16-bit and 32-bit OS/2 is that the 16-bit system maintains user exception handlers on a per-process basis, whereas the 32-bit system provides user exception handling on a per-thread basis. The general protection fault exception, which is raised when a protection violation occurs, cannot be handled by users in 16-bit OS/2 and results in process termination. However, 32-bit OS/2 allows users to handle general protection faults, since the latter are useful in lazy parameter validation schemes. Lazy parameter validation is discussed further in Chapter 7, with respect to exception management.

When an exception occurs, control is transferred through the IDT to the *trap manager dispatch routine,* with interrupts disabled and the trap number identified. The trap manager dispatch routine calls *EnterKMode* to preserve the thread's user context, and then dispatches the thread to the appropriate trap handler according to the trap type. The trap handler either blocks by calling *ProcBlock,* or completes and returns to the trap manager dispatch routine. The trap manager dispatch routine then calls *ExitKMode* to restore the user context and to resume execution. Unlike interrupts, exceptions are handled on the kernel stack of the thread that caused the exception. They are handled there because the current thread caused the exception. Also, unlike interrupts, exceptions do not nest, so the amount of stack space required is limited.

Exceptions that can be potentially handled by user mode threads are routed to a special trap handler called the *user exception dispatcher,* which implements the exception APIs and user exception routing. User exceptions are not dispatched immediately. Instead, the user exception dispatcher builds an exception stack frame on the current thread's user mode stack that will simulate an exception in the current thread when that thread returns to user mode. When the trap manager dispatch routine finally calls *ExitKMode* to restore the thread's context, the thread will resume automatically in the context of the user exception handler the next time it is scheduled. If the exception was not handled by a user handler, the kernel processes the default action. If the default action is process termination, a bit is set in the process's force flags that forces the process to terminate itself the next time one of its threads exits the kernel.

5.5.9 Timeslicing

The timeslicing function of the system provides an environment where each thread runs for a short time and is then preempted for a rescheduling cycle. The length of time each thread gets to run is called a *timeslice,* and the timeslice value is configured when the system is started. Since OS/2 implements preemption in user mode, a thread is not always permitted to run for a complete timeslice. This section describes how the scheduler and dispatcher components interact to provide the basic timeslicing function.

The timeslice is counted using a real-time clock external to the processor. OS/2 uses ticks from the clock to calculate timeslice intervals. A timeslice can be anywhere from 34 milliseconds to 9999 milliseconds. However, the clock is set to a tick granularity finer than the timeslice, so that other timer services can be provided to applications.

The scheduler manages the states and priorities of threads and calculates real-time processor usage. Timer ticks are recorded when the clock device interrupts the processor. The clock interrupt causes the system to enter interrupt mode and to dispatch the interrupt to the clock device driver interrupt handler. The clock interrupt handler calls the scheduler entry point for recording timer ticks, *SchedClock. SchedClock* calls the routine *SchedTick* for timeslice accounting, and various other components of the kernel that rely on real-time aging algorithms.

SchedTick adds the elapsed time to the current thread's processor usage field, and checks to see whether the thread has run for a timeslice. If the thread has completed a timeslice, *SchedTick* sets the *ReSched* flag, resulting in a forced rescheduling cycle occurring the next time the thread exits the kernel. In either case, *SchedTick* returns to the clock interrupt handler, which ultimately returns to the interrupt dispatcher.

As in all interrupts, the interrupt dispatcher checks whether the interrupted context was in interrupt mode (i.e., resulting in a nested interrupt), kernel mode, or user mode. If it was in interrupt mode or kernel mode, the interrupted context is restored directly, since these are nonpreemptible modes. Ultimately, when the thread finishes running nonpreemptible code and exits the kernel, the forced reschedule cycle (timeslice) occurs. If the interrupted context is user mode, then the interrupt dispatcher calls *EnterKMode* followed by *ExitKMode* to force a reschedule. In this scenario, the preemption is called a timeslice.

5.5.10 ProcBlock/ProcRun

The low-level dispatcher routines responsible for moving a thread from the running state to the blocked state, and from the blocked state to the ready-to-run state, are called *ProcBlock* and *ProcRun,* respectively. Threads executing in kernel mode either complete their service or block awaiting a resource or an external interrupt. Threads can also block when they incur page faults or segment-not-present faults, waiting for the I/O to load the memory.

The *ProcBlock* routine requires three parameters: an event identifier, a timeout value, and flags. The event identifier is a token that represents the event on which the blocked thread is waiting. OS/2 maps the event identifiers onto system virtual addresses. Typically, a thread calling *ProcBlock* uses the address of a major data structure related to the block request. The timeout value allows a thread to specify the maximum amount of time that the thread should block waiting on the event. The flags parameter specifies whether the block is interruptible by signals. Because both the timeout and flags parameters are used, blocked threads are prevented from being blocked forever.

ProcBlock is allowed to be called only in kernel mode (top half), never in interrupt mode (bottom half). When a thread in kernel mode calls *ProcBlock,* the thread is moved into the blocked state, is inserted on the appropriate timeout and block queues, and executes *SchedNext* to force another thread to be run. The timeout value is aged by *SchedClock,* discussed previously in this chapter. If a thread's timeout occurs before *ProcRun* is issued on the event, the thread is moved automatically into the ready state, and the *ReSched* flag is set.

The *ProcRun* routine requires one parameter: an event identifier. Since event identifiers are mapped onto system virtual addresses, they are not unique. Therefore, *ProcRun* must wake up all threads blocked on a given event identifier. This requirement is a side effect of using system virtual addresses for event identifiers. Multiple threads waiting on a single event cannot be distinguished from multiple threads waiting on different events using the same address for the event identifier. Therefore, *ProcRun* marks all the threads waiting on the event as ready, sets *ReSched,* and returns to the caller. *ProcRun* can be called in kernel mode, but is most often called from interrupt mode.

The use of system virtual addresses for mapping event identifiers leads to other side effects in the system. Since more than a single thread can be blocked using a single event identifier, when a thread awakens and returns from *ProcBlock*, it must check whether the intended event has occurred. Also, since *ProcRun* can be called at interrupt time, interrupts must be disabled before the condition of the event is checked. The management of the state of the interrupt flag during calls to *ProcBlock* is critical, since the state is used to guarantee mutually exclusive access to data and code shared by the top half and bottom half of the kernel. Figure 5.13 illustrates how *ProcBlock* is called.

If all threads awaken, *race conditions* arise in the kernel, because all the awakened threads are rescheduled according to priority. All the awakened threads, except for the one that finds its event satisfied, will be rescheduled long enough for their conditions to be checked and for *ProcBlock* to be called again. This practice is avoided where possible by careful selection of event identifiers by the system, but it cannot be avoided in some cases. The mapping of events to system virtual addresses also has the potential to cause logic and correctness problems to occur in unexpected areas. In Chapter 7, we shall examine the effect this race condition has on the performance of 16-bit semaphores.

An interesting comparison to the UNIX system can be made in this area. The *ProcBlock* and *ProcRun* routines closely parallel the UNIX *sleep* and *wakeup* routines. Both systems use addresses for event identifiers; both suffer from the same side effects. However, the 32-bit version of OS/2 introduces a different architecture that uses unique event identifiers and allows the caller of *ProcRun* to request single or multiple thread wakeup. This distinction enables the system to wake up a single thread of highest priority among a group of threads blocked on an event identifier. The capability to wake up multiple threads when that is the intention also is retained. This capability allows the system to eliminate race conditions and wasted processor cycles, and to provide a consistent wake-up time no matter how many threads block on an event.

The 32-bit dispatcher uses a hash table to store and search event block ids so that the performance of *ProcBlock* and *ProcRun* is consistent no matter how many threads in the system are blocked. Each hash entry contains a pointer to a list of TCBs blocked on one or more event ids. There can be more than one event id in the same hash entry, since more than one unique event id can be hashed to the same value. The list of TCBs blocked on an event id is sorted in order of priority.

5.5.11 Voluntary Preemption

Since a thread running in kernel mode is not preemptible, it would seem that a thread in the kernel could continue running and effectively exclude other threads from running. This situation is especially problematic given the existence of time-critical threads. Although most system calls and kernel services complete rapidly or block the requesting

```
Disable interrupts
While (need to block)
    ProcBlock (Event, TimeOut, Flags)
```

Fig. 5.13 ProcBlock calling sequence.

thread, there are a few situations in which large lists must be searched, or long sequences of instructions must be executed, in order to complete the service. For instance, in the 16-bit system, the memory manager performs compaction, an expensive process in which segments are copied between areas of physical memory.

OS/2 guarantees that a time-critical thread that is made ready to run will be dispatched within 4 milliseconds. To ensure that ready time-critical threads will get a chance to run within 4 milliseconds, the kernel implements a type of voluntary preemption called a *yield*. So that this criterion is met, there is a secondary version of the *ReSched* flag, called the *TCReSched* (for time-critical) flag. The *TCReSched* flag is set whenever a thread in the time-critical class moves to the ready state. In specific areas in the kernel where an operation may take longer than 4 milliseconds, the code is written to call periodically a dispatcher interface named *TCYield*. *TCYield* examines the state of the *TCReSched* flag and forces a context switch if *TCReSched* is set by calling a special entry point in the *SchedNext* routine.

Since the yielding thread can potentially own resources, it is important that execution return to the yielding thread after the time-critical thread has run. To ensure this return, *TCYield* boosts the priority of the yielding thread to a priority level just below the lowest time-critical priority. Note that these critical sections of code in the kernel that can potentially yield the processor must be written to be reentrant, and are in effect small sections of coarsely preemptible code in the kernel. Full preemption, instead of voluntary preemption, would require the entire kernel to be written such that a preemption cycle could occur at any time, not just at specifically defined points where it is necessary. A symmetric multiprocessor version of the kernel would have to be reentrant and to allow concurrent execution of multiple threads in the kernel.

In the example of copying 64KB of memory, the 16-bit memory-manager code that performs the operation is written to copy as much of the segment as is possible in 4 milliseconds, to call *TCYield* to allow time-critical threads to run, then to continue the operation after the time-critical threads have run.

5.6 Multitasking API

Table 5.1 lists the 16-bit and 32-bit multitasking API calls.

SUMMARY

This chapter presented OS/2's multitasking architecture. The basic elements of the architecture are processes and threads; they are managed by the multitasking API. The scheduling model that threads use in OS/2 is a multilevel priority scheme with round-robin scheduling within a priority level. The kernel contains most of the critical portions of the system, and the multitasking components that provide the system's concurrency features. The task manager, scheduler, dispatcher, and interrupt manager work together to provide the fundamental multitasking functions of context switching, dispatching, and scheduling.

16-bit API name	32-bit API name	Description
DosCreateThread	*DosCreateThread*	Create a thread
DosCWait	*DosWaitChild*	Wait for child process termination
N/A	*DosWaitThread*	Wait for thread termination
DosEnterCritSec	*DosEnterCritSec*	Disable thread switching within process
DosExecPgm	*DosExecPgm*	Create child process and load program
DosExit	*DosExit*	Terminate thread/process
DosExitList	*DosExitList*	Register process termination handler
DosGetInfoSeg	*DosGetInfoBlocks*	Get process/thread info
DosGetPrty	N/A	Get execution priority
DosKillProcess	*DosKillProcess*	Send termination signal to process
N/A	*DosKillThread*	Kill thread within process
DosSetPrty	*DosSetPriority*	Set execution priority
DosGetPID	N/A	Get process/thread IDs
DosGetPPID	*DosGetPPID*	Get parent process ID
DosPTrace	*DosDebug*	Debug program/process
DosResumeThread	*DosResumeThread*	Resume a thread
DosSuspendThread	*DosSuspendThread*	Suspend a thread
DosGetEnv	N/A	Get process environment
DosScanEnv	*DosScanEnv*	Scan process environment

Table 5.1 Multitasking API calls.

TERMINOLOGY

API requests
asynchronous I/O operation
blocked
blocking
CALL FAR instruction
call gate
child process
clock device-driver interrupt handler
context
context switching
critical section
daemon thread
device interrupt handler
device I/O

dispatcher
DOS compatibility
DosCreateThread
DosCWait
DosKillProcess
DosExecPgm
DosExit
DosExit API
DosPTrace
dynamic link import
dynamic link library
dynamic priority variation
EnterKMode
event

ExitKMode
exception
exception handler
exitlist procedure
external reference
fault
flat linear address space
file handle
foreground
foreground boost
general protection fault
idle loop
idle priority class
incoming thread
inDOS
input focus
I/O boost
interprocess communication
interrupt
interrupt descriptor table (IDT)
interrupt dispatch latency
interrupt management
interrupt manager
interrupt mode
interrupt table
kernel
kernel mode
kernel space
kernel stack
maskable interrupt
massive parallelism
massively parallel
master/slave relationship
memory management
memory protection
module table entry (MTE)
multilevel priority architecture
multitasking
multitasking API
multithread process model
nested interrupt
open file handle
outgoing thread
page table

parent process
per-task data area (PTDA)
priority boost
privilege level 0
process
process ID (PID)
process termination handler
process virtual address space
program
program loader
queue
ready
reentrant
regular priority class
ReSched
resume
round-robin scheduling
SchedNext
scheduling algorithm
scheduler
segment-not-present fault
semaphore
session
sibling process
SIGBREAK
SIGCTRLC
signal
signal handler
SIGTERM
single-thread process model
stack-based calling convention
stack-based linkage
starvation boost
supervisor
suspend
system call interpreter
system clock
system interrupt stack
system timer
system virtual address space
tasking manager
task state segment (TSS)
thread
thread control block (TCB)

thread ID (TID)
thread 1
thread swappable data (TSD)
thread termination
time-critical priority class
time-critical thread
timeslice
timeslicing
translation lookaside buffer (TLB)
trap

trap dispatcher
trap manager
unblocking
user exception
user exception dispatcher
user space
user stack
worker routine
yield

EXERCISES

5.1   Explain how, even though DOS is not a multitasking operating system, it is still possible for applications to provide their own multitasking.

5.2   What are the primary resources contained by a process?

5.3   Why can a process not access another process's memory or the system's memory?

5.4   How are processes created in OS/2?

5.5   Explain OS/2's hierachical process structure. Discuss the notions of parent, child, and sibling processes, and of the root of the process tree.

5.6   What do we mean when we say that a child process runs synchronously relative to its parent? What do we mean when we say that a child process runs asynchronously relative to its parent?

5.7   How are processes terminated in OS/2?

5.8   What is an exitlist handler? How does the kernel know which handlers are associated with a particular process?

5.9   What is a signal? In what three ways may a process respond to a signal?

5.10   Is it true that OS/2 processes do not run? Explain your answer.

5.11   Explain the various thread states (i.e., running, ready, and blocked), and describe the various transitions that may occur between thread states.

5.12   List advantages to the multithread process model over the traditional single-thread process model found in systems such as UNIX and MVS.

5.13   How does the multithread process model promote greater overlapping of I/O requests?

5.14   Why is OS/2's multithread process model important in the context of multiprocessor systems?

5.15   Unlike processes, OS/2 threads are not hierarchical. What implication does this have for the relationships among the threads of a process?

5.16   Discuss the special significance of thread 1.

5.17   How does OS/2 guarantee mutually exclusive access to shared data among the threads of a process?

5.18   What do we mean when we say that a set of threads within a process have a master/slave relationship?

5.19   Describe OS/2's multilevel priority architecture. Explain dynamic priority variation and round-robin scheduling.

5.20   Is it possible for a thread's execution to be postponed indefinitely? Explain your answer.

5.21   An OS/2 thread may set its own priority. In some operating systems, allowing individual activities to control their own destiny in this manner is frowned on. Why is such a capability reasonable in OS/2?

5.22   Distinguish among time-critical threads, regular-priority-class threads, and idle-priority-class threads.

5.23   What guarantees does the system give to time-critical threads?

5.24   In OS/2, timeslicing is driven by a system clock and can be configured by the user. Values for the quantum may be set between 34 milliseconds and 9999 milliseconds. What are the consequences of selecting far too large a quantum? What are the consequences of selecting far too small a quantum? How might a user tune the quantum to an appropriate value for a given system?

5.25   Define each of the following terms in the context of OS/2 multitasking: foreground, input focus, background, foreground boost, I/O boost, starvation boost.

5.26   What are the key functions performed by the OS/2 kernel?

5.27   Describe the functions of each of the following kernel components involved in the management of multitasking: the tasking manager, the dispatcher, the scheduler, the interrupt manager, and the trap manager.

5.28   Explain how the dichotomy between user mode and kernel mode helps to ensure protection in OS/2's multitasking environment.

5.29   What might cause a general protection fault? How does the system typically respond to such a condition?

5.30   What is kernel mode? Under what circumstances might a thread make the transition from user mode to kernel mode?

5.31   Why do you suppose threads running in kernel mode are not preemptible?

5.32   How might a thread be executing at privilege level 0, yet not be in kernel mode?

5.33   When can context switches occur?

5.34   In the operating systems literature, the data structure that serves as a central depository for all information about a process is called the process control block (PCB). What data structure in OS/2 corresponds to the PCB?

5.35   How is the PTDA of the current process located in 16-bit OS/2? How is the PTDA of the current process located in 32-bit OS/2?

5.36   What is the idle loop?

5.37   Distinguish between process context switching and thread context switching. What operations are performed to accomplish each type of context switch?

5.38   Can a thread that has called an API in a dynamic link library, and is currently executing in that dynamic link library, be preempted? Explain your answer.

5.39   Describe the sequence of events that occurs in OS/2 from the initiation of a system call request by an application, through the processing of the system call by the kernel, to the resumption of the application.

5.40 What do we mean when we say that, in OS/2, although the kernel is nonpreemptible, it is interruptible?

5.41 What is a maskable interrupt? What does it mean to enable or disable maskable interrupts?

5.42 Describe the communications that occur between an Intel 8259 controller and a host 80X86 processor when an interrupt occurs.

5.43 Why does the OS/2 interrupt table potentially have multiple interrupt handlers per interrupt level?

5.44 How might a nested interrupt occur?

5.45 Distinguish among the three exception types on the 80X86 architecture: faults, traps, and aborts.

5.46 Under what circumstances might the current thread block during the handling of a system exception?

5.47 Why are exceptions, unlike interrupts, handled on the kernel stack of the thread that caused them?

5.48 Explain how OS/2 implements timeslicing.

5.49 How is 32-bit OS/2's algorithm for thread-wakeup superior to UNIX's algorithm?

5.50 Discuss the operation of OS/2's voluntary preemption technique, called a yield. How does the yield capability help to ensure rapid response to the needs of time-critical threads?

5.51 Give an example of an application that is inherently parallel. Explain why programming such an application with multiple threads is more natural than is programming it with a single thread.

5.52 In what sense are all the threads of a process identical? In what sense are they different?

6
Memory Management

The fancy is indeed no other than a mode of memory
emancipated from the order of time and space.

Samuel Taylor Coleridge

'Tis in my memory lock'd,
And you yourself shall keep the key of it.

William Shakespeare

A great memory does not make a philosopher,
any more than a dictionary can be called a grammar.

John Henry, Cardinal Newman

Outline

6.1 INTRODUCTION

This chapter describes the memory management aspects of OS/2. We begin with a look at the terminology necessary to understand OS/2 memory management. *Physical memory* is primary memory, or the range of real addresses within a computer. For example, the DOS system allows a program to access physical addresses in the range from 0KB to 640KB. OS/2 systems allow far more physical storage to be accessed than do DOS systems.

A major feature of most multitasking systems such as OS/2 is to utilize *virtual memory*. The key to virtual memory is that it allows the addresses referenced in a running program to be disassociated from the addresses available in primary storage. A processor's memory management unit (MMU) provides this feature, which is called *address translation*. The MMU translates virtual addresses into physical addresses as instructions are executed. The range of virtual addresses available is called the virtual address space; the range of physical addresses available is called the physical address space. Virtual memory systems have the characteristic of allowing a program or process to be independent of its actual position in physical memory, whether all or part of that program or process is in physical memory. The address translation between virtual and physical addresses occurs at run time and must be extremely fast—otherwise, the performance of the system would be degraded severely. Another attribute of virtual memory systems is that the range of the virtual address space can be independent of the range of real memory. In other words, the virtual address space can be far larger than the real address space. Typically, secondary storage media, such as disks, are used as swapping devices for saving the portions of a program that are not resident in physical memory at the time that the program is running.

In a multitasking, virtual memory system, protection is another major feature usually provided by the memory management unit of the processor. There are two forms of protection that are required in a multitasking system. The first is protection among the processes in the system, which allows each process to have an isolated memory environment in which to run. This memory environment is called the process virtual address space, as we saw in Chapter 5. By allocating a process virtual address space to each process, we protect the individual processes in the system from one another. The architecture of the process virtual space defines what the memory model of a system is, or how memory looks to the processes in the system. The second type of protection provides isolation of the system from the user processes. In the implementation of this protection scheme, the system virtual address space encompasses the kernel memory and all the process virtual address spaces. The system virtual address space is accessible only by a thread running in kernel mode.

Relating these factors to what we discussed in Chapter 5, a thread running in user mode can access only memory mapped by its own process virtual address space; it cannot access memory within another process's virtual address space unless memory sharing between the processes has been set up. A thread in user mode also cannot access kernel memory. However, a thread in kernel mode can access all process virtual address spaces and kernel memory. In summation, both kinds of protection are necessary in any multitasking system to guarantee the integrity of concurrent applications.

The memory management component of the system is responsible for allocating process virtual address spaces and for setting up the required hardware structures to enable processes to be protected from one another and from the system. The memory management API allows threads within a process to manipulate the contents of the process virtual address space. It also provides functions for manipulating memory objects within the process virtual address space. OS/2 provides functions for object allocation, deallocation, and sharing.

6.2 OS/2 1.X MEMORY MANAGEMENT

In this section, we describe the motivations for the architecture of 16-bit OS/2 memory management. The 16-bit OS/2 version targets the 80286 processor platforms. The main goals with respect to memory management in 16-bit OS/2 are to break the 640KB barrier associated with DOS systems and to provide a protected environment for multitasking. Another major goal is to allow applications to allocate more memory than physically is present in the computer. Finally, a powerful memory sharing capability is necessary to permit multiple processes to communicate through shared memory and to support dynamic link libraries.

6.2.1 Memory Model

When the 80286 processor is placed in protected mode, it provides virtual segmented addressing. The addresses within the virtual address space of the processor are not contiguous because they are divided into variable-sized portions called *segments*. Segments can have sizes from 1 to 64KB. Each segment must be mapped by a descriptor or a general protection fault will occur when the memory is accessed. The OS/2 memory model for 80286 processor systems is called the *segmented memory model*.

Unlike in real-mode DOS systems, segment arithmetic cannot be performed on the protected mode virtual segmented addresses. Segment arithmetic occurs when a DOS program takes advantage of the fact that a single memory location can be addressed using different *segment:offset* combinations or aliases. Recall from Chapter 2 that, on an 8088 architecture, the values loaded into the segment registers are directly related to the generated physical address. In the 80286 environment of 16-bit OS/2, the segment values are specific selectors that map descriptors, and each segment can be addressed only by a unique selector. Therefore, the segment protection of the 80286 automatically prohibits segment arithmetic. Segment protection is accomplished using the protection ring architecture discussed in Chapter 2. Segment swapping allows more physical memory than is available in the computer to be allocated by applications.

The system address space is common to all processes and is mapped by the GDT at privilege level 0. Each process has an LDT that represents its process virtual address space. A process can access only memory mapped by the GDT or by its own LDT. Because each process has its own LDT, the process virtual address spaces are encapsulated and isolated. Threads running in user mode cannot access the descriptors in the LDT or the GDT. Furthermore, each LDT's descriptors are divided into private and shared descriptors, in order to differentiate between addresses (not storage) private to a process and addresses that are shared across processes. Figure 6.1 illustrates the usage of the descriptor tables for the system and process virtual address spaces.

6.2.2 Memory Objects

Memory objects in 16-bit OS/2 are segments. A segment is from 1 to 64KB, is physically contiguous, and is addressable via a 16-bit selector value in combination with a 16-bit offset. This fully qualified virtual address is also called a 16:16 address (selector:offset). Segments are also relocatable in physical memory and are swappable. Since there are only four segment registers available on the 80286 processor, all the segments within a process's virtual address space cannot be addressed simultaneously. To establish addressability to a segment, a thread must load a segment register with the selector for that segment.

Segments are classified according to type of virtual address, type of storage, and what kind of segment it really is. Segments can be *fixed, movable, swappable,* and *discardable*. Most of the kernel itself is fixed memory, and only the kernel can allocate fixed memory. Fixed memory never moves, is never swapped, and is resident in physical memory. Memory that is movable can be relocated. However, this relocation is transparent to applications, since segments are relocatable through their descriptor tables. Swappable segments are those that can be swapped to disk if physical memory is

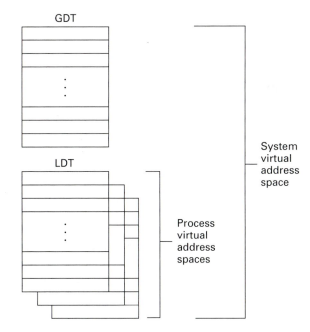

Fig. 6.1   16-bit virtual address spaces.

in short supply. Discardable segments are those that can be reloaded from their executable files when they are referenced during execution. Examples of discardable segments are application code segments and data segments that are read-only. Unless segment swapping or segment motion is disabled when the system is started, all application data segments are swappable and moveable.

Segments can share their virtual addresses, their contents, or both. Each process virtual address space has separate shared and private selector regions within the LDT. Actually, the selectors are interleaved within an LDT to allow the smallest LDT size possible. Selectors that map to descriptors in the private part of the LDT are called *private selectors;* those that map to descriptors in the shared portion of the LDT are called *shared selectors.* The selector type is independent of whether the contents of the segment are shared. Therefore, there are four possible combinations of the virtual-address-space and storage-type attributes.

Segments with private addresses and private storage are those allocated by the memory management API, and read-write data segments that are loaded from executable files. Segments with private addresses and shared contents are executable code and read-only data segments. Thus, executable EXE code and read-only data segments can be shared by all processes that are running the same EXE.

Shared address segments are managed differently from private address segments since they can be accessed by multiple processes concurrently. Whereas the 80286 hardware places no constraints on whether processes map shared segments using the same LDT descriptor, OS/2 shared segments are mapped at the same address in all processes. Thus, all processes use the same virtual address when accessing shared addresses.

Since code segments have fixups to other segments that must be resolved when the code segments are loaded into memory, these fixups must be valid in all contexts in which the code segment will be used. Placing all shared segments and EXE code segments at the same address in all contexts meets this criterion. The same address is provided in each process's context by use of the same LDT selector/descriptor pair for the shared segments. Thus, OS/2 divides an LDT into private and shared descriptors, and reserves shared descriptors in all LDTs when a shared segment is allocated by any process.

Shared addresses with shared storage segments are *shared segments.* In other words, there is a single physical segment that is referenced in the context of multiple processes. Shared memory is allocated either at run time using the shared memory APIs, or at load time when a dynamic link library's code and global data segments are loaded. Shared address private storage segments are called *instance segments.* Instance segments are mapped using shared addresses; however, a different copy of the segment exists for each process in physical memory. Instance segments are allocated by dynamic link libraries when they are loaded, and contain per-process data defined by the library. Table 6.1 illustrates the possible combinations of segment types.

6.2.3 OS/2 1.X Memory Management API

This section describes the functions of the 16-bit OS/2 memory management API.

Address type	Storage type	Origin
Private	Private	EXE read-write data or private memory API
Private	Shared	EXE code or EXE read-only data
Shared	Private	DLL instance read-write data
Shared	Shared	DLL code, DLL read-only data, DLL shared data, or shared-memory API

Table 6.1   Memory object types.

6.2.3.1 Private Memory

Private memory is allocated by a call to *DosAllocSeg*. *DosAllocSeg* allows the requestor to allocate a segment of up to 64KB, and returns an LDT selector to the allocated segment. Allocation flags that are supplied during requests allow the requestor to determine whether the memory is to be private, or is to be shared through the *give-get* mechanism (discussed in Section 6.2.3.2). A segment is freed by a call to *DosFreeSeg*.

  DosReallocSeg allows the requestor to change the size of a segment. Private segments can be grown or shrunk, whereas shared segments are usually only grown. If a shared segment is of the give-get variety, its size can be reduced if a special bit was set in the allocation flags when the segment was created by *DosAllocSeg*. A segment reallocation request can cause a segment to be relocated in physical memory.

  Since segments have a maximum size of 64KB, a special type of construct, called a *huge segment,* exists in 16-bit OS/2 to allow a memory object larger than 64KB to be allocated. *DosAllocHuge* allows a huge object to be constructed. A huge object consists of a series of LDT selectors, each of which maps a segment of the huge object. The LDT selectors for a huge object are mathematically related by a value called the *huge increment* or *huge shift factor.* The huge increment is applied to one of the LDT selectors that maps a portion of a huge object, allowing applications to address different 64KB portions of the huge object. The huge-segment arithmetic is reminiscent of segment-value arithmetic in DOS. The huge increment must be determined by a call to *DosGetHugeShift. DosReallocHuge* supports resizing of huge objects.

6.2.3.2 Shared Memory

The shared memory API provides functions for manipulating global shared segments. Global shared segments use shared LDT addresses and shared storage. As the section on 16-bit memory objects explained, in the traditional shared memory scheme, a single copy of a segment is shared within the context of multiple processes. There are several ways to manage global shared memory. The first method is *named shared memory*. Named shared memory is created by issuance of a *DosAllocShrSeg* request. One of the parameters in the request to create the named shared segment is a name in the

\SHAREMEM\XXX format. This name is entered into the name space of the file system using an entry in the directory \SHAREMEM. Since any name in the file system name space is global to all processes, any process that knows the name of the segment can gain access to that segment by calling *DosGetShrSeg*. *DosGetShrSeg* causes the named shared segment to be mapped into the requesting process's LDT, and returns the selector for accessing the segment. Recall that the selector for a given shared segment is the same in all processes. Named shared memory is typically used between loosely coupled peer processes as an interprocess communication mechanism.

Another type of global shared memory is called *give-get shared memory*. Give-get shared memory is allocated using *DosAllocSeg* with the giveable and getable flags set in the allocation flags as an input parameter. If the giveable flag is set, the segment may be given to another process by a call to *DosGiveSeg*. If the getable flag is set, the segment may be gotten by another process a by call to *DosGetSeg*. This strategy allows a process either to give addressability to a segment to another process, or a process to get address-ability to a segment in another process. For example, if process A allocates some shared memory that is giveable, it specifies the PID of process B to give that segment to pro-cess B when invoking *DosGiveSeg*. This specification establishes a mapping in process B's process address space (LDT). Conversely, if the segment was getable, process B could get access to process A's segment by calling the *DosGetSeg* API and providing the selector of the segment in process A's context. In both cases, the process gaining access to the shared segment must become aware of the selector for addressing the seg-ment through an interprocess communication mechanism. Give-get shared memory is typically used by closely coupled peer processes that need to pass data to each other. Figure 6.2 illustrates 16-bit memory sharing.

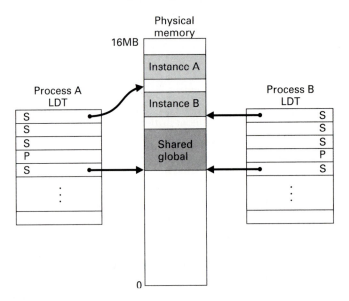

Fig. 6.2   16-bit memory sharing.

DosFreeSeg is used for freeing all segments in the system, whether they are shared or private. For each shared segment, the system maintains a usage count that represents the number of times a segment has been shared. Each time a segment is freed, the usage count is decremented. The actual shared segments are freed when their usage count reaches 0. When a process terminates, the system automatically frees any allocated memory that has not already been deallocated.

6.2.3.3 Memory Suballocation

Since the system must track each segment that is allocated, it is expensive to allocate a segment for small memory objects (1 byte to 2KB). Allocating a segment for every small object can slow down the process, since segment management is performed by kernel APIs, and the process must continually reload segment registers to change addressability to each small segment. When the size of a segment is smaller than the size of the data structures that the system maintains for that segment, memory as a resource is not being used in an optimal fashion. Allocating a segment for each small object needed also causes the LDT selectors that compose the process virtual address space to be consumed excessively. Furthermore, allocating a segment for each object requires segment registers to be loaded whenever the segment is addressed, a slow operation compared to accessing memory within a segment that is already addressed.

To reduce this overhead and fragmentation, OS/2 provides a memory-suballocation subsystem that provides management for memory objects within a segment. The memory-suballocation subsystem runs in user mode and resides in a dynamic link library. Therefore, the memory-suballocation API functions are extremely fast compared to the kernel API functions, and run preemptibly. A segment that is suballocated in this fashion is also known as a *heap*. *DosSubSet* initializes a segment for use as a *memory pool.* Memory objects allocated from the pool are of variable length and are byte-granular. Memory is allocated from the heap using *DosSubAlloc,* and is deallocated using *DosSubFree*. Since the memory objects reside within the same segment, access is much faster because a segment register does not have to be reloaded to address different objects in the memory pool. A memory pool or heap can be used with private or shared segments. Since the suballocation APIs are serialized, a heap can be accessed concurrently by multiple threads in different processes.

6.2.3.4 Dynamic Linking

DosExecPgm is used to load programs, as described in Chapter 5. The memory for a program or a library that is allocated while the latter is being loaded is called *load-time memory*. Memory that is allocated while a program or library is being executed using an API is called *run-time memory*. When an executable (EXE) file is loaded into memory, segments are allocated for the contents of the executable file and for the segments of any associated dynamic link libraries (DLLs). The only time that instance data can be allocated is when a DLL is being loaded.

Dynamic linking occurs at load time and at run time. Chapter 5 described how load-time dynamic linking occurs when a process is created using *DosExecPgm*. However, there are several functions in the memory management API that allow a process explicitly to load or attach to a specific DLL module at run time. *DosLoadModule* loads a selected DLL and any resources it needs to complete its load at run time. The process loading or attaching to the library is returned a handle to the loaded module. Generally, handles are used by user processes to specify system-managed objects in API calls. Once a process has loaded a module, the handle can be used on subsequent *DosGetProcAddr* calls to retrieve the address of entry points within the module. When the process has finished using the library, *DosFreeModule* is invoked with the module handle to notify the system that the process has finished using the module.

6.2.4 OS/2 1.X Memory Management Kernel

The OS/2 kernel provides most of the memory management functions. The memory management portion of the kernel consists of four components: the *virtual memory manager,* the *loader,* the *physical memory manager,* and the *swapper.* The virtual memory manager is responsible for providing the memory management API, and for handling the descriptor table for mapping virtual memory to physical memory. The loader is responsible for program loading, dynamic linking, and demand loading of segments from executable files and dynamic link libraries. The physical memory manager is responsible for the management of physical memory resources and of compaction to reclaim physical memory fragments. The swapper extends the physical memory resource by storing currently unneeded segments in a swap file and restoring them when they are referenced.

6.2.4.1 Virtual Memory Management

The virtual memory manager is responsible for providing the memory management API used by processes to manipulate segments within their process virtual address spaces. It is also responsible for the management of the descriptor tables, of shared addresses, and of memory-overcommit accounting. Finally, the virtual memory manager maintains data structures representing user segments and handles segment-not-present faults.

6.2.4.1.1 Overcommit Accounting   Overcommit accounting is necessary to ensure that the system always has enough memory to run, and that the total allocated resources do not exceed the size of the swap file. The 80286 has four segment registers, and each segment register can map a single 64KB segment at a time. Since a single instruction can cause an access of two more segments at a time, such as a call through a call gate between privilege levels, a total of 6 x 64KB, or 372KB, of physical memory must be available in order to guarantee that a process can run. So that a process does not thrash the system attempting to load its segments into memory when it exits the kernel, a special routine is used to load all the process's segments atomically. Fixed kernel memory and locked user segments in the system reduce the amount of memory available for a process to run. Fixed kernel allocations and long-term locks fail if the total memory remaining is too small for a single process to run.

6.2.4.1.2 Descriptor Management   The 80286 descriptor tables are managed by the virtual memory manager. The GDT is used to map the system virtual addresses to physical memory. The GDT contains the descriptors for the kernel's code and data, for the device drivers' code and data, and for the call gates to the kernel. Free GDT descriptors are linked into a free list using the fields of the descriptor fields that are unused when a descriptor is invalid. The kernel provides simple functions for allocating and freeing GDT descriptors when necessary.

Each process virtual address space is mapped by an LDT. Each LDT is a segment that is grown dynamically as the size of the largest LDT in the system increases. Each LDT maps all the segments allocated at load time and run time on behalf of a given process. When context switches occur between processes, the dispatcher calls the virtual memory manager to switch LDTs. Figure 6.1 illustrates the descriptor tables.

The LDT is divided into private and shared selectors (or descriptors). In OS/2 1.0, the shared and private selectors are interleaved in a ratio of one shared selector to one private selector (1:1). However, OS/2 1.1 changed this ratio to three shared selectors to one private selector (3:1). Shared and instance objects are allocated at common shared addresses in the process virtual address spaces, because processes tend to need more shared virtual addresses than they do private virtual addresses. The selector type is independent of whether the segment contents are shared. The private selectors within an LDT are used to map segments that are private to a process, including code and data segments from the EXE file and API-allocated private segments. Even though EXE code and read-only objects are private, they are shared with each instance of the same program. Since a process can dynamically attach to a shared library, shared selectors are used to map segments from dynamic link libraries. Code, global shared data, and instance data segments are mapped using shared selectors. Shared selectors are also used for API-allocated shared memory, both named and give-get.

As stated previously, all shared segments, whether code or data, occur at the same virtual address in all process virtual address spaces. This single address simplifies the task of tracking shared memory usage in different processes. The virtual memory manager uses a systemwide bitmap for handling the reservation of shared selectors across all LDTs in the system. Each bit in the bitmap corresponds to a descriptor or selector in the LDT. The bits for the private selectors in the bitmap are set to indicate that the selectors are not available, and the bits representing shared selectors are clear to indicate that these selectors are free. When a shared segment is allocated, a slot for the shared descriptor is found by consultation with the system LDT bitmap, and the descriptor is reserved across all processes by setting of the entry in the bitmap. Private LDT descriptors are managed in the same way as GDT descriptors. Free LDT descriptors within an LDT are linked in a free list using the fields of the descriptor that are unused when the descriptor is invalid.

Dividing the LDT into shared and private descriptors reduces virtual memory consumption. If each process's code were mapped using shared selectors, then every time a process was started, the system would have to update and grow every LDT in the system to accommodate the new segments. This strategy would force each LDT to be larger than necessary. Splitting the process virtual address space into private and shared addresses eliminates this side effect. However, another side effect is introduced by the sharing of memory at the same virtual address in all contexts. If a single process uses many shared objects or segments, it can consume shared address space in another process's LDT.

Code segments from executable files and dynamic link libraries always share their contents or storage. For this scheme to work, the virtual memory manager must ensure that the same selector is available in all contexts for mapping the shared code. For shared libraries, the LDT bitmap reserves selectors across processes. However, this mechanism does not work for code from an executable file, since it is mapped using private selectors. The system guarantees that the same private selectors are available each time a given process is loaded, since the LDT is empty at the time a program is loaded.

6.2.4.1.3 Object Management   The major data structure that is used by the virtual memory manager for tracking system objects and user segments is called the *handle table*. Each memory object in the system is assigned a 16-bit *handle*. The handle of a memory object is an index into the virtual memory manager's handle table. A handle selects a *handle table entry (HTE)* that represents the memory object. Each HTE contains permanent information on segments, indicating whether they are present in physical memory, in the swap file, or in an executable file or dynamic link library. Figure 6.3 illustrates the contents of a handle table entry.

The handle table has a semaphore associated with it that is used to serialize access to the handle table when it is grown. The only times that two different threads try to modify the handle table concurrently are when one thread tries to access an object in interrupt mode while another thread is accessing it in kernel mode during a system call, or while a thread in kernel mode has voluntarily yielded the processor. This is due to the nonpreemptible nature of the OS/2 kernel.

Each HTE has a flags field that indicates whether the object is shared or private, and whether it is moveable, fixed, swappable, or discardable. The flags also indicate whether the memory object must reside in physical memory above or below 1MB. The latter indicator is significant with respect to how the system provides DOS compatibility. It allows the virtual memory manager to be flexible enough to allocate memory so that the memory is addressable when the processor is in real mode running a DOS application. Another bit in the HTE flags is used to indicate when an operation is in progress for the object. This bit is used as a per-object semaphore for allowing a thread to gain ownership of a handle for the duration of an operation on a specific memory object. If an operation is in progress when a thread attempts to access a handle, it blocks using the address of the HTE as a block identifier.

In addition to the HTE flags, each HTE also contains the physical address of an object when that object is present in physical memory and is mapped by a descriptor. The selector field in the HTE indicates the descriptor used to map the segment. The lock count field

← 32 bits →	
Handle flags	PhysAddr (low)
PhysAddr (high) / Lock count	Primary selector

Fig. 6.3   16-bit handle table entry (HTE).

indicates the number of outstanding locks on the object. Locks are used by the kernel and device drivers to fix discardable or swappable memory segments in physical memory. Some of the fields for physical address in HTEs are overlapped by other information when an object is not present, as we shall describe in a moment. Locks are discussed in more detail in Chapter 8. Some of the fields in HTEs are overlapped by other information when an object is not present, as we shall also examine now.

Each object in the system has an owner field that identifies from where the memory object came. In other words, the owner field indicates whether the segment is a discardable one that can be reloaded from an EXE or DLL module, or is a swappable API-allocated one that resides on the swap file. If the memory object is discardable, the owner is the handle to the MTE of the module that contains the segment. If it is swappable, the owner is a handle to the PTDA of the process.

There are two prinicipal types of memory objects mapped by the handle table: *system objects* and *user objects*. System objects are always present and fixed, and have special reserved handle values for their owner fields. Examples of system objects are PTDAs, MTEs, and LDTs. Each PTDA has an HTE that contains its physical address, and a special owner value that tells the virtual memory manager that the system object is a PTDA. A different owner-field value (handle) is reserved for MTEs, LDTs, and other system-object classes.

System objects are mapped dynamically; in other words, they are not allocated permanent descriptor mappings, and are not accessible until they are mapped explicitly. The distinction between an object and a segment in 16-bit OS/2 is that an object does not necessarily have a descriptor mapping it, whereas a segment is always mapped. Since there are so many system objects, allocating to each system object a permanent descriptor would cause a huge growth in the GDT, and would result in a significant reduction in the number of GDT selectors available for other purposes. Therefore, each system object is mapped by an HTE to a physical address, instead of being mapped by a descriptor, to conserve GDT selectors. This mapping strategy also allows references to these system objects to use 16-bit memory object handles instead of 24-bit physical addresses or 32-bit 16:16 virtual addresses, resulting in a memory savings in kernel data structures. These fixed objects are dynamically mapped and unmapped by the virtual memory manager whenever they need to be accessed.

For example, if an MTE needs to be addressed, the MTE handle is passed to a mapping routine called *MemMapMTE*, which allocates a GDT descriptor that maps the physical address contained in the HTE for the MTE. When the MTE no longer needs to be addressed, *MemUnmapMTE* is called to deallocate the descriptor mapping. Any references to the MTE in other kernel data structures use the 16-bit memory-object handle for that MTE.

User objects also are mapped by the handle table. User objects are either API-allocated segments or segments that reside in an EXE or DLL file. Note that user objects are called segments since they always have a virtual memory mapping in an LDT. The owner field of a user object is either an MTE handle or a PTDA handle, based on whether the segment comes from an EXE or DLL file, or whether it is allocated by an API request. The rest of the contents of the HTE of a user memory object depend on whether or not the segment is present in physical memory. In the case of system objects, segments are always present. User objects, however, can be present or not present.

Figure 6.4 illustrates the 16-bit virtual memory management data structures for three segments. Segment A is a discardable segment that resides in the EXE file of the process when it is not in memory. Segment B is a swappable segment that resides in the swap file when not in memory. Segment C is a swappable present segment in physical memory.

If a segment is present, the HTE's physical address field contains the 24-bit physical address of the segment in physical memory. Although, at first glance, this address appears redundant, since the present descriptor also contains the physical address, it is needed because the memory manager may be called in real mode as the result of an interrupt occuring while a DOS application is running, and because the owner field is saved by the physical memory manager to save space. Chapter 10 discusses in more detail the requirements of the DOS compatibility component on the kernel.

The lock field in the HTE is valid for counting locks that are made by device drivers or other portions of the kernel for I/O operations that require the object to be fixed. A lock forces a segment to be fixed, and prevents the segment from being moved or swapped until it is unlocked. A present segment also has a descriptor allocated to it, and the descriptor points to the physical memory that is allocated by the physical memory manager. The selector field of the HTE indicates which descriptor was allocated for the segment. In Fig. 6.4, segment C is a present swappable segment.

If a segment is not present, the HTE is used to store information that can be used to determine how to reload the segment when a segment-not-present fault occurs. If a segment is not present, the descriptor contains the memory handle of the HTE that represents the memory object. When a segment-not-present fault occurs, the virtual memory manager uses the memory handle in the faulting descriptor to get to the permanent information for the memory object. If the object is swapped (segment B in Fig 6.4), the physical address field is overlaid with a *swapID* that is passed to the swapper for loading in the image from the swap file. If the segment is discarded (segment A in Fig. 6.4), the physical address is overlaid with the MTE handle of the originating module, and the MTE handle and selector are passed to the loader so that it can demand load the segment from the module.

All the allocation of physical memory occurs as a result of segment-not-present faults. This style of physical memory resource commitment is called *lazy segment allocation*. Postponing physical memory allocation until the latest possible moment results in a reduction in the number of I/O operations that occur when segments are demand loaded from their load modules or from the swap file. The following example illustrates the events that occur when an application allocates a segment by invoking *DosAllocSeg*. From the virtual memory manager's perspective, this is an allocation request for swappable *allocate-on-demand* memory. An HTE is allocated for the segment, as is an LDT descriptor. Overcommit accounting is performed to ensure that the system can satisfy the request with swap space at a later time. The descriptor is marked not present and is filled with the memory object handle for the allocated HTE. The selector allocated is returned to the thread requesting the memory. When the thread attempts to use the

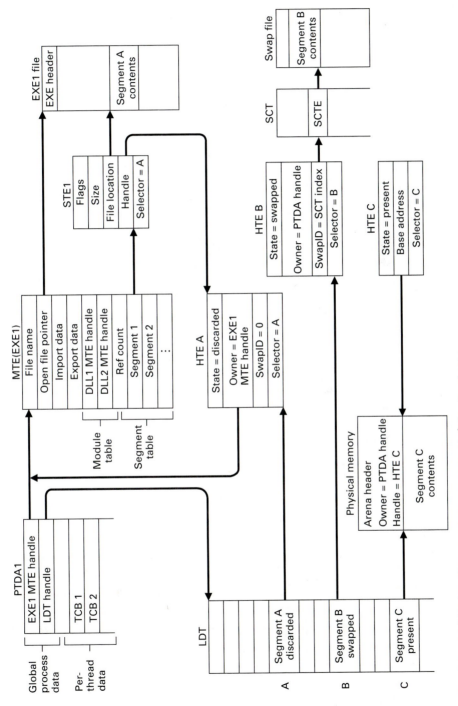

Fig. 6.4   16-bit virtual memory management data structures.

selector by loading the latter into a segment register, a segment-not-present fault occurs, causing the segment-not-present fault handler to be called in the virtual memory manager. The segment-not-present fault handler then calls the physical memory manager to allocate physical storage for the object. After the physical storage is allocated, the physical address returned by the physical memory manager is inserted into the HTE and the descriptor, and the object owner and handle are saved by the physical memory manager. The faulting instruction is restarted, and the process continues.

6.2.4.2 *Loader*

The loader is responsible for program loading and for the management of dynamic linking API. It manages the EXE and DLL modules that are loaded into memory, as well as the segments from these modules. Although both EXE and DLL modules are "executable files," EXEs are programs, whereas DLLs are shared libraries. The loader also provides for demand loading of segments from DLLs and EXEs. The OS/2 loader preresolves at load time all external references that might be called during execution. Figure 6.5 illustrates the file format for 16-bit executable files.

The primary data structure used to track modules and their segments is called the *module table entry (MTE)*. Every load module in the system, whether it is an EXE or a DLL module, has an MTE that describes it. As mentioned previously, from the viewpoint of the virtual memory manager, an MTE is a system object that contains the memory representation of the executable file control information. When the loader allocates an MTE, the virtual memory manager allocates a handle table entry and physical memory for the MTE, since the latter is a fixed system object. Therefore, MTEs are referenced using a 16-bit handle, and are dynamically mapped into the system virtual address space when accessed.

When a process is created with *DosExecPgm,* the loader allocates an MTE, stores the MTE handle in the PTDA of the new process, and maps the MTE into memory. The loader then reads the executable header from the module being loaded into the MTE. All the MTEs in the system are linked in a graph. Since an EXE usually contains references to DLLs, all the DLL modules that are loaded as a result of loading of an EXE module

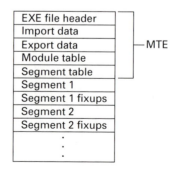

Fig. 6.5   16-bit executable file format.

are linked together. Thus, the MTEs that represent EXE files are head pointers or roots into the system's graph of MTEs.

Each MTE also contains a reference count of the number of times each program module is loaded. During the program load process, the loader first scans the MTEs in the system to see whether the module is already loaded. If it is, then the new process attaches to the module by incrementing the reference count in the MTE and calling the virtual memory manager to attach the module's segments to the new process. Figure 6.4 contains an illustration of an MTE.

The MTE also contains the module file name and an open file pointer for accessing the load file. The import data contain information on references to other modules; the export data contain the module's public definitions. The module table portion of an MTE contains MTE handles of the modules that have been loaded to resolve this module's dynamic link imports.

The portion of the MTE that maps the segments of a module is called the *segment table*. The segment table contains *segment table entries (STEs)*. Each STE contains the flags that describe the attributes of the segment, the size of the segment, a file offset into the load module from which the segment can be loaded, the virtual memory handle for the segment, and the selector used to map the segment. Figure 6.4 contains an illustration of an STE.

When *DosExecPgm* is called, the loader calls multitasking to allocate a process with an LDT and a PTDA. Next, the loader reads the EXE header to determine the size of the MTE; this step is necessary because the MTE is of variable length, depending on the size of the load module. Once the size of the MTE is known, the loader calls the virtual memory manager to allocate an MTE as a system object. Once the MTE object is mapped, the loader then calls the file system to read the MTE into memory from the load module file. The next step in program loading is to load the DLLs referenced by the import table. If these DLLs are already loaded for another process, then the EXE's MTE is linked to the MTE of the loaded DLL.

The last portion of program loading is to process the segments in the segment table. The loader allocates virtual memory for each segment, and the descriptors are marked not present. If the load module is being attached to only the new process, the virtual memory manager attaches the segments to the process virtual address space by editing the LDT. Segments that are required by the user to be loaded when the program is loaded are called *preload segments*. The default alternative to a preload segment is a *demand load segment* that is loaded when a thread accesses the descriptor and causes a segment-not-present fault.

Demand loading occurs when the loader is called by the virtual memory manager during a segment-not-present fault to load in a segment that resides in an EXE or DLL module. Recall from Section 6.2.4.1 that, when a segment-not-present fault occurs, the descriptor for the segment contains the handle for the object. In the case of a demand-loadable object, the handle table entry indicates that the segment resides in a load module and contains the MTE handle of the originating module. The segment-not-present fault handler allocates physical memory for the segment based on the size in the descriptor, sets the base address field in the faulting descriptor, then passes the MTE handle and the faulting selector to the loader. From this information, the loader can map the appropriate MTE, and can search the segment table for the segment allocated to the same selector. Once the correct STE is found, the loader calls the file system to load the segment from the load module into physical memory. The loader then performs any necessary fixups on the segment, validates the descriptor, and returns to the faulting instruction.

To provide preload segments, the loader calls a virtual memory manager interface that simulates a segment-not-present fault for the preload segments. This fault causes the loader to demand load the segments before the module's entry point is executed. The simulated-fault approach is used, since the virtual memory manager is already prepared to perform lazy allocation of the physical memory for segments.

6.2.4.3 Physical Memory Management

The physical memory manager manages the system's physical memory resource. It consists of two components: the physical allocator and the compactor. The physical allocator manages free and allocated blocks of physical memory in the system's physical address space. So that free blocks that are small and fragmented within the physical address space can be reclaimed, compaction is implemented. The compactor runs only as a result of a request for allocation of physical memory.

Figure 6.6 illustrates the physical memory layout of the system. The system is partitioned into those portions that are necessary for DOS compatibility, and those that are not. The 1MB boundary is a critical mark, since physical addresses above 1MB can be accessed only when the processor is in protected mode. Portions of the system that must be accessed while a DOS program is running must be in contiguous memory below 1MB, since the system runs DOS applications in real mode. However, in OS/2 1.3, the DOS environment can be swapped when it is moved to the background. Chapter 10 discusses the memory requirements of the DOS environment in more detail.

The main data structure used by the physical memory manager to track physical memory is called an *arena header*. Each arena header describes a tree or in-use physical memory block. There are two double-linked lists of arena headers in the system: one that links all arena headers, and one that links all arena headers for free blocks. The free

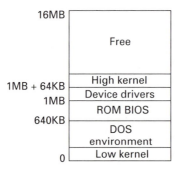

Fig. 6.6   16-bit physical memory map.

list is used by the physical allocator when satisfying allocation requests, and the in-use list is used by the compactor when attempting to reclaim free space by copying segments around physical memory. The *physical arena* refers to all the free and allocated physical memory and arena lists. Figure 6.7 illustrates the layout of an arena header.

Each arena header contains a next and a previous field, a next-free and a previous-free field, the size of the object, the handle table entry of the object, the owner of the object, a lock count for the object, some flags, and a timestamp. The timestamp indicates the last time that the object was accessed.

The handle and owner fields that are in the arena header are kept there on behalf of the virtual memory manager for two reasons. When a segment is present in memory and is mapped by a descriptor and a handle table entry, the owner and handle must be saved by the physical memory manager for later use by the virtual memory manager when the segment is swapped out or discarded. Recall that there is no room in an HTE for this information if a segment is present. The second reason is that they are needed by the compactor to tell the virtual memory manager which descriptors to update when a segment is moved in physical memory. From the HTE, the virtual memory manager can find all the descriptors in all contexts that map a given physical block.

The arena headers are linked using 32-bit physical pointers, and are physically located adjacent to the physical block that they describe. When the arena is traversed, the 32-bit physical address link fields are converted to 16:16 virtual addresses using GDT selectors reserved by the physical memory manager. Effectively, each arena header is in its own segment, since a segment register must be reloaded when a link is traversed. Furthermore, none of the arena headers have permanent descriptors to map them, so the dynamic GDT mapping occurs between links also. The layout of the arena data structures in physical memory is illustrated in Fig. 6.8.

Compared to placing the arena headers in a table, this approach at first appears nonoptimal. Placing the arena headers in a table would still require 32-bit link fields unless the table were restricted to 64KB (a single segment). More complex descriptor management would be needed for setting up the table, as well as logic to deal with growing and shrinking the table dynamically. However, there are also positive side effects associated with placing the arena headers throughout physical memory. Translating any virtual

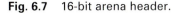

```
         ◄──────── 32 bits ────────►
        ┌───────────────────────────┐
        │           Next            │
        ├───────────────────────────┤
        │         Previous          │
        ├───────────────────────────┤
        │         Next free         │
        ├───────────────────────────┤
        │       Previous free       │
        ├───────────────────────────┤
        │           Size            │
        ├─────────────┬─────────────┤
        │   Handle    │    Owner    │
        ├─────────────┼─────────────┤
        │   Flags     │  LockCount  │
        ├─────────────┴─────────────┤
        │       LRU timestamp       │
        └───────────────────────────┘
```

Fig. 6.7   16-bit arena header.

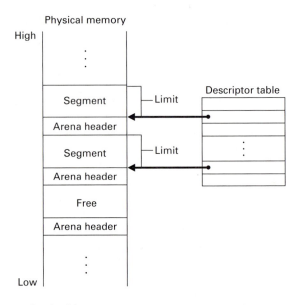

Fig. 6.8   16-bit arena physical layout.

address into the address of an arena structure is simple, since the beginning of the arena structure is located directly beside and below the segment in physical memory. Subtracting the size of an arena header from the base address in a descriptor yields the physical address of the arena header for the segment.

We now describe a typical physical memory allocation scenario. A thread running in user mode attempts to access a segment allocated with *DosAllocSeg,* but a segment-not-present fault occurs. The virtual memory manager handles the fault and checks the handle table entry to determine whether the segment is allocate on demand, discarded, or swapped. The physical allocator is called to allocate physical memory for the segment, and employs a *first-fit* allocation strategy. The physical allocator scans the free list of arena headers, searching for a block big enough to service the request. If a free block is found that can fulfill the request, the arena header is removed from the free list. The handle and owner of the segment previously stored in the HTE for the segment are passed to the physical allocator as parameters of the allocation request, and are placed in the allocated arena header. The physical address of the allocated block is returned to the virtual memory manager. The virtual memory manager then completes the transaction by updating the descriptor with the allocated base address. If the segment is discarded or swapped, the loader or swapper is called to swap the segment into memory: if the segment is allocate on demand, no segment loading is necessary. Finally, the virtual memory manager validates the descriptor by setting the present bit; it then restarts the original faulting instruction.

The scenario changes if the physical allocator fails to find an arena header on the free list for a block large enough to satisfy the physical allocation request. Since the allocation and freeing of small segments can cause fragmentation in the physical address space, there may exist enough free physical storage to satisfy the request, but it may not be in contiguous blocks. So that enough free physical storage to satisfy the request can be created, the compactor portion of the physical memory manager is called. The compactor attempts to reclaim free storage by moving (copying) physical blocks and thus creating a free block large enough to satisfy the allocation request. If the compactor fails to reclaim enough storage to satisfy the request, it either discards or swaps out enough segments to create a large-enough block. Physical memory allocations can potentially block, and also can drive the compaction and swapping of segments in the system.

Compaction is needed because variable-length segments can fragment physical memory. To reduce this fragmentation and to reclaim physical memory, the compactor performs *segment motion*. A segment can be moved invisibly to the processes using it, since the segment is referenced via a descriptor. The compactor interacts with the virtual memory manager to update the base address field of the descriptors referencing moved segments. The compactor executes only as a result of a physical allocation request; it is serialized to move only one segment at a time. Since copying of segments can be a lengthy operation, when the compactor is copying large segments, it yields the processor using the TCYield interface discussed in Chapter 5. Compaction can be disabled when the system is started.

Segments are aged in a *least recently used (LRU)* fashion to determine the best candidate for swapping or discarding. The timestamp field of an arena header is used to record the age of a segment, and is initialized with the time at which a physical allocation occurs. Approximately four times per second, the *SchedClock* routine (discussed in Chapter 5) calls the physical memory manager to age swappable segments in the GDT. Swappable segments in the GDT can be allocated by device drivers and file systems. Whenever a process is being context switched out, one-quarter of the process's LDT is aged before the new LDT is switched in. Segments are aged by scanning the segment descriptors and checking the accessed bit to see whether the segment has been referenced since the last time its age was recorded. If the accessed bit is set, the time is recorded in the timestamp field of the arena header for the segment, and the accessed bit is reset. The timestamp field of an arena header is also reset whenever a segment is swapped in.

When the compactor determines that a swap out or discard operation is necessary to satisfy an allocation request, it constructs an ordered list of the oldest segments in the system. The compactor then discards or swaps out the segments on the list until enough free storage is available to satisfy the original physical allocation request. If the swap file is full and cannot be grown, the system attempts to find enough discardable segments to create sufficient free storage.

6.2.4.4 Segment Swapping

OS/2 implements segment swapping; it does not use program swapping, as used in UNIX systems. Compaction is not a complete solution, since it does not allow more physical memory to be allocated than exists in the computer. Swapping does soften the physical memory barrier, and does allow programs to use more memory than is present. A situation in which memory is 25 percent overcommitted usually performs acceptably.

However, the relatively slow disk speeds on most 80286 systems (on the order of 20 to 80 milliseconds) prevent true demand segment swapping from being feasible in heavily overcommitted situations. Like compaction, swapping can be disabled when the system is started.

There are basically two routines in the swapper, called *SwapOut* and *SwapIn*. *SwapOut* is called only as a result of an allocation request, as described in the previous section. *SwapIn* is called as the result of a segment-not-present fault on a swapped-out segment. Swapping occurs on a thread different from the thread that causes the fault. The swapper thread is a special kernel thread that executes at privilege level 0.

The major data structure of the swapper is called the *swap control table (SCT)*. The SCT is composed of swap control table entries (SCTEs). Each SCTE contains flags describing the segment and the offset in the swap file of the segment. The size of a segment that is swapped out is maintained in the not-present descriptor(s) for the segment. Figure 6.9 illustrates the swapper data structures.

When *SwapOut* is called, the swapper allocates an SCTE for the segment and writes the segment to the swap file. The index into the SCT for the allocated entry is called the *swapID* and is stored by the virtual memory manager in the handle table entry for the segment. The virtual memory manager marks the descriptor not present, and puts, into the descriptor the handle to the segment, so that the segment can be located later. During a segment-not-present fault, the virtual memory manager calls *SwapIn* and provides the swapID of the desired segment and an address into which the swapper can read the segment.

The swap file is managed by the file system rather than by the swapper. Some systems allow the swapper to perform direct I/O to the swap device for better performance, but this approach also has drawbacks. The swapper must have intimate knowledge of the layout of the physical swap device (usually a disk), and growing the swap file without reformatting the swap device is difficult. The OS/2 approach keeps the swapper simple and allows the file system to manage the swap disk. Under the FAT file system, it can lead to some swap file fragmentation at a physical level, but the HPFS file system supports a physically contiguous swap file. Even on a FAT system, the user can move the swap file to its own partition, resulting in a contiguous swap file.

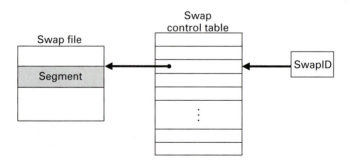

Fig. 6.9   16-bit swapper data structures.

Since the swapping of small segments in an overcommitted system can lead to excessive performance overhead, a *swap cache* is used to reduce the number of disk operations for swapping. The swap cache resides in a fixed buffer on the order of 16KB. When *SwapOut* is called with a small segment, the swapper merely copies the segment into the swap cache. When the swap cache is full, it is written to the swap file in a single operation. Each small segment still retains its own swapID and SCTE.

6.3 OS/2 2.X MEMORY MANAGEMENT

The primary motivation behind the design of OS/2 2.X is to ensure portability. For OS/2 2.X to compete with other high-end workstation operating system platforms such as UNIX, OS/2's 32-bit applications, its dynamic link libraries, and the OS/2 2.X system itself must be retargetable to other processor platforms. This requirement is especially significant given the current trend toward generic RISC processor engines in workstations. This design goal represents a major departure from the design philosophy of OS/2 1.X, which emphasizes exploitation of the 80286 processor.

The memory model of an operating system is key in providing the capability for applications, dynamic link libraries, and the system to be recompiled when a new processor architecture is being retargeted. The initial implementation of OS/2 2.X is targeted at the 80386 processor and 80486 processors. It takes full advantage of the capabilities of these processors that are common with most 32-bit processor engines, and makes use of features specific to the Intel processors only in areas of DOS and 16-bit OS/2 compatibility (see Chapter 10).

OS/2 2.X defines a 32-bit memory model that is designed to be portable to any 32-bit uniprocessor or multiprocessor architecture including RISC platforms. Another major design goal of the memory model for OS/2 2.X is to provide memory objects that are greater than 64KB or larger than physical memory. The 16-bit version of OS/2 allows segments up to only 64KB, forcing applications to add logic for managing the segmented virtual address space. OS/2 2.X provides all the same memory sharing and memory allocation functions as does 16-bit OS/2.

6.3.1 Memory Model

The main features of the 80386 and 80486 processors are paged virtual memory and 32-bit-wide segments, which are up to 4GB in size. A weakness with the Intel segmentation scheme is that its memory architecture combines addressing and protection in a unique way that is different from the scheme used by most processors. Segmentation also forces applications to have code that implements processor-dependent addressing. A segmented virtual address space is not contiguous and, therefore, provides an unnatural memory addressing model. However, a 32-bit segment can be used to simulate a large, flat 32-bit virtual address space that is contiguous. The flat 32-bit virtual address space is a common feature on many processors, and it is portable.

In 80286 addressing, a segmented virtual address (selector:offset) is translated by a descriptor into a physical address. However, on the 80386 with paging enabled, another level of address translation exists between the descriptor mapping and physical memory; it is called the linear address space (see Chapter 2). On the 80386, a segmented virtual address (16:16 or 16:32) is translated by descriptors into a 32-bit (flat) linear address, which in turn is mapped to a 32-bit physical address by page tables. If a pair of code and data descriptors is created that maps the entire linear address space, and is loaded into the segment registers and never changed, the virtual address space is "flattened" and segmentation is masked from applications. This memory model is called the *flat memory model,* and is used in 32-bit OS/2.

Since segments on the 80386 have 32-bit sizes, any byte within the linear address space can be accessed using only a 32-bit linear address without changing the segment registers. In the flat model, a linear address is a virtual address. A flat model virtual address is also called a 0:32 address, since the segment value is never changed and the offset value is a 32-bit offset. In addition to being portable, the flat model provides superior performance over any segmented model, since it does not require segment registers to be reloaded every time addressability to a different memory object needs to be established.

The system virtual address space is mapped by a pair of GDT code and data descriptors with limit fields of 4GB. When a thread is executing in kernel mode or at privilege level 0, the segment registers contain selectors for the entire 32-bit linear address space.

The process virtual address space is mapped by a pair of GDT code and data descriptors with limit fields of 512MB. The 512MB limit is due to the implementation of 16-bit OS/2 compatibility and will be removed in future versions. The segment limit of the process virtual address space is used to protect the system memory from threads running in user mode. The system provides an independent 512MB linear address space to each process by giving each process its own set of page tables. Like the 16-bit process virtual address spaces, the 32-bit process virtual address space is partitioned into private and shared regions that grow toward each other. Page tables, rather than LDTs, are used to provide the same level of sharing found in the 16-bit system. Although LDTs are not used for the flat model, they are used for providing compatibility for 16-bit OS/2 applications and are discussed in Chapter 10. Figure 6.10 illustrates the virtual address spaces present in the flat model of OS/2 2.X.

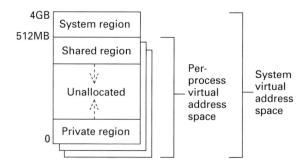

Fig. 6.10   32-bit virtual address spaces.

6.3.2 Memory Objects

The smallest memory unit in the flat model is a page (4KB on the 80386), compared to a byte in the 16-bit segmented model. Thus, the flat model is *page-granular*. A memory object is not a segment in the flat model, but rather is a range of contiguous linear pages within the process virtual address space. The base address of a memory object is aligned on a page boundary, and the size of a memory object is a multiple of the page size. Unlike in the segmented system, all memory objects are addressable simultaneously. No segment registers need to be loaded, which results in optimal performance for an 80386 in protected mode. Also, since no application logic is tied to a processor-dependent memory model, the portability requirement is met. Memory objects in the flat model are nonrelocatable, and the pages that compose memory objects are swappable.

The use of paging allows memory objects to be larger than 64KB, and larger than physical memory; it also allows more efficient swapping and memory overcommit algorithms. Paging also allows *sparse objects* to be allocated. Sparse objects have some pages that are present and some pages that are invalid. Since the flat model "flattens" the segmented architecture, page-level protection is used to provide separation of code and data within a process virtual address space. Each page is assigned the read-only or read-write attribute. Although the granularity of memory protection is a page, rather than a byte as in the segmented model, illegal memory accesses by flat-model programs are reported with byte-granular accuracy.

As in the 16-bit system, there are basically four types of objects that are classified according to the attributes of virtual address type, storage type, and the type of pages that back that storage. Besides the method of addressing memory objects and the attributes of pages, the memory object types in the OS/2 32-bit flat model are equivalent to those found in the 16-bit segmented model.

Pages are also classified according to whether they are *fixed, resident, swappable, discardable, invalid,* or *guard*. Fixed and resident pages exist only in kernel space and are always present in physical memory. Swappable and discardable pages are allocated by applications and by dynamic link libraries. Invalid pages are not mapped. Accessing an invalid page causes a fault that is the equivalent of a general protection fault in the 16-bit system. Pages are also classified according to whether they are read-only (code pages), or read-write (data pages), and whether they are accessible from user or supervisor (kernel) mode. When a memory object is allocated, all the pages have the same attributes. However, page attributes can be changed dynamically using a function of the memory management API.

Sparse objects are a natural subset of page-granular memory objects. A sparse object consists of pages that have varying attributes. The flat model API allows an application to reserve linear memory without physical memory. The virtual address space for the object is reserved and the pages are set to invalid. Linear pages that have been reserved and set invalid are said to be *uncommitted*. When the application needs to utilize some uncommitted but reserved pages, it can dynamically request the system to *commit* the pages for usage. When a page is *committed,* the system then reserves physical or swap memory for backing up that page, and the page is accessible by the requestor. If an application accesses an uncommitted page, the result is the same as a general protection fault in 16-bit OS/2, since the page is invalid.

A guard page is a special type of committed page used to allow user thread stacks to grow dynamically. Thread stacks are sparse objects with a guard page between the stack pages that have been committed and those that are uncommitted. When an instruction causes the guard page to be accessed, the system removes the guard attribute from the faulting page, resulting in a regular committed page. Then, an exception is generated that allows the thread to commit the next page in the stack as a guard page, and then to resume the faulting instruction. The use of guard pages, user thread stack growth, and the associated exceptions are discussed further in Chapter 7.

As in the 16-bit segmented model, there are both private and shared virtual address-es, and private and shared storage. Instead of the private and shared addresses being defined by different descriptors in an LDT, they are represented by contiguous regions in the process virtual address space that grow toward each other. The level of sharing in the segmented system is achieved using a set of page tables, instead of an LDT, for each process virtual address space.

API-allocated objects and EXE read-write data objects are private-address and private-storage objects. Private addresses and shared storage are used for mapping EXE code and read-only objects, as in the 16-bit system. Shared-address objects also have the classifications found in the 16-bit system. Shared-address objects are mapped at the same virtual address in all processes. Analogous to reserving shared LDT descriptors in the 16-bit segmented model, the linear pages representing objects in the shared address region are reserved across all processes to allow shared objects to reside at the same address in all contexts. Shared objects with shared storage are allocated using the shared memory API or during the load-time allocation of dynamic link libraries' shared code and data objects. Instance data objects also exist in which there is a shared address with a private storage copy of the object for each process that has attached to it for dynamic link libraries. As in the 16-bit system, instance objects are used by DLLs for per-process data structures.

6.3.3 OS/2 2.X Memory Management API

This section describes the functions of the 32-bit OS/2 memory management API.

6.3.3.1 Private Memory

Private memory is allocated using *DosAllocMem. DosAllocMem* allows the requestor to allocate an object up to the size of available memory in the process virtual address space, and returns a 32-bit offset to the start of the allocated memory object. The memory allocation granularity of the system is a 4KB page. All memory objects are aligned on linear page boundaries, and their sizes are rounded up to the closest multiple of 4KB.

Memory objects allocated with *DosAllocMem* are composed of swappable pages. Allocation flags that are supplied during requests allow the requestor to determine the memory object's attributes, such as read-only, read-write, committed, decommitted, or guard. All the pages within an object have the same attributes when the object is allocated. If the pages are not committed when the object is allocated, the system reserves only linear address space, creating a sparse object. If uncommitted pages are accessed by a user-mode thread, a protection fault is generated.

Private memory is deallocated by a call to *DosFreeMem*. The base address of a valid memory object is the only valid parameter accepted by *DosFreeMem*. Since flat memory objects are not relocatable, there is no memory object reallocation API, as there is in the 16-bit system. Since movement of objects within the address space does not occur, applications use sparse objects and commit pages dynamically in situations where data structures or memory pools must be extended.

6.3.3.2 Shared Memory

Shared-memory objects are allocated from the shared address region of the process virtual address space. As in the 16-bit system, the shared-memory APIs provide support for both named and give-get shared memory. Both API-allocated shared-memory types use shared addresses and shared storage. The functions of the 32-bit shared-memory API are similar to those of the 16-bit shared-memory API, but there are some differences. The API performs operations on flat memory objects that are referenced by a 0:32 virtual address, instead of segments that are referenced by a 16:16 virtual address. Also, the API function names refer to memory objects, instead of to segments.

The previous paragraph stated that the 16-bit and 32-bit APIs are similar but not identical. All shared memory—whether it is named or give-get—is allocated using the *DosAllocSharedMem* function. Allocation flags passed to *DosAllocSharedMem* indicate whether the shared object is giveable or getable, and whether the pages are initially committed or uncommitted. An object-name parameter can be used optionally to create a named shared-memory object. Give-get shared objects are unnamed; attempting to create one with a name results in an error. Also, API-allocated shared-memory objects can be allocated as sparse (uncommitted) objects, and contain swappable pages.

Named shared-memory objects are accessed by processes other than the creator by a call to *DosGetNamedSharedMem*. Giveable shared objects are given to other processes using *DosGiveSharedMem,* and getable shared objects can be mapped into a process's virtual address space by a call to *DosGetSharedMem*. Since each process has its own set of page tables for mapping the shared-memory object, each process that attaches to the shared memory can set its own attributes for the pages in the shared object. *DosFreeMem* is used to free shared memory-objects as well as private memory objects. Except for the basic shared memory allocation API, the shared-memory APIs are the same as the 16-bit versions.

6.3.3.3 Memory Object Control

Each page within a flat-model memory object can have its own set of attributes. *DosQueryMem* allows a thread to query the attributes of a linearly contiguous range of pages within a process virtual address space. *DosQueryMem* accepts a base address parameter and size that define the region of pages to be queried. This memory management API is the only one that accepts an address range that is not entirely within a single memory object. *DosQueryMem* scans the region of pages beginning at the base address until the entire range of pages is scanned, a page with a nonmatching set of attributes is encountered, or the first page of a memory object is encountered. *DosQueryMem* returns the attributes of the pages in the region and the size of the region scanned. Therefore, all the pages ultimately scanned in a single request have the same attributes. Attributes returned indicate whether the range of pages is committed, free (never allocated and therefore invalid), reserved (uncommitted), read-only, execute-only, read-write, or guard.

DosSetMem performs the complementary function of setting the attributes of a range of pages within a memory object. *DosSetMem* can be used to create a sparse object by committing and decommitting pages within a memory object. It also can be used to change the page type. Both *DosQueryMem* and *DosSetMem* can be used on shared and private memory objects. When a shared page is committed, it is committed in all contexts that have attached to it. The page access protection applied to a committed page in another context is the same access protection as that specified when the object was originally allocated or attached to that context. A page in a shared object cannot be decommitted unless a control flag is set when the object is allocated that explicitly allows pages to be decommitted.

6.3.3.4 Memory Suballocation

The memory suballocation API also exists in the 32-bit system to manage small memory objects, which are less than one page (4KB). Since the granularity of allocation in the flat-model system is a page, a page is the minimum-sized object that can be allocated. If an application requires many small memory objects smaller than one page, a heap or memory suballocation pool should be used to divide a large object into many small ones. This strategy prevents fragmentation of the process virtual address space and waste of system resources, which would occur if whole pages were used for each small object.

The memory suballocation API in 32-bit OS/2 is similar in basic function to its 16-bit counterpart, but has several added features. Since the flat model supports memory objects larger than 64KB, a suballocation pool can be arbitrarily large. Also, the programmer has the option of using sparse heaps, in which the pages within the heap object are committed dynamically by the suballocation API as needed. This dynamic commitment is in contrast to requiring all the pages in the heap to be committed at all times. Although the 16-bit version has always provided serialization of threads so that shared heaps are supported, serialization is an option for increasing performance when the heap is a private one.

DosSubSetMem is used to initialize a heap inside a memory object. When *DosSubSetMem* is called, flags are provided that tell the suballocator whether the object is sparse, or whether serialized access to the heap is required. The flags also indicate whether the heap is being created for the first time, or whether another process is attaching to a shared heap. Unlike in the 16-bit version of suballocation, if a shared heap is being used, all processes must attach to the shared memory in which the heap resides, and must call *DosSubSetMem* to notify the system. Also contained in the flags is a bit that allows a current heap to be grown.

DosSubAllocMem is used for allocating memory from the heap, and *DosSubFreeMem* is used to free memory allocated from the heap. *DosSubUnsetMem* allows the memory suballocator to clean up the resources used to manage the heap. Like the 16-bit memory-suballocation API, the 32-bit version resides in a DLL and runs in user mode.

6.3.3.5 Dynamic Linking

The 32-bit dynamic linking APIs are essentially the same as the 16-bit versions. *DosExecPgm* is used to load programs, as described in Chapter 5, and the program loader performs all load-time memory allocations. As in the 16-bit system, dynamic linking occurs at both load time and run time.

The 32-bit run-time dynamic linking API is a flat-model analogue of the 16-bit version. *DosLoadModule* loads a selected DLL and any other modules it needs to complete its load at run time. The process loading or attaching to the library is returned a 32-bit handle to the loaded module. Once a process has loaded a module, the handle may be used on subsequent *DosQueryProcAddr* requests to retrieve the address of entry points within the module. When the process has finished using the shared library, it calls *DosFreeModule,* supplying the handle to notify the system that the process has finished using the module.

6.3.4 OS/2 2.X Memory Management Kernel

The 32-bit kernel is based on the flat memory model, rather than the segmented model of the 16-bit kernel. Also, a greater percentage of the 32-bit kernel is swappable than of the 16-bit kernel, due to paging. The kernel consists of basically the same memory management components: the virtual memory manager, loader, physical memory manager, and swapper. However, the physical memory manager is replaced by the *page manager* and the swapper is replaced by the *page swapper*. The virtual memory manager is responsible for implementing the memory management API, kernel memory allocators, descriptor table management, virtual address space management and object management. The loader is responsible for program loading, dynamic linking, and demand loading of pages from executable and dynamic link library files. The page manager controls the paged physical memory resource, and the page tables that map linear addresses onto physical addresses. The page swapper is used to extend the physical memory resource so that more physical memory can be allocated than exists in a machine.

6.3.4.1 Virtual Memory Management

The OS/2 2.X virtual memory manager provides the flat-model memory management APIs. As described in the API section, these APIs have the equivalent functions of the segmented APIs, but they are for flat memory objects. The virtual memory manager provides kernel memory allocators, which are used to manage kernel memory. It also performs descriptor management to map the system virtual address space and the process virtual address spaces to linear memory. The virtual memory manager maintains regions of linear address space for the private and shared regions within a process, and for the system region that contains the system memory. Object records are used for tracking system and user memory objects that are mapped into the address spaces. When allocating an object, the virtual memory manager calls the page manager to reserve page tables for the virtual memory. The page manager is also called when virtual pages are committed and uncommitted, and during context switch operations.

6.3.4.1.1 Kernel Memory Allocators   Kernel memory allocators are used to manage kernel memory and to reduce fragmentation of memory within the kernel. They are used by most kernel components such as multitasking and interprocess communication. There are three kernel memory allocation interfaces—the *block management package (BMP)*, the *resident heap*, and the *swappable heap*. The BMP routines manage kernel memory pools of fixed-length objects. The use of the BMP reduces fragmentation within the kernel by allowing objects to be packed within a page. The BMP also supports sparse arrays, where pages within a large array are committed and decommitted dynamically. Memory pages are fixed once they are allocated and committed through the BMP. The BMP provides initialization, allocation, free, query, and set interfaces for other kernel components to use.

The resident heap is used for managing variable-length kernel memory objects within the kernel. All objects allocated from the resident heap are packed into fixed pages. The resident heap manager provides UNIX-like *malloc* and *free* style interfaces for allocation and deallocation of memory. The swappable heap is used to manage variable-length kernel memory objects that can be swapped. The kernel components that use swappable kernel memory must deal with the fact that they can be preempted when attempting to access that memory. The swappable heap manager also provides interfaces, called *smalloc* and *sfree,* similar to those of the resident heap manager. There are separate read-write and read-only versions of both the resident and the swappable heaps.

6.3.4.1.2 Descriptor Management   The descriptor management performed by the virtual memory manager is much simpler than that of the 16-bit version of OS/2. The GDT is used to map the process and system virtual address spaces to linear memory. However, no LDTs are necessary in the 32-bit system, although they exist for 16-bit OS/2 compatibility. The usage of LDTs in the 32-bit system is described further in Chapter 10.

The system address space maps the current process virtual address space and the system memory region, which contains the kernel's code and data. The current process virtual address space is a subset of the system virtual address space. The system is protected from the user-mode threads using segment-limit protection. If a user-mode thread attempts to use an address past the limit of the process virtual address space (512MB), a general protection fault occurs. Since each address space has both a code and a data segment alias, separation of read-only (code) and read-write objects within the process virtual address space is implemented using page-level protection attributes instead of segment attributes.

The system and process virtual address spaces are mapped using four descriptors to emulate two large segments. The first pair of descriptors, one code and one data, is privilege level 0 with a limit of 4GB. These two descriptors are loaded into the segment registers when a thread is in kernel mode, and represent the system virtual address space. The other pair of descriptors, also code and data, is privilege level 3 and has limits of 512MB. This pair of descriptors is loaded into the segment registers when a thread is executing in user mode. The limitation of 512MB for each process virtual address space is due to the 16-bit OS/2 compatibility implementation; it is discussed further in Chapter 10. Figure 6.10 illustrates the 32-bit virtual address spaces.

Only the one pair of user space GDT descriptors is used for all processes in the system. Descriptors point to linear memory, and the linear memory is in turn mapped to the physical memory by page tables. Since each process has its own linear address space, only one set of descriptors is needed. Because a separate linear address space defined by page tables is provided for each process, processes are encapsulated and are protected from one another. During a context switch, the page manager switches the per-process page tables and flushes the TLB; no segment register reloading is necessary.

6.3.4.1.3 Linear Address Management   In the 32-bit version of OS/2, arenas are used by the virtual memory manager to manage regions of linear address space. Arenas are similar to the physical arena used to manage physical memory found in 16-bit OS/2. However, in the 32-bit system an arena represents a contiguous subset of virtual (instead of physical) address space, and there are several arenas in the system. There are three arena types: the *system arena,* the *shared arena,* and the per-process *private arenas.* Figure 6.11 illustrates the arenas in the system.

The system arena maps the range of system linear addresses above the process virtual address space. The system arena is backed by a single set of page tables that is shared in the context of all processes. System memory objects are accessible only by a thread in kernel mode or privilege level 0, and are mapped into the system arena.

Each process has its own private arena that is used for mapping private objects, such as API-allocated data and EXE code. The private arena maps the private addresses of a process much as do the private selectors in a process's LDT in the 16-bit system. The private arena begins at the low addresses in each process virtual address space, and is guaranteed to contain a minimum of 64MB of available private address space when a process is created. Since the private arena starts at the low addresses, EXE code is guaranteed to be loaded at the same virtual address in all process contexts. Therefore, if the same program is loaded into multiple processes, the EXE code is loaded into the same private virtual address in each context, and a single copy of the code is shared. Recall that EXE code is a private-address, shared-storage memory object.

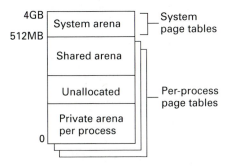

Fig. 6.11   32-bit arena structures.

The shared arena maps shared-address objects such as DLL code and data in the process virtual address spaces. The shared arena is shared by all processes and is analogous to the shared LDT selectors in the 16-bit system. Using a single shared arena ensures that all shared address memory objects have the same virtual addresses in all process contexts. The shared arena begins at the top of the process virtual address space and grows toward lower addresses and the private arena. The minimum size of the shared arena is 64MB of shared address space.

Each process has its own set of page tables that maps the private and shared arenas. This strategy allows per-process instance shared objects and per-process selective access to the memory objects in the shared arena.

The private and shared arenas grow toward each other. The 64MB minimum arena size guarantee serves several purposes. Since shared objects have the same address in all contexts, growth of the shared arena can restrict the maximum possible size of a new process's private arena. Also, a process with a large amount of private memory can potentially prevent from being loaded a future process that dynamically links to a huge amount of shared memory, since the shared arena cannot grow "lower" than the largest private arena. This side effect also occurs in the 16-bit system, and is handled by setting of the ratio of shared memory to private memory at 3:1 (shared selectors to private selectors). The 32-bit arena implementation guarantees a large amount of shared and private virtual address space, and lets float the ratio of shared to private memory, depending on the dynamics and requirements of the processes in the system.

An arena is represented by a circular double-linked list of *arena records* sorted in ascending order of base virtual address. Arena records serve a purpose similar to that served by arena headers in the 16-bit system, but are much more specialized than their counterparts. Arena records are allocated out of a fixed sparse array managed by the BMP. So that space in data structures that reference arena records is conserved, a maximum of 64K arena records exist in the system. This allows each arena record to be accessed by a 16-bit handle, which is an index into the array of arena records. As a result of the 16-bit handle, instead of a 32-bit linear address, being used, there is large memory savings in structures that reference or link to arena records, including the arena records themselves. Figure 6.12 illustrates the layout of an arena record.

Since arena records are double linked, each arena record has a previous and a next link that together form a 16-bit handle to an arena record. The flags in the arena record

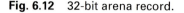

←	32 bits	→
Previous	Next	
Flags	Virtual page number (base linear address)	
Size		
Object handle	Context handle or PTDA handle	

Fig. 6.12   32-bit arena record.

indicate the type of arena record and the disposition of the fields within the record. The virtual page number field of the arena record indicates the base linear address of the allocated region, and the size represents the size of the allocated region in 4KB pages. The object handle and context/PTDA handle fields are used to cross-link the arena record with the data structures representing the memory object allocated at the base virtual address. This linkage is described in more detail in Sections 6.3.4.1.4 and 6.3.4.1.5.

Each arena record maps allocated linear memory—there are no arena records for unallocated linear memory. Free regions are represented by consecutive arena records that are not contiguous; that is, the base linear address plus the size of the *n*th record is less than the base linear address of the *n+1st* record. The calculation for finding free space is efficient and results in fewer arena records. Figure 6.13 illustrates the layout of the private and shared arenas for three processes.

There are three types of arena records that are differentiated using the arena flags field: *regular, sentinel,* and *arena boundary.* Regular arena records represent allocated linear address space. Each private arena in the system is headed by an arena sentinel record that is referenced by each PTDA. The last regular record in each private arena is linked back to the start sentinel. The start sentinel also contains the highest private address used and points to the arena boundary record that represents the beginning of the shared arena. If the the base virtual address and size of the arena boundary record are

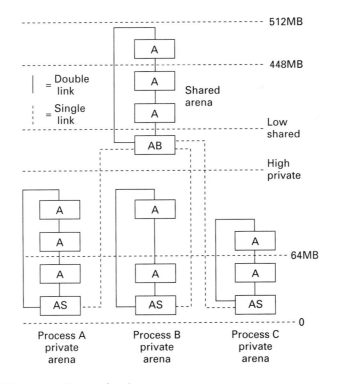

Fig. 6.13 32-bit arena layout for three processes.

varied, the boundary between the private and shared arenas is moved dynamically as necessary. The arena boundary record also is the head of the shared arena, and the last regular record in the shared arena is linked to the arena boundary. When the virtual memory manager must determine whether a virtual address is in the shared or private arena, the address is compared to the virtual address values represented by the sentinel for the private arena and the arena boundary.

6.3.4.1.4 Object Management   The *system object table* is used to track memory objects and their attributes. Like the arena records, *object records* are also managed using the BMP. The system supports a maximum of 64K object records, and each object is referenced using a 16-bit handle which is an index into the *system object table array*. Each object record is cross-linked with an associated arena record that represents the virtual address space of the memory object. Figure 6.14 illustrates the layout of an object record.

Each object record contains an arena record handle, which links the object to the arena record that maps the linear address space occupied by the memory object. The object flags indicate the type of object, the way the object was allocated, and the initial attributes assigned to the pages within the object. Each object is associated with an owner, as in the 16-bit system. If the object is defined by a load module and is shared, the record contains the MTE handle of the module. The object chain field is used to track shared objects in the shared arena that are accessed in multiple contexts. The object semaphore is used to serialize operations on the object, and the lock count fields denote outstanding long-term and short-term locks on the object. Locks are counted on a per-object basis. Lock requests force pages within a record to be fixed until the object is unlocked. There are both long-term and short-term locks. Device drivers use short-term locks on memory objects for some I/O operations.

In the flat model, memory objects are allocated with page granularity. However, since system objects such as PTDAs and MTEs are substantially smaller than the 4KB page size, it would be a waste to allocate an entire page for each of these small structures. Also, these objects require 32-bit addresses where they are referenced by other structures. To overcome the problem of fragmentation due to small structures and excessive data structure sizes, the virtual memory manager defines *pseudo objects*. A pseudo object has an object handle just like a regular object; however, the object record flags have a bit set, indicating the object is a pseudo object. The object record for a pseudo

← 32 bits →	
Arena record handle	Object chain
Object flags	Object owner
MTE handle	Semaphore
Lock counts	

Fig. 6.14   32-bit object record.

object contains the object's 32-bit linear address, and is not linked to a corresponding arena record. Pseudo objects in the 32-bit system perform the same roles as that of system objects in the 16-bit system. Pseudo objects enable objects smaller than a page to be packed on pages to reduce fragmentation, and allow these objects to be referenced using a 16-bit memory object handle to reduce data structure sizes.

Most internal virtual memory management functions receive a virtual address as input that the virtual memory manager needs to validate and then convert into an object record. The virtual memory manager uses a bitmap associated with each arena to indicate which virtual pages within the arena contain the first page of an object. The bitmap for each private arena is in the process's PTDA. When a virtual address is input, the virtual memory manager determines whether the address resides in the current process's private arena or the shared arena. The virtual page number is broken out of the virtual address and is used as an index into the appropriate arena bitmap. The bitmap is then scanned in reverse to find a bit that is set, indicating the beginning of an object. That bit in the bitmap is then used as an index and converted into a virtual page number that represents the base virtual address of an object.

In the next step, the virtual memory manager searches the arena records in the selected arena for a record with a matching base virtual address. Since performing this search sequentially results in inconsistent and nonoptimal performance, a hash table is used to speed the search. The arena records within an arena are linked into a hash table using the hash field of the arena record. The hash algorithm takes advantage of the fact that arena records are linked in ascending order, and provides fast, consistent search times. Once an arena record is found that contains the base virtual address of the object, the virtual memory manager verifies that the original input address actually is within a valid object.

So that an object in the shared arena can be mapped into multiple contexts at the same address, another record is required to iterate these references. The data structure that provides this information is called the *context record*. Like arena and object records, context records are managed by the BMP as a large sparse array. There are a maximum of 64K context records in the system, and a context record is referenced by a 16-bit handle that is an index into the context array. As is true of arena and object records, this scheme reduces the size of structures that link and reference context records. Context records are chained from a shared arena record that represents an object's linear address in all contexts. Each context record contains a PTDA handle and a link to the next context record. It also contains flags to indicate the initial permissions of the object's pages in each context. Figure 6.15 illustrates the layout of a context record.

Fig. 6.15   32-bit context record.

6.3.4.1.5 Arena-Object Linkages   There are four user object types, depending on the address-type and storage-type attributes. This section describes how arena records, object records, and context records are linked together for the four basic types of memory objects.

The first category of object is *private-address, private-storage* objects. They are mapped into the private arena, are read-write objects, and use private storage. Thus, only a single copy of the data exists, and it is referenced by only one process. Both load-time EXE read-write memory objects and API-allocated private objects (i.e., those allocated by *DosAllocMem* at run-time) are in this class. They are mapped into the private arena by an arena record, and are represented by an object record that is cross-linked to the arena record. Figure 6.16 illustrates the linkage of the data structures for a private address-private storage object allocated by *DosAllocMem*.

In Fig. 6.16, the object record owner field contains the handle to the PTDA of the process that allocated the memory. If the memory object had been allocated as the result of loading the process's EXE, the owner would be the MTE handle of the originating module. The MTE handle field references the MTE of the EXE that contains the program loaded by the process.

The next object category is *private-address, shared-storage* objects, such as EXE code and EXE read-only objects. These objects are shared by linkage of arena records in different private arenas to a single object record. Each private arena into which the read-only object is mapped has an arena record that indicates the linear address space where it is allocated. Since only EXE load-time allocations fit into this category, the same address is available in all private arenas for mapping these objects. Figure 6.17 illustrates the data structures for private-address, shared-storage objects.

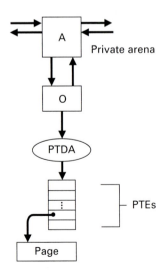

Fig. 6.16   Private-address, private-storage object.

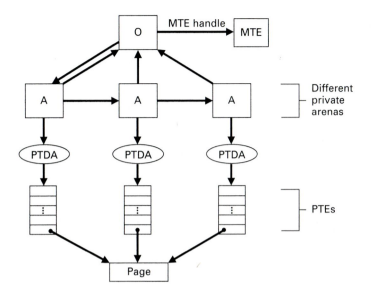

Fig. 6.17   Private-address, shared-storage object.

The arena records in different private arenas are chained to the same object record that represents the object using the link field in the arena record. Since there are many processes using the memory object but only one object record, the memory object is freed when the MTE is freed, not when the process is freed. Therefore, the MTE becomes the owner and the object record contains an MTE handle instead of a PTDA handle. Each arena record contains a PTDA handle that leads to the page tables for that process. The page tables in the different processes that map a private-address, shared-storage object are mapped to shared page frames.

The third object category is *shared-address, shared-storage* objects. In this category are DLL read-write data, DLL read-only or code objects, and API-allocated shared memory objects. They are mapped into the shared arena by an arena record that contains a context chain to iterate the multiple process contexts that share the memory. A single object record is used, since there is only a single object in the system that is being shared. Figure 6.18 illustrates the data structures for shared-address, shared-storage objects.

The fourth type of object is the *shared-address, private-storage* object. The only type of memory object in this class is DLL read-write instance data. This object is mapped in the shared arena, and there is a copy of the object for each process that references it. Instance objects are mapped into the shared arena by an arena record, and there is one object record per instance. The object records for the instances are linked using the object chain field of the object record. Each object record points back to the shared arena record that maps the linear address space. Also, each object record contains the handle of the MTE for loading the instance data from the DLL. Figure 6.19 illustrates the linkage of data structures for a shared-address, private-storage object.

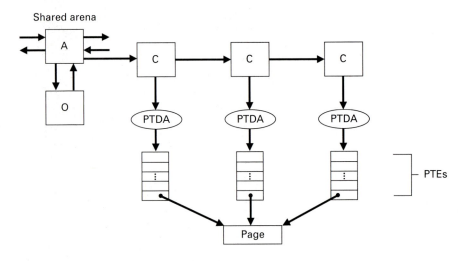

Fig. 6.18   Shared-address, shared-storage object.

6.3.4.2 Loader

The loader is responsible for program loading, the dynamic linking API, and the demand loading of pages from EXE and DLL modules for the page manager. It manages loaded modules and the memory objects within loaded modules. The loader supports a 32-bit executable file format different from the 16-bit format. The 32-bit executable files are

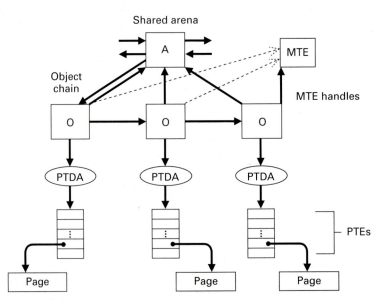

Fig. 6.19   Shared-address, private-storage object.

organized into pages instead of segments, and the fixup information is organized on a per-page basis. The linker relocates 32-bit EXE files to a base address of 64KB instead of 0, and reserves the first 64KB of the virtual address space to contain invalid pages. This scheme allows null pointer (0) references to be trapped by applications and libraries. As a result of 32-bit EXEs being relocated by the linker to a fixed base address, the EXEs have no fixups in them except for external dynamic link references. A file thus can have more *pure pages*—pages with no fixups—that can be read directly into memory when referenced. However, 32-bit DLL files retain most of their fixup records, so that they can be relocated in the shared region at load time. The 32-bit load module format supports 0:32 fixups for 32-bit dynamic linking.

As in the 16-bit loader, MTEs are used to track modules and modules' memory objects. MTEs are allocated from the kernel swappable heap and are mapped by pseudo-object records. MTEs are linked into a graph with executable file MTEs as head pointers into the graph. Each MTE contains a reference count to indicate how many processes have loaded a program module. The MTE also has a module filename, open file pointer, import data, export data, and a module table, much the same as in the 16-bit system. However, instead of a segment table, the 32-bit MTE has an *object table* that contains each object's attributes, such as flags, size, the block number in which the object can be found, and a handle to the memory object. The block number for the object is used by the loader to determine the executable file offset from which the object can be retrieved.

During *DosExecPgm* requests, the loader calls the multitasking component to allocate a process with an empty process virtual address space. The executable file header is read into memory to determine the size of the MTE, and then the virtual memory manager is called to allocate an MTE pseudo object. The file system is called to read the executable file header into the MTE in memory. The loader then processes the DLL references made in the import table section of the MTE. If a DLL module is already loaded for another process, the DLL is attached to the process by a call to the virtual memory manager. Otherwise, the loader loads the referenced DLL. In either case, the MTE for the EXE is ultimately linked into the MTE graph.

When the loader allocates the virtual memory for each object, it passes the MTE handle and the block number of the object within the executable file to the virtual memory manager allocation routine. The MTE handle is saved by the virtual memory manager inside the object record, and the block number is passed on by the virtual memory manager to the page manager so that the correct page can be found in the executable file when a page fault occurs. The page table entries that are allocated for each object are marked not-present, and the preload pages of the module are touched after they are allocated by the loader, to force preloading of pages.

The loader component also performs demand paging on behalf of the page manager during page faults. When a page fault occurs, the loader is passed an MTE handle, a block number, and the virtual address of a page frame into which to load the page. The MTE handle is used by the loader to determine from which module to load the page. The block number indexes the executable *page table map,* a page map in the 32-bit executable file header that tells the loader where in the executable file this object is stored. The relative page number indicates where within the object the page is found. From there, the loader can call the file system to load the page into memory, perform any fix-ups necessary, and then return to the faulting instruction. Demand paging from the executable file allows the system to provide fast program loading.

6.3.4.3 Page Management

The page manager manages the physical memory resource, which is divided into page frames when paging is enabled. It is also responsible for the overcommit calculations and the management of the secondary storage provided by the swapper. Unlike in 16-bit OS/2, the overcommit calculation occurs in the physical memory management layer, instead of in the virtual memory management layer. The overriding policy of the page manager is to postpone commitment of actual physical memory as long as possible, via a *lazy allocation* scheme. In a lazy allocation scheme, physical memory pages are allocated only as the result of a page fault. The scheme is called lazy because physical memory allocation is postponed until the last possible moment. This scheme results in postponement of I/O operations for the demand loading of pages from load modules and the swap file, and potentially results in a reduction in the number of I/Os necessary to keep the system running.

The page manager provides interfaces for allocating and deallocating pages, committing and uncommitting pages, attach and detach operations for sharing pages, and lock and unlock operations for fixing pages in physical memory (pinning). Internally, the page manager maintains both hardware-specific data structures for supporting paged address translation, and system data structures for tracking the contents and disposition of the paged memory resource. The principal data structures are the *page tables,* the *page frame* array, and the *virtual page* structures. The page tables are used to map linear addresses to physical addresses, and to provide selective access to shared pages. A virtual page structure exists for each committed page in the system. The page frame array contains entries for each physical page of memory in the system.

There are four types of pages: *fixed, swappable, discardable,* and *invalid.* Fixed pages are the same as resident pages: They never move, and they are always mapped by a page table. Swappable, discardable, and invalid pages are similar to their 16-bit segment counterparts. Pages also can be read-only or read-write, and can be accessed by the user or supervisor (kernel).

6.3.4.3.1 Page Tables   The paging mechanism of the 80386 processor was discussed in Chapter 2. As mentioned there, the page size for the 80386 is 4KB, and the hardware data structure for converting 32-bit linear addresses into 32-bit physical addresses is called the *page table (PT).* Each page table contains 1024 (1K) 32-bit *page table entries (PTEs)*, each of which maps a 4KB page of physical memory. A page table is a page itself and is 4KB. A single page table can map 4MB (1K * 4KB per page) of memory. The CR3 control register of the 80386 points to the system *page directory,* the top-level page table in the system. The 1K PTEs of the page directory are also called *page directory entries (PDEs)*, since they map page tables in the two-level page address translation. Since each entry in the page directory maps 4MB of memory, the processor can map 4GB (1K * 4MB per page table) of linear memory to physical memory at a time.

Multiple independent linear address spaces can be implemented via provision of a set of page tables for each 4GB linear address space, and via switching of page directory contents when context switching is performed between linear address spaces. Whenever a PTE is changed or a linear address space is switched, the 80386 translation lookaside buffer (TLB) cache must be flushed by reloading of CR3. Figure 2.16 in Chapter 2 illustrates the 80386 paging data structures.

The page tables representing the system region are shared. When the system is started, enough linear memory is reserved for the system page tables to map the maximum size of the system arena. Each process has its own set of page tables that maps the process virtual address space in the range from the 0 to 512MB. So that all the page tables of the system can be addressed, linear address space in the system arena is reserved for page tables for 256 512MB processes (128MB of system linear address space). Each 512MB process requires 128 page tables, each of which maps 4MB of linear memory. This setup results in 512KB of linear memory reserved for the page tables of each process. Each process's PTDA contains variables that point to the page tables that map the private and shared arenas for that process, and that indicate how many page tables are actually in use at the shared and private ends of the 512MB process virtual address space. The process page tables can also be thought of as a sparse array of per-process page tables, where each entry contains the memory for a single process's page tables. When a process is created, one of the 256 blocks of linear memory is allocated for the new process's page tables. All interfaces of the page manager exported to the virtual memory manager and loader accept a PTDA parameter that indicates on which set of page tables the page manager should operate. The parameter is ignored by the page manager for linear addresses in the system arena.

Rather than allocate a page directory for each process, the OS/2 page manager uses a single directory for the entire system, since each process usually is much smaller than 512MB. Having a page directory for each process would add an unnecessary overhead to the amount of memory used by the system. When a single page directory is used, the page tables being used by a process are copied in and out of the page directory when a context switch occurs. This single directory results in memory savings, since there is no need for a directory for each process. Since most processes use relatively few of the available page tables, the operation of copying the in-use shared and private page table addresses is fast. The TLB is flushed after the context switch, since its contents may represent invalid mappings.

The OS/2 page manager allows page tables to be swappable like normal page frames. However, the system must keep track of how many PTEs within a page table are in use by the page manager, and how many of the in-use PTEs are currently present. When the present count of the number of PTEs in a page table falls to 0, the page table can be swapped. If the number of PTEs in use falls to 0, the page table is freed.

6.3.4.3.2 Page Table Entries Each committed page in the system may be referenced by one or more PTEs. Multiple PTEs referencing the same page may be independently marked present or not present. The PTE contains different information, depending on whether the page is present. If the page is present, the PTE contains a physical page

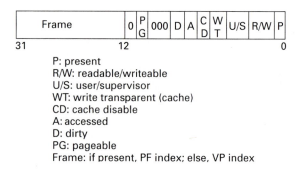

P: present
R/W: readable/writeable
U/S: user/supervisor
WT: write transparent (cache)
CD: cache disable
A: accessed
D: dirty
PG: pageable
Frame: if present, PF index; else, VP index

Fig. 6.20   Page table entry (PTE).

number and the attributes of the page in a format defined by the 80386. Figure 6.20 illustrates the definition of a PTE.

If a page is present, the attributes defined by the 80386 indicate whether the page is read-only or read-write, whether the page has been accessed (referenced) or dirtied (written), and how the page should be treated with respect to caching. Most pages are set up for transparent, write-through caching. However, pages representing memory-mapped I/O devices must be disabled from the hardware external caching scheme. Note that the cache bits in the 80386 PTEs are for external cache control, not for the internal translation lookaside buffer on the processor. If a page is not present, the page manager defines the content of the unused 31 bits of the PTE to contain information for determining a course of action on a page fault. Since the PTE is not large enough to contain all the information for processing a page during a page fault, the page manager uses the virtual page data structure to represent each committed page of memory. Not-present PTEs for valid pages contain pointers to virtual page structures.

6.3.4.3.3 Page Frames   Each page of physical memory in the system is represented by a *page frame (PF)*. The PFs are stored in an array indexed by physical PF number. Each PF contains flags that indicate what type of physical memory constitutes it, and whether it is eligible for page replacement. For example, the PF may be fast (planar) or slow (channel-attached) memory, and may be above the 1MB or 16MB physical memory addresses. Figure 6.21 illustrates the contents of a PF array.

A page frame can have one of three states: *in use, idle,* and *free.* A PF is in use if there are any present PTEs in the system that reference the frame. A PF for an in-use page contains a pointer to the associated *(virtual page)* structure (explained in

Fig. 6.21   Page frame (PF) array entry.

Section 6.3.4.3.4), long- and short-term lock counts, and a reference count that indicates the number of present PTEs that point to the page frame. The file offset field of a PF contains a *swapID* or *loader block number* of the page for finding the page on disk when the page is in use.

The next type of PF is a *free page frame*. When the system is started, all the fixed pages representing the system are mapped as present and in use. However, the rest of the pages are marked as free and available for paging. The PF *free list* is a doubly linked list with fast PFs at one end and slow PFs at the other. When a PF is allocated, the page manager attempts to allocate fast memory before slow memory. Also, when a PF is freed, fast frames are placed on the fast end of the list, and slow frames are placed on the slow end of the list.

When the system is in an overcommitted situation and the free PF resource decreases below a low-water mark, the *page ager* begins aging pages in the system. As a result of page aging, PFs that contain data that have not been used recently change from the in-use state to the idle state. A page frame is idle if no PTEs reference a PF, but the data inside the page are reclaimable. A reclaimable PF is still linked to a valid virtual page structure (see Section 6.3.4.3.4). All the idle PFs in the system are on a doubly linked list called the *idle list*. The page ager makes sure that no PTEs reference a PF before marking the PF idle. Figure 6.22 illustrates the free list and the idle list.

The idle list contains idle PFs, which are dirty or clean, and are reclaimable if a PTE is faulted on that indirectly references the page through a virtual page structure. The idle list is doubly linked and is accessed by the LRU or MRU (most-recently-used) end. When the page manager allocates a PF to satisfy a page allocation request as a result of a page fault, the page manager first attempts to allocate a free PF. If there are no free PFs, a PF is allocated (stolen) from the idle list. If the page is dirty, then the contents must be swapped out before the PF is stolen to satisfy the request. Discardable pages are never dirty, since they are code or read-only data pages.

6.3.4.3.4 Virtual Pages   Whenever the virtual memory manager allocates a committed page, a *virtual page (VP)* is allocated. The VP structure is necessary, since the page manager allows more pages to be committed than can be held simultaneously in physical memory. The page manager extends the physical memory resource of the system by demand loading discardable pages from load modules, and by swapping pages to the swap file. The VP structure also stores the permanent information for each page that describes the disposition of a page, regardless of whether that page is in memory. A VP

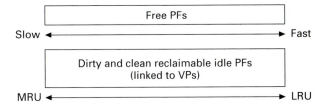

Fig. 6.22   Free and idle page frame lists.

◄──────────── 32 bits ────────────►

Frame pointer	Flags
Object-relative page number	Object handle
PTE reference count	

Fig. 6.23 *Virtual page (VP) structure.*

is an extension of the contents of a not-present PTE, since a not-present PTE is not large enough to contain all the necessary information.

At any time, the disposition of an allocated committed page is one of allocate-on-demand, in physical memory, or on disk. If a page is on disk, it is either swapped in the swap file or demand loadable from a load module. Allocate-on-demand disposition implies that a PF is to be allocated when the page is referenced. A VP exists independent of whether a PF has been allocated to satisfy an allocation or commit request. Overcommit accounting is performed when a VP for committed swappable memory is allocated, since the system guarantees backing store for the request. Figure 6.23 illustrates the contents of a VP structure.

Each VP contains a reference count of the number of present and not-present PTEs that reference the VP. The VP contains an object handle and an object-relative page number passed in by the virtual memory manager; these data are used to enumerate all references to the page and to process page faults. The flags in the VP indicate the state of the page, the action to be taken on the page for page faults, and the contents of the frame field of the VP. The flags also provide bits used for per-VP semaphores to serialize access to each VP.

When a page in a memory object is committed, a PTE and a VP are allocated. The PTE for the page is set to not-present and contains the VP index, which is a pointer to the VP. The VP flags indicate whether the page is allocate-on-demand, swapped, discarded, swappable-on-write, copy-on-write, dirty, or idle. Figure 6.24 illustrates the layout of the page data structures for an initially allocated committed page.

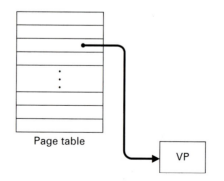

Fig. 6.24 Page structures for initially allocated committed page.

When a thread accesses the virtual address mapped by the PTE, a page fault occurs and the system immediately processes the VP referenced in the PTE. The VP flags determine the source of the data for the page, if there are any. The page is loaded from the swap file, loaded from a load module, or supplied by the page manager.

The frame value within the VP has different meanings depending on whether the page is present. If a page is present, the frame value contains the physical page number, which is also the PF array index of the corresponding PF. When the page is present, the frame value for locating the page contents when the page is not present is stored in the associated PF. If the page is not present, the VP frame field contains either a swapID or a loader block number, depending on whether the page is swapped or discarded. If it is neither swapped nor discarded, the page is allocate-on-demand and the frame field has a flag indicating whether the page should be zero-initialized.

6.3.4.3.5 Overcommit Calculations   The page manager is also responsible for overcommit calculations. Overcommit calculations are made when a swappable or fixed page is committed—when a VP is allocated for swappable or fixed memory. Discardable pages are not part of the overcommit calculation, since they are not swapped. If the total number of swappable committed pages in the system exceeds the size of the swap file, then the system attempts to grow the swap file. If the swap file cannot be grown, the allocation fails. Page tables are included in the overcommit calculation.

6.3.4.3.6 Page Operations   Page table allocation occurs when the virtual memory manager calls the page manager to allocate or reserve linear pages for an object. If an object is allocated and linear address space is merely reserved (not committed) for it, then the PTEs are marked invalid, and page tables are allocated to map them. Accessing an invalid page causes the current thread to receive a general protection fault, which results in process termination if the fault is not handled by the faulting thread. If fixed memory is committed, a VP and a PF are allocated, and they are cross-linked. A PTE is allocated and marked present, and it points to the PF. Except for fixed allocations and lock requests, all PF allocations occur during page faults.

If a swappable or discardable page is committed, a VP is allocated, a PTE is allocated and marked not present, and the PTE is pointed to the VP. The VP reference count is set to 1, and the VP frame contains the loader block number passed in by the loader when memory was allocated if the object is initially discarded. The VP also stores the handle of the object in which the page is located. No physical memory is allocated until the VP is referenced by a page fault.

Page sharing occurs when the virtual memory manager calls the page manager to attach one page to another page. Page sharing allows multiple PTEs to reference the same VP. Attach requests are honored by copying of the contents of the source PTE to the target PTE and incrementing of the VP count. If the original PTE referenced a present page, then the PF reference count is incremented also. Attach requests commonly occur when the virtual memory manager services shared memory API requests and shared module load requests.

When a page is deallocated, the PTE is zeroed out, and the VP reference count is decremented. If the PTE references a present page, the PF reference count is decremented also. If the VP reference count falls to 0, both the VP and the PF can be freed. However, if the PF reference count falls to 0 and the VP reference count is still greater than 0, then not-present PTEs still reference the virtual page. In this situation, the PF is in the idle state, and can be ultimately stolen or reclaimed.

6.3.4.3.7 Page Faults   Page faults are handled by the page manager *page fault handler*. When a fault occurs, the 80386 hardware provides the system with the virtual address that was faulted on. The virtual address is used to look up the PTE that caused the fault. If the page is valid, the PTE contains a link to the VP that describes the page's disposition and state. If the VP is linked to a PF, then the page is reclaimed from the idle list. If the page is not reclaimable, then a PF must be allocated, and must be filled with the data as specified in the VP flags.

When a PF is needed, the page manager first attempts to allocate a PF from the fast end of the free list. If a free PF exists, the PF immediately satisfies the requests and is cross-linked to the faulting VP. If there are no free PFs available, as is common in a memory-stressed system, the page manager steals a PF from the LRU end of the idle list. When a PF is stolen, it is effectively stolen from one VP and linked to the faulting VP.

For a PF steal to be performed, the flags in the VP associated with the PF to be stolen are checked to determine how the page should be stolen. If the page to be stolen is a clean swappable page with a valid image on the swap file, or is a discardable page, then it can be stolen without further processing. If it is a swappable page that has been written to since the last write to the swap file, it is dirty and must be swapped out before the PF can be stolen. The PF steal is completed when the link between the old VP and PF is severed, and a link between the faulting VP and the PF is established.

Once the faulting VP is linked to a PF, the page's data are loaded as specified in the flags of the faulting VP. If the page is a new swappable page, it is zeroed out. If the VP flags indicate that the VP is swapped, then the VP contains the swapID and the swapper is called with the swapID to bring in the page. If the VP flags indicate that the VP is a discarded loader page, then the VP link to the object record is used to obtain the MTE handle of the originating module. The MTE handle, loader block number, and a linear address for loading the page are passed to the loader to demand load the page. After the contents of the page have been loaded, the faulting PTE is marked present and contains the physical page number of the allocated PF. The VP frame field is saved in the file off-set field of the PF, and then is set to reference the allocated PF. The PF reference count is set to 1, and ultimately the faulting instruction is restarted, resuming the thread at the start of the faulting instruction. Figure 6.25 illustrates the layout of the page data structures after a page fault has caused a page to be allocated.

The page manager uses *copy-on-write* and *swap-on-write* for optimizing page allocation. When the virtual memory manager commits a swappable page that originates in an executable module (i.e., private EXE data), it requests the page manager to allocate the pages swap-on-write. The page manager allocates a VP for the page and sets the VP flags to indicate that the page is discarded (can be reclaimed from an executable module), but that the page should be made swappable when written to. The PTE for the page

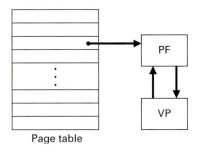

Fig. 6.25   Page structures after page fault.

is set to read-only. When the page is written to, a page fault occurs and the page manager changes the page to a swappable page, performs overcommit accounting, and changes the PTE to read-write. This postpones reservation of space on the swap device until the page is made swappable during a page fault.

Copy-on-write is used for managing multiple copies of a page in multiple contexts. When the virtual memory manager needs to allocate a new copy of an existing read-write page (i.e., attaching to some instance data in a DLL), it sets the copy-on-write attribute when it calls the page manager to commit or create the copy. The page manager allocates a VP for each copy-on-write page, and sets the PTE for the page to point to the original page. However, the allocation of the PF for the new copy of the original page is delayed as long as possible. All PTEs that reference a copy-on-write page are set to present and read-only. When a copy-on-write page is written to, a page fault occurs, since the PTE is marked read-only. If the VP referenced by the faulting PTE is copy-on-write, the page fault handler allocates a PF, copies the contents of the original PF to the new PF, links the VP and PTE to the new PF, marks the PTE present, and restarts the faulting instruction. Thus, the actual allocation of a PF for the original request to allocate a copy of a page is delayed until the page is written to.

Recall from Chapter 2 that the 80386 allows any page to be written (even if the page is marked read-only) if the access is made in supervisor mode. Since the 80386 defines supervisor mode to be privilege levels 0, 1, and 2, a read-only page can be written to be a thread running at privilege level 2. Since OS/2 allows user-mode threads to execute with I/O privilege at privilege level 2, a copy-on-write or swap-on-write page can be written to inadvertently by a thread running at privilege level 2. Therefore, the page manager does not implement copy-on-write or swap-on-write on the 80386. However, the 80486 allows read-only page protection in all rings, enabling copy-on-write and swap-on-write to be performed on an 80486.

6.3.4.4   Page Aging

A special thread called the *page ager* exists for aging pages in the system so that the system can replace page frames on an LRU basis. The page ager thread is a kernel thread and runs at privilege level 0. The ager thread is blocked until the system's idle and free page count reaches a low-water mark, which indicates that the system is running low on memory resources. At this time, the page ager's priority is increased until the page ager ultimately is allowed to run. It implements a *single-hand clock algorithm*, in which it examines the present PTEs of processes. As stated previously, present PTEs contain the physical PF number of the present page, which is also an index into the PF array for the corresponding physical page information.

If a scanned PTE is present, the ager examines the accessed and dirty bits to see whether this page has been accessed since the last time the page ager scanned it. If the page has not been accessed, then the PTE is marked not present, and is pointed to the appropriate VP referenced by the PF, and the reference count in the PF entry is decremented. If the PF reference count falls to 0, then the page is linked onto the idle list. If the page is dirty and is swap-on-write, then it is marked swappable. Read-only pages are never dirty or swap-on-write. Figure 6.26 illustrates the page data structure when a page has been idled.

So that the number of PTEs scanned by the ager is minimized, the count per-page table of the number of present pages is used when each process's page tables are scanned. This is a global aging scheme, in that processes do not page against themselves, but rather page against the working set of the entire system.

6.3.4.5 Page Swapping

Page swapping is executed on the context of the faulting thread, unlike in 16-bit OS/2, where there is a separate kernel swapper thread used for swap I/O. The swap file is managed by the file system, and the swap manager uses a bitmap to manage space within the swap file. Each bit in the bitmap corresponds to a *disk frame (DF)* in the swap file. The index in the bitmap of a DF is used as a swapID when a page is marked swappable. The 32-bit swapper also implements multiple swap outs, or group paging. When it is time to allocate a page from the idle list, and the LRU page on the idle list is dirty, the page's contents must be swapped out before the frame can be stolen to satisfy the current

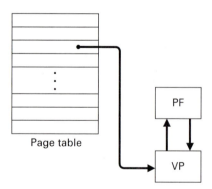

Fig. 6.26   Page structures for idle page.

request. In this situation, the page allocation routine looks for more dirty pages on the idle list that need to be swapped out, and swaps out several pages at a time. This strategy takes advantage of the scatter-gather disk hardware that exists to support I/O in a paged environment.

6.4 SEGMENTED VERSUS FLAT MEMORY MODEL

The performance of the flat memory model is far better than that of the segmented memory model, since segment registers do not need to be loaded when a new memory object is addressed. Also, the flat memory model allows objects to be larger than 64KB, and lends itself more easily to a portable environment, whereas the segmented model forces nonportable programming constructs on application programmers. Both models have the equivalent level of memory protection. However, the flat model uses page-granular protection; while the segmented model uses byte-granular protection. Another difference in the memory models is the type of pointer used in API calls for returning data to the requestor. If the 32-bit system had used a segmented model, API pointers would have been 16:32 pointers with a selector and a 32-bit offset. When pushed on the stack, a pointer parameter would require 64 bits, leading to slower API performance and larger user thread stacks. Also, validating pointers would require segment register loads, further slowing down the system.

6.5 MEMORY MANAGEMENT API

Table 6.2 summarizes the 16-bit and 32-bit memory management API calls.

6.6 DYNAMIC LINKING API

Table 6.3 summarizes the 16-bit and 32-bit dynamic linking API calls.

SUMMARY

This chapter explained the architecture, APIs, and design of OS/2 16-bit and 32-bit memory management. The 16-bit version of OS/2 uses a segmented memory model that results in the system having a segmented API and process virtual address space. Due to the segment size limitation of 64KB, 16-bit OS/2 programs tend to be dependent on the memory architecture of the 80286 processor. The 32-bit version of OS/2 uses a flat memory model that provides a large, contiguous process virtual address space that can be addressed naturally using offset pointers. As a result, the 32-bit system and programs can be ported to any 32-bit architecture that supports large, flat, paged virtual address spaces. Both systems provide virtual memory solutions for protecting memory and for extending the physical resources of a system using secondary storage devices as swap media.

16-bit API name	32-bit API name	Description
DosAllocSeg	*DosAllocMem*	Allocate memory
DosAllocShrSeg	*DosAllocSharedMem*	Allocate shared memory
DosGetShrSeg	*DosGetNamedSharedMem*	Access shared memory
DosGetSeg	*DosGetSharedMem*	Get shared memory
DosGiveSeg	*DosGiveSharedMem*	Give shared memory
DosReallocSeg	N/A	Reallocate memory
DosFreeSeg	*DosFreeMem*	Free memory
DosAllocHuge	N/A	Allocate huge memory
DosGetHugeShift	N/A	Get huge shift count
DosReallocHuge	N/A	Reallocate huge memory
DosCreateCSAlias	N/A	Create code alias
DosMemAvail	N/A	Query system memory
DosSizeSeg	N/A	Get segment size
DosSubSet	*DosSubSetMem*	Initialize heap
DosSubAlloc	*DosSubAllocMem*	Allocate heap memory
DosSubFree	*DosSubFreeMem*	Free heap memory
N/A	*DosSubUnsetMem*	Uninitialize heap
N/A	*DosQueryMem*	Query process memory
N/A	*DosSetMem*	Set process memory

Table 6.2   Memory management API.

16-bit API name	32-bit API name	Description
DosLoadModule	*DosLoadModule*	Load DLL module
DosFreeModule	*DosFreeModule*	Free DLL module
DosGetProcAddr	*DosQueryProcAddr*	Resolve fixup to DLL
DosGetModHandle	*DosQueryModuleHandle*	Query module handle
DosGetModName	*DosQueryModuleName*	Query module name
DosQAppType	*DosQueryAppType*	Query application type
DosGetResource	*DosGetResource*	Get application resource

Table 6.3   Dynamic linking API.

TERMINOLOGY

allocate-on-demand page
arena boundary record
arena header
arena record
arena sentinel record
block management package (BMP)
call gate
committed page
compaction
compactor
context record
copy-on-write page
demand loading
demand-load segments
demand paging
descriptor
dirty page
discardable page
discardable segment
disk frame (DF)
DLL module
DLL read-write instance data objects
dynamic linking
dynamic link
80286 descriptor tables
EXE code segment
EXE module
export data
FAT file system
fault
fixed page
fixed segment
fixup
flat memory model
flush cache
fragment
fragmentation
free
free list
free page frame
give-get mechanism
give-get shared memory

global aging scheme
global infoseg
global shared segment
group paging
guard page
handle table
handle table entry
heap
HPFS file system
huge increment
huge segment
huge shift factor
idle list
idle page
idle page frame
import data
import table
infoseg
instance segment
in-use page frame
invalid page
lazy allocation scheme
least recently used (LRU)
loader
load-time memory
local infoseg
long-term lock
LRU page replacement
LRU segment replacement
malloc
memory management unit (MMU)
memory overcommit
module table entry (MTE)
movable segment
named shared memory
object record
open file pointer
page ager
page directory
page directory entry (PDE)
page fault
page frame (PF)

EXERCISES

6.1   What is the key aspect of virtual memory that makes the latter fundamentally different from physical memory?

6.2   Explain the notions of virtual address space and real address space.

6.3   What relationship, if any, exists between the size of a system's virtual address space and the size of that system's real address space?

6.4   Can one process reference portions of another process's virtual address space?

6.5   What address spaces can a thread in kernel mode access?

Questions pertaining to OS/2 1.X systems:

6.6   What are the main goals of memory management in 16-bit OS/2 systems?

6.7   Explain the architecture of the segmented memory model.

6.8   Can threads running in user mode access descriptors in the LDT or GDT? Explain your answer.

6.9   Why are not all segments in a process virtual address space simultaneously addressable? How is addressability to a segment established?

6.10   Distinguish among fixed segments, movable segments, swappable segments, and discardable segments.

6.11   What are private selectors and shared selectors?

6.12   How are instance segments mapped and allocated?

6.13   Private segments can be grown or shrunk, but shared segments are usually only grown. Explain why shared segments are not shrunk.

6.14   Explain the notion of a huge segment.

6.15   How is named shared memory accessed?

6.16   What is give-get shared memory?

6.17   What kind of shared memory is appropriate for interprocess communication between loosely coupled peer processes? What kind of shared memory is appropriate for passing data between closely coupled peer processes? Explain your answers.

6.18   What technique is used to allocate small memory objects? What is a heap?

6.19   What are infosegs? What kinds of information appear in the global infoseg? What kinds of information appear in local infosegs?

6.20   Distinguish between load-time memory and run-time memory.

6.21   Explain the operation of each of the main components of the memory management portion of the kernel—namely, the virtual memory manager, the loader, the physical memory manager, and the swapper.

6.22   What is overcommit accounting?

6.23   All shared objects, whether code or data, occur at the same virtual address in all process virtual address spaces. Why are they placed in this way?

6.24   Why does dividing the LDT into shared and private descriptors (selectors) reduce virtual memory consumption?

6.25   What is the handle table? What is the significance of the flag indicating "above or below 1MB" in each handle table entry?

6.26   Under what circumstances will two different threads try to access an object?

6.27   What is lazy segment allocation?

6.28   Explain the relationship between loader and module table entries (MTEs).

6.29   Discuss how program loading is accomplished.

6.30   Distinguish between preload segments and demand-load segments.

6.31   When a segment-not-present fault occurs, what does the descriptor for the segment contain?

6.32   Discuss the operation of the two components of the physical memory manager—namely, the physical allocator and the compactor.

6.33   Under what circumstances can physical memory above 1MB be accessed?

6.34   Describe how arena headers are used to track free and in-use memory blocks.

6.35   Effectively, each arena header is in its own segment. Why is this so?

6.36   Give positive and negative side effects of placing arena headers throughout physical memory.

6.37   Describe a typical physical memory allocation scenario. Indicate situations in which the compactor and the swapper will be needed.

6.38   Why can segments be moved invisibly to the processes that reference them?

6.39   How is LRU aging of segments implemented to determine the best candidate for swapping?

Questions pertaining to OS/2 2.X systems:

6.40   The primary motivation behind the design of OS/2 2.X is to ensure portability. List several aspects of OS/2 2.X memory management that facilitate portability across a wide variety of platforms.

6.41   List several aspects of segmentation that detract from the portability of OS/2 2.X.

6.42   Why does the flat memory model provide performance superior to that of the segmented memory model?

6.43   Discuss each of the following page attributes: fixed, resident, swappable, discardable, invalid, and guard.

6.44   Distinguish between committed pages and uncommitted pages.

6.45   How is memory suballocation implemented?

6.46   Describe each of the kernel memory allocation interfaces: the block management package (BMP), the resident heap, and the swappable heap.

6.47   Discuss each of the following arena types: the system arena, the shared arena, and the private arena.

6.48   Discuss each of the following object types: private-address, private-storage objects; private-address, shared-storage objects; shared-address, shared-storage read-write objects; and shared-address, private-storage read-write objects.

6.49   Discuss the use of each of the following key data structures by the page manager: the page table, the page frame array, and the virtual page structure.

6.50   Why is the TLB flushed after a context switch?

6.51   Discuss each of the states in which a page frame may be: in-use, idle, and free.

6.52   Describe how the page ager operates to increase the number of free page frames. In particular, discuss the single-hand clock algorithm used.

6.53 Trace the complete processing of a page fault.

6.54 Distinguish between copy-on-write pages and swap-on-write pages.

6.55 Explain OS/2's notion of group paging.

6.56 Compare and contrast the flat memory model of OS/2 2.X and the segmented memory model of OS/2 1.X.

7
Interprocess Communication

Many shall run to and fro, and knowledge shall be increased.

Daniel 12:2

A person with one watch knows what time it is; a person with two watches is never sure.

Proverb

The path of duty lies in what is near, and man seeks for it in what is remote.

Mencius

Outline

7.1 INTRODUCTION

OS/2 is a multitasking operating system. The existence of multiple processes and asynchronous concurrent threads implies the need for mechanisms to allow processes to exchange data and to synchronize the execution of their threads. Interprocess communication primitives provide these basic features for data sharing and thread synchronization. This chapter describes various aspects of *interprocess communication (IPC)* in the 16-bit and 32-bit OS/2 systems.

The IPC facilities of the OS/2 system are organized into a tiered hierarchy based on the complexity of the IPC mechanism. The simplest IPC mechanisms are *shared memory, semaphores, signals,* and *exceptions.* These constructs are classified as simple constructs, since the processes that use them must communicate with one another explicitly. More abstract IPC mechanisms higher in the hierarchy are built out of the low-level mechanisms. *Queues* and *named pipes* are examples of higher-level abstractions that allow processes to exchange data and to synchronize their execution. However, the usage of low-level IPC constructs, such as shared memory and semaphores, is masked from the users of queues and named pipes. The highest-level abstraction of IPC mechanisms is the API call. Since each API function defines an abstraction and a level of information hiding, these functions manage the usage of any necessary IPCs from requestors. The API abstraction is often used by application programs that build their own API functions into dynamic link libraries that are tailored to their specific needs. Clients of the API are not sensitive to the underlying IPC usage of the dynamic link library, that allows it to be used by multiple processes and threads.

7.2 SHARED MEMORY

Shared memory is the simplest type of IPC mechanism. Its functions are similar in both 16-bit and 32-bit versions of OS/2. Chapter 6 described the types of shared memory that OS/2 supports. This chapter describes shared memory in terms of its role in IPCs.

Run-time shared memory is allocated while a thread is running, whereas *load-time shared memory* is allocated when a process is loaded into memory by *DosExecPgm,* or when a library is loaded by *DosLoadModule.* There are two types of run-time shared memory: *named shared memory* and *give-get shared memory.* Named shared memory has the name of the shared memory registered in the file-system name space. It creates a directory entry in the file system that allows access to the named shared memory by loosely coupled peer processes. These peer processes can access the shared memory by knowing the name of the memory. Chapter 6 discussed the named-shared-memory API calls.

Give-get shared memory is anonymous; no name is associated with the memory. Giveable memory is allocated by a process and is passed to another process explicitly by specification of the address of the memory and the PID of the process that is being given the memory. Conversely, gettable memory is acquired by specification of the memory address from the process that allocated the memory. Ultimately, access is passed directly from process to process. Chapter 6 discussed the give-get shared-memory API functions.

The give-get shared-memory model is safer to use than is the named shared-memory model, since access to the memory in the former is controlled directly by the sharing processes.

Load-time shared memory is allocated when a process's EXE file and associated DLLs are loaded into memory. It consists of shared code and shared data. All code in the OS/2 system, whether it comes from an EXE file or a DLL, is shared and is reentrant. It is mapped at the same address in every virtual address space (as is all shared memory) in both the 16-bit and 32-bit systems. The writer of shared code must keep in mind that shared code accessing shared resources, such as shared data, must be able to handle being preempted at any time.

Specifying the sharing granularity of memory is a way of classifying memory according to how it is accessed. *Thread memory* (also called *local memory*) is memory that consists of the thread's user stack. It is local to the thread and is mapped within the process virtual address space. *Process memory* is memory mapped within the process virtual address space; it is accessed and shared by the threads of the process. No API calls are necessary to set up this sharing—it is part of the multitasking model introduced in Chapter 5. *Shared memory* is accessed and shared by threads in different processes, and is mapped into the shared portion of the process virtual address space.

Process and shared memory usually need some type of serialization if the memory is accessed concurrently by multiple threads. In other words, if threads within a process are all using process memory that is not their own stacks or thread local memory, then the threads need to access that memory in a controlled fashion to guarantee the integrity of the shared data. When multiple threads in different processes attempt to access shared memory, the same situation arises.

Shared-address, private-storage memory objects, which are used for *instance data* in dynamic link libraries, usually need no serialization unless they are being accessed by more than one thread within the same process. Instance memory is used for per-process data within a dynamic link library.

Although shared memory is conceptually simple, it has several weaknesses. The protocol and layout of the shared memory must be understood by all threads accessing that memory. Also, since there are multiple threads accessing the memory, semaphores or flags usually are needed to control concurrent access to the shared region.

7.3 SEMAPHORES

When multiple threads concurrently execute shared code that accesses shared data or serially reusable shared resources, those threads need mutually exclusive access to the shared resources. Semaphores are special protected variables with a defined set of operations that allow threads to synchronize their execution. OS/2 provides two basic types of semaphores: *mutual exclusion semaphores* and *event synchronization semaphores*.

A *critical section* of code is a portion of code in which a thread accesses shared, modifiable data. Only one thread at a time can be allowed to access the modifiable data, and that thread must exclude other threads from executing the critical section of code simultaneously. Threads not in the critical section continue to run. So that threads waiting to get into the critical section are not blocked for a long time, critical sections should be as short and fast as possible, and threads should not block within critical sections if possible.

Critical sections as described here are not to be confused with the *DosEnterCritSec* and *DosExitCritSec* API calls (described in Chapter 5) that enable and disable thread switching within a process. These API calls provide a coarse granularity of synchronization that is valid only for threads within a process. Disabling thread switching within a process can also have bad side effects on threads within a process. Semaphores provide a more reliable and robust mechanism for managing critical sections.

A *mutual exclusion semaphore* is used to serialize access of threads to shared modifiable data or resources. When a thread wants to enter the critical section, it requests ownership of the semaphore. If the semaphore is unowned, then there is no thread in the critical section; the requesting thread is given ownership of the semaphore and proceeds to execute the critical section of code. If, while this thread is in the critical section, another thread attempts to enter that critical section, the second thread's request for semaphore ownership blocks until the first thread exits the critical section and releases ownership of the semaphore. At the time the thread within the critical section exits, the highest-priority thread that has blocked requesting ownership of the semaphore is awakened and is given ownership of the semaphore.

Event synchronization semaphores are used when one or more threads need to wait for a single event to occur. Event semaphores have no concept of ownership. They have two possible states: set or clear. When a thread needs to wait for an event to occur, it performs a wait operation on an event semaphore. If the event semaphore is in the set state, the thread blocks until the event occurs and the semaphore is cleared. If more than one thread is waiting on the event when the semaphore is cleared, all the threads waiting on the event are notified that the event has occurred, and the threads are made runnable. Another type of event synchronization is the *muxwait* operation; it is used when a thread needs to wait on multiple semaphores simultaneously.

Like shared memory, semaphores also have several drawbacks for IPCs. Processes sharing the resources must understand the semaphore semantics and the shared-memory format. Queues and pipes are higher-level IPC abstractions that utilize semaphores and shared memory in a way that is transparent for the requestors.

7.3.1 OS/2 1.X Semaphores

Three types of semaphores are supported in the 16-bit OS/2 system. Each has its own sharing, performance, and protection characteristics. OS/2 1.X offers both hardware-based and software-based semaphores. The hardware-based semaphores are *RAM* and *fast-safe RAM (FSRAM) semaphores.* RAM and FSRAM semaphores depend on the hardware to provide an uninterruptible *test-and-set instruction* to prevent preemption during semaphore operations. Software-based semaphores are called *system semaphores;* they rely on the nonpreemptibility of kernel mode for implementing atomic semaphore operations.

RAM and system semaphores can be used for mutual exclusion (mutex) or event synchronization operations. FSRAM semaphores can be used only for mutex operations.

The same API calls are used for manipulating RAM and system semaphores; FSRAM semaphores use two different special API calls. RAM, FSRAM, and system semaphores are accessed by a 32-bit *semaphore handle.*

If a program or library has a critical section in which it accesses some shared resource, and it needs to serialize concurrently executing threads accessing that shared resource, the *DosSemRequest* and *DosSemClear* API calls are used to provide mutually exclusive access to the critical section. *DosSemRequest* receives the handle of the semaphore being used for serializing access to the critical section, and a timeout value. If the semaphore is unowned, there is no thread within the critical section; the requesting thread gains ownership of the semaphore and enters the critical section. Subsequent requests for the semaphore while it is owned cause threads to block or, in the case of no timeout, to return immediately. When the thread in the critical section executes *DosSemClear* to release semaphore ownership and to exit the critical section, the highest-priority thread that blocked requesting the semaphore gains ownership of the semaphore and is the next thread to execute the critical section. This strategy ensures that only one thread at a time accesses the shared resource; sequential access guarantees the integrity of the shared resource.

FSRAM semaphores use API calls different from those of system or RAM semaphores for their mutex operations. These additional API functions are necessary to allow the system to distinguish between RAM and FSRAM semaphores. The FSRAM API functions, *DosFSRamSemRequest* and *DosFSRamSemClear,* have the same semantics as do *DosSemRequest* and *DosSemClear.*

Event operations are used for synchronizing threads. An event semaphore has no concept of ownership; it is in either the clear or the set state. *DosSemClear* clears an event semaphore; *DosSemSet* sets an event semaphore. When a thread wishes to wait on an event semaphore, it issues a *DosSemWait* request. If the semaphore is clear, *DosSemWait* returns immediately. If the semaphore is set, *DosSemWait* blocks the thread until the semaphore is cleared. When the semaphore is cleared, all threads waiting on the semaphore are made runnable. A timeslice can occur between calls to *DosSemSet* and *DosSemWait,* so a thread can miss *DosSemClear* operations, since the event semaphore has a binary nature. Therefore, *DosSemSetWait* can be used atomically to set-and-wait on an event semaphore. Event operations wake up all threads waiting on a semaphore, whereas mutex operations give ownership to only one thread and make only that thread acquiring semaphore ownership ready-to-run.

The *timeout parameter* used in *DosSemRequest, DosFSRamSemRequest, DosSemSetWait,* and *DosSemWait* allows threads to control their semaphore waiting semantics. During a mutex semaphore request operation, the timeout describes the action to be taken when the semaphore is owned by another thread. During an event semaphore wait operation, the timeout describes the action to be taken when the semaphore is set. If the timeout value is 0, there is no timeout, and the API call returns immediately if the semaphore is owned or set. If the timeout value is −1, the requesting or waiting thread will wait indefinitely until the semaphore is cleared. Otherwise, a timeout value is a positive number that indicates the number of milliseconds that the thread remains blocked if the semaphore is owned or set. If a *DosSemClear* operation does not occur before the timeout expires, the API call returns to the requestor or waiter with a timed-out return code.

7.3.2 OS/2 1.X Semaphore API

Table 7.1 summarizes the 16-bit semaphore API.

7.3.2.1 RAM Semaphores

A RAM semaphore consists of a 32-bit double word in user memory. It can reside in shared memory or private memory, and the system supports an unlimited number of RAM semaphores. A RAM semaphore is a binary semaphore—it is in either the owned or unowned state. The RAM semaphore is initialized to zero to indicate that it is unowned. The semaphore handle to a RAM semaphore is the address of the semaphore in user memory. Therefore, since all user memory in 16-bit OS/2 is addressed through the process's LDT, all RAM semaphore handles have an LDT selector for the high word.

The system does not save the owner of a RAM semaphore. Therefore, if a thread terminates while owning a RAM semaphore, threads that are blocked requesting the semaphore may remain blocked forever, depending on their timeout values. Since the system does not retain the information of which thread owns the semaphore, the system cannot help to notify those requesting the semaphore when the owner terminates. Therefore, RAM semaphores are preferred for providing mutually exclusive access to a resource shared by threads within a process, since only that process is harmed if a thread terminates owning the semaphore. Using RAM semaphores in shared memory to provide mutually exclusive access to a resource shared by threads in different processes is dangerous and should be avoided. RAM semaphores are also used for event

API name	Description
DosSemClear	Clear semaphore
DosSemRequest	Request semaphore ownership
DosSemSet	Set semaphore
DosSemSetWait	Set and wait on semaphore
DosSemWait	Wait on semaphore
DosMuxSemWait	Wait on multiple semaphores
DosCreateSem	Create system semaphore
DosOpenSem	Open system semaphore
DosCloseSem	Close system semaphore
DosFSRamSemRequest	Request fast-safe RAM semaphore ownership
DosFSRAMSemClear	Clear fast-safe RAM semaphore ownership

Table 7.1 OS/2 1.X semaphores API.

synchronization operations among threads within a process. RAM semaphores are fast and are useful for threads within a process.

The RAM semaphores API runs in user mode and resides in a system DLL. The 80286 XCHG instruction is used to provide an uninterruptible atomic test-and-set operation for claiming the semaphore. Because this instruction is used, there is no need to enter the kernel to protect the thread from preemption while attempting to gain ownership of the semaphore. The kernel is called only in the case when the RAM semaphore is already owned and the thread needs to be blocked. There being no kernel call this results in a significant performance gain when an unowned semaphore is claimed, compared to implementing semaphore operations in the kernel. The semaphore can be requested or cleared by any thread with addressability to the semaphore.

Figure 7.1 illustrates how the system interprets the contents of a RAM semaphore. The high-order word is a 16-bit value that is used for saving the *eventID* used when a thread blocks, awaiting a clear operation. The low-order word consists of a wait flags field and a busy field that indicates whether the semaphore is owned. The wait flags signify whether there are any threads in the kernel blocked on the semaphore.

When *DosSemRequest* is issued, the XCHG instruction is done on the owner field to determine whether the semaphore is owned. If the semaphore is not owned, the XCHG instruction claims ownership of the semaphore, and *DosSemRequest* returns. If the semaphore is owned, the kernel is called to block the thread. Once the thread enters the kernel, a unique eventID for this RAM semaphore is constructed from the semaphore handle and an internal counter, and a portion of it is saved in the high-order word of the RAM semaphore itself. Since the eventID used for blocking the thread can be reconstructed from the semaphore contents, the kernel does not allocate any memory or maintain any block information. The wait flags are set to indicate that a thread is blocked on the semaphore in the kernel; then, the dispatcher routine *ProcBlock* is used to block the thread on the RAM semaphore.

DosSemClear clears the owner field of the RAM semaphore. *DosSemClear* then checks the wait flag field of the RAM semaphore to see whether there are any threads blocked on this RAM semaphore in the kernel. If there are threads blocked in the kernel, the kernel is called. The kernel executes a *ProcRun* after regenerating the eventID using the blockID stored in the RAM semaphore and the handle of the semaphore. Subsequently, the wait flag field in the RAM semaphore is cleared.

Several race conditions may arise inside the path of the RAM semaphores. As mentioned in Chapter 5, 16-bit OS/2 has a race condition built into the dispatcher because of the way *ProcBlock* and *ProcRun* work. Since all threads that are blocked on a given

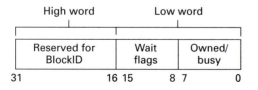

Fig. 7.1   RAM semaphore structure.

eventID are awakened when a *ProcRun* is issued, all the threads must check to see whether the condition for which they went to sleep has been satisfied. In the case of *DosSemRequest,* all of the threads requesting the semaphore that are blocked in the kernel are blocked on the same eventID. All the blocked threads are awakened when the semaphore is cleared by *DosSemClear*. However, only the highest-priority thread (the first one dispatched) blocked in *DosSemRequest* will find the semaphore unowned; the others will find the semaphore owned and will go back to sleep. This method of allocating ownership expends excess processor cycles and is a race condition.

Another race condition exists since the RAM semaphore API code runs in user mode and kernel mode. When *DosSemRequest* is invoked and a RAM semaphore is unowned, there is a chance that there may be threads blocked on the RAM semaphore in the kernel that are at a higher priority. This situation can occur because the code in the DLL that implements *DosSemClear* is preemptible. *DosSemClear* clears the RAM semaphore in user mode, then calls the kernel to wake up any threads blocked on the semaphore. Therefore, an interrupt or timeslice can occur between the time the owner field is cleared in user mode and the time the threads blocked on the semaphore in the kernel are awakened. If the clearing thread is preempted during this window by a timeslice or an interrupt, the thread that is dispatched by the system can request and successfully gain ownership of the semaphore, since the owner field is clear. However, the threads blocked in the kernel may be of higher priority than the new owner; due to the race condition, however, they effectively miss the *DosSemClear* and do not get an opportunity to compete fairly for the semaphore on a priority basis. To overcome this condition, *DosSemRequest* checks to see whether the wait flags in the RAM semaphore are set. If they are, it calls the kernel to give those other threads previously blocked on the semaphore a chance to compete for the semaphore with the current requesting thread.

The usage of RAM semaphores for events is much simpler. *DosSemSet* sets the owner field of the semaphore. *DosSemWait* tests the owner field of the semaphore, and returns immediately if the field is clear. Otherwise, it calls the kernel to block the thread in much in the same way as *DosSemRequest* does, except that the threads do not attempt to claim the semaphore when they are awakened. *DosSemClear* does the same thing as it would for a mutex operation on a RAM semaphore: It clears the owner field and calls the kernel to wake up any blocked threads. *DosSemSetWait* is an atomic set-and-wait operation. It allows a thread to set the RAM semaphore and then to wait for the event to occur, in a single operation. There is a chance that a semaphore could be cleared between the set and wait operations, causing the subsequent wait to return immediately when a thread anticipates blocking. *DosSemSetWait* allows a thread to control the situation, since the 16-bit event model does not allow the user to detect the number of clears between set operations.

7.3.2.2 System Semaphores

The 16-bit OS/2 system supports 255 system semaphores. System semaphores exist in kernel space and are accessed using the same API calls as are used for RAM semaphores. However, when the API code for semaphores in user mode detects that a handle is to a system semaphore, the API code immediately calls the kernel. Since system semaphores are accessible only in kernel mode, they are slower than RAM semaphores. However, they are completely protected, and ownership is tracked by the system. Each process has its own *open system semaphore table* in its PTDA. Open semaphore handles, but not semaphore ownership, are inherited by child processes.

Unlike RAM semaphores, system semaphores must be created using an API call since they reside in the kernel. *DosCreateSem* creates a system semaphore. Every system semaphore must have a name, and these names are mapped within the file system name space using a directory entry. This allows system semaphores to be accessed by peer processes using the global name of the semaphore. *DosOpenSem* is used by processes to gain access to an existing system semaphore. *DosCloseSem* is used to close a semaphore; when all processes referencing a system semaphore have performed close operations, the semaphore is freed by the system.

System semaphores use the same API calls as do RAM semaphores for mutex and event operations, but the system semaphore has a different type of handle. This difference allows the system DLL that contains the user-mode layer of the semaphores API to decide if the semaphore operation should be serviced in user mode or kernel mode, depending on the type. RAM semaphore handles have an LDT selector as the high-order word of their semaphore handle. System semaphores ensure that the LDT bit or table indicator bit of the selector used as the high-order word of the system semaphore handle is clear. Therefore, system and RAM semaphores can always be distinguished by a quick test operation on the semaphore handle. Figure 7.2 illustrates the kernel structures for tracking system semaphores.

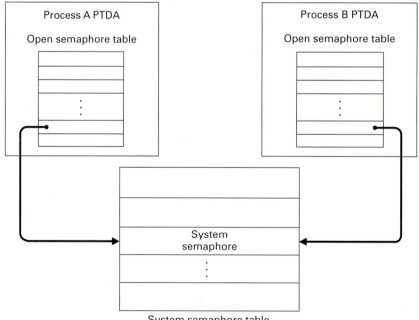

System semaphore table

Fig. 7.2   System semaphore tables.

The system semaphore can be accessed by any thread in any process that has opened the semaphore. The system maintains an open and close count for each system semaphore in the system. This count is incremented when a process opens a semaphore; it is decremented when a process closes a semaphore. When the count falls to 0, a semaphore is freed. The system also saves the owner of a system semaphore to provide better cleanup facilities than RAM semaphores provide. Figure 7.3 illustrates the system semaphore data structure.

When a process terminates while owning a system semaphore, since in this case the system knows the owner of the semaphore, the system performs deadlock recovery, so that threads blocked on the semaphore do not wait forever. This deadlock recovery mechanism is called *owner died notification*. When a process terminates while owning a system semaphore, the owner died notification is sent to the thread that next acquires the semaphore through *DosSemRequest*. The blocked threads are awakened, and they return from their pending *DosSemRequest* calls with an error code indicating that the semaphore owner has died. This implies to the blocked requestors that the resource protected by the semaphore is corrupted and that the threads should close the semaphore so that it can be released.

So that the fatal owner died recovery cycle can be prevented, a system semaphore can be cleaned up during the exitlist processing that occurs when a process dies. Exitlist processing occurs before the owner died notification is sent, to allow the semaphore to be cleared and the resource potentially restored. Since exitlist handling is performed on the context of thread 1 of a process, the system allows thread 1 to claim ownership of a system semaphore during execution of an exitlist handler even if another thread in the terminating process owned the semaphore. The semaphore can then be cleared and the shared resource can be restored so that operations on the shared resource can continue. In this case, the exitlist handling avoids the owner died notification by cleaning up the semaphore and shared resource.

There are two types of system semaphores: exclusive and nonexclusive. *Exclusive system semaphores* are used for mutex operations among threads in different processes. Exclusive semaphores are owned by a thread, not by a process, and can be cleared only by the thread that owns them except during the execution of an exitlist handler. They are counting semaphores in that the system provides a count that indicates how many times the semaphore has been requested. The thread that owns the semaphore may request the semaphore recursively. Each request operation increments the request count; each clear operation decrements the request count. Recursive request and clear operations must nest, and the semaphore is not clear until the count falls to 0.

16 bits	
Owner	
Flags	Reference count
Request count	Name pointer

Fig. 7.3   System semaphore structure.

Nonexclusive system semaphores are used for thread event signaling among threads that are in different processes. Since nonexclusive semaphores can be requested only once, subsequent requests by the owner cause the thread to block. Any thread in any process that has opened the semaphore can clear the semaphore.

Since system semaphores also rely on the dispatcher's *ProcBlock* and *ProcRun* routines for low-level block and unblock primitives, the race condition encountered in the RAM semaphores API also arises for system semaphores.

7.3.2.3 MuxWait Semaphores

Muxwait semaphores give threads the capability to wait until one or more semaphores are cleared. A *muxwait list* consists of up to 16 semaphore handles. *DosMuxSemWait* allows a thread to wait on all the semaphores in a muxwait list. When one of the semaphores in the muxwait list is cleared, *DosMuxSemWait* returns. After a clear operation, threads *muxwaiting* run even though the semaphore may be reset before the awakened thread actually runs. Threads that are part of a muxwait condition have wakeup priority over threads that are waiting on the same semaphore from a single *DosSemRequest* or *DosSemWait* operation. Muxwait semaphores have the same race conditions as those associated with the other 16-bit semaphores.

7.3.2.4 Fast-Safe RAM Semaphores

A *fast-safe RAM semaphore (FSRAM)* is a modified RAM semaphore. It is designed to give the performance of RAM semaphores with the protection of system semaphores. FSRAM semaphores are similar to RAM semaphores in that they exist in user space and their API is implemented in both user mode and kernel mode. However, the owner of the semaphore and a request count are maintained by the system in the user-provided FSRAM semaphore structure. Figure 7.4 illustrates the FSRAM semaphore structure.

Like that of a RAM semaphore, the semaphore handle of a FSRAM semaphore is the address of the structure. However, *DosSemClear* and *DosSemRequest* are not used for FSRAM semaphores, since these semaphores' handles cannot be distinguished from those of RAM semaphores. Therefore, there are different API functions for requesting and clearing FSRAM semaphores—namely, *DosFSRamSemRequest* and *DosFSRamSemClear*. These two calls are identical to *DosSemRequest* and *DosSemClear* for RAM semaphores, except that *DosFSRamSemRequest* retains the unique PID:TID values of the thread that owns the semaphore in the FSRAM semaphore data structure.

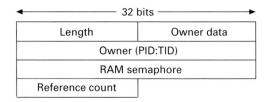

Fig. 7.4　Fast-safe RAM semaphore structure.

If a process terminates while one of its threads owns the FSRAM semaphore, its exitlist handler can look at the FSRAM semaphore and detect whether the semaphore is owned by a thread in the terminating process. If a thread in the terminating process does own the semaphore, the exitlist handler can clear the semaphore and restore the shared resource, allowing other threads blocked on the resource to continue running. The owner of a FSRAM semaphore may request and clear the semaphore multiple times, since there is a request count built into the semaphore structure. FSRAM semaphores are used only for mutex operations and have semantics that are equivalent to exclusive system semaphores.

Since the FSRAM semaphore API code runs in user mode, it needs some method of atomically setting several fields in the FSRAM structure. Since it cannot do this task in a single instruction, some other means must be used to ensure atomic semaphore operations in a preemptible environment. Therefore, the code for the FSRAM semaphores API resides in a special type of code segment called an *IOPL segment*. As pointed out in Chapter 2, IOPL on an 80286 is the privilege level necessary to use the trusted I/O instructions such as IN, OUT, CLI, and STI. OS/2 sets IOPL to be privilege level 2. This setting allows any code segment at privilege level 2 to execute the CLI and STI instructions that enable and disable interrupts. The FSRAM semaphore code disables interrupts while claiming semaphore ownership to prevent any interrupt or timeslice from occurring while the semaphore is being taken. When this practice is used, any segments that need to be addressed in the section of code with interrupts disabled must be loaded into the segment registers beforehand. Otherwise, a segment-not-present fault may occur if the segment is swapped, and the critical section of code may be reentered by another thread while the swap I/O occurs. IOPL is strictly an 80X86 feature; it is not portable to other architectures. For certain special cases, it allows the flexibility needed to provide high performance without calling the kernel.

Like the other semaphore models in the 16-bit version of OS/2, FSRAM semaphores also use the *ProcBlock* and *ProcRun* primitives of the dispatcher to block and run threads. Therefore, the same race conditions found in the rest of the 16-bit semaphore APIs arise for FSRAM semaphores also. Table 7.2 summarizes the uses of the different types of 16-bit OS/2 semaphores.

7.3.3 OS/2 2.X Semaphore Models

The OS/2 2.X semaphore models are all completely protected and portable. The 32-bit semaphores reside in kernel space and are manipulated using kernel API calls. There are no RAM semaphores in the 32-bit version of OS/2, since they are not portable to

Usage	Threads in the same process	Threads in different processes
Mutual exclusion	RAM semaphore	FSRAM semaphore or exclusive system semaphore
Event signaling	RAM semaphore	Nonexclusive system semaphore

Table 7.2   OS/2 1.X semaphore model usage.

multiprocessor architectures. RAM semaphores are not portable because they are mapped in user memory, and, depending on the multiprocessor architecture, they may not be naturally addressable by all processors. Therefore, RAM semaphores are not carried forward into the 32-bit semaphore architecture. All 32-bit semaphores are software-based and rely on kernel mode for providing atomic nonpreemptible semaphore operations. The 32-bit OS/2 semaphore architecture provides two semaphore classes with different sharing, protection, and performance characteristics: *private semaphores* and *shared semaphores*.

There are 64K private semaphores allowed per process in the system. They are used for semaphore operations among threads within a process. Private semaphores have no names and are accessed by handle. There also are 64K shared semaphores allowed in the system. They are used for semaphore operations among threads in different processes. Shared semaphores may be named or unnamed. If they are named, the names are entered into the file system name space, as in 16-bit OS/2. Unnamed, shared semaphores are accessed by handle.

The 16-bit semaphores API is overloaded, since the same API calls are used for both mutex and event semaphore operations. The 32-bit semaphores API, in contrast, is not overloaded. The private and shared semaphore classes are further divided into three semaphore types: *mutual exclusion semaphores, event semaphores,* and *muxwait semaphores.* Mutual exclusion (mutex) semaphores are used for managing critical sections, event semaphores are used for thread synchronization, and muxwait semaphores are used for constructing compound semaphore conditions. Each semaphore type has its own set of API functions for creating, opening, closing, querying, and operating on a semaphore. The APIs are named for the semaphore type on which they operate—private or shared semaphores.

The mutex semaphores API allows a thread to gain ownership and release ownership of a mutex semaphore. A mutex semaphore is created using *DosCreateMutexSem.* If the semaphore is private, there is no name parameter to *DosCreateMutexSem.* However, if the created semaphore is shared, there may optionally be a name parameter, which is entered into the file system name space with a directory entry. *DosCreateMutexSem* returns to the created semaphore a semaphore handle that is used on subsequent API requests. If the semaphore is shared, other processes obtain access to the semaphore by issuing *DosOpenMutexSem* API requests. If the semaphore is named, the name is used as an input parameter. Otherwise, the semaphore is anonymous, and the handle returned from the create API is used as an input parameter for identifying the semaphore. The semaphore handle is returned to the caller of *DosOpenMutexSem.* So that recursive code is supported, a semaphore can be opened up to 64K times. In the case of a private semaphore, it is not necessary to open the semaphore at all, since once the semaphore is created, it is accessible by all threads within the process. However, nested open and close operations are supported in both the private and the shared cases. A mutex semaphore is closed using *DosCloseMutexSem.* When the number of close operations is equal to the number of open operations, the system frees the semaphore. Process termination closes all private semaphores, and decrements reference counts for all shared semaphores. A mutex semaphore can be queried by invocation of *DosQueryMutexSem*. The create, open, close, and query operations described for mutex semaphores are the same, but there are different names for event and muxwait semaphores. *DosRequestMutexSem* is used to request ownership, and *DosReleaseMutexSem* is used to release ownership, of a mutex semaphore. Table 7.3 summarizes the 32-bit semaphores API.

The event semaphore API calls are used for thread synchronization. The terminology used in the 32-bit event semaphores is different from that used for 16-bit events. *DosResetEventSem* is similar to the 16-bit *DosSemSet*, and is used to initialize an event semaphore before waiting for the event to occur begins. *DosPostEventSem* is similar to the 16-bit *DosSemClear* and is used to signal that an event has occurred or has been posted. *DosWaitEventSem* is used to wait on an event to be posted; it is similar to the 16-bit *DosSemWait*. Thus, the 32-bit event semaphores use the terms *reset* and *post* to mean the same as *set* and *clear* mean in the 16-bit event model.

The muxwait semaphores API allow a thread to wait on a list of semaphores to be posted or released. They are similar to the 16-bit *DosMuxSemWait* API function, but provide a richer muxwait semaphore type. The muxwait API allows a thread to define a muxwait semaphore with a list of up to 64 muxwait events. Entries in a *muxwait list* can be added and deleted dynamically using the *DosAddMuxWaitSem* and *DosDeleteMuxWaitSem* API calls. A muxwait list can contain event or mutex exclusion semaphores, but cannot contain both. Private and shared semaphores may be mixed in a muxwait list if the muxwait semaphore is private. *DosWaitMuxWaitSem* is used for a thread to wait on a muxwait semaphore.

API name	Description
DosCreateXXXSem	Create semaphore (XXX = Mutex, Event, or MuxWait)
DosOpenXXXSem	Open semaphore
DosCloseXXXSem	Close semaphore
DosQueryXXXSem	Query semaphore state
DosRequestMutexSem	Request/wait mutex semaphore
DosReleaseMutexSem	Release mutex semaphore
DosPostEventSem	Post event semaphore
DosResetEventSem	Reset event semaphore
DosWaitEventSem	Wait event semaphore
DosAddMuxWaitSem	Add semaphore to muxwait list
DosDeleteMuxWaitSem	Delete semaphore from muxwait list
DosWaitMuxWaitSem	Wait for muxwait list

Table 7.3 OS/2 2.X semaphores API.

7.3.3.1 Semaphore Handles

All 32-bit semaphores are accessed by 32-bit semaphore handles. The kernel uses the semaphore handle to differentiate between private and shared semaphores, and to locate the associated semaphore data structure during semaphore API requests. Except for the semaphore-creation API calls, all the semaphore API calls require the kernel to translate a semaphore handle to a kernel-space semaphore structure. Due to its frequent use, this operation significantly affects the performance of the 32-bit semaphores API. Therefore, the internal semaphore data structures used by the kernel to track instances of private and shared semaphores are important. Since the limits on the number of semaphores allowed are determined by class (private or shared) instead of by type (mutex, event, or muxwait), there are two semaphore handle spaces. The high-order bit (bit 31) in the semaphore handle is used to indicate whether the semaphore is private or shared.

Since private semaphores are accessed by threads only within a process, the kernel uses a per-process array of semaphore structures for mapping semaphore handles into semaphore structures. The semaphore handle of a private semaphore has the private bit set in the high word of the handle, and the low word of the handle is an index into the per-process private semaphore array. The private semaphore array contains pointers to the actual semaphore structure for each private semaphore. Only the actual semaphore structure is sensitive to the type of semaphore. Figure 7.5 illustrates the mapping of private semaphore handles to the internal semaphore data structure. Each private semaphore has an *open count* that indicates how many times the private semaphore has been opened by the threads in the process.

Shared semaphore handles are accessed by threads in different processes. The kernel must track which processes have access to each shared semaphore, and how many times each process has opened the shared semaphore. The kernel allocates a per-process bitmap that is used to track which shared semaphores are in use by each process. The semaphore handle of a shared semaphore has the shared-private bit set to shared in the high word, and an index into the per-process *open shared semaphore bitmap* in the low-order word. The bitmap index is used to verify that a process has access to a semaphore, and also is used as an index into the system's *shared semaphore array*. The actual semaphore data structure is pointed to by an entry in the shared semaphore array, and each shared semaphore structure has an open queue for tracking the number of opens

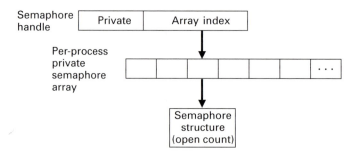

Fig. 7.5   Private semaphore structures.

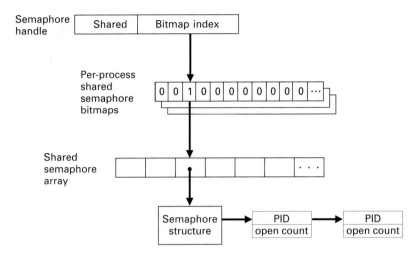

Fig. 7.6   Shared semaphore structures.

performed by each process. Figure 7.6 illustrates the data structures used for shared semaphores in the 32-bit kernel.

7.3.3.2 Mutual-Exclusion Semaphores

Mutex semaphores are used for serializing access to shared data structures or for managing critical sections in programs and shared libraries. They have performance characteristics that are similar to those of 16-bit FSRAM semaphores, and they are protected. Each mutex semaphore has a request count, like that used in the exclusive 16-bit system semaphore model. Therefore, a thread that owns a mutex semaphore can recursively call *DosRequestMutexSem* and *DosReleaseMutexSem* in a nested fashion. Each mutex semaphore has a field for flags, a muxwait queue for muxwait events, a request count indicating the number of requests, an open count or open queue indicating the number of opens, and an owner. Figure 7.7 illustrates the 32-bit mutex semaphore structure.

Mutex semaphores can be recovered when the owner dies by use of a process termination exception handler (explained later in this chapter) or an exitlist handler. If the semaphore is not recovered during process termination, then the system closes the

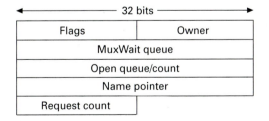

Fig. 7.7   Mutual-exclusion (mutex) semaphore structure.

semaphore for the terminating process and returns the owner died return code to all threads blocked in the *DosRequestMutexSem* API call. The threads receiving the owner died return code from *DosRequestMutexSem* then perform deadlock recovery by closing the semaphore and the resource. As part of the owner died termination processing, the system closes all semaphore references for the terminating process.

Unlike the 16-bit semaphores, all the 32-bit semaphores utilize the 32-bit single wakeup mechanism in the dispatcher, which was described in Chapter 5. This mechanism ensures that there are no race conditions when the system wakes up the highest-priority thread that has blocked waiting for mutex semaphore ownership. When *DosReleaseMutexSem* is called, only the single highest-priority thread that has blocked on the semaphore by calling *DosRequestMutexSem* is made runnable. The *DosQueryMutexSem* can be used to determine the semaphore owner.

When a process terminates while owning a mutex semaphore, the system performs deadlock recovery so that threads blocked on the semaphore do not wait forever. The deadlock recovery mechanism is called *owner died notification*. When a process terminates while owning a system semaphore, the owner died notification is sent to all threads blocked on the semaphore. The blocked threads are awakened, and they return from their pending *DosRequestMutexSem* calls with an error code indicating that the semaphore owner died. This error code indicates to the blocked requestors that the resource protected by the semaphore is corrupted and that the threads should close the semaphore so that it can be released. As in the 16-bit system, the owner died recovery cycle can be avoided, and the semaphore and shared resource can be restored by use of exitlist handlers. The exitlist handlers manage the condition of a process that terminates while owning a mutex semaphore. In the 32-bit system, a process termination exception handler also can be used to manage termination conditions. The 32-bit exception management and process termination exception are described later in this chapter.

7.3.3.3 Event Semaphores

Event semaphores are used for signaling events and synchronizing thread execution. Whereas the 16-bit event semaphores are binary, the 32-bit event semaphores are counting semaphores. The system retains the number of times an event has been signaled or posted, and returns this post count when the semaphore is reset or queried. When a thread wishes to set an event semaphore so that a subsequent wait operation will block the thread until the event is posted, *DosResetEventSem* is called. When a thread wishes to signal an event, it invokes *DosPostEventSem*. *DosWaitEventSem* is used to block a thread waiting for an event to be posted. When *DosPostEventSem* is called to signal the event, all threads blocked on the event by calling *DosWaitEventSem* are made runnable. The awakened threads remain runnable even if the event semaphore is reset before they are dispatched. If a thread calls *DosWaitEventSem* and the event has been posted already, the thread returns immediately without blocking. Figure 7.8 illustrates the event semaphore data structure.

The post count maintained by the system for each event semaphore enables the communicating threads to detect exactly how many post operations occur between reset operations. The binary nature of 16-bit event semaphores creates the possibility that clear (post)

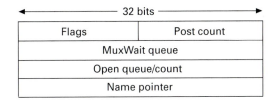

Fig. 7.8   Event semaphore structure.

operations can be missed. A timeslice may occur between *DosSemSet* and subsequent *DosSemWait* calls, allowing the event to be cleared (posted) by another thread before the original thread waits. Since there is no count of clear (post) operations in the 16-bit events, it is not known how many clear (post) operations occur before a thread waits on the event. Therefore, the 16-bit system provides *DosSemSetWait* to atomically allow a thread to set an event and to block on it. With the addition of the post count, the 32-bit event semaphores API does not require an atomic reset-and-wait operation.

7.3.3.4 *MuxWait Semaphors*

The muxwait semaphore architecture provides a special compound semaphore model that allows lists of events or mutex semaphores to be waited on in a single operation. *DosCreateMuxWaitSem* is used to create a muxwait semaphore. A muxwait semaphore can be private or shared, and is composed of a list of either event or mutex semaphore handles called a *muxwait list*. Shared muxwait semaphores can have only shared semaphores in the muxwait list. Private muxwait semaphores can have private and shared semaphores of the same type in the muxwait list. Figure 7.9 illustrates the data structure used for a muxwait semaphore.

Each muxwait semaphore contains a flags field, a count of the number of semaphores in the muxwait list, the muxwait list itself (composed of semaphore records), an open count or queue, and a wait count. Muxwait semaphores have an attribute set when they are created that describes whether the semantics of the muxwait semaphore are *wait-any* or *wait-all*. Depending on whether the muxwait list contains mutex or event semaphores, the semantics of *DosWaitMuxWaitSem* are different. The wait-any attribute implies that a thread blocking on a muxwait semaphore will wait until

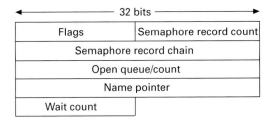

Fig. 7.9   Muxwait semaphore structure.

any one of the semaphores is released or posted. Wait-all implies that the thread will wait until all semaphores in the muxwait list are released or posted.

With mutex semantics, the wait-any attribute will cause threads to block until any one of the mutex semaphores in the muxwait list is released. Ownership of the released semaphore is given to the highest-priority blocked thread in a *DosWaitMuxWaitSem* request. *DosWaitMuxWaitSem* returns the semaphore handle of the released semaphore after a successful wait-any request. If a thread is blocked in the wait-all condition, the thread will return only when all the semaphores in the muxwait list are released. The thread does not incrementally take ownership of the semaphores in the muxwait list. This averts any indefinite postponement or deadlock conditions that may occur when a thread attempts to claim multiple resources. Only when all semaphores in the muxwait list are released does the thread claim ownership of the muxwait semaphore. As in the 16-bit system, threads waiting on muxwait semaphores have wakeup priority over threads blocked in a single mutex operation.

The kernel prevents race conditions between single mutex semaphore *DosRequestMutexSem* requests, and between *DosWaitMuxWaitSem* requests on a muxwait semaphore that have the same mutex semaphore in its muxwait list. To prevent race conditions, the kernel detects when mutex semaphores are part of muxwait operations, and gives muxwait operations priority over single semaphore operations when the semaphore is released. If the owner of one of the semaphores within a muxwait list dies while owning a mutex semaphore, *DosWaitMuxWaitSem* returns with the owner died return code. Then, *DosQueryMutexSem* can be used to find the semaphore within the muxwait list that has been corrupted.

The event semantics for *DosWaitMuxWaitSem* are different. With event muxwait semaphores, the wait-any attribute will cause threads to block on a *DosWaitMuxWaitSem* operation until any one of the event semaphores in the muxwait list is posted. When the post occurs, all threads waiting on the muxwait event are made runnable. *DosWaitMuxWaitSem* returns the semaphore handle of the posted semaphore after a wait-any request. If the wait-all attribute is used with an event muxwait list, the threads remain blocked in *DosWaitMuxWaitSem* until all the event semaphores in the muxwait list are simultaneously in the posted state. In this case, if one of the events in the list is posted and then is reset immediately, and then the other event semaphores in the list are posted, the muxwait semaphore remains in the reset state, since one of the semaphores is not posted.

7.4 SIGNALS

Signals are used for asynchronous event notification between processes. To the process that receives a signal, a signal is a simulated external interrupt to the flow of instruction execution. A signal is sent to a process by direct user keyboard interaction or by the actions of asynchronous processes. Signals are an archaic leftover from the command-line-oriented interfaces of the UNIX and DOS command shells. Since most OS/2 programs are PM programs that do not utilize the command-line interface architecture, and there are better constructs for performing interprocess communications, signals do not play a large role in 16-bit OS/2 applications. Signals exist mainly as an aid to tty-style and text-based applications being ported to 16-bit OS/2 from the DOS and UNIX environments.

Another by product of the 16-bit OS/2 signals implementation is that the source code that uses the signals architecture is not portable to other processor architectures. The signal handler calling conventions require applications to code some of their signal handlers using assembler, and the context in which signal handlers run is poorly defined. Therefore, signals were not continued in the 32-bit version of OS/2. The signal functions that were needed were integrated into the portable 32-bit exception architecture. The UNIX system integrates all exceptions and signals into a single, large, signal mechanism.

The signals available in the OS/2 16-bit system are break (SIGBREAK), interrupt (SIGINTR), termination (SIGTERM), and user-defined flag events. SIGBREAK and SIG-INTR occur when the ctrl-BREAK or ctrl-C key sequences are typed on the keyboard. SIGTERM is sent to a process when *DosKillProcess* is called with the target process's PID. *DosSendSignal* sends SIGBREAK or SIGINTR to another process. *DosFlagProcess* sends a user-defined flag signal to another process. *DosHoldSignal* can be used to disable signals in critical sections. Signals can be sent to a single process or to an entire process tree.

The kernel maintains a signal vector and signal dispositions within each PTDA in the system. A process's signal disposition describes how a given signal should be handled when received. The disposition can be to take a default action, to ignore the signal, or to handle the signal by calling a user-supplied signal handler. The default action for all signals is forced process termination. When a process is created, all signals are set to take the default action of termination. *DosSetSigHandler* allows a process to change the state of a signal's disposition, or to set a signal handler. Table 7.4 summarizes the signals API in 16-bit OS/2.

Signals are applied to a process or to a process tree, as described in Chapter 5. Since a process can consist of more than a single thread, and the signal architecture is built on the process model, OS/2 must define a protocol for signals that takes into account a process with multiple threads. Any thread in a process can issue any of the signal API requests and thus alter that process's signal vectors and disposition. This ability follows from the process architecture, which allows the threads of a process to share the process's resources. OS/2 defines the first thread of a process, thread 1, as the thread that receives signals. Therefore, thread 1 must be the last thread in a process to die, ensuring that the signals are handled.

API name	Description
DosHoldSignal	Disable signal dispatching
DosSetSigHandler	Register signal handler
DosSendSignal	Send signal
DosFlagProcess	Send signal flag

Table 7.4   OS/2 1.X signals API.

As described in Chapter 5, signals are dispatched when a thread exits kernel mode, not at the time the signal is "sent." It is during the *ExitKMode* routine that the kernel consults the process force flags to see whether any signals need to be handled when the thread is dispatched. If the exiting thread is *thread 1,* the kernel dispatches the signal after checking to make sure that there is not a hold-signal condition from a *DosHoldSignal* API call. If the signal disposition indicates that a user signal handler exists, the signal is dispatched via building of an 80286 interrupt frame on the thread 1 user stack, followed by return to user mode at the address of the signal handler. The signal handler can return to the interrupt instruction by executing an IRET instruction.

7.5 QUEUES

Queues are a form of peer-process interprocess communication. The queueing model of OS/2 is a mailbox scheme in which multiple processes may write to the queue and a single owner process may read the queue. The process that owns the queue is usually called the *server process;* the processes that write to the queue are called *client processes.* A return receipt function enables processes that write to the queue to detect that their element has been read from the queue by the owner. The queueing functions are nearly identical in the 16-bit and 32-bit OS/2 systems.

Queues are created by a call to *DosCreateQueue.* Each queue has a unique name within the file system name space, mapped by a directory entry that allows peer processes to access the queue by name in the *DosOpenQueue* API call. A queue is closed by a call to *DosCloseQueue.* A queue is deleted by the system when all processes referencing that queue have closed the queue or terminated.

When a queue is created, it can be defined to use different element-ordering schemes based on the needs of the application. A *FIFO queue* implements elements that come and go in first-in-first-out protocol. A *LIFO queue* is similar to a stack, since elements are read from the queue in last-in-first-out order. A *priority queue* allows each element to be assigned a priority that is used to order the queue elements. Like most OS/2 objects, queues are accessed using a *queue handle* returned by *DosCreateQueue* or *DosOpenQueue.* Figure 7.10 illustrates several processes using a queue.

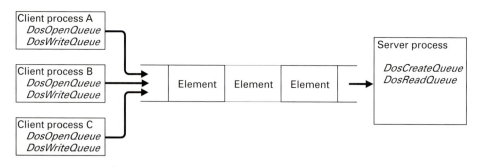

Fig. 7.10   IPC queue.

DosReadQueue and *DosWriteQueue* are used for reading elements from and writing elements to a queue. The messages passed through a queue are actually 4-byte queue elements whose contents are defined by the communicating processes. They are chained together to form a queue by the queueing subsystem. Usually, these 4-byte elements are pointers to shared memory elements. If shared memory is used for passing messages through a queue, the sharing of the memory containing the elements must be established by the communicating processes, not by the queueing subsystem. Usually, named shared memory is used for queue elements, and the name of the shared memory parallels the name of the queue. Since shared memory is involved, queues cannot be used across a network.

DosPeekQueue can be used to take a look at the next element to be read from the queue without removing that element. *DosPurgeQueue* allows a queue owner to clear all the elements from a queue. *DosQueryQueue* can be used by owners and clients to find out what the status of the queue is. Table 7.5 summarizes the OS/2 queueing API calls.

The queueing API calls reside in a system DLL. They run in user mode, are preemptible, and use the memory suballocation API to manage queue and element data structures in shared memory. Fast-safe RAM semaphores are used for serializing access to the shared memory representing queue and element structures. The queueing DLL registers an exitlist handler each time a process attaches to it, so that it can clean up per-process queue resources and semaphores during process termination.

7.6 PIPES

A pipe is a data connection between two processes. OS/2 provides two different types of pipes in both the 16-bit and 32-bit systems: anonymous and named pipes.

7.6.1 Anonymous Pipes

An *anonymous pipe* or *unnamed pipe* is a FIFO file. The origins of anonymous pipes lie with the UNIX system and its command line shell architecture. Anonymous pipes are used to pass data between *filters,* which are utility programs such as *more* and *sort* that

16-bit API name	32-bit API name	Description
DosCreateQueue	*DosCreateQueue*	Create queue
DosOpenQueue	*DosOpenQueue*	Open queue
DosCloseQueue	*DosCloseQueue*	Close queue
DosPeekQueue	*DosPeekQueue*	Peek queue
DosPurgeQueue	*DosPurgeQueue*	Purge queue
DosQueryQueue	*DosQueryQueue*	Query queue
DosReadQueue	*DosReadQueue*	Read queue
DosWriteQueue	*DosWriteQueue*	Write queue

Table 7.5   OS/2 Queueing API.

read standard input, to process the data, and to write to standard output. The command interpreter can set up a chain of filters that are connected by pipes, so that the filters are not aware they are reading and writing pipes instead of files. This strategy allows data to be redirected transparently between files and filter processes due to the convention of using the standard I/O streams.

In OS/2, an anonymous pipe is a FIFO character stream between two related processes. Anonymous pipes can be accessed only by processes that are descendants of the creating process. There are no directory entries associated with anonymous pipes, and the pipes are not in the file system name space. Open pipes are passed between related processes using the process creation inheritance mechanism. When a process creates another process, the child inherits the parent's open file table. This inheritance scheme allows a child to gain access to pipes created by the parent. Data in pipes are accessed sequentially. Pipes have one reading end and one writing end; thus, they are half-duplex. Pipes are accessed using file system APIs. Figure 7.11 illustrates two processes communicating over an anonymous pipe.

Anonymous pipes are created using *DosCreatePipe*. *DosCreatePipe* creates the pipe structures and allocates two file descriptors from the open file table in the PTDA of the requesting process. One is the read descriptor and one is the write descriptor. The read and write descriptors may subsequently be used in *DosRead* and *DosWrite* calls to perform file I/O on the pipe. They may also be used in *DosClose* when they are finished being used. *DosDupHandle* is used to manipulate the descriptors within the open file table of a process. *DosDupHandle* is used in combination with open-file-handle inheritance mechanism to set up filters among parent and child processes. The system performs I/O synchronization when I/O is performed to pipes. A *DosRead* request on a pipe blocks until the pipe has data or until the writer dies. A *DosWrite* request to a pipe blocks if there is not enough room in the pipe for the data, or until the reader dies.

7.6.2 Named Pipes

Named pipes allow message data streams to be passed between peer processes. They are helpful in the *client-server* computing environment, where processes may be remotely connected by a network. Named pipes provide local and remote network transparency

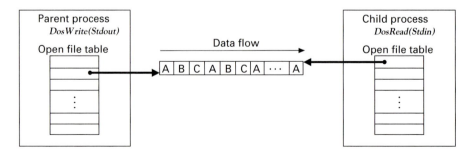

Fig. 7.11   Anonymous pipe.

through the *network redirector,* as described in Chapter 11. Named pipes provide basic connection and data transfer services, as well as functions for *remote procedure calls* and *transaction processing.* They can be accessed by peer processes, not just by processes within a process hierarchy. They can be multiplexed, allowing a single named pipe to have multiple instances. Using multiple instances, multiple paths can be set up for different sets of requestors on a single pipe. A named pipe can run full- or half-duplex. That is, a named pipe can be bidirectional and have a single handle used for reading and writing operations. Named pipes can also be accessed transparently using the *DosOpen, DosRead, DosWrite,* and *DosClose* file system API calls.

The creator of a named pipe is typically called a *server process.* The server provides service for clients using the named pipe as a medium of data exchange. Named pipes are created using the *DosCreateNPipe* call. Their names are taken from the file system name space. A directory entry is created for each named pipe that allows peer processes to access the named pipe by using the name. *DosCreateNPipe* returns the *pipe handle* for accessing the pipe. It also sets the pipe mode and number of instances. The capability of having multiple instances of a pipe allows a server to service more than one client using a single named pipe.

The use of named pipes is best described by an example interchange between a server and a client process. Once the server creates the named pipe, it calls *DosConnectNPipe* to listen for a client attempting to access the named pipe. When a client process calls *DosOpen* using the name of the named pipe, it is connected to the named pipe, and the server process is notified that a client has established a connection with the named pipe instance. If there are no pipe instances available when a client process issues *DosOpen, DosWaitNPipe* can be used by the client to wait for the next instance to become available. Figure 7.12 illustrates a named pipe with three instances.

I/O is performed across pipes with *DosRead* and *DosWrite* using the handle of the named pipe. The pipe can be configured to perform *blocking I/O* or *nonblocking I/O* when it is created. *DosPeekNPipe* is used to support peek operations by the server process on the contents of the pipe. *DosTransactNPipe* is the equivalent of a *DosWrite* followed by a *DosRead* across a named pipe. Although the separate *DosWrite* and *DosRead* operations perform the same actions as does *DosTransactNPipe,* in a situation where the named pipe represents a connection across a network, combining the two operations into one provides a significant performance savings. This savings is the reasoning behind the *DosCallNPipe* API function. This function is the equivalent of a

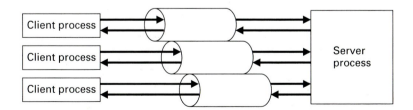

Fig. 7.12   Named pipe (three-channel full duplex).

DosOpen, DosWrite, DosRead, and *DosClose* sequence of operations on a named pipe. It causes almost exactly the same actions as occur when a remote procedure call is issued to a process running on another machine. The named pipe API calls (see Table 7.6) are basically the same in the 16-bit and 32-bit OS/2 systems.

7.7 EXCEPTIONS

Exceptions are used to deliver synchronous events caused by the current thread of execution. In this section, the 16-bit and 32-bit OS/2 exception architectures are described separately, since they are so different.

7.7.1 OS/2 1.X Exception Architecture

Chapter 2 described the 80286 exception architecture. Under OS/2, the exceptions that can occur on an 80286 are further classified into *system exceptions* and *user exceptions.* System exceptions are handled by the kernel. User exceptions can be handled by the applications that cause them; if a user exception is not handled, the kernel takes a default action of terminating the process that caused the exception. Table 7.7 illustrates the 80286 exceptions and classifies them according to system or user types.

The kernel maintains an *exception vector* in each PTDA for handling the user exceptions. The user-handleable exceptions for 16-bit OS/2 are divide overflow, overflow, bound, invalid opcode, numeric coprocessor (NPX) not available, and NPX error.

16-bit API name	32-bit API name	Description
DosMkPipe	*DosCreatePipe*	Create anonymous pipe
DosMakeNmPipe	*DosCreateNPipe*	Create named pipe
DosConnectNmPipe	*DosConnectNPipe*	Connect named pipe
DosDisConnectNmPipe	*DosDisConnectNPipe*	Disconnect named pipe
DosWaitNmPipe	*DosWaitNPipe*	Wait named pipe
DosPeekNmPipe	*DosPeekNPipe*	Peek named pipe
DosQNmPHandState	*DosQueryNPHState*	Query named pipe handle state
DosQNmPipeInfo	*DosQueryNPipeInfo*	Query pipe information
DosQNmPipeSemState	*DosQueryNPipeSemState*	Query Named Pipe Semaphore State
DosSetNmPHandInfo	*DosSetNPHState*	Set named pipe handle state
DosSetNmPipeSem	*DosSetNPipeSem*	Attach semaphore to named pipe
DosCallNmPipe	*DosCallNPipe*	RPC transaction
DosTransactNmPipe	*DosTransactNPipe*	Write/read transaction

Table 7.6   OS/2 pipes API.

Exception description	Type
Divide by zero	User
Single step	System
Nonmaskable interrupt (NMI)	System
Breakpoint	System
INTO overflow	System
Bound range exceeded	User
Invalid opcode	User
NPX not available	User
Double fault	System
NPX error	User
Invalid TSS	System
Segment not-present	System
Stack overrun	System
General protection fault	System

Table 7.7   16-bit exceptions.

Debugged processes rarely cause exceptions—most exceptions are the result of error conditions. Usually, these error conditions are fatal, so the default action for a user exception is to terminate the process immediately. However, there are cases when a process needs notification that an exception has occurred. For example, a process computing a mathematical limit may use an algorithm that indicates that it is completed when a divide-by-zero operation occurs. Also the NPX exceptions are used by floating-point emulation libraries when a coprocessor is not present. A process can register an exception handler using the *DosSetVec* API call. The exception handler address is provided to *DosSetVec,* and the address of the handler previously installed in the PTDA exception vector is returned. The exception vectors for a process are shared by all threads in the process, and are used regardless of which thread causes an exception.

As Chapter 5 described, when an exception occurs, the kernel trap manager builds an exception frame on the stack of the thread that caused the exception, and then resumes thread execution in user mode at the exception handler address stored in the PTDA. To the exception handler, the stack frame looks like the thread has been interrupted, thereby requiring an IRET instruction to return to the point of the interruption. The exception handler runs within the context of the thread that caused the exception. Since there is only a single set of exception vectors in each PTDA for the threads of a process, multiple threads in the same process may inadvertently corrupt the contents of the exception vectors. If each thread is executing an API that uses different DLLs, and both DLLs attempt to register a handler for the same exception, the last one to register sets the exception vector for the exception. If the first thread then causes the exception, the wrong handler will be executed. This shortcoming in the 16-bit exception architecture is addressed in the 32-bit architecture. However, it is not too critical, since the limited user handleable exceptions are rarely encountered.

The system trap manager handles most of the system exceptions. The most important system exceptions are the general protection fault and the segment-not-present exception. The segment-not-present exception is passed to the virtual memory manager so that the segment can be brought into memory. A GP fault can occur in any situation in which the segment protection semantics of the 80286 are violated. When a GP fault occurs, the system terminates the process and prints the fault information on the screen for debugging.

A major shortcoming of the 16-bit exception architecture is that GP faults cannot be handled by the process. This restriction has side effects on API parameter passing and parameter validation. If a process calls a kernel API and passes a bad address as a parameter, the kernel detects the fault and terminates the process without returning from the API. Another option would be to detect the bad parameter and to return a return code from the API to the requestor, but this option is not supported. Since the process is terminated, the requestor has no opportunity to perform resource cleanup except during an exitlist handler. The thread that causes the fault is not necessarily aware of what other threads in the process are doing, and can cause resource cleanup and rollback problems for other threads. For example, if one thread is updating a remote database while another thread causes a forced termination of the process, the transaction with the remote database can be left in an indeterminate state. Although the exitlist handler for the remote transaction API's DLL does get a chance to clean up, its options are limited due to the overhead of tracking the states of the threads that use it.

Following the example set by the kernel APIs, APIs implemented in DLLs perform practically no address parameter validation. If a DLL API is passed an invalid address parameter, the DLL uses the address in good faith and causes a GP fault. Although this algorithm for treating invalid addresses makes the behavior of the kernel and DLL API calls consistent, it is undesirable.

Ideally, the entire API should be changed such that all API requests are guaranteed to return. When invalid pointers were passed to a kernel API, a bad parameter error code would be returned. If GP faults could be handled by user-mode threads, a DLL API could perform lazy parameter validation by registering a GP fault exception handler, and handling the exceptions caused when invalid address parameters are passed in. Although it is not necessarily obvious at first, there is an underlying assumption that any 80286 GP fault must be restartable. Unfortunately, many of the 80286 chips shipped to date have an erratum that causes the CX register to be corrupted during a GP fault. This corruption effectively prevents the system from restarting instructions that cause GP faults. Since 16-bit OS/2 is targeted for the 80286 processor, the design of the system had to take into account all the errata inherent in the 80286. The 80286 dependencies of the 16-bit OS/2 exception architecture also prohibit portability.

7.7.2 OS/2 2.X Exception Architecture

The 32-bit exception architecture is portable, is machine independent, and provides the fundamental building blocks for resource recovery. The 32-bit exception architecture carefully defines the exception handler context and handles exceptions on a per-thread basis. GP faults can be handled by user-mode threads to provide better lazy parameter validation in DLLs. The exceptions are generalized into machine-independent categories that can be implemented on any architecture. Support for user-defined exceptions and system-reserved exceptions allow applications to define their own exceptions also.

Two new guard page exceptions exist to allow dynamic growth of user stacks. Also, the functions for dealing with the SIGINTR and SIGBREAK signals from the 16-bit signal API are integrated into exception management. A new exception, called the *process termination exception,* is used by threads to handle individual thread termination. *Unwind* operations allow a thread to backtrack and to unwind exception handlers that have been registered during nonlocal goto operations. The 32-bit exception architecture supports frame-based language strategies, in which an exception handler is set for each activation frame on the user stack. This allows better resource cleanup in nonlocal branching (goto) operations such as *longjump* and *setjump* in the C language. Table 7.8 lists the 32-bit OS/2 exceptions.

Exception description	Type
Divide by zero	User
Debug	System
Nonmaskable interrupt (NMI)	System
Breakpoint	System
INTO overflow	System
Bound range exceeded	User
Invalid opcode	User
NPX not available	User
Double fault	System
NPX error	User
Invalid TSS	System
Segment not present	System
Stack overrun	System
General protection fault	User
Page fault	System
Guard page fault	User
Guard page allocation fault	User
Process termination	User
SIGBREAK	User
SIGINTR	User
SIGTERM	User

Table 7.8   32-bit exceptions.

For each thread in the system, there is a chain of exception handlers in user space that is headed by a pointer in the thread information block (TIB). *DosSetExceptionHandler* and *DosUnsetExceptionHandler* are used for the registration and deregistration of exception handlers on a thread's exception chain. When an exception occurs, control transfers to the *kernel trap manager*. The kernel trap manager determines whether the exception is handled by a user mode thread or the system. If the exception is a user exception, the trap manager transfers control to the *user-mode exception dispatcher*. The user-mode exception dispatcher then processes the exception handler chain based off the TIB by calling each exception handler. Figure 7.13 illustrates the per-thread exception chain.

When each exception handler is called, the exception dispatcher passes to the handler information that describes the exception. Since the exception architecture is portable, exception handlers can be written in high-level languages without any machine dependence. However, there is also a machine-specific structure attached to the exception handler information that allows machine-specific operations if they are desired. The exception handler either handles the exception or does not handle the exception, and then returns to the exception dispatcher. If the exception was handled, it is restarted at the address specified by the exception handler. If it was not handled, the exception dispatcher continues processing the exception chain until it has exhausted all exception handlers. If none of the exception handlers handles the exception, then the default system action for the exception is taken. The default action for all exceptions except guard page exceptions is process termination. The exception dispatcher also supports nesting of exceptions in case an exception handler causes another exception.

DosRaiseException raises an exception in the context of the current thread. *DosUnwindException* unwinds exception handlers on the thread exception handler chain up to a certain point. The unwind causes each exception handler to be called with an indicator that an unwind request is being processed. *DosSendSignalException* is used for sending the SIGINTR and SIGBREAK signal exceptions to other processes. These signal exceptions are fielded as exceptions, not as signals. The *DosSetSignalExceptionFocus* enables a process to receive the signal exceptions.

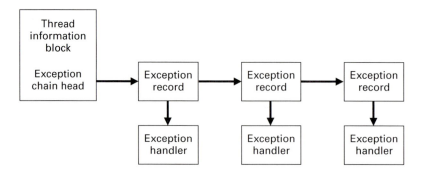

Fig. 7.13   Per-thread exception chain.

As a result of the addition of the process termination exception and the unwind operations, process termination is much more robust than in the 16-bit system. When a single thread dies by calling *DosExit*, it receives the process termination exception, followed by an unwind operation. This process termination exception is of the synchronous variety. If a thread causes a forced termination of the entire process, then all threads in the process receive a process termination exception followed by an unwind exception, and then the process exitlist handlers are called. This type of delivery of the process termination exception is called asynchronous, since it is not caused by the threads receiving the exception, except for one. Asynchronous delivery gives 32-bit DLLs the ability to provide much better resource cleanup in forced-termination situations. The process termination exception also provides to DLLs the ability to ensure that critical operations in independent threads are completed. Handling of the process termination exception allows the termination of an individual thread to be deferred. Since the GP fault to be handled by user-mode exception handlers, fewer involuntary forced termination situations are encountered. Table 7.9 summarizes the OS/2 exception APIs.

7.8 SYSTEM INTEGRITY ISSUES

Protection and security are two different system integrity issues. Security is discussed in Chapter 11. This section examines protection from the standpoint of interprocess communications. For instance, any device driver can totally destroy the system, since it has addressability to the kernel memory space. However, this possibility is more a security issue than a protection issue, since in a secure system only a user with permission to alter the system configuration files could load a device driver. Protection and integrity describe how the system prevents from occurring deadlock situations, such as a thread waiting on an event that will never occur. In the DOS system, there is almost no protection. If a DOS application disables interrupts and goes into a spin loop, the system hangs. If an application destroys the memory containing an interrupt vector, control is transferred to an unknown location when the interrupt occurs. Since the DOS system is not protected, faults do not occur, and protection violations usually result in the system crashing.

16-bit API name	32-bit API name	Description
DosSetVec	*DosSetExceptionHandler*	Register exception handler
N/A	*DosUnsetExceptionHandler*	Deregister exception handler
N/A	*DosRaiseException*	Raise exception
N/A	*DosUnwindException*	Unwind exception handlers
N/A	*DosSendSignalException*	Raise signal exception in another process
N/A	*DosSetSignalExceptionFocus*	Enable process to receive signal exceptions
N/A	*DosAcknowledge Signal Exception*	Acknowledge signal exception

Table 7.9   OS/2 exceptions API.

In the protected environment of OS/2 with multiple processes and threads concurrently executing and sharing resources, a more sophisticated means of deadlock recovery exists. The underlying theme for protection revolves around the process model. If a process accidentally or maliciously causes errors, the errors affect only that process. Processes that are hung can be shut down from the user interface. Also, termination handlers exist to allow DLLs to do resource housekeeping during termination. Properly debugged libraries and programs in OS/2 do not deadlock the system. An improperly debugged program can harm only itself, and an improperly debugged library can harm only its client processes.

There are several categories of integrity breaches that can cause an OS/2 process to execute some kind of recovery scheme. If a signal arrives and the signal handler does not return to the interrupted code, a critical section can perhaps be interrupted. This could cause a semaphore to be in an owned state even though the owner died. Another possible situation is that a process can kill another process using *DosKillProcess*. In 16-bit OS/2, a process can incur a GP fault or a nonrecoverable exception. A process can also fail to release a semaphore due to a coding error. However, all these situations can be avoided using the appropriate interprocess communication constructs and the right combination of termination housekeeping and resource cleanup. Having exitlist and process termination exception handlers allows semaphores to be cleaned up and ensure that threads are never blocked waiting for conditions that will never occur. However, if these handlers do not exist, the threads that are blocked will be notified using the owner died logic of the 16-bit system semaphores or the 32-bit semaphores discussed previously. This notification allows recovery and cleanup to occur, so that the processes can be terminated gracefully without the loss of data.

SUMMARY

This chapter described the OS/2 interprocess communication features. Shared memory is one of the simple IPC constructs, as are semaphores, signals, and exceptions. Anonymous pipes, named pipes, and queues are more complex IPC structures. IPC mechanisms are used by DLLs and programs to facilitate sharing of data resources and integrity management. OS/2 provides a rich set of IPC constructs; selecting the correct mix of such constructs is critical to writing successful programs for the OS/2 system.

TERMINOLOGY

anonymous pipe	counting semaphore
asynchronous concurrent threads	critical section
asynchronous event notification	data sharing
atomic set-and-wait operation	deadlock
binary semaphore	deadlock recovery
blocking I/O	event ID
client-server computing	event semaphore

event signaling
event synchronization semaphore
exception
exception dispatcher
exception handler
exception vector
exclusive system semaphore
exitlist handler
fast-safe RAM (FSRAM)
filter
general protection (GP) fault
give-get shared memory
graceful process termination
guard page
guard page exception
hardware-based semaphore
inheritance mechanism of
    process creation
instance memory
interprocess communication (IPC)
IOPL segment
kernel mode
kernel trap manager
load-time shared memory
local memory
LTD selector
more filter
mutual exclusion (mutex)
mutual exclusion semaphore
mutually exclusive access to
    shared resources
muxwait
muxwait list
muxwait semaphores
named pipe
named shared memory
network redirector
nonblocking I/O
nonexclusive system semaphore
numeric coprocessor (NPX)
open file handle inheritance
open file table
open system semaphore table
owner died logic

owner died notification
owner died return code
peek operation
peer-process interprocess communication
per-process open shared
    semaphore bitmap
per-task data area (PTDA)
pipe handle
pipe mode
post a signal
private semaphore
queue
race condition
RAM semaphore
remote procedure call (RPC)
reset
run-time shared memory
segment-not-present exception
segment-not-present fault
semaphore
semaphore handle
server process
shared address private memory
shared memory
shared semaphore
SIGBREAK
signal
signal handler
SIGINTR
SIGTERM
16-bit event semaphore
software-based semaphore
sort filter
synchronous event
system exception
system semaphore
system trap manager
test-and-set instruction
thread exception handler chain
thread memory
thread 1
thread synchronization
transaction processing
unnamed pipe

unwind operation   user-mode exception dispatcher
user exception   XCHG instruction
user mode

EXERCISES

7.1   Discuss the notions of run-time shared memory, load-time shared memory, named shared memory, and give-get shared memory.

7.2   Distinguish among thread memory, process memory, and shared memory.

7.3   Give several weaknesses of shared memory.

7.4   Explain the notions of critical section and mutual exclusion.

7.5   Distinguish between mutual exclusion semaphores and event synchronization semaphores. Describe a muxwait operation.

7.6   Discuss the usage of each of the three types of semaphores that are supported in 16-bit OS/2: RAM semaphores, fast-safe RAM (FSRAM) semaphores, and system semaphores.

7.7   Distinguish between binary semaphores and counting semaphores.

7.8   What instruction is used on the 80286 to claim a RAM semaphore? What attribute of this instruction eliminates the need to enter the kernel to protect the thread from preemption while attempting to gain ownership of a semaphore?

7.9   Describe several race conditions that may develop with the use of RAM semaphores.

7.10   Explain the use of owner died notification. How is this mechanism useful in deadlock recovery?

7.11   Distinguish between exclusive system semaphores and nonexclusive system semaphores.

7.12   Why are there no RAM semaphores in the 32-bit version of OS/2?

7.13   Distinguish between 32-bit OS/2 private semaphores and shared semaphores.

7.14   Explain the use of mutual exclusion semaphores, event semaphores, and muxwait semaphores in 32-bit OS/2.

7.15   How does 32-bit OS/2 prevent deadlocks between threads awaiting muxwait semaphores?

7.16   What are signals? Why were signals omitted from 32-bit OS/2? How is signal processing performed in 16-bit OS/2?

7.17   How are queues used for peer-process communication among client and server processes?

7.18   Distinguish between named pipes and anonymous (unnamed) pipes. Which processes may access an anonymous pipe? When would a read operation from a pipe block? When would a write operation to a pipe block?

7.19   Explain the use of named pipes to establish communication among remote processes in a networked environment.

7.20   List several advantages of named pipes over anonymous pipes.

7.21   Describe an example interchange over a named pipe between a client and a server process.

7.22   Discuss the respective exception architectures of 16-bit and 32-bit OS/2. Why is the 32-bit architecture superior?

8
I/O Management

I can only assume that a "Do Not File" document is filed in a "Do Not File" file.

Senator Frank Church
Senate Intelligence Subcommittee Hearing, 1975

Gather up the fragments that remain, that nothing be lost.

John 6:12

A form of government that is not the result of a long sequence of shared experiences, efforts, and endeavors can never take root.

Napoleon Bonaparte

A fair request should be followed by the deed in silence.

Dante

. . . the latter, in search of the hard latent value with which it alone is concerned, sniffs round the mass as instinctively and unerringly as a dog suspicious of some buried bone.

William James

Outline

8.1 INTRODUCTION

This chapter describes file and device I/O management in OS/2. OS/2 I/O can be divided into two categories: *system I/O* and *user I/O*. Processes use system I/O to perform file-level I/O to secondary storage devices managed by file systems, and to perform device-level I/O to devices managed by device drivers. System I/O is programmed using the *file system API*. Processes utilize user I/O to interact with the user by employing the keyboard, mouse, and display. User I/O is programmed using the *keyboard (KBD)*, *mouse (MOU)*, and *video (VIO)* subsystems, or the *Presentation Manager (PM)*. This chapter concentrates on the file system and device driver architectures. The discussion in this chapter describes the device driver model that supports the user-I/O device subsystems at the lowest level. Chapter 9 describes how processes interact with the user I/O devices and the associated subsystems.

8.2 DEVICES

OS/2 has two types of devices: *block devices* and *character devices*. Block devices usually have random access characteristics and transfer blocks of data between devices and memory. Block devices comprise secondary storage media, such as hard disks, diskettes, and optical disk devices. Character devices transfer sequential streams of characters to and from devices such as the serial port, keyboard, or parallel port.

Each device in the OS/2 system has a name that is used to access it via the file system API. Device names depend on whether the device is a block or a character device. Character device names have up to seven characters, such as *COM:* and *LPT:*. Block devices can be partitioned into one or more *logical block units*, also called *logical drives*. Logical drives are named using the letters of the alphabet—*A:*, *B:*, through *Z:*. File systems manage the storage of files on logical block devices. Block device drivers manage the mapping of logical block devices to physical drives, and the low-level I/O on behalf of file systems. Data structures similar in function to the device chain of DOS (discussed in Chapter 4) are used to link the logical drive unit letters and character device names to the device drivers that support them.

8.3 INSTALLABLE FILE SYSTEM ARCHITECTURE

OS/2 has an *installable file system (IFS)* architecture, introduced in Version 1.2, that allows the coexistence of multiple file systems. Since each logical block unit can have its own file system, different file systems are usually used for block devices that have different characteristics. For example, write-once-read-many (WORM) and CD/ROM devices need file systems different from those used by random access hard disks.

Each file system supports the management of *file system objects*, such as *files* and *directories*, in a hierarchical fashion. File system objects and devices are managed and accessed by processes using a common file system API. Since the file system API is not sensitive to any of the file system naming conventions, each file system can have its own name structure for the file system objects it supports. Figure 8.1 illustrates the installable file system architecture.

The OS/2 kernel *installable file system router* routes file system API requests to the appropriate file system based on the logical unit addressed by the requesting process. Each file system is called a *file system driver (FSD)*. FSDs service file system API requests by issuing I/O requests to the device drivers. System services are available for FSDs in the form of *file system helper (FSHelp)* functions.

The *device manager* is responsible for the mapping of logical block units to block device drivers and file system drivers. It also provides routines used by file system drivers and the rest of the kernel for issuing device driver requests. The *volume manager* provides control for supporting removable block media, such as diskettes. It ensures that the correct volume is mounted on removable media block devices by invoking the responsible device driver to manage the state of the removable media. For example, the volume manager ensures that the correct diskette is in a diskette drive, and detects when the diskette drive door has been opened and closed, so that it can perform volume verification.

8.4 FILE SYSTEM NAME SPACE

The *file system name space* is the domain of named objects in the system. It is used to ensure the uniqueness of object names for objects that are addressed through the file system API. The file system name space is used for naming files and directories, as well as for naming non-file-system objects such as semaphores, shared memory, queues, and

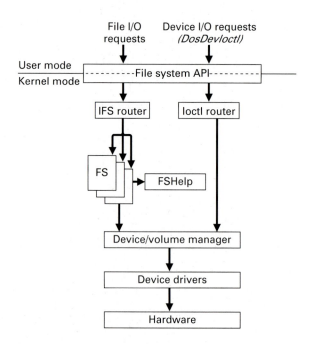

Fig. 8.1   File and device I/O subsystem.

named pipes. Since each of these named objects must be able to guarantee that its name is unique, the names are taken from the file system name space.

The 16-bit and 32-bit versions of OS/2 provide both the FAT file system and the *high performance file system (HPFS)*. The file system name space of the FAT file system uses the traditional *8.3 naming format*, with up to eight characters in a file name followed by an optional three-character suffix. Also, FAT file system names are not case sensitive—they use only uppercase characters. HPFS allows names to be up to 256 characters in length, and supports case preservation of file names. The file system name space is used in conjunction with security access models to associate access permissions with objects that are mapped in the file system name space.

8.5 FILE SYSTEM OBJECTS

The most common file system objects are files and directories. Files contain user data. Directories contain files and other directories. Files and directories have attributes such as size, time of creation, and time of last update, as well as extended attributes that can be manipulated by user programs. Files and directories are managed in a hierarchical fashion: A tree represents a file system's directory structure. The topmost directory in a directory tree is the *root directory,* signified by the " \ " character. Since each block unit is managed by a file system, each has its own directory tree and root directory.

The kernel tracks the *current logical block unit,* also called the *current drive,* of each process in that process's PTDA. Associated with each logical drive is a *current directory,* which maintains the process's position within the directory tree for each logical drive unit. Therefore, each process is always "at" a location in a directory tree based off the current logical block unit (or drive). Using the file system API, a process can traverse directory structures by changing the current directory or logical drive.

Pathnames describe the location of a file in the hierarchical directory structure. Pathnames can be absolute or relative. *Absolute pathnames* are valid no matter where in the directory tree a process is. For example, *D:\TMP\MYFILE* is the absolute pathname for file *MYFILE* in the *TMP* directory on logical drive *D:*. There are some special directory names associated with all file systems. *Relative pathnames* are specified by using special directory names for the current directory, signified by the "." character, and for the *parent directory,* signified by the ".." character sequence. Relative pathnames describe the location of a file relative to a process's current directory and logical drive. The *PATH* and *DPATH* configuration commands are used to specify a search path used by OS/2 when executable files are loaded and when data files are opened. The *LIBPATH* configuration command is used to locate dynamic link library files.

8.6 FILE SYSTEM API

The file system API is used for file and device I/O. *DosOpen* is used for opening both files and devices. *DosOpen* takes the name of the file or device as a parameter, along with other parameters that tell the system how the device or file is being used. The *open mode* tells the system the desired *access mode* and *sharing mode* for the file. The access mode specifies the type of access needed by the process performing the open—it indicates whether *read-write, read-only,* or *write-only* access to the file is desired. The sharing mode specifies the type of access to the file that other processes may have. For example, a sharing mode of *deny-write* prevents other processes from opening the file for write access, but still allows them to read it.

In the case of opening a device, the open mode specifies whether the device should be opened exclusively for the requesting process. The exclusive open mode is used so that a process can ensure that it is the only process accessing the device at a given time. Another input parameter is the *open flag*. The open flag tells *DosOpen* what action to take based on whether the file exists. The open flag specifies whether *DosOpen* should fail if the file does not exist, or whether the file should be created. The open flag also specifies whether the file should be opened or replaced if it already exists.

DosOpen returns a *handle* that the process uses to access the file or device in subsequent file system API requests. File and device handles are 16 bits in OS/2 1.X, and are 32 bits in OS/2 2.X. *DosOpen* also returns information that reports the action taken based on the open flag. Once a file is open, it is accessible by all threads within the process that opened it.

DosRead and *DosWrite* are used for reading from and writing to open files and devices. In the 16-bit system, single I/O transfers can be up to 64KB. The 32-bit system supports I/O transfers of more than 64KB. For each process that opens a file, the system maintains a *logical file pointer*. The logical file pointer indicates where in the file the next *DosRead* or *DosWrite* operation will occur. The logical file pointer can be changed by issuance of *DosSetFilePtr* requests. A file is closed by a call to *DosClose*.

The system maintains an *open file table* for each process in its PTDA. When a file is opened, a descriptor is allocated from the open file table of the process. The index of the allocated descriptor is returned to the user in the form of a *file handle* that is used in subsequent file system API requests for accessing the file. Unlike shared memory addresses and 32-bit semaphore handles, handles to files are not reserved across all processes. Therefore, if two processes both open the same file, each may use a different file handle to access the file. Each open file table entry points to a *system file table (SFT)* *entry* that contains information specific to each logical open reference to a file. The SFT contains the per-process logical file pointer associated with the open file, the file size, time and date of the last modification, and a pointer to a *master file table (MFT) entry*. An MFT is allocated for each unique open file in the system, and is used for controlling file sharing and file locking. Each PTDA also contains a *current drive structure (CDS)* array used for tracking the per-process current drive and directory information. The SFTs, MFTs, and CDSs also contain links to file-system-specific information. Figure 8.2 illustrates the file-system-independent data structures for two processes.

In Fig. 8.2, each process has opened a unique file, and both processes have opened a file that is being shared, for a total of three unique open file instances. For each logical open there is an SFT, and for each unique file open there is a single MFT. The shared file has a single MFT that is referenced by two SFTs. Thus, each process has its own logical file pointer into the shared file, but access according to the open sharing mode and file locks is controlled by the MFT.

DosDupHandle can be used to manipulate the location of descriptors inside the open file table. It is usually used when filters and pipes are being set up between two processes, so that the standard input and standard output file descriptors can be redirected

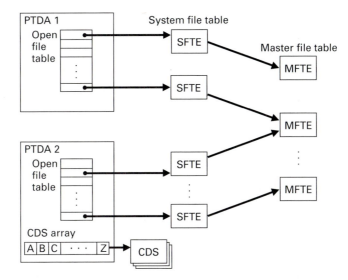

Fig. 8.2   File and path management file system data structures.

from the keyboard and screen to pipes, files, and devices. *DosDupHandle* can also be used to force a child process to share a logical file pointer with that process's parent process. *DosDupHandle* creates multiple references to a single SFT within a process or across processes.

If two processes have a file open with write access, they must synchronize their access to the file. Although each process usually has its own logical file pointer, it is possible for one process to update a portion of the file while another process is trying to read that same portion. Problems can occur if the processes do not manage their access carefully. To enable processes to share portions of a file in a controlled fashion, the *DosSetFileLocks* API call allows a process to obtain exclusive access to a specific region of a file.

Devices are also accessed using *DosOpen* with a device name instead of a file name. Device I/O requests are then issued by invocation of *DosRead* or *DosWrite*. The *DosDevIOCtl* system call is used to communicate directly with the device driver that monitors and controls the device. *DosDevIOCtl* is used to perform functions whose protocols do not fit the file I/O model. The operations and protocol are determined by the device driver and the requesting applications. For example, issuing *DosOpen* in the *E:* logical block device enables a process to issue low-level disk I/O commands directly to the device driver. This type of interface is used, for example, by the disk formatting utility. Similarly, the serial and printer device drivers can be accessed directly using *DosDevIOCtl*. The user I/O subsystems for keyboard, mouse, and video shield their requestors from the device driver interfaces by performing *DosDevIOCtl* requests on behalf of high-level user I/O requests. The role of these subsystems is discussed in Chapter 9.

DosQueryCurrentDisk and *DosQueryCurrentDir* are used to query the process's current logical drive and directory. The complementary functions *DosSetCurrentDisk* and

DosSetCurrentDir are used to change the current logical drive and directory. A file's open mode can be queried and set at run time by a call to the *DosQueryFileMode* and *DosSetFileMode* API functions. The *DosFindFirst, DosFindNext,* and *DosFindClose* calls are used to scan and search directories for files that have matching attributes. Table 8.1 summarizes the file system API calls for both the 16-bit and the 32-bit systems. The calls for the two systems are similar in function, but some of the 32-bit API function names have been altered to be more consistent with the rest of the system API.

8.7 OS/2 1.X FILE SYSTEM DRIVERS

File system drivers are trusted modules that run at privilege level 0 in kernel mode. They are loaded when the system is started. The two primary FSDs that are shipped with OS/2 1.X are the FAT file system and HPFS. The FAT file system is the same as that in the DOS system, except for enhancements for supporting partitions larger than 32MB. Providing the FAT file system in OS/2 allows users to migrate from DOS-based systems to OS/2 without having to convert file formats. Although the FAT file system does not provide caching, the disk device driver does provide disk block caching for logical block units managed by the FAT file system. However, if the system swap file is located on a FAT partition, I/O requests from the swapper are not cached.

HPFS is a highly cached file system that supports the multitasking environment of OS/2 and large disk volumes of up to 2GB. It performs overlapped I/O operations and attempts to keep files contiguous on the secondary storage media to maximize system performance. HPFS reduces I/O operations by managing a write-behind cache (optionally write-through), and a read-ahead cache. HPFS provides its own cache management, since it has more information than does the disk device driver on how the file system data are organized on the block media. Therefore, the disk device driver does not provide caching for logical block units managed by HPFS. Like the FAT file system, HPFS provides an interface for swapper I/O that does not perform caching.

Since the DOS environment uses the OS/2 file system, DOS applications can access files transparently on a logical drive managed by HPFS. HPFS also allows *long file object names* up to 254 characters. Programs that support long file names can run on either the FAT or HPFS environments. For compatibility with applications that rely on the FAT 8.3 naming convention, FSDs support a superset of the FAT's 8.3 name format.

The OS/2 FSDs maintain a standard set of information, called *attributes,* on file objects. Examples of a file's standard attributes are the name, file size, and the time and date of creation, last access, and last write. HPFS and the file system API allow applications to attach additional information, called *extended attributes,* to file objects. Extended attributes can be used to store application-specific notes about file objects, or to append additional data to the file in the form of *extents.* A file's extended attributes effectively become part of the file, and are accessed when the file is opened. If a file is copied or deleted, the extended attributes are copied or deleted with the file. Extended attributes are not accessible to DOS programs.

FSDs implement the file system API for the logical block units to which they are attached. The IFS router component of the OS/2 kernel dispatches file system API

16-Bit API Name	32-Bit API Name	Description
DosBufReset	*DosResetBuffer*	Flush file(s) cache buffers
DosChDir	*DosSetCurrentDir*	Set current directory
DosChgFilePtr	*DosSetFilePtr*	Move file I/O pointer
DosClose	*DosClose*	Close file or device
DosDelete	*DosDelete*	Delete file
DosDevIOCtl2	*DosDevIOCtl*	Device-level I/O request
DosDupHandle	*DosDupHandle*	Duplicate file handle
DosEditName	*DosEditName*	Search/edit file object names
DosFileIO	*N/A*	Multiple file-level I/O requests
DosFileLocks	*DosSetFileLocks*	Lock/unlock range of file
DosFindClose	*DosFindClose*	Close find handle
DosFindFirst	*DosFindFirst*	Find first matching file object
DosFindNext	*DosFindNext*	Find next matching file object
DosFSAttach	*DosFSAttach*	Attach/detach device to FSD
DosFSCtl	*DosFSCtl*	File system I/O control
DosMkDir	*DosCreateDir*	Create directory
DosMove	*DosMove*	Move file
DosNewSize	*DosNewSize*	Change file size
DosOpen	*DosOpen*	Open file or device
DosQCurDir	*DosQueryCurrentDir*	Get current directory
DosQCurDisk	*DosQueryCurrentDisk*	Get current logical drive
DosQFileInfo	*DosQueryFileInfo*	Get file information
DosQFileMode	*DosQueryFileMode*	Get file mode
DosQFSAttach	*DosQueryFSAttach*	Query attached FS information
DosQFSInfo	*DosQueryFSInfo*	Query file system information
DosQHandType	*DosQueryHType*	Query handle type
DosQPathInfo	*DosQueryPathInfo*	Get file or directory info
DosQSysInfo	*DosQuerySysInfo*	Get system information
DosQVerify	*DosQueryVerify*	Query verify setting
DosRead	*DosRead*	Read from file or device
DosReadAsync	N/A	Asynchronous read
DosRmDir	*DosDeleteDir*	Delete directory
DosSearchPath	*DosSearchPath*	Search path for file name
DosSelectDisk	*DosSetDefaultDisk*	Set default drive
DosSetFHandState	*DosSetFHState*	Set file handle state
DosSetFileInfo	*DosSetFileInfo*	Set file information
DosSetFileMode	*DosSetFileMode*	Set file mode
DosSetFSInfo	*DosSetFSInfo*	Set file system information
DosSetMaxFH	*DosSetMaxFH*	Set max# of open file handles
DosSetPathInfo	*DosSetPathInfo*	Set file or subdir attributes
DosSetVerify	*DosSetVerify*	Enable file write verify
DosWrite	*DosWrite*	Write to a file or device
DosWriteAsync	N/A	Asynchronous write

Table 8.1 File System API.

requests to the correct FSD, based on the drive being accessed. FSDs run in kernel mode, and call block device drivers via the device manager to carry out their I/O operations. When a thread issues a file system I/O, the request may have to be broken up into several I/O requests if the data are not contiguous on the block media. The I/O interface presented by 16-bit device drivers allows each thread to make a single I/O request between a contiguous range of logical sectors on a logical block unit, and a physically contiguous buffer. Usually, the device driver blocks the requesting thread until the I/O completes. Although each thread can perform only a single I/O transaction at a time, multiple I/O requests from different threads can be overlapped concurrently.

The FSHelp interface is used by FSDs to access system services provided by the kernel. FSHelp functions are invoked by placement of a function number and parameters in registers, then a call to the FSHelp entry point provided to the FSD when it is installed. Thus, FSHelp is a statically linked, kernel-level interface.

8.8 OS/2 2.X FILE SYSTEM DRIVERS

The 32-bit version of OS/2 enhances the I/O architecture of the 16-bit system to exploit intelligent I/O subsystem hardware, and to perform I/O in the demand-paged environment. Intelligent I/O subsystems are programmable at a higher level of abstraction than are existing I/O devices. They are used to offload I/O device handling from the operating system, thus enhancing performance. Some intelligent devices also include support for executing I/O command chains, and for managing hardware-based I/O caches. Modifications to the I/O architecture are also needed to deal with the paged environment, in which physical memory buffers are not contiguous.

Cache management has been added to the FAT file system, so the disk device driver no longer performs any caching. Since the file system has more knowledge about the layout of data on block devices, it can perform caching algorithms more effectively than can the disk device driver. Providing caching in the file system also eliminates read requests to the disk device driver when data are in the cache, reducing I/O path lengths. The file system can also more accurately perform cache heuristics, such as read-ahead and lazy write. File systems also have the capability to manage I/O caches located on intelligent I/O subsystems, and to preload anticipated data into an external cache.

Many intelligent I/O subsystems support *I/O command chaining*. Devices that support command chaining allow multiple commands to be submitted to the device for processing at a time. For file systems, command chaining minimizes the path length for accessing files that are discontiguous on the secondary storage media. Command chaining can also reduce the number of interrupts processed by the system for a set of I/O operations.

A paged memory environment poses a problem for devices that rely on DMA for data transfers. Most existing DMA devices assume that physical memory is contiguous. In the paged environment, however, I/O buffers that are contiguous in the virtual address space are usually composed of discontiguous physical pages. *Scatter-gather I/O* is a mechanism for transferring blocks of data to and from a buffer whose pages are physically discontiguous. A *gather-write* operation writes a physically discontiguous I/O buffer to a contiguous range of sectors on the secondary medium. A *scatter-read* operation reads a contiguous range of sectors from the secondary medium to a physically discontiguous I/O buffer. I/O buffer addresses are supplied to devices that support scatter-gather I/O using *scatter-gather lists*.

Both the FAT file system and HPFS provide interfaces for performing *page swapper I/O*. The page swapper I/O interfaces support a contiguous swap file, and I/O operations that are not cached. The page swapper can request multiple page-in and page-out operations to occur in a single command in a specific sequence.

Whereas the implementation of the FSDs uses 16-bit code, the FAT and HPFS FSDs both use an extended device driver interface to manage intelligent I/O devices, and the paged environment. If a block device does not support intelligent I/O or the paged environment, the existing 16-bit device driver interfaces are used. The extended interface supports I/O command chains, scatter-gather I/O, and a better I/O dispatching model that optimizes asynchronous I/O and allows a single thread to issue multiple chained I/O requests before blocking.

8.9 DEVICE DRIVERS

Device drivers are device dependent modules that provide the low-level I/O support for a device. They are trusted modules—they run at privilege level 0 and have access to the kernel. Device drivers must be reentrant to support overlapped asynchronous I/O operations requested by the kernel. To support the OS/2 multitasking model, device drivers relinquish control of the processor when forced to wait for I/O operations to complete. Device drivers are loaded and initialized when the system is started. There are two types of device drivers in the system: *base device drivers,* which are included with the system, and *installable device drivers,* which the user can install through CONFIG.SYS when the system is started.

The OS/2 device driver model is a segmented 16-bit model, and the device driver interfaces are accessed using register-based calling conventions. Thus, most device drivers are written in assembler to meet performance requirements in this environment. The same device driver model is used in the 16-bit and 32-bit versions of OS/2. There are some differences in the implementations due to the different DOS compatibility architectures of 16-bit and 32-bit OS/2, and to the need to support intelligent I/O devices in the paged environment. Chapter 10 describes the influence on device drivers of DOS compatibility requirements.

8.10 HARDWARE DEVICE STRUCTURE

Each hardware device in a personal computer has a *controller* that is interfaced to the system bus. The controller is attached to the actual peripheral device, and operates the device on behalf of the system. For example, the keyboard controller is connected to the keyboard, and the disk controller is attached to a hard disk drive. The main processor operates devices by programming their controllers. For example, the hard disk drive is connected to the hard disk controller, which is programmed by the main processor. Each controller contains internal registers used to program the device. Command operations, status operations, and data transfers with the device are initiated by programming of the controller through its registers.

The granularity of data transfer between a device and the processor determines whether the device is a character or block device. For example, the asynchronous port transfers one or several bytes at a time in a stream—clearly, this is a character device. The hard disk transfers data one or more sectors at a time. Since each sector is a block of 512 or more bytes, the hard disk is classified as a block device.

The data access characteristics of a device determine whether that device is sequential or random access. Character devices—such as the asynchronous communications port, the keyboard, and the mouse—are sequential, since their data are transferred as a stream of characters or events that are ordered as they are generated. The hard disk is a random access device—any specified sector can be accessed directly without having to read sequentially from a starting point. Therefore, the disk device driver can order the requests for data transfers to and from the disk according to an algorithm that optimizes disk access performance (De90). However, not all character devices are accessed sequentially, and not all block devices are accessed randomly.

Controllers also contain device buffers for data transfer. For example, the hard disk controller contains the registers for programming hard disk operations, and a disk buffer. When a read operation occurs, the processor programs the controller to perform a read from the hard disk. The controller initiates the operation, and reads the data to the disk buffer within the controller. The data in the disk buffer are later transferred across the bus to the memory location specified in the read request to the device driver.

Another example is the video controller. The video controller has a *video RAM (VRAM)* buffer that is scanned by the video hardware for the images to be placed on the screen. The video controller is programmed via accessing of the video controller's internal registers. However, I/O to the video buffer is performed by execution of memory write operations to the video buffer. The video hardware picks up the contents of the video buffer, and traces them on the display screen. A final example is the keyboard controller, which is programmed via its internal registers, and which contains a special data register for transferring data typed on the keyboard.

8.11 HARDWARE DEVICE ATTRIBUTES

There are three major attributes that can be used to describe any hardware device:

- Device addressing
- Device control and status
- Data transfer

Each of these attributes is independent of the others. Devices can have any combination of these attributes.

Device addressing describes how a device is addressed by the main processor. It depends on how the controller for the device is connected to the bus, and on the nature of the device. The two methods of device addressing used in personal computers are *memory mapping* and *I/O mapping*. *Memory-mapped devices* have their controller's registers mapped into the memory address space of the processor. Thus, processor-initiated memory operations to and from the memory-mapped range of addresses actually cause accesses to the internal registers and buffers of a memory-mapped device's controller. *I/O-mapped devices* are addressed through the I/O port architecture of the Intel processors. They are programmed by using the I/O instructions described in Chapter 2.

Device control and status describes how the processor communicates with the device controller to determine the current status of the device, and to initiate operations or control the device. There are two major protocols: *polled* and *interrupt driven*. A *polled device* is one in which the system must periodically check whether the device needs servicing. Polled devices are not suitable for multitasking, since the operating system must dedicate processor cycles to determine whether the device needs servicing. Polled devices provide synchronous I/O. *Interrupt-driven devices* are more appropriate for multitasking. With interrupt-driven devices, the system is notified by an interrupt when a device needs servicing. This notification scheme allows the system to perform other tasks while I/O operations are in progress, without having to poll devices for status intermittently. When an interrupt occurs, the system stops what it is doing and services the device. Since the system continues to run between interrupts, interrupt-driven I/O operations are classified as asynchronous.

Data transfer refers to the strategy employed by a device for moving data from the device to memory, and vice versa. There are three primary device data transfer strategies:

- Programmed I/O
- Direct memory access (DMA)
- Bus mastering

Programmed I/O is used when data are moved between the device and memory under control of the processor. The processor executes I/O instructions that move the data between the device and memory using the processor as an intermediary. Since the data transfer occurs under processor instruction control, the processor cannot perform other tasks while the data are being transferred. An example of a programmed I/O device is the ST-506 hard disk controller used in PC/ATs. To perform a disk read, the controller is programmed to read the data from the disk into the buffer on the disk controller. At the completion of this operation, the disk controller interrupts the processor to notify the latter that the data are ready for transfer. The processor executes the *REP INS* instruction, which causes the processor to read repeatedly from an I/O port to a main memory address until the transfer is complete. The *REP INS* instruction causes the data to be read from the disk controller, moved across the bus into the processor, and then moved by the processor across the bus to memory.

Direct memory access (DMA) is a technique in which a special DMA controller is programmed to move data directly between devices and memory, without any interaction from the processor. DMA operations are initiated by the processor, but do not require the processor for the data transfer. Instead, the processor can continue executing instructions while the DMA controller performs the data transfer. The DMA controller moves the data across the bus by *stealing bus cycles* from the processor. When the transfer is complete, the DMA controller interrupts the processor to notify the processor of the transfer status. Since the processors in today's systems have prefetch instruction queues to maximize instruction fetch performance, they can continue executing instructions while DMA transfers occur. Thus, DMA allows a low-level form of hardware parallelism. In most personal computers, a DMA controller is included on the system planar. The DMA controller provides multiple channels that are dedicated to DMA devices in the system.

Bus mastering is a special protocol that allows multiple controllers with their own associated DMA controller to compete for bus cycles. The bus must arbitrate among those bus masters that are attempting to use the bus resource. Bus master data transfer is similar to DMA data transfer, except that a DMA controller on the bus master device, the system DMA controller, is used for data transfer. The Micro Channel Architecture described in Chapter 3 provides *bus arbitration* to support an environment in which bus master, programmed I/O, and DMA data transfers can coexist.

8.12 HARDWARE DEVICE INDEPENDENCE

DOS device drivers utilize ROM BIOS to access the actual hardware device, instead of directly programming the hardware. ROM BIOS is built into the system planar, and insulates DOS device drivers from the underlying hardware architecture and device controller dependencies. This insulation is useful when an engineering change to a component of the hardware system occurs between production runs of a computer. If a controller has a slightly different interface, the ROM BIOS is altered to support the new part, and DOS continues to run on the system without any changes.

ROM BIOS is mapped into the 640KB to 1MB range of the PC address space. ROM BIOS also has an associated ROM BIOS data area at physical address 400H, used to store device information accessed by the ROM BIOS routines. ROM BIOS is accessible in only real mode, and is not reentrant. ROM BIOS is suitable for the DOS environment, but its lack of reentrancy and its real-mode dependencies render it unusable for a protected-mode operating system.

When the PS/2 systems were developed, IBM saw a need for a new type of BIOS, called *advanced BIOS (ABIOS)*. ABIOS supports real-mode, protected-mode, and bimodal operating environments. It is reentrant and extendable. To differentiate between the two BIOS modules in the system ROMs, the developers renamed the original real-mode BIOS *compatibility BIOS (CBIOS)*. OS/2 device drivers have the options of programming directly to the hardware, or of using ABIOS.

The development of *intelligent I/O subsystems* capable of independent operation led to the definition of IBM's *Subsystem Control Block (SCB)* architecture. Intelligent I/O subsystems usually are bus masters; they have their own processors, local memories, and DMA controllers. Although ABIOS relieves the restrictions of the original CBIOS, it is not designed to run optimally in an environment with intelligent I/O subsystems.

The SCB architecture is used on IBM's intelligent SCSI adapters, and on the PS/2 Models 90 and 95.

The SCB architecture is an interface used by device drivers on the main processor for accessing intelligent I/O processors in a device-independent fashion. It frees the main processor from the burden of staging I/O operations that generate interrupts. The SCB architecture raises the level of device abstraction, so work for completing multiple related requests is offloaded from the main processor. It also provides the capability of addressing and programming intelligent I/O subsystems in a uniform way.

SCBs are used for communication between the main processor and I/O processors. SCB I/O operations are issued by allocation of an SCB, and transmission of that SCB to the local memory of an intelligent I/O subsystem. The I/O subsystem then performs the operations described in the SCB without interrupting the main processor until the operations are complete. SCBs can also be chained, allowing a list of I/O operations to be submitted to an I/O subsystem in a single request. The SCB architecture also supports scatter-gather I/O transfers for environments that have paging enabled.

8.13 OS/2 1.X DEVICE DRIVERS

In OS/2 1.X, only one DOS application is supported by the DOS compatibility environment, and it runs in real mode. Furthermore, the DOS environment runs only when it is in the foreground—it is suspended when in the background. When the DOS environment is in the foreground, other OS/2 programs can run in the background in protected mode. The system mode switches between real mode and protected mode as necessary. However, so that mode switching is minimized, portions of the OS/2 system and the OS/2 1.X device drivers need to be able to run in real mode and in protected mode. Code that is executable in both real mode and protected mode is *bimodal code;* the OS/2 1.X device drivers are *bimodal device drivers.*

Since bimodal code and the data it accesses must be addressable in both real mode and protected mode, bimodal code is loaded in physical memory addresses below 1MB. Recall from Chapter 6 that the 16-bit system takes special care to load device drivers and portions of the kernel into low physical memory, so that they can be executed in real mode. The system is partitioned to minimize the amount of low memory taken from the DOS environment, yet to provide acceptable performance in critical operations such as interrupt management and context switching.

Since a device driver for an interrupt-driven device can initiate an I/O request in one mode and have the request complete in the opposite mode, buffer transfer addresses are converted to physical addresses by the device driver. The physical addresses are converted to virtual addresses sensitive to the processor mode when the device driver accesses memory.

8.14 DEVICE DRIVER STRUCTURE

OS/2 device drivers are packaged in specialized EXE files. They contain at least one code segment and one data segment, and are loaded into low physical memory. A device driver can also contain other segments that are loaded into high memory, above the 1MB boundary. Figure 8.3 illustrates the device driver file structure.

Each device driver has a special set of entry points used by the OS/2 system to request service. The *strategy routine* is the main entry point for requests from the kernel. The kernel passes a pointer to a *request packet* that describes the request to the strategy routine. The request packet pointer is referenced by the *ES:BX* registers when the strategy routine is called. Strategy routines run in kernel mode, and on the stack of the requesting thread. The strategy routine can be thought of as the *top half of the device driver,* the same way that there is a top half of the OS/2 kernel. The strategy routine either completes the request and returns the packet to the kernel, or blocks the thread until the request is completed. This routine allows other threads to continue running while a device is busy when a request is made.

Each interrupt-driven device also usually has a *hardware interrupt handler* associated with it. The interrupt handler is called by the interrupt manager when an external hardware interrupt on a specific interrupt level occurs. Usually, when the device driver is initialized, it registers a hardware interrupt handler if it needs one. The interrupt handler is responsible for clearing the interrupt controller hardware, and for checking the status of the interrupting device. It runs in interrupt mode on the interrupt stack of the system (see Chapter 5). This stack corresponds to the *bottom half of the device driver* in the top-half-bottom-half model. Access to structures shared by the strategy routine and the hardware interrupt handler must be serialized, since interrupts can occur during the strategy routine. Device drivers synchronize the top-half and bottom-half by enabling or disabling the 80X86 interrupt flag.

In the 16-bit system, use of interrupt mode implies that the processor is in either real mode or protected mode due to the mode switching architecture of the DOS environment. Therefore, request packets and I/O buffer transfer addresses provided in the request packets must not be sensitive to the processor mode. Furthermore, interrupt-driven device drivers save I/O buffer addresses as physical addresses, since a request may complete in the context of a process other than the one that initiated it.

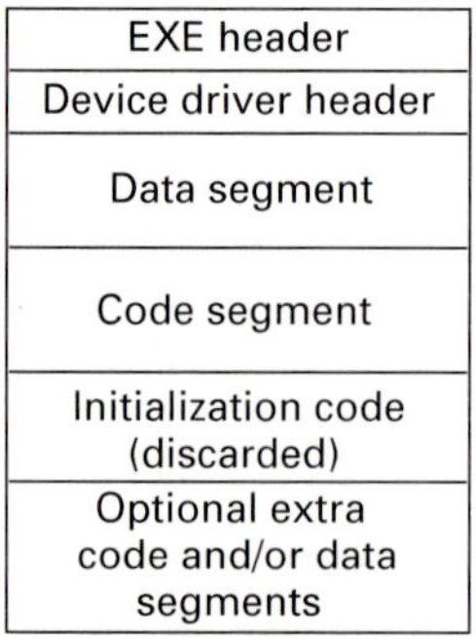

EXE header
Device driver header
Data segment
Code segment
Initialization code (discarded)
Optional extra code and/or data segments

Fig. 8.3   Device driver file structure.

Some devices have timing constraints. For instance, for diskette operations, the diskette drive must be accelerated to full speed before the next step of the operation can occur. Since it takes a known time interval to bring the disk to full speed, the device driver needs to set a *timer handler*. A timer handler is used for devices that need to perform intermittent services, such as accessing polled devices or accelerating the diskette drive motor. Timer handlers are registered by device drivers as needed, and run in interrupt mode.

Device drivers request system services to assist in performing requests in the form of *Device Help (DevHelp)* functions. *DevHelp* is a statically linked interface that allows device drivers to call a special set of kernel routines available to device drivers. *DevHelp* and the associated functions are described in detail in Section 8.19. Figure 8.4 illustrates the logical components of a device driver.

In 16-bit OS/2, ROM BIOS software interrupt services are provided by the device drivers that service the respective devices. If a device driver provides ROM BIOS support, it registers an entry point for BIOS service—called a *ROM BIOS handler*—when it is initialized. When DOS applications running on the 16-bit system make BIOS requests, the appropriate device driver ROM BIOS handler is called in real mode—also called *DOS Mode* in OS/2 publications. Since ROM BIOS is not reentrant, and the system multitasks protected-mode applications in the background while a DOS application is in the foreground, the system must provide a means of preventing preemption of a DOS application that has entered ROM BIOS. The kernel provides the *DevHelp(ROMCritSection)* function to allow a device driver to indicate that it is about to use ROM BIOS code, and to disable preemption temporarily until the DOS application exits ROM BIOS. The final device driver entry point is the *inter-device-driver communications handler*. It is used for private communication between device drivers, and has no mode restrictions.

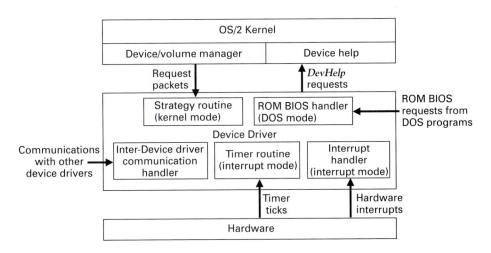

Fig. 8.4   OS/2 1.X device driver interfaces.

8.15 DEVICE DRIVER HEADER

Each device driver has a *device driver header* at the start of the first segment in the device driver executable image (Fig. 8.5). Therefore, the device driver data segment is always the first segment of the device driver executable file image.

The header has a field used for chaining together the device drivers, similar to the device chain described in Chapter 4. The header contains fields used to locate the strategy and inter-device-driver communication entry points, and the name of the device. For character devices, the name is an 8-byte ASCII string. For block devices, the name is the number of logical block units supported by the block device driver.

8.16 DEVICE ATTRIBUTE FLAGS

The *device attribute flags* are part of the device driver header (Fig. 8.6). They determine which commands are serviced by the device driver strategy routine. The flags determine whether the device is block or character, and whether the device driver provides inter-device-driver communication support. The flags also specify whether a block device is for fixed media, such as hard disks, or for removable media, such as diskettes. This distinction is important, since the file system makes specific strategy requests based on whether the device medium is removable. The flags also determine whether the device driver supports *open* and *close* strategy commands. They thus allow the device driver writer to choose whether the device driver should be called when device level *DosOpen* and *DosClose* requests are made to the device name. The flags have a function-level field that describes the earliest version of OS/2 that the device driver supports. Other bits in the flags indicate whether the device is the *system null device, standard output device, standard input device,* or *clock device.*

8.17 REQUEST PACKETS

Requests packets are used by the OS/2 kernel to communicate the parameters of a request to a device driver strategy routine (Fig. 8.7). Request packets are resident in

Next device driver pointer	DWORD
Device attributes flags	WORD
Offset to strategy routine	WORD
Offset to IDC entry point	WORD
Name or blocks units	8 BYTES
Reserved(0)	8 BYTES

Fig. 8.5 Device driver header.

CHR	IDC	IBM	SHR	OPN	0	Level	0 0 0	CLK	NUL	SCR	KBD
15	14	13	12	11	10	9 8 7	6 5 4	3	2	1	0

Fig. 8.6   Device driver attribute flags.

kernel memory, and are variable in length depending on the command issued. Request packets contain the command information for processing by the strategy routine.

The request packet is divided into two sections: a static portion and a variable-length portion. The static portion contains the length of the packet, the block unit for which the packet is intended (if it is for a block device driver), the specific command number, and a field for returning status to the system. Also, there is a queue linkage field used for linking request packets. The variable-length portion of the request packet provides the command-specific data.

Since request packets need to be addressable in both real mode and protected mode in the 16-bit OS/2 system, they are allocated special *tiled virtual addresses*. If an address is tiled, it means that a single virtual address in real mode and protected mode accesses the same physical memory location. For example, the ROM BIOS data area is a tiled region of memory. It exists at virtual address 40:0, or physical address 400H in real mode. To make this a tiled data region, the descriptor for selector 40 in the GDT has a base address of 400H. Therefore, any reference to virtual address 40:0 will result in accessing of physical address 400H, regardless of whether the access is in real mode or protected mode. Chapter 10 describes tiling and DOS compatibility issues in more detail.

8.18 STRATEGY COMMANDS

The device driver strategy routine is called for the first time when the device driver is being installed by the system. The request packet command code indicates that this request is an *initialization* request, and the strategy routine dispatches to the code that handles the initialization of the device driver. The initialization routine runs in a special

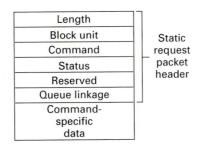

Fig. 8.7   Device driver request packet format.

mode called *initialization mode,* because the system is not fully initialized and cannot support all operations that the driver can perform. Initialization mode executes at privilege level 3 so that device drivers can use several of the system API functions, for tasks such as accessing files or printing status messages on the console. Initialization routines usually prepare the device for I/O, register an interrupt handler if necessary, and initialize device driver data structures. The initialization routine is passed the address of the *DevHelp router* as part of its initialization of command-specific data. This address is saved by the device driver so that it can be used later when the device driver makes calls to other *DevHelp* services.

In general, most strategy routine commands, except the initialization command, are called in kernel mode. The strategy routine then dispatches (through a table based on the command number specified in the request packet) to the code that is used to handle the command. Strategy requests either are completed immediately and returned to the kernel, or are blocked until the operation can complete. For random access devices such as hard disks, request packets can be queued by the strategy routine, and ordered into the most efficient combination of disk accesses. The strategy routine runs on the kernel stack of the requesting thread and is not preemptible, since it runs in kernel mode. Thus, the strategy routine has critical sections only where data that can be modified by the interrupt handler are accessed. Access to these data must be serialized using *CLI* and *STI* instructions.

Depending on the nature of the device, most of the commands serviced by a strategy routine, except for *read* and *write,* can be processed immediately. If the block device is busy, read and write request packets are linked onto a device service queue, and the requesting thread is blocked until the I/O completes. The request packet for the read and write operations contains the physical address of a locked I/O buffer, the starting sector number, and the count of sectors to be transferred. Physical addresses are used due to the 16-bit mode switching environment. Since I/O interrupt-driven operations can be started in protected mode and completed in real mode, or vice versa, the addresses stored by the device driver need to be independent of the processor mode. Furthermore, the addresses stored by a device driver that services an interrupt-driven device need to be accessible in the context of any process, since often a process other than the requestor is running when a queued request is completed. Although GDT virtual addresses in the kernel space are not process sensitive, they cannot be used by bimodal interrupt handlers executing in real mode without mode switching.

Therefore, the file systems lock the segment containing the I/O buffer to obtain a physical address for read and write commands. Locking of the memory is necessary since the device driver stores physical addresses and cannot determine whether the memory is moved or swapped. The physical address is converted to a processor mode-dependent system virtual address that is usable in any process context by the device driver using the *DevHelp(PhysToVirt)* function.

The kernel uses the *generic IOCtl* to pass user *DosDevIOCtl* API requests to device drivers. *DosDevIOCtl* is used for device-level I/O, and the interface between applications and a device driver's *IOCtl* routine is defined by the device driver. The generic *IOCtl* request packet contains the user's parameters from the *DosDevIOCtl* call in the variable-length portion of the request packet. Since the format of the IOCTL request packet is not known by the kernel, the kernel cannot lock the addresses before the packet is presented to the device driver. The device driver must lock any referenced segments using *DevHelp(Lock)*, which returns a physical address that can be used at interrupt time in the context of any process. After the I/O operation is complete, the device driver unlocks the segment by calling *DevHelp(Unlock)*. Table 8.2 summarizes the device driver strategy commands.

8.19 DEVHELP SERVICES

DevHelp services are provided by the kernel to assist device drivers in servicing request packets. They are called indirectly through the address passed to a device driver in the latter's initialization routine. The *DevHelp* functions use register-based parameters. The calling conventions for *DevHelp* services require a static linkage to functions

Command	Description	Device type
Initialization	Initialize device driver.	Block/char
Media check	Check if removable media changed.	Block
Build BPB	Build BPB for new media.	Block
Read(input)	Read from device.	Block/char
Nondestructive read	Peek data from device (no wait).	Char
Input status	Check input queue status.	Char
Input flush	Flush input queue.	Char
Write(output)	Write to device.	Block/char
Write with verify	Write to device w/verify (format).	Block/char
Output status	Check output queue status.	Char
Output flush	Flush output queue.	Char
Device open	Device-level *DosOpen* request.	Block/char
Device close	Device-level *DosClose* request.	Block/char
Removable media	Check if media is removable.	Block
Generic IOCtl	*DosDevIOCtl* request.	Block/char
Reset media	Reset driver media status.	Block
Get logical drive map	Get logical-physical drive map.	Block
Set logical drive map	Set logical-physical drive map.	Block
Partitionable hard disks	Query number of hard disks supported.	Block
Get logical unit map	Get hard disk-logical unit mapping.	Block
Get device support	Get device and volume information.	Block

Table 8.2   Device driver strategy commands.

in the kernel through the *DevHelp router*. The device driver places the number of the service in one register, and the parameters for the service in other registers, and then indirectly calls *DevHelp* using the *DevHelp* router address. *DevHelp* functions are mode sensitive. That is, whether a device driver can call a specific *DevHelp* function is determined by the current mode of the device driver—kernel mode, interrupt mode, DOS mode, or initialization mode. For instance, since there is no real thread context at interrupt time, a device driver cannot call *DevHelp(Block)* at interrupt time to put a thread to sleep.

The *DevHelp* services are divided into the following categories:

- Process management
- Semaphore management
- Request queue and request packet management
- Character queue management
- Memory management
- Interrupt management
- Timer services
- System services

The *process management DevHelp* functions allow device drivers to control multi-tasking. The functions *Block, Run, Yield,* and *TCYield,* are analogous to the functions described in Chapter 5. The *semaphore management DevHelp* functions allow access to 16-bit semaphores. The *request-queue and request-packet management DevHelp* services provide routines for managing request packets, and for managing queues of request packets. The *character queue management DevHelp* calls allow character queues to be managed for supporting asynchronous and keyboard devices.

The *interrupt management DevHelp* services provide functions for setting and unsetting hardware and software interrupt handlers, and for managing the programmable interrupt controller. The *timer services DevHelp* functions allow device drivers to register timer handlers and to modify the frequency at which they are called. *System services DevHelp* is a general category for other *DevHelp* services that fall into miscellaneous areas, such as retrieving system variables, switching modes, and accessing ABIOS services.

Memory management is perhaps the most important *DevHelp* service provided by the system. The *memory management DevHelp* services provide segmented 16-bit memory management functions for virtual and physical address translation, lock and unlock operations, memory allocation and deallocation functions, and descriptor management services. Table 8.3 summarizes the *DevHelp* functions for the OS/2 1.X systems. The calling mode in which each *DevHelp* is accessible is included, using the following abbreviations:

- I: interrupt mode
- K: kernel mode
- S: system initialization mode
- D: DOS (real) mode

Name	Description	Modes
Process management		
Block	Block thread on event	K,D
Run	Unblock thread(s) on event	K,I,D
Yield	Yield processor if *ReSched* set	K
TCYield	Yield to time-critical (*TCReSched*)	K
DevDone	Device I/O complete	
16-bit semaphore management		
SemRequest	Claim semaphore	K,D
SemClear	Release semaphore	K,I,D
SemHandle	Get semaphore handle	K,I
Request packet and queue management		
PushReqPacket	Add request packet (RP) to list	K
PullReqPacket	Remove next RP from list	K,I
PullParticular	Remove specific RP from list	K,I
SortReqPacket	Insert RP in sorted order to list	K
AllocReqPacket	Get request packet	K
FreeReqPacket	Free request packet	K
Character queue management		
QueueInit	Initialize character queue	K,I,D,S
QueueFlush	Clear character queue	K,I,D
QueueWrite	Put character in queue	K,I,D
QueueRead	Get character from queue	K,I,D
Interrupt management		
EOI	Send end-of-interrupt	I,S
SetROMVector	Set software interrupt handler	K,S
SetIRQ	Set hardware interrupt handler	K,S
UnSetIRQ	Unset hardware interrupt handler	K,I,S
Timer services		
SetTimer	Set timer handler	K,S
ResetTimer	Unset timer handler	K,I,S
TickCount	Modify timer handler frequency	K,I,D,S
System Services		
GetDOSVar	Access system variable	K,S
SendEvent	Send signal event	K,I
ROMCritSection	ROM BIOS critical section	D
AttachDD	Attach to a device driver (IDC)	K,S

(continued)

Table 8.3 DevHelp functions.

(continued)

Name	Description	Modes
InternalError	Halt system and signal error	K,I,D,S
RealToProt	Switch processor to protected mode	K,I
ProtToReal	Switch processor to real mode	K,I
Register PDD	Register PDD (32-bit only)	S
RegisterStackUsage	Indicate kernel stack usage	S
16-bit memory management		
Lock	Lock segment	K,S
Unlock	Unlock segment	K,S
PhysToVirt	Create virtual to physical mapping in system virtual address space (GDT)	K,I,S
VirtToPhys	Convert virtual address to physical	K,S
PhysToUVirt	Create virtual to physical mapping in process virtual address space (LDT)	K,S
AllocPhys	Allocate physical memory	K,S
FreePhys	Free physical memory	K,S
AllocGDTSelector	Allocate GDT descriptor(s)	S
PhysToGDTSelector	Map GDT descriptor to physical address	K,I,D,S
UnPhysToVirt	Invalidate *PhysToVirt* mapping	K,I,S
VerifyAccess	Check memory accessibility	K

Table 8.3   DevHelp functions.

8.20 OS/2 2.X DEVICE DRIVERS

The 16-bit device driver model of OS/2 1.X is enhanced in OS/2 2.0 to provide support for intelligent I/O devices, command chaining, and scatter-gather I/O, and to allow OS/2 2.X DOS compatibility. In OS/2 2.X, the 80386 virtual 8086 mode and paging are used to manage multiple concurrently executing DOS environments, called *virtual DOS machines*. Since the virtual 8086 mode is a subset of protected mode, the OS/2 2.X DOS compatibility does not use the 80386 real mode. Thus, bimodal code is not necessary for device drivers, since they are always called in protected mode. Bimodal 16-bit device drivers continue to be supported in the 32-bit system, but are called in only protected mode.

The 16-bit device driver model was changed for OS/2 2.X, so that DOS device support would be separated from OS/2 device support. This division resulted in two types of device drivers: *physical device drivers (PDDs)* and *virtual device drivers (VDDs)*. PDDs are the same as existing OS/2 1.X device drivers without their bimodal code and ROM BIOS support. VDDs utilize a new 32-bit driver model, and provide virtual DOS device I/O emulation. VDDs interact with PDDs when they need to perform actual I/O on behalf of a virtual DOS machine by calling the PDDs' *VDD handler*. Thus, the 32-bit system has fewer requirements regarding low physical memory addresses, no bimodal code is needed, and the system and device drivers no longer use mode switching to support a bimodal environment. Existing bimodal device drivers that provide ROM BIOS support still run on the 32-bit system, but their ROM BIOS handlers are never called, and they do not provide any DOS support. Chapter 10 provides more detail on DOS compatibility and its relationship to the rest of the system. Figure 8.8 illustrates the structure of the device driver interfaces for OS/2 2.0.

The device driver architecture has also been enhanced to provide a new *extended strategy interface*. It provides an alternative I/O model for FSDs that supports intelligent I/O devices, command chaining, scatter-gather I/O, and a better asynchronous I/O model. An FSD determines whether a block device driver supports the extended strategy interface by calling the device driver's old strategy routine. If the device driver supports the extended strategy interface, the address of the extended strategy entry point is returned. The extended strategy interface supports four operations:

- Read
- Write
- Write with verify
- Prefetch

The read, write, and write-with-verify operations are similar to their counterparts in the old strategy interface, but they support chained operations and use scatter-gather lists for addressing I/O buffers. The prefetch command allows an FSD to manage the contents of an external cache associated with a block device, such as the 1MB cache on the IBM SCSI disk controller. The prefetch command can be used by an FSD implementing a read-ahead heuristic. It causes data to be read from the disk to the cache without any system bus or memory activity.

When an I/O request is executed in the 32-bit system, the file system locks the pages of the I/O buffer, and generates scatter-gather lists containing physical addresses for the pages of the I/O buffer. The buffer must be locked, since the scatter-gather list

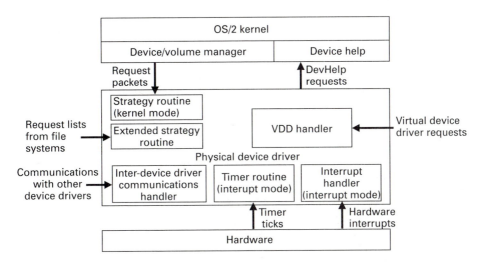

Fig. 8.8   *OS/2 2.0 extended device driver interfaces.*

contains physical addresses that are not updated if the pages are discarded or swapped. FSDs then issue requests to the extended strategy interface using *request lists* instead of request packets. Request lists are composed of *request list entries* that describe each operation in a command chain. Each request list entry contains the scatter-gather list for the I/O buffer, the starting logical block number, and the count of logical blocks to be transferred. Figure 8.9 illustrates the format of a request list.

The extended strategy interface queues incoming requests on per-device service queues, and then immediately returns to the caller without blocking. This allows the requestor, usually an FSD, to determine when the thread should be blocked. Consequently, a single thread can initiate multiple chained I/O requests before blocking. Each request list contains I/O notification fields that enable the device driver to call the requestor when the request list or specific request entry is complete. The notification routine usually unlocks the memory and unblocks the requesting thread. The extended strategy interface provides FSDs with a faster and more flexible I/O model for performing asynchronous I/O.

The *DevHelp* services are extended in OS/2 2.0 to support the paged memory environment (Table 8.4). Functions are provided for locking memory, managing scatter-gather page lists, and performing address translation. Also, the *DevHelp(Block)* and *DevHelp(Run)* interfaces to the dispatcher support single-wakeup thread dispatching, as described in Chapter 5.

SUMMARY

This chapter described OS/2 file and device I/O management. The architecture of file systems, the file system API, and the use of device drivers by file systems was explained. The device driver architecture was described in terms of the entry points supported by device drivers, the operations they perform, the interfaces the device drivers have with other components of the system, and the way that device drivers operate.

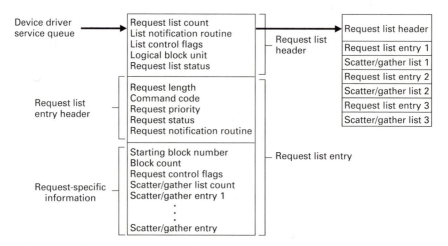

Fig. 8.9   Request list.

Name	Description	Modes
32-Bit Memory Management		
VMAlloc	Allocate memory	K,S
VMSetMem	Set memory attributes	K,S
VMFree	Free memory	K,S
VMLock	Lock linear address range	K,S
VMUnlock	Unlock linear address range	K,S
VMProcessToGlobal	Create system mapping of process memory	K
VMGlobalToProcess	Create process mapping of system memory	K
VirtToLin	Convert virtual to linear address	K
LinToGDTSelector	Map selector to linear address	K
FreeGDTSelector	Free GDT selector	K
GetDescInfo	Return descriptor information	K
LinToPageList	Build pagelist from linear address	K
PageListToLin	Map pagelist to linear address	K
PageListToGDTSelector	Map selector to pagelist	K
Miscellaneous		
RegisterPDD	Register PDD VDD handler	S

Table 8.4   32-bit DevHelp functions.

The OS/2 device driver model is more sophisticated and richer than is the DOS device driver model. Its two-layer architecture is similar to that found in UNIX systems. However, the *DevHelp* interface provides a much more robust feature set than is provided in most UNIX systems, and is consistent across all OS/2 releases.

TERMINOLOGY

absolute path name
access mode
advanced BIOS (ABIOS)
"\" character
base device driver
bimodal code
bimodal device driver
block device
bottom half of the device driver
bus arbitration
bus mastering
character device
character queue management

clock device
COM:
compatibility BIOS (CBIOS)
controller
current directory
current drive
current logical block unit
cycle stealing
data transfer
deny-write sharing mode
device addressing
device attribute flags
device control and status

system file table (SFT)
system I/O
system null device
system service
tiled virtual address
timer handler
timer service

top half of the device driver
user I/O
video (VIO)
video RAM (VRAM)
virtual device driver (VDD)
volume manager
write-only access

EXERCISES

8.1 Distinguish between system I/O and user I/O.

8.2 Differentiate between block devices and character devices. Give several examples of each, and discuss the naming conventions used for each.

8.3 Discuss the notion of the installable file system (IFS) architecture. Explain the purpose of each of the following in the context of IFS: file system API, IFS router, file system driver, file system helper (FSHelp) functions, device manager, and volume manager.

8.4 Explain the organization of the file system's directory structure. Distinguish between absolute path names and relative path names.

8.5 It is possible for one process to update a portion of a file while another process is trying to read it. How do processes deal with this situation to avoid indeterminate results?

8.6 What techniques are used in the high performance file system (HPFS) to achieve better performance in an OS/2 environment than is possible with the FAT file system?

8.7 In OS/2 2.X, cache management has been added to the FAT file system. Discuss several ways in which this addition improves performance.

8.8 Explain how I/O command chaining is performed. Discuss several ways in which it improves performance.

8.9 Why does a paged memory environment pose a problem for most existing DMA devices? How is this problem handled in OS/2?

8.10 Why must OS/2 device drivers be reentrant?

8.11 Why do OS/2 device drivers relinquish control of the processor when forced to wait for I/O operations to complete?

8.12 Distinguish between memory-mapped devices and I/O-mapped devices.

8.13 What problem associated with polled devices makes them inappropriate for multitasking environments? How do interrupt-driven devices solve this problem?

8.14 Explain each of the following device data transfer strategies: programmed I/O, direct memory access (DMA), and bus mastering.

8.15 In what sense does DMA allow a low-level form of hardware parallelism?

8.16 How are DOS device drivers insulated from the underlying hardware architecture and device controller dependencies?

8.17 List several ways in which advanced BIOS (ABIOS) differs from compatibility BIOS (CBIOS).

8.18   What motivated the development of Subsystem Control Block (SCB) architecture? How is a typical SCB I/O operation performed? How are performance improvements realized, compared to with the use of ABIOS?

8.19   Why is bimodal code loaded in physical memory addresses below 1MB?

8.20   Discuss the functions performed by the top half of a device driver, and those performed by the bottom half of a device driver. Explain what an inter-device-driver communications handler is.

8.21   Why must the 16-bit OS/2 system provide a means of preventing preemption of a DOS application that has entered ROM BIOS?

8.22   Explain what a tiled virtual address is. Give an example of a data area that is a tiled area of memory.

8.23   What is initialization mode? Why does initialization mode execute at privilege level 3?

8.24   Why do the addresses stored by a device driver that services an interrupt-driven device need to be accessible in the context of any process?

8.25   Give a brief example of a function that is performed by each of the following categories of *DevHelp* services: process management, semaphore management, request queue and request packet management, character queue management, memory management, interrupt management, timer services, and system services.

8.26   Why does OS/2 2.X DOS compatibility not use 80386 real mode?

8.27   Distinguish between physical device drivers (PDDs) and virtual device drivers (VDDs).

8.28   What is the extended strategy interface? What operations does it support? What is the operation of the prefetch command? How does this command improve performance?

8.29   When an I/O request is executed in the 32-bit system, why does the file system lock the pages of the I/O buffer?

9
Presentation Management

One picture is worth more than ten thousand words.

Chinese proverb

Seeing is believing.

Proverb

Nothing ever becomes real till it is experienced — even a proverb is no proverb to you till your life has illustrated it.

John Keats

Outline

9.1 INTRODUCTION

This chapter describes the *presentation management* in the OS/2 system. It discusses the role of *sessions,* and the way applications access the user I/O devices. It also explains the windowing and graphics architecture of the OS/2 *Presentation Manager (PM).*

9.2 SESSION MANAGEMENT

Sessions, or *screen groups,* are managed by the *session manager,* a component of OS/2. Each session contains a *logical keyboard,* a *logical mouse,* a *logical display,* and a collection of processes that share the logical user I/O devices. Figure 9.1 illustrates the structure of a session. The *user shell* allows users to start and stop applications, and to select the *foreground session.* The OS/2 user initiates session switching using the *hot key* or mouse device, and then tells the OS/2 user shell which session to activate. When sessions are switched, the user-I/O subsystems switch logical device contexts, by changing the per-session, logical-to-physical user I/O device mappings. We shall find it is easiest to understand OS/2 session management by examining the evolution of OS/2 user I/O.

OS/2 1.0 did not provide the PM. Although it has the capability for graphics, OS/2 1.0 is basically a text-mode system. It provides three different types of sessions: *full screen, DOS,* and *detached.* Full-screen sessions are used to run OS/2 protected-mode or DOS programs. The per-session logical user I/O devices are managed for full-screen sessions by the *video, keyboard,* and *mouse subsystems.* Because applications are run in separate sessions, the user is given the appearance of multiple full-screen consoles, one per application. The single DOS full-screen session contains the 16-bit DOS environment. The DOS compatibility component provides the logical user I/O devices for the DOS application(s) running in the DOS environment. A single *detached session* contains background processes that have been detached. Processes in the detached session run without the user I/O devices. Typically, programs that wake up occasionally to perform minimal housekeeping duties are run in the detached session.

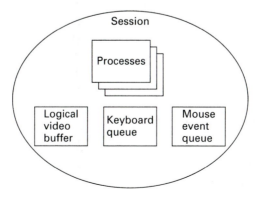

Fig. 9.1   Session structure.

Figure 9.2 illustrates the *session* and *process hierarchy* in OS/2 1.0. The user shell runs in the topmost session of the hierarchy. The user shell in OS/2 1.0 is called the *program selector*. It is a text-mode application that provides two text-mode windows, one for starting programs, and one for switching among active programs. When the user shell starts a program, it calls *DosStartSession* to run a program in a new child session. Descendants of a process are inherited automatically by the session in which the process is running. The *DosSelectSession* API call is used by the user shell to switch the active foreground session. The Ctrl-Esc and Alt-Esc keyboard sequences are reserved for use as user-shell hot keys. The Ctrl-Esc sequence returns the session with the user shell to the foreground, so that the user can start new programs or switch between running programs. The Alt-Esc sequence is used to toggle between active sessions. An OS/2 text-mode command processor, similar to COMMAND.COM of DOS, is provided; it is called CMD.EXE.

OS/2 full-screen sessions run OS/2 full-screen programs. They are characterized by their use of the video, keyboard, and mouse subsystems for their user I/O. Each of these subsystems provides per-session logical user I/O devices for full-screen sessions. Each subsystem resides in a dynamic link library, and its API functions run in user mode. The subsystem converts API requests into *DosDevIOCtl* requests to the appropriate device drivers. *DosWrite* API requests to standard output are routed to the video subsystem, and *DosRead* API requests from standard input are routed to the keyboard subsystem. C applications can use either the OS/2 full-screen user I/O functions, or the C run-time-library standard I/O functions. The C standard I/O library functions use *DosRead* and *DosWrite*, which are ultimately serviced by the keyboard and video subsystems unless standard input

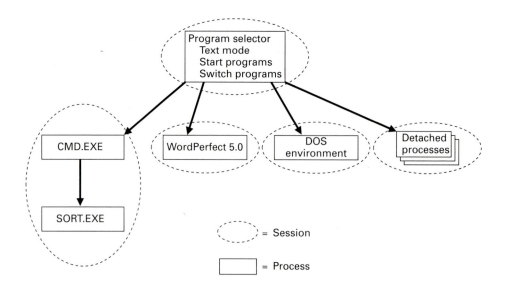

Fig. 9.2   OS/2 1.0 session and process hierarchy.

or standard output has been redirected to a file or device. The user I/O subsystems are replaceable on a per-session basis. System extensions can register with the individual subsystems to handle requests on a per-session basis, enabling each session ultimately to have its own user I/O device management. Figure 9.3 illustrates the user I/O subsystem architecture for OS/2 1.0.

The video subsystem API calls are named using the *VIO* prefix. Thus, full-screen programs are also called *VIO applications*. The video subsystem provides BIOS-level output functions for full-screen programs, the equivalent of TTY-style text output to CGA, EGA, and VGA devices. It maintains a *logical video buffer* for each session in the system, and switches logical video buffers when the session manager switches sessions. It uses the video device driver to map the logical video buffer in the process virtual address space onto the physical video buffer when a session is switched into the foreground. The video API runs in user mode in an IOPL segment, which enables it to access the video controller directly from user mode. Therefore, the video subsystem runs entirely at privilege levels 2 and 3, and accesses the video buffer directly by writing to the video RAM. It provides capabilities for font loading, for setting the mode of the display, and for cursor shape and positioning. It also enables applications to access the logical video buffer directly. Thus, applications can perform their own graphics.

The keyboard subsystem API calls are named using the *Kbd* prefix. The keyboard subsystem provides BIOS-level keyboard support for full-screen programs. It manages a *logical keyboard queue* for each session, and converts keyboard API requests into *DosDevIOCtl* calls to the keyboard device driver.

The mouse subsystem API calls are named using the *Mou* prefix. The mouse subsystem provides BIOS-level mouse support for full-screen programs. It manages a

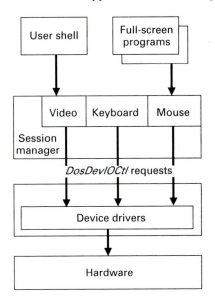

Fig. 9.3   Full-screen user-I/O subsystem architecture.

logical mouse event queue for each session, and converts mouse API requests into *DosDevIOCtl* calls to the *mouse device driver*.

The PM was introduced in OS/2, Version 1.1; it is the graphical user interface used in all subsequent OS/2 releases. It uses several new session types, the main one being the *PM session*. The PM session contains the user shell, and programs that use the graphical user interface. It contains all PM applications, including a graphic user shell that consists of the *desktop manager*, the *task manager*, and the *file manager*. *Subsessions* are used within the PM session to manage processes that share the PM session's user I/O devices. The PM manages the sharing of logical user I/O devices among programs, and organizes them into windows on the display. It provides a device-independent message-based user I/O model for PM programs. PM also allows text-mode OS/2 full-screen programs to run inside of a standard window using *windowed sessions*. Only text-mode full-screen applications can run in a windowed session. These applications are also called *VIO windowable applications*. Full-screen applications that access the logical video buffer directly can be run only in full-screen sessions. Figure 9.4 illustrates the session and process hierarchy with the PM.

In OS/2 2.0, several new session types were added because of the extended support for DOS applications. Since OS/2 2.0 supports multiple DOS applications, each DOS application is run in its own session. These sessions can contain text or graphics, and can be full

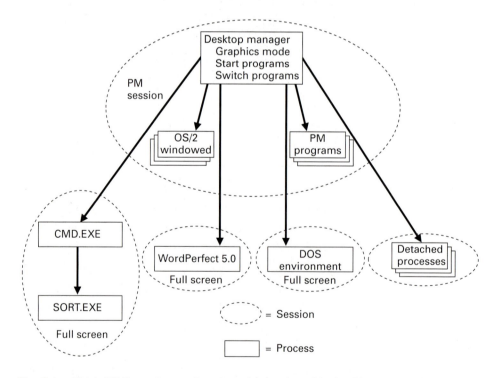

Fig. 9.4   16-bit OS/2 session and process hierarchy with the PM.

screen or windowed. *DOS full-screen sessions* run DOS programs in full-screen mode, and use the DOS compatibility component to provide the per-session logical user I/O devices. Chapter 10 describes how support for DOS application user I/O is implemented. *DOS windowed sessions* allow DOS applications to run in the PM session within a standard window. Figure 9.5 illustrates the OS/2 session and process hierarchy in the OS/2 2.0 system.

OS/2 2.0 also introduces a new object-oriented user shell, called the *workplace shell*. The workplace shell allows users to interact seamlessly with applications and data files using intuitive *drag-and-drop* operations. The object model allows users to perform work without having to understand hierarchical file system layouts, and allows programs to participate in an object-oriented action paradigm. The workplace shell can also be configured to look like the DOS shell, the Windows user interface, or the OS/2 1.X desktop manager, to ease user migration.

9.3 PRESENTATION MANAGER

The PM is the graphical user interface of OS/2. It extends the functionality of the base user I/O services to include a windowed user interface and device-independent graphic presentations. In a graphical user interface environment, the screen becomes a source of user input. Users use the mouse and keyboard to manipulate intuitive graphic controls

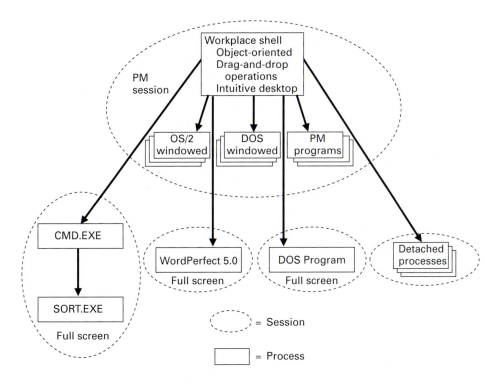

Fig. 9.5   OS/2 2.0 session and process hierarchy.

displayed on the screen. Examples of these controls are *pull-down menus, dialog boxes, icons, buttons,* and *scroll bars.* The PM allows programs to have a consistent user interface, since the controls for these programs are built into the PM, not into the user programs. The PM is the strategic user interface of IBM's *Systems Application Architecture (SAA).* It conforms to the *Common User Access (CUA)* specification of SAA, and the PM API implements the presentation functions of the SAA *Common Programming Interface (CPI).* SAA, CUA, and CPI are discussed in more detail in Chapter 12. The PM architecture contains essentially the same functions in the 16-bit and 32-bit versions of OS/2, except where noted in this chapter.

The PM API is divided into two functional groups: the *windows API* and the *graphics API.* The windows API was derived from the windowing architecture of *Microsoft Windows.* The graphics API integrates technologies from the *IBM Graphics Data Display Manager (GDDM),* the *IBM 3270 Graphics Control Program (GCP),* and the *Microsoft Windows Graphics Device Interface (GDI).* Although these technologies form the foundation for the PM's architecture, the PM integrates them into the OS/2 protected multitasking environment. The PM is an extension to the base OS/2 architecture, and runs on top of the OS/2 kernel in the PM session. The PM is a collection of dynamic link libraries and executable programs that runs in user mode. The PM API is object oriented. Like the base system, it uses handles to manipulate objects such as messages, message queues, and windows.

The PM session contains the user shell, called the desktop manager, and PM programs. The PM session is displayed in *graphics mode,* and can support most *all-points-addressable (APA)* display devices. Most text-mode full-screen programs can be run in the PM session using a *standard window,* except for those that directly write to the logical video buffer. These programs cannot be run in the PM session, since the PM manages the sharing of the session's logical video buffer among programs in the PM session.

The PM user I/O model consolidates the mouse, keyboard, and display devices. The user I/O interfaces for full-screen programs are called *procedural,* since applications call the system and wait on user input. The PM uses an *event-driven, message-based I/O architecture* to connect the user interface to PM applications. It translates user events into messages that are routed to per-application *message queues,* which are then later processed by functions that manage windows. Examples of messages are keyboard and mouse input, window modifications, and window repainting. Windows receive messages from the windows API, and perform output using the graphics API. The PM does not manage a logical video buffer for each window. Each window is responsible for redrawing itself when the PM indicates that the window needs to be redrawn. Since graphical information takes large amounts of memory to store, this scheme achieves a significant savings.

9.4 WINDOWS ARCHITECTURE

Windows provide a means of sharing, subdividing, and organizing the screen. A window is a rectangular area used to receive user input, and to display output. A windowed user interface is commonly compared to a "messy desktop," in which windows are similar to papers and files on a desktop. They may be overlapped, obscured, resized, and moved to the foreground.

The PM windows architecture is an *object-oriented programming (OOP)* architecture. A *window* is an object that is used as the focus for user input, and as the frame for user output. Each window is associated with a *window procedure (WinProc)* that manages all messages coming to that window. The window procedure determines how the window responds to messages, and paints the window's contents on the display. In OOP terminology, window procedures are *methods* that are applied to *objects* (windows). Methods are applied to windows by messages being sent to the message queue of the thread that created the window. The messages in the queue are dispatched by the thread to the correct window procedure using a *callback mechanism*. Message routing and the callback mechanism are discussed further in Section 9.5.

The *window class* determines which window procedure is used to process messages coming to a window. The window-class mechanism allows a group of windows to share a single window procedure. Therefore, windows that have the same style and contents will differ only in the data processed by the window procedure. The class mechanism also supports *object inheritance*. This facility allows a new window to be created based on an existing window without the entire original window procedure being incorporated in the new one. Creating new window classes based on existing window classes is called *window subclassing*. A window class can be *private* or *public*. *Private window classes* are usable only by a specific PM program, whereas *public window classes* can be shared among PM programs. The PM provides several *system-defined window classes* for built-in window types, such as the standard window, menus, scroll bars, and dialog boxes.

Like all PM objects, windows are accessed using handles that are assigned when windows are created. The coordinate space of a window ranges from ±32KB, and its origin (0,0) is *lower left*. Windows have a hierarchical relationship, and are located relative to the origin of their parent windows.

The *window hierarchy* describes how the windows on the desktop are related to one another. The windows have a parent/child relationship similar to that used for processes. At the top of the hierarchy is the *desktop window*. It is the topmost window in the PM session, and it occupies the entire screen (it looks like the background). The PM user shell—the desktop manager—provides two windows that are children of the desktop window. The *program manager* window allows the user to organize and start programs. The *task manager* window allows the user to switch between running programs. Figure 9.6 illustrates the PM window hierarchy.

Children of the desktop window are called *top-level windows* or *main windows*. They are created by applications, and can be overlapped, obscured, or minimized. Operations by the user affect only the main window that is active (in the foreground). Only one main window is active at a time on the screen. The top-level windows are child windows of the desktop window, and can create subordinate windows of their own in the parent/child fashion. Child windows are completely contained within a parent window. They are always *clipped* to be displayed within the parent. They remain in the same position relative to the parent unless moved. Also, if a parent is minimized,

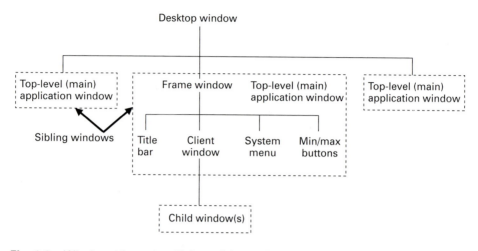

Fig. 9.6   Window hierarchy. (Adapted from "Programming the OS/2 Presentation Manager," Copyright 1989 by Charles Petzold. Reprinted with permission of Microsoft Press.)

maximized, hidden, or destroyed, so are its children windows. Windows that share the same parent are *sibling windows*. Siblings can overlap on the screen.

Control windows are used to receive user input from the screen. They are provided by several predefined window classes in the PM. Their messages are handled by window procedures inside the PM. However, the messages for control windows come through the message queue for the application that created the window. Examples of control windows are the *title bar, system menu icon, minimize-maximize buttons,* and *sizing borders.* The 32-bit version of PM contains support for more controls, such as *spinbuttons, notebooks,* and *sliders.*

A *standard window* is a collection of several windows that as a unit provides a consistent user interface for applications. The top-level window of a standard window is called the *frame window.* The frame window has several children: the control windows and the client window. The frame window is the parent and the owner of the control windows and the client window. The *client window* is the portion of the standard window that is defined by the application. The class of the client window is registered by the application, and messages to the client window are handled by the window procedure defined for the class. Figure 9.7 illustrates a standard window with menu bar and scroll bars.

Window ownership is used to manage message routing between windows. When the control windows of the standard window are activated by the user, they send the message to the owning frame window for processing. The frame window performs the actions determined by the messages, such as minimizing the window or resizing its border. Owners are not required, and are rarely used, for client windows.

Window redrawing is performed by window procedures when they receive the *WM_PAINT message* from PM. This message is sent to a window whenever a part of a

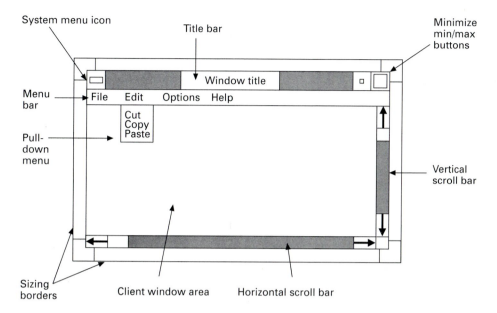

Fig. 9.7   Standard window with menu bar and scroll bars.

window is invalid on the display as a result of user actions. For example, if a window is minimized and then maximized, the window must be repainted, since the PM does not save the contents of the window. If a window is overlapped by another window and then is brought back to the foreground, portions of the window must be restored by the window procedure. Since window procedures redraw windows on demand, the PM does not have to save the graphical data contained in a window, resulting in a substantial memory savings.

9.5 MESSAGE ARCHITECTURE

As stated previously, the PM has an event-driven, message-based I/O architecture. That is, messages are delivered to programs as a result of events occurring at the user interface. All input consists of messages delivered to window procedures. Window procedures are effectively message filters that perform work on windows. Figure 9.8 illustrates the overall PM message architecture.

The keyboard and mouse device drivers place input event messages in the *system input queue* in order of occurrence when the PM session is in the foreground. The system input queue is used to manage the delivery of synchronous and asynchronous messages to application message queues. It serializes events so that they are presented in correct sequence to applications. Each PM application has a message queue for receiving user interface event messages. The message queue is associated with the thread that creates it. It receives all messages going to windows created by the thread that created the message queue. The *message router component* of the PM moves messages from the

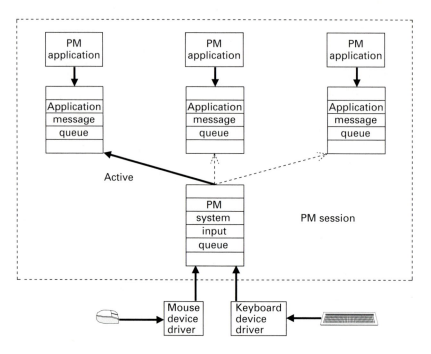

Fig. 9.8   PM message architecture.

system input queue to the correct application message queues. Keyboard messages are routed to the window with the keyboard focus, and mouse messages are routed to the active window. Also, messages can be generated by the PM itself and placed in an application's message queue.

Messages have a simple structure. Each message contains the handle of the window that receives the message, the message type, and the data of the message. If the message contains large numbers of data, it contains pointers to the message data. Since messages and their data can be passed between processes, the data is located in give-get shared memory (described in Chapter 6). Examples of messages follow:

- *WM_CREATE* (create window)
- *WM_SIZE* (resize window)
- *WM_CHAR* (route keyboard input to window)
- *WM_PAINT* (redraw window)

After initializing itself, creating a message queue, defining window classes, and creating the main window, each PM application executes an *application message loop* that processes messages arriving at the message queue. The message loop is actually a spin loop in which the application calls *WinGetMsg* to retrieve a message from the queue, and then calls *WinDispatchMsg* to dispatch the message to the proper window. This loop drives message delivery to window procedures from the application message queue. *WinGetMsg* removes messages from the application message queue, and blocks if there are no messages. It returns the *WM_QUIT message* when there are no more messages. *WinDispatchMsg* causes the *window dispatcher* component of the PM to look up the target window, and to call the correct window procedure for the message. *WinDispatchMsg* does not return until after the message is processed by the invoked window procedures. If a window procedure does not handle the message, it calls *WinDefWindowProc* for default window message processing. Figure 9.9 illustrates the application message loop.

Not all messages arrive at window procedures through the message queue. Window procedures can also be called directly by the PM and by other window procedures. The message queue is used for *queued messages,* such as keyboard input, mouse input, timer messages, and menu selections. However, *nonqueued messages* also exist, such as those sent to a window when it is created or destroyed. Because both queued and nonqueued messages come to window procedures, a window procedure can be called directly, even while the thread that created the window is blocked in *WinGetMsg*. Also, messages can generate more messages. Thus, window procedures must be reentrant.

WinSendMsg is used to call a window procedure directly with a message. Using it is similar to hand delivering the mail. For example, if a window procedure receives a message and wants to send that message to one of its sibling or child windows, it calls *WinSendMsg*. *WinSendMsg* does not return to the caller until the target window procedure finishes processing the message. *WinSendMsg* is used for sending a message directly to a window procedure.

WinPostMsg is used to put a message into a message queue associated with a specific window. If a window procedure calls *WinPostMsg,* the call is similar to putting a letter in a mailbox for later delivery. The message is placed into the message queue associated with the target window, and *WinPostMsg* returns immediately. *WinPostMsg* is used for sending a message asynchronously to a window procedure.

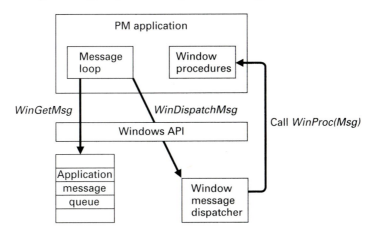

Fig. 9.9   PM application message loop processing.

9.6 GRAPHICS ARCHITECTURE

There are two principle types of graphics technologies used today: *raster graphics* and *vector graphics*. Raster graphics utilizes bitmapped images on *all-points-addressable (APA)* graphical output devices. Vector graphics are constructed using lines and patterned areas. The PM is fundamentally a vector graphics system, but it can display graphics on both vector-based and raster-based hardware. The PM also contains some raster functions for bitmaps that are supported for only raster output devices. When using vector-based output devices, the PM translates graphics commands into device-specific vector commands. When using raster-based output devices, the PM translates graphics commands into pixels using simulations.

The graphics architecture of the PM utilizes two basic constructs: *presentation spaces* and *device contexts*. A presentation space defines an abstract output device, and is used to assemble graphics for outputting to a given device. The graphics API allows high-resolution graphics and text to be mixed in a presentation space. It provides functions for constructing graphics objects built out of graphics primitives such as lines, patterned areas, text, and images. The graphics API also provides operations for graphical transformations such as scaling and inversion. The *graphics engine* component of the PM is responsible for mapping device-independent presentation spaces onto device-specific device contexts. In OS/2 2.0, a 32-bit version of the graphics engine is used to increase the performance and responsiveness of graphic operations. Figure 9.10 illustrates the PM device-independent graphics architecture.

A presentation space defines a device-independent output device. Associated with the presentation space are fonts for text output, and a device context that provides the device-dependent information for the output of the graphics drawn in the presentation space. The presentation space coordinate system is measured in pixels, and the origin is *lower left* in the presentation space. The PM API provides mechanisms that allow windowed graphics to be displayed correctly no matter what the current dimensions of the window are.

Device contexts define the characteristics of unique output devices. Each window can have a unique device context. The default device context for a window is the display. An application paints a window by allocating a presentation space that is linked to a device context, writing to the presentation space using the graphics API, and then deallocating the presentation space.

Presentation drivers are used by the graphics engine to map device-independent I/O requests to specific output devices. Presentation drivers are not the same as device drivers—they are 16-bit dynamic-link libraries that run at ring 2 using IOPL segments. Presentation drivers exist for displays, printers and plotters. Depending on the nature of the output device, a presentation driver may have a corresponding device driver component that it uses for performing I/O to the device.

9.7 RESOURCES

Resources are graphical user interface objects such as icons, menus, dialog boxes, bitmaps, strings, and fonts. They are read-only data and are stored in the EXE or DLL

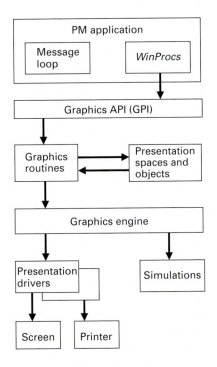

Fig. 9.10   PM device-independent graphics architecture.

files of PM applications. Since resources are read-only data, they are discardable, and can be shared by multiple instances of a given PM program. Resources are created using either *resource editors* or *resource scripts*. A resource script is a text file that contains information for defining resources. It may also contain references to other files that contain resources created by resource editors. The PM toolkit provides a *resource compiler* and three resource editors: the *dialog box editor, font editor,* and *icon editor.* The resource compiler converts resource scripts into a binary image that is appended to EXE or DLL files that use the resources. Applications are not sensitive to resource formats, since the PM provides API functions for loading, processing, and displaying resources.

Metafiles are supported by the PM for storing pictures. The *Mixed Object Document Control Architecture (MODCA)* interchange standard is used to store metafiles in the PM environment. Each metafile contains graphics instructions for creating pictures on a device-independent graphics device.

Bitmaps are arrays of data organized into rows and columns in which the bits correspond to the pixels of a raster-based graphics device. Bitmaps are highly device dependent because pixel resolution varies across graphics devices. Therefore, some level of device-dependence is inherent in a bitmap. Bitmaps are manipulated using *bit-blt* operations. The *GpiBitBlt* API call can be used for transferring portions of bitmaps, and performing transformations on them. The icon editor provided with the PM toolkit can also be used to make bitmaps. Bitmaps are accessed by handles like most PM objects, and are stored in binary format like other resources.

Dialog boxes are pop-up windows that receive input from the user. They usually contain radio buttons, entry fields, icons, text, list boxes, check boxes, and push buttons as controls that allow the user to input the information. They can be built from templates using the dialog editor and resource compiler provided with the PM toolkit. List boxes are variants of dialog boxes that are used when an application has a set of selectable items too large for the client area of a window.

9.8 APPLICATION DATA EXCHANGE

There are two primary mechanisms used for data exchange between PM applications: the *clipboard* and *dynamic data exchange (DDE)*. The clipboard is a temporary storage area for user-initiated data transfers between PM applications. Clipboard operations are usually specified on the *edit menu* of a PM application. Four basic operations are defined for the clipboard: *mark, cut, copy,* and *paste.* The mark operation is used to delineate an area of data in a window that the user desires to transfer to another application. The marked area is either cut or copied to the clipboard. If it is cut, it is deleted from the source application. The copy operation moves a copy of the data from the source application to the clipboard. A paste operation is used to place the contents of the clipboard into a destination PM application window. Both text and graphics data can be transferred using the clipboard. However, both the source and destination application must understand the format of the data being transferred. The clipboard can hold only one item at a time, and access to the clipboard is serialized by the PM API functions used by applications to access it.

The dynamic data exchange protocol defines how applications can access one another's data. It is intended for use by future PM applications for linking documents, spreadsheets, and graphical data. For example, if a word processor imports a graphical file from another application, it does not need to retrieve the file—instead, it can have only a DDE link to that file.

9.9 MULTITASKING ISSUES

PM and Microsoft Windows share the same basic windowing and message passing architecture, but they exist in different environments. OS/2 is a preemptive, timeslicing, multitasking environment, whereas Windows is a nonpreemptive, nontimeslicing, single-tasking environment based on the DOS operating system. In the Windows environment, a program runs until its message queue is empty; only then does Windows switch to another program with a nonempty message queue. Therefore, all Windows applications but one are always suspended in the *WinGetMsg* API function. This setup presents a problem if a program takes too long to process a message. For example, if the user clicks on the recalculation option when working with a large spreadsheet, other applications are postponed until the message that initiated the recalculation is processed. In fact, *WinDispatchMsg* also does not return until the message is processed. It does not return because multitasking is performed by applications that are not aware of one another in the Windows environment.

At first glance, it appears that the multitasking features of OS/2 solve this problem, since multiple applications can process their message queues concurrently. However, processing of long messages by a PM application can still affect other applications in the OS/2 environment due to the PM's use of the message-based architecture. When the PM's window architecture and messaging architecture were inherited from the original Microsoft Windows system, other underlying problems existed that were not apparent in the single-tasking Windows environment.

To illustrate the problems in the OS/2 environment, we can assume that a PM program with a single thread takes a long time to process a message. It could be a spreadsheet attempting to do a recalculation, or a word processor generating a large document. Recall that a window procedure always executes in the context of the thread that created the message queue and the window. Thus, the window procedure does not read a new message from the message queue until it finishes processing the previous message.

If the user attempts to use the keyboard to switch applications while a long message is being processed, the thread that must process the keyboard message for the window is still working on the previous message. Furthermore, the mouse cannot be used to switch to a different program, because the keyboard and mouse input are serialized through the PM system event queue. These messages are serialized so that type-ahead and mouse-ahead operations work correctly. Therefore, keyboard and mouse messages are routed to application message queues one at a time. Even if another program could get a keyboard or mouse message delivered to its message queue, the PM sends a message to the window losing the focus. In this case, the window losing the focus cannot process the message because it is still processing the previous long message. If a message takes longer than a 0.1 second to be processed, system responsiveness to the user is reduced. If a window procedure enters an infinite loop while processing a message, the system is effectively hung.

Therefore, the problems associated with PM programs that take a long time to process their messages originate from two sources: the program is single-threaded, and messages are not interrupts. It is important to realize that messages do not preemptively interrupt a thread and start its execution somewhere else. Window procedures receive messages only as a result of calls to *WinSendMsg, WinDispatchMsg,* and *WinPostMsg.* A window procedure can be called recursively, but not as a result of new messages arriving. Rather, recursive calls are the result of a window procedure sending messages that result in messages coming back to it.

The OS/2 multithread process model solves all these problems. By dedicating a single thread to servicing the user interface, and using other threads as workers for time-intensive operations, an application can be assured that user messages will be processed promptly. The threads used by a PM application for completing time-intensive operations are called *non-message-queue threads,* since they are not associated with a message queue. Therefore, they cannot create windows, send messages, or call functions that cause window procedures to be invoked. However, non-message-queue threads can utilize the base OS/2 API.

SUMMARY

This chapter described the user I/O in the OS/2 system. It discussed the role of sessions, and the way full-screen applications access the user I/O devices. It described the evolution of the OS/2 session and process hierarchy from the 16-bit system through the current 32-bit system. The design of OS/2's graphical user interface, the Presentation Manager, was described with respect to window management, device independence, and the message-based I/O architecture.

TERMINOLOGY

all-points-addressable (APA) display
   device
Alt-Esc sequence
application message loop
application message queue
bit-blt operations
bitmap
button
callback mechanism
client window
clipboard
clipped
common user access (CUA)
control window
copy
Ctrl-Esc sequence
cut
desktop manager
desktop window
detached session
device context
device-independent graphics
device-independent presentation space
dialog box
dialog box editor
DosDevIOCtl
DOS full-screen session
DosRead
DosSelectSession
DOS session
DosStartSession
DOS windowed session
DosWrite
dynamic data exchange (DDE)
edit menu

event-driven, message-based I/O
   architecture
font editor
foreground session
frame window
full-screen session
GpiBitBlt
graphical user interface (GUI)
Graphics Data Display Manager (GDDM)
graphics engine
graphics mode
hot key
IBM Graphics Data Display Manager
   (GDDM)
IBM 3270 Graphics Control Program
   (GCP)
icon
icon editor
KBD subsystem
keyboard queue
keyboard (KBD) subsystem
logical display
logical keyboard
logical mouse
logical mouse event queue
logical video buffer
main window
mark
message-based, event-driven architecture
message queue
message router
method
Microsoft Windows
Microsoft Windows Graphics Device
   Interface (GDI)

minimize-maximize buttons
Mixed Object Document Control
    Architecture (MODCA)
mouse
mouse device driver
mouse event queue
mouse (MOU) subsystem
non-message-queue threads
nonqueued message
object
object inheritance
object-oriented programming (OOP)
paste
PM session
presentation driver
presentation management
presentation manager (PM)
presentation space
private window class
program manager
program selector
public window class
pull-down menu
queued message
raster graphics
resource
resource compiler
resource editor
resource script
SAA common programming interface
    (CPI)
screen group
scroll bar
session
session hierarchy
session management
session manager
session and process hierarchy
sibling window

sizing border
standard window
subsession
system-defined window class
system input queue
system menu icon
system menu window
systems application architecture (SAA)
task manager
title bar window
top-level window
user shell
vector graphics
video (VIO) subsystem
VIO application
VIO windowable application
window
window class
window dispatcher
window hierarchy
window management
window ownership
window procedure (*WinProc*)
window redrawing
window subclassing
windowed session
window API
WinDefWindowProc
WinDispatchMsg
WinGetMsg
WinPostMsg
WinProc
WinSendMsg
WM_CHAR message
WM_CREATE
WM_PAINT message
WM_QUIT message
WM_SIZE message

EXERCISES

9.1 Explain the notion of a session. Discuss the structure of a typical session.

9.2 Discuss the types of sessions in OS/2 1.0—namely, full-screen sessions, DOS sessions, and detached sessions.

9.3 Briefly describe the functions of the video, keyboard, and mouse subsystems.

9.4 How does the PM help to ensure that programs have consistent user interfaces?

9.5 In what sense is the PM strategically important to IBM?

9.6 Explain the notions of events, messages, and message queues in the context of the PM's event-driven, message-based I/O architecture.

9.7 Discuss the object-oriented nature of the PM. In particular, consider each of the following: window procedures, windows, messages, message queues, window classes, object inheritance, and window subclassing.

9.8 Briefly explain each of the following types of windows: desktop window, top-level (or main) window, sibling window, control window, standard window, frame window, and client window.

9.9 Distinguish between queued messages and nonqueued messages.

9.10 Explain the two principal types of graphics technologies—namely, raster graphics and vector graphics.

9.11 Discuss the PM notions of presentation space, device context, graphics engine, and presentation driver.

9.12 In the context of the PM, what are resources?

9.13 Discuss the operation of the two primary mechanisms used for data exchange between PM applications—namely, the clipboard and dynamic data exchange (DDE).

9.14 Compare and contrast the environments in which the PM and Microsoft Windows operate.

9.15 Explain how the processing of a long message can cause problems in the PM. From what two sources do these problems originate?

10
Compatibility

E pluribus unus.
(One composed of many.)

Virgil

For there is no friend like a sister
In calm or stormy weather;
To cheer one on the tedious way,
To fetch one if one goes astray,
To lift one if one totters down,
To strengthen whilst one stands.

Christina Rossetti
Goblin Market

Can two walk together, except they be agreed?

Amos 3:3

Outline

10.1 INTRODUCTION

This chapter describes *compatibility* in the OS/2 system. "Compatibility" refers to the capability of an operating system to run applications developed for previous versions of the system, or for other operating systems. Providing compatibility for existing software protects customers' investments in software when the customers migrate to an operating system of higher functionality and performance. The retention and reuse of the existing code base encourages users to migrate to the new, more powerful system.

There are two principal types of compatibility: *binary compatibility* and *source compatibility*. Binary compatibility is the capability of running existing applications without modification. Systems that provide source compatibility allow existing application source code to be recompiled for a new system without changes. Binary compatibility is more desirable than is source compatibility, since it does not require applications to be recompiled and redistributed. Furthermore, most software developers do not ship, in standard user distributions, source code and tools for building their products.

OS/2 provides binary compatibility for DOS applications on both the 16-bit and 32-bit versions of the system. The 16-bit system allows a single DOS application to run with OS/2 protected-mode applications, and the 32-bit version allows multiple DOS applications to coexist with OS/2 protected-mode applications. The 32-bit system also provides binary compatibility for Windows 3.0 applications, and for existing OS/2 16-bit applications and dynamic-link libraries.

10.2 DOS COMPATIBILITY

This section describes what the characteristics of DOS applications are, and what it means to be *DOS compatible*. DOS applications execute in the real mode of Intel 80X86 processors, and can address up to 1MB of physical memory. They perform segment arithmetic on the segment register values, and assume that segmented addresses are directly related to the physical addresses generated by the processor. DOS and BIOS services are accessed using the software interrupt mechanism of the 8086. DOS applications have full control of the machine, and can access the hardware directly since there is no protection. DOS can be extended using terminate-and-stay-resident modules, device drivers, and other DOS add-on technologies. DOS programs that use EMS and XMS to access more than 640KB of memory must manage the extra memory explicitly, further complicating the memory management duties already necessary due to the 16-bit segmented addressing scheme of the 8086.

10.3 80286 DOS COMPATIBILITY

There are two primary strategies used for providing DOS application compatibility with a protected-mode host operating system on the 80286 platform:

- Run DOS applications in protected mode.
- Run DOS applications in real mode using mode switching.

The first alternative makes it difficult for the protected-mode host operating system and the DOS environment to coexist. When DOS applications access the segment registers with real-mode semantics in protected mode, they generate general protection faults unless a descriptor that maps the desired memory exists. These faults occur because DOS and its applications believe that the segment register values are directly related to the physical addresses generated. In protected mode, however, the segment-register values are selectors, which are indices into descriptor tables. When DOS is emulated in protected mode on an 80286, these faults are serviced by the host operating system. The fault is processed by allocation of the descriptor that maps the desired memory that the DOS application intended to access, and restarting of the DOS application at the point of the fault.

There are several problems with this approach. Due to an 80286 erratum, the contents of the CX register are destroyed when a general protection fault occurs. Therefore, instructions that cause general protection faults cannot be restarted on many 80286 processors. Although this problem can be circumvented by replacement of the defective 80286 chips, this solution is not desirable due to another limitation. When a DOS application generates a fault, the host system must allocate and initialize a specific descriptor based on the address that the DOS application tried to access. Since there is no way to predict the addresses that a DOS application might need, the DOS application's addressing conflicts with the management of descriptors for the protected-mode portion of the host system. Therefore, descriptors cannot be dedicated to the protected-mode host operating system and its applications while a DOS application is running.

Another variation on this alternative entails the use of a special test instruction called *LOADALL,* which allows the entire register set, including the hidden segment descriptor caches, to be initialized in one instruction. *LOADALL* can be used to set any descriptor to perform the desired DOS access in protected mode, but the segment mappings it establishes are valid only until the segment registers are touched. However, the *LOADALL* alternative cannot be used on 80286 processors with the erratum that destroys the CX register on general protection faults. Thus, running DOS applications in protected mode on an 80286 is neither realistic nor feasible.

The second approach is to run DOS applications in real mode, and to emulate the DOS system using the protected-mode host operating system. This approach allows DOS applications to run in real mode in low memory (0 to 1MB) physical addresses, just like they do under DOS in real mode. The protected-mode host operating system and its applications are loaded in the high memory (1 to 16MB) physical address range. Part of the host system runs in both real mode and protected mode, and is loaded into low memory with the DOS application. The low memory used by the DOS application is not moved or swapped by the protected-mode operating system while a DOS application is running. The host operating system switches between real mode and protected mode to emulate DOS services, and multitasks the protected-mode programs. Since the 80286 processor does not support a mode switch from protected mode to real mode, such a switch must be done by external hardware, as described in the following section.

10.3.1 Mode Switching

Switching an 80286 from real mode to protected mode is accomplished simply via setting of the protected-mode flag in the machine status word. However, the 80286 is not
designed to switch from protected mode to real mode. This capability should have been
built into the 80286 as a special instruction executable only at privilege level 0 in protected mode. The only way to switch an 80286 processor from protected mode to real
mode is to cause the 80286 to *reset*. Resetting the 80286 and resuming execution in real
mode requires external hardware support.

The 80286 can be reset on a PC/AT using the keyboard controller. The keyboard
controller is connected to the *reset line*. Issuing a special command to the keyboard controller causes the reset line of the 80286 to be toggled. This operation effectively quickly
turns the 80286 off, and then on, causing the 80286 to be restarted. When the power is
dropped to the reset pin of the 80286, the RAM of the system is *refreshed* while the processor is being reset. This refresh operation ensures that the contents of memory are pre-
served during the reset operation.

The PS/2 introduced a faster method of resetting the 80286 without using the keyboard controller. A special I/O port in 80286-based PS/2s is used to reset the 80286 with
an I/O instruction. This method is faster than is using the keyboard controller, since the
controller must decode and process the command to reset the 80286. An 80286 can also
be mode switched by a *triple fault*. To cause such a fault, the operating system must
cause a fault, force the fault handler to cause a double fault, and have the double fault
handler cause yet a third fault. Compared to the other alternatives, this process is a slow
one. Mode switching from protected mode to real mode on an 80386 requires just one
special instruction executable at privilege level 0, and is faster than the preceding methods since it does not require a reset.

When an 80286 is reset or is turned on, it immediately begins executing instructions
at the top of memory in real mode. Mapped into the top of memory of all personal computers is a small stub of code that branches into the system ROMs. Once in the system
ROMs, the *power-on self-test* (*POST*) routine begins executing. POST normally tests the
memory and devices present in the system, initializes ROM BIOS, and calls BIOS to
read and execute the bootstrap sector from the media in the boot device. To support
mode switching, POST must be able to differentiate between when the system has been
turned on, and when the system has been intentionally reset for a mode switch to real
mode. In the case of a mode switch, POST must stop executing, and branch to a prepro-
grammed location so that the system can continue executing in real mode.

To support this, a CMOS RAM chip that retains its contents without power is used
to maintain the *shutdown status* of the 80286. POST checks the shutdown status in the
CMOS RAM to determine whether a mode switch is in progress, or whether the system
was just turned on. If the shutdown code indicates that power was just turned on, the
normal POST cycle is executed, and the standard boot cycle occurs. If the shutdown
code indicates a mode switch from protected mode to real mode, it dispatches directly to
an address saved in the CMOS RAM chip.

Although Intel did not provide a mode switch capability on the 80286, the designers of the IBM PC/AT—the first PC to use the 80286—recognized the need for mode switching. They invented and provided the rudimentary mode switching support through the keyboard controller, POST, and CMOS RAM architecture. Were it not for the foresight of these designers, mode switching on an 80286 would not be possible.

10.3.2 System Structure

The 16-bit version of OS/2 uses the mode switching strategy to implement DOS compatibility on an 80286. The most recent version of the system, OS/2 1.3, provides compatibility for DOS 4.0. It provides the capability to execute one DOS application in real mode. The DOS application runs in the foreground; it is frozen when it is in the background. OS/2 cannot run DOS applications in the background since excessive mode switching could disrupt protected-mode applications. Also, the 80286 architecture does not allow OS/2 to virtualize the devices used by DOS applications. Therefore, the DOS application does not get hardware interrupts in the background under OS/2, which is why applications such as communications programs may not run in the 16-bit DOS compatibility environment. OS/2 allows protected-mode applications to run in the background while the DOS application is running in the foreground. The system switches between real and protected-mode as needed while the DOS application is in the foreground.

Since mode switching is a relatively slow operation, OS/2 attempts to minimize the mode switching on critical paths, such as interrupt management and context switching. OS/2 also attempts to maximize the amount of memory available to DOS applications below 1MB by partitioning the system in an intelligent fashion. Figure 10.1 illustrates the 16-bit OS/2 physical memory layout with DOS compatibility installed.

The system's physical memory is divided into two areas: low memory, below 1MB and high memory, above 1MB. All OS/2 applications and most of the kernel are loaded into high memory and executed in protected mode only. The DOS application is loaded into low memory. Also loaded into low memory are the portions of OS/2 that need to run in both protected mode and real mode. Code that runs in both protected mode and real mode is called *bimodal code*. The bimodal portions of OS/2 loaded into low memory in the following:

- Device management
- Interrupt management
- Mode switching
- Context switching
- Device drivers

Memory management, the file system, and most of the OS/2 kernel are in high memory to reduce the impact on DOS application memory. This strategy leaves approximately 520KB for DOS applications under OS/2 1.3. Also in low memory is a stub DOS kernel used to route requests for DOS services from DOS applications to the

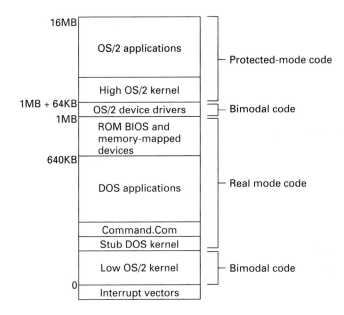

Fig. 10.1   16-bit physical memory layout with DOS compatibility.

protected-mode kernel in high memory. Therefore, all DOS file I/O is emulated by switching to protected mode, calling the file system in high memory, performing the I/O, and switching back to real mode. This overhead is acceptable, since file I/O is slow compared to the performance of a mode switch. Since the file system is in high memory, more memory is available in low memory for DOS applications.

The region from 1MB to 1MB + 64KB is known as the *A20 wrap area*. Due to the segmented scheme for generating 20-bit physical addresses on an 8088, it is possible for a DOS program to generate physical addresses in the range from 1MB to 1MB + 64KB. On an 8088 system, these addresses wrap to the low 64KB of physical memory. However, 80286 physical addresses are 24 bits. The *twenty-first* address line of the 80286 is called the *A20 line,* and its setting determines whether real-mode programs wrap low physical memory, or directly access the range from 1MB to 1MB + 64KB. When an 80286 is started, the A20 line is disabled, causing the 80286 to emulate the 8088 environment. When the 80286 is switched to protected mode, the A20 line is enabled, since the protected mode of the 80286 generates 24-bit physical addresses. However, the A20 wrap area can be addressed in real mode if the A20 line is enabled manually. OS/2 can thus use the memory in the A20 wrap area for bimodal code by managing the state of the A20 line. When running a DOS application in real mode, OS/2 disables the A20 line to force the 8088 segment wrapping semantics on DOS applications. When accessing bimodal code in the range from 1MB to 1MB + 64KB in real mode, the OS/2 kernel enables the A20 line.

The DOS system services are emulated by the OS/2 system. The DOS system does not run in low memory—only a DOS application does. A stub DOS kernel is used for applications that jump directly into DOS without calling INT 21. DOS services are emulated by the low part of the kernel if possible; otherwise, the system switches to protected mode to perform the operation. Since DOS applications use the OS/2 file system, they benefit automatically from the installable file system architecture. Thus, DOS applications can access FAT files and HPFS files, and can share file resources with protected-mode programs.

DOS applications also use the ROM BIOS services by executing software interrupts. BIOS requests are emulated by real-mode code in the device drivers and the kernel. As we saw in Chapter 8, *DevHelp(SetROMVector)* is used by 16-bit physical device drivers to hook BIOS software interrupts. The device driver then either emulates the BIOS functions, or uses BIOS to provide the function. When BIOS is used, the device driver calls *DevHelp(ROMCritSection)* to tell the system to delay context switching until the BIOS request is complete. It is necessary to prevent preemption when the DOS environment is executing BIOS, since background protected-mode programs can potentially issue requests to the same device. These requests cannot proceed when BIOS is being used, since BIOS is not reentrant, and the device drivers compete with BIOS to program the same hardware.

Since the system multitasks protected-mode applications in the background when a DOS application is in the foreground, and since mode switching is performed so that all these programs apparently can run concurrently, interrupt-driven device drivers may get in one mode interrupts for requests that were started in the other mode. For example, a background protected-mode application may make a device driver request, and the thread may be blocked until an interrupt occurs. Since the system is multitasking between the DOS application in the foreground and real-mode and protected-mode programs in the background, the interrupt for the I/O request can occur when the processor is in real mode. To make the buffer addresses used in device I/O requests accessible in both modes, interrupt-driven device drivers save the buffer addresses as physical addresses instead of mode-sensitive virtual addresses. The physical addresses are converted to virtual addresses by the device driver at interrupt time using *DevHelp(PhysToVirt)*. When the device driver is done using the temporary mapping, it calls *DevHelp(UnPhysToVirt)*.

Device driver interrupt handlers also may need to access memory above 1MB in real mode at interrupt time to transfer data from requests initiated in protected mode. On PC/AT architectures, a special Intel test instruction, called *LOADALL*, is used by *DevHelp(PhysToVirt)* to establish a mapping to memory above 1MB in real mode. However, while the *LOADALL* instruction is in effect, the segment registers cannot be altered. On fast mode-switching architectures, such as any PS/2 or 80386 machine, *DevHelp(PhysToVirt)* switches to protected mode to access the memory above 1MB, and *DevHelp(UnPhysToVirt)* switches back to real mode to complete service of the interrupt.

Interrupt table shadowing is used to detect when DOS applications *hook hardware interrupts*. The *OS/2 protected-mode interrupt manager* detects changes to the *interrupt vector table* made by DOS applications when the system switches from real mode to protected mode. If the hooks placed into the interrupt vector table are not in conflict with devices owned by protected-mode applications and device drivers, the interrupt manager restores the state of the interrupt vector table when the processor switches back to real mode. If there are any conflicts, however, the DOS application is not allowed to hook the interrupt when the system switches back to real mode.

10.3.3 Tiled Memory

Another mechanism used for optimizing access to memory objects used by bimodal code is *tiled memory*. Tiling lets bimodal code execute correctly regardless of the processor mode. It allows the same virtual address to access the same physical memory regardless of whether the processor is in real mode or protected mode. This is done by reserving specific selectors, and setting the base address within the descriptors to be the selector*16. For example, the ROM BIOS data area is mapped into the physical memory of a personal computer at 400H. Therefore, the real-mode virtual address of physical memory 400H is 40:0. Tiling the ROM BIOS data area results in virtual address 40:0 accessing physical address 400H in protected mode also. Tiling achieves this result by allocating the GDT descriptor referenced by selector 40, and setting the base address in the descriptor to physical address 400H. Thus, subsequent uses of the address 40:0 in real mode and protected mode cause physical address 400H to be accessed. Figure 10.2 illustrates tiling.

Tiled memory objects and the bimodal code that accesses them are in low physical memory. Tiled objects include the following:

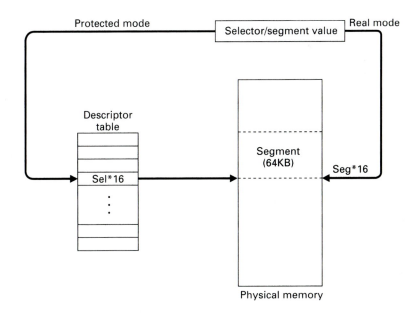

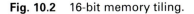
Fig. 10.2   16-bit memory tiling.

- Low kernel code and data segments
- ROM BIOS data area
- Device driver request packets

The device driver code and data segments that exist in low memory are not tiled. The kernel sets the segment registers to the correct values for the current mode before the strategy and interrupt entry points are called.

10.3.4 Analysis

The successful coexistence of the DOS application with the protected-mode applications of OS/2 is a significant achievement on the 80286 architecture. Incorporating compatibility for an unprotected system such as DOS within a protected system is difficult, especially since the 80286 was never intended to support protection.

Due to the 80286 architecture, DOS compatibility is limited. The system cannot protect itself from ill-behaved DOS applications, since there is no protection from real mode. Only a single DOS application can run in the foreground, and some DOS communications applications do not run in the compatibility environment since they do not get interrupts in the background. There is no XMS, EMS, VCPI, or DPMI support, since these all conflict with the management of memory above 1MB by the protected-mode OS/2 kernel.

10.4 80386 DOS COMPATIBILITY

The 80386 provides features that overcome the DOS compatibility limitations of the 80286 architecture. The 80386 incorporates *virtual 8086 (v86) mode* to allow 8086-based systems and applications to run in a protected environment. Running in virtual 8086 mode is equivalent to running in protected mode with real-mode instruction and addressing semantics at privilege level 3. Therefore, v86 mode enables a DOS environment to be encapsulated, and thus to coexist with a protected-mode system and applications without the problems of mode switching and system integrity. Applications running in v86 mode cannot directly access supervisor functions or perform I/O without causing general protection faults. These general protection faults are then serviced by the protected-mode operating system. Memory-mapped and I/O mapped device I/O can be trapped by the underlying protected-mode operating system, and can be emulated.

Software and hardware interrupts in v86 mode cause the 80386 to switch to protected mode. Therefore, the system never uses real mode. The address space accessible when the processor is running in v86 mode corresponds exactly to that of an 8086 with the same real-mode semantics for processing the values placed in segment registers. The v86 mode feature provides fast switches between protected mode and virtual 8086 mode.

The paging feature of the 80386 processor allows multiple virtual 8086 address spaces to coexist. Each virtual 8086 mode task can be allocated its own linear address space by allocation of one page table per v86 task. Paging also enables the emulation of EMS and XMS. Thus, the 80386 supports true DOS multitasking without the use of real mode. A protected operating system such as OS/2 can provide DOS multitasker functionality without compromising its system integrity.

Each v86-mode task effectively has its own virtual PC. It has its own v86 virtual address space and virtual devices, and it performs virtual I/O. Whether DOS applications running in v86 mode receives real or virtual interrupts is a policy decision, made by the protected-mode operating system that provides the compatibility. Real interrupts are delivered when the interrupt occurs, whereas virtual interrupts are delayed until the intended v86 mode task is the current running task. If v86-mode tasks are given only virtual interrupts, then they can also be paged. If they are given real interrupts, however, they cannot be paged, since the interrupt handler may be paged out. It is too complex and slow to have the system block to bring in pages for a DOS application's interrupt handler at interrupt time. Furthermore, if real interrupts are delivered to a v86-mode task, the v86-mode task can breach the integrity of the system.

There are two approaches to DOS compatibility on the 80386 utilizing v86 mode. The first is running DOS in a v86-mode task. DOS is loaded into a v86-mode address space, and provides all DOS services for the DOS application running in the v86-mode task. The host operating system provides emulation services to provide a virtual PC environment in which DOS and its applications can run. The v86-mode task emulates device level hardware I/O and BIOS-level I/O services. This approach allows for absolute DOS compatibility. However, it does not allow the host operating system to control polling in the DOS kernel, resulting in wasted processor cycles. Also, the memory taken up by the DOS kernel uses memory in the v86-mode address space that could be used by DOS applications. This approach also makes file sharing with the host operating system difficult, since direct hardware and BIOS I/O to the block devices that contain the files must be intercepted and routed through the network redirector interface.

The second approach to providing DOS compatibility on an 80386 using v86 mode is to emulate DOS in a v86 task. All DOS application interfaces are emulated using the host operating system, and virtual hardware and BIOS support are provided for each v86-mode task. This approach allows the host operating system to control the DOS environment completely. It allows the system to reduce polling and wasted processor cycles caused by the DOS kernel and its applications. More memory is available for DOS applications, since the DOS kernel is not mapped within the v86-mode address space. Since DOS I/O requests are serviced by direct DOS emulation, instead of via trapping of BIOS and hardware I/O requests generated by the DOS kernel, this approach achieves better performance than does the alternative of running DOS. This performance advantage is due to a reduction in the number of traps between v86 mode and protected mode. However, the system must be revised when the contents of the DOS system changes.

10.4.1 Multiple Virtual DOS Machines

OS/2 2.0 uses *multiple virtual DOS machine (MVDM)* technology on the 80386 to provide DOS compatibility. Each DOS application runs in a *virtual DOS machine (VDM)* in v86 mode. A VDM is a v86-mode variant of an OS/2 single-thread process. Each VDM executes a DOS application and emulates the functions of DOS in a virtual PC environment.

VDMs run within their own sessions, and can be multitasked with OS/2 protected-mode programs. DOS text and graphics applications can run in either full screen sessions or windowed sessions using a standard PM window. MVDM architecture uses the DOS emulation approach, and is compatible with DOS 5.0. However, since the PC hardware and BIOS emulation is so complete, MVDM technology also has the capability of booting the actual DOS operating system into a DOS environment. This facility gives users the capability of running DOS applications that are DOS version specific.

The MVDM architecture provides a protected execution environment for DOS applications, to prevent ill-behaved DOS applications from disrupting the system. The paging feature of the 80386 is used to emulate EMS and XMS, and DOS applications are paged with OS/2 applications. Since the DOS emulation approach is used for DOS compatibility, a large amount of application memory is available to DOS applications. Also, the emulation layers provide compatibility for DOS communications and NetBIOS applications.

The MVDM architecture is layered, allowing the virtual DOS environment to be custom-tailored and extended. It also does not allow DOS applications to access the block devices directly, since these devices are managed by the OS/2 file systems. However, DOS applications benefit from the OS/2 installable file system environment, and can access and share files on both FAT and HPFS logical drives.

The MVDM kernel extends the existing OS/2 kernel to support virtual DOS machines. It runs entirely in protected mode, and uses the dispatcher's *EnterKMode/ExitKMode* services for dispatching VDMs in the same fashion as regular OS/2 processes. Figure 10.3 illustrates the MVDM architecture.

As Fig. 10.3 shows, the MVDM kernel consists of the following major components: *VDM management, DOS emulation, 8086 emulation,* and *virtual device drivers (VDDs).* VDM management is responsible for creating and terminating VDMs. It manages system resources for all VDMs and provides *virtual device helper (VDHelp)* services for virtual device drivers.

The DOS emulation component emulates the function of DOS on a per-VDM basis. Each VDM effectively has its own DOS and virtual PC. DOS services either are provided directly by the *stub virtual DOS kernel* loaded into each VDM, or are routed to the OS/2 protected-mode kernel. The DOS emulation component also provides compatibility for undocumented DOS interfaces.

The 8086 emulation component is responsible for 8086 instruction decoding. It controls the per-VDM *I/O permission map (IOPM)* that is used for specifying the I/O ports a VDM can access. The per-VDM IOPM structure is defined by the 80386, and is mapped into the system TSS when a VDM is being executed. The 8086 emulation component provides routing services for traps caused by software interrupts and virtual I/O device accesses, to allow the latter to be emulated correctly.

VDDs are used to emulate DOS devices at the hardware and BIOS level on a per-VDM basis. They use *VDHelp* functions to obtain services from the system. VDDs use *protected-mode physical device drivers (PDDs)* to access the hardware. VDDs simulate virtual hardware interrupts at task time into VDMs, instead of allowing VDMs to get hardware interrupts at interrupt time.

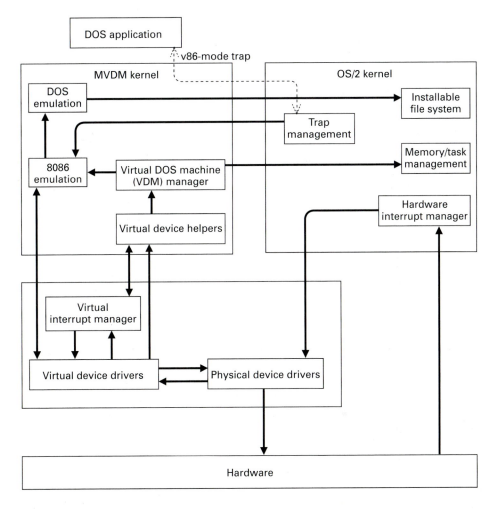

Fig. 10.3 MVDM architecture. (Adapted from OS/2 Notebook, Copyright 1990, Microsoft Corporation. Reprinted by permission of Microsoft Press.)

10.4.2 VDM Management

The *VDM manager* is responsible for the creation, termination, and control of virtual DOS machines. It loads and initializes virtual device drivers, provides *VDHelp* functions for virtual device drivers, and accesses system resources for VDMs. The VDM manager provides a compatible DOS environment that supports a standard hardware configuration. It utilizes the installable, customizable virtual device driver layer to perform the virtual I/O and BIOS services for the VDMs. VDM management also calls the virtual device driver VDM-creation entry points when VDMs are created.

VDM creation supports per-VDM configurations. For example, each VDM can have its own CONFIG.SYS that describes how it should be configured. When a VDM is created, the VDM manager calls the OS/2 kernel to create a process and the associated structures, such as a PTDA, TCB, and TSD. It then calls memory management to create an arena for the VDM, and creates an I/O permission map for the VDM. The 8086 emulation component is initialized for the VDM, and all the VDD per-VDM initialization entry points are called. The last part of VDM creation is to call DOS emulation to initialize the DOS device drivers and the DOS arena, and to load the COMMAND.COM shell or whatever program the user specifies through the configuration.

VDM termination occurs when a DOS application running in a VDM terminates, or when the VDM is terminated by the user through interaction with the desktop manager. When a VDM terminates, the VDD per-VDM termination handlers are called so that they can clean up their per-VDM data structures. The VDM manager then calls normal process cleanup routines in the OS/2 kernel for reclaiming resources used by the VDM, such as files. VDMs are also terminated by the MVDM kernel when invalid operations occur in a VDM.

The session manager notifies the VDM manager when screen switches occur. The VDM manager notifies the mouse, keyboard, and video VDDs to allow them to reset their virtual-to-real device mappings. When a VDM is switched, the VDM manager is also responsible for changing the IOPM for the process. The OS/2 memory manager edits the page directory to context switch VDM address spaces.

The VDM process address space, or *v86 address space,* is similar to a regular flat model 32-bit program that has a special 4MB private arena. When a VDM runs in user mode, it is in v86 mode. Each VDM has 4MB of linear address space that are mapped by a single page table. This 4MB linear address space for each VDM is reserved in the system arena. The current VDM is mapped at linear addresses 0 to 4MB by editing of the page table entry for that range of addresses into the page directory. Page 0 of each VDM contains the interrupt vector table, ROM BIOS data area, DOS communications area, and the virtual DOS kernel stub. Figure 10.4 illustrates the VDM process address space.

The A20 wrap area in Fig. 10.4 is used to emulate the behavior of real-mode applications accessing addresses between 1MB and 1MB + 64KB. On an 8086, it is possible to generate physical addresses between 1MB and 1MB + 64KB using real-mode virtual addresses (e.g., FFFFH:FFFFH). However, since an 8086 has only 20 bits of address lines, some of these addresses wrap into the first 64KB of physical memory. In a VDM, the wrapping of these addresses is emulated by the page table entries for the range between 1MB and 1MB + 64KB being set to be the same as the page table entries for the first 64KB of the VDM.

The memory between the top of the A20 wrap area and 4MB is the *per-VDM memory area.* It is used for per-VDM data allocated by the VDM kernel, and also for per-VDM instance data allocated by the VDDs. It is not accessible to applications running in v86 mode, since it is out of the v86-mode address space. This memory is used for maintaining the virtual video buffer, and for emulating expanded memory.

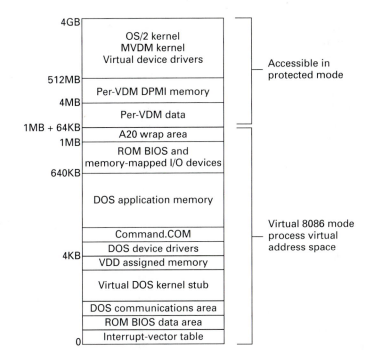

Fig. 10. 4 Virtual DOS machine memory layout.

VDM events are used by VDDs to sequence and control the execution of VDMs. There are two kinds of events: *global events* and *local events*. Global events are called the next time any OS/2 process runs. Local events are called when a specific VDM is dispatched. The events are implemented in a manner similar to the force flags described in Chapter 5 for regular OS/2 processes. The VDM kernel and VDDs run in kernel mode, except when receiving hardware interrupts from physical device drivers. When they need to set local and global event handlers, they call *VDHelp* interfaces in the MVDM kernel to register the event handlers. The *ExitKMode* routine of the dispatcher detects the presence of registered event handlers and processes them before dispatching to user (v86) mode. Event handlers are commonly used by VDDs to simulate interrupts into VDMs at task time.

10.4.3 8086 Emulation

The 8086 emulation component manages communication between the VDM 8086 in-struction stream and the virtual device drivers. It controls the execution flow of VDMs with respect to I/O-sensitive instructions, and provides routing of software interrupts and I/O instruction traps to VDDs. All exceptions, traps, and faults caused in v86 mode are routed to the 8086 emulation component by the OS/2 kernel trap manager. The 8086 emulation component enables virtual device drivers to emulate BIOS-level and hardware-level I/O in a VDM.

IOPL is the minimum privilege level needed to use I/O-sensitive instructions in protected mode. It was discussed in Chapter 2 with respect to the protected-mode architecture of Intel's 80X86 processors. I/O-sensitive instructions, or IOPL-sensitive instructions, are those that can alter the state of the interrupt flag: IN, OUT, CLI, STI, POPF, PUSHF, INT, and IRET. If the current privilege level is numerically greater than the IOPL, a general protection fault occurs when I/O-sensitive instructions are executed. IOPL for OS/2 applications is set at privilege level 2. The privilege level for an application running in v86 mode is 3. IN and OUT instructions are not I/O sensitive in v86 mode since the IOPM in the TSS is used to manage access to I/O ports in v86 mode.

The IOPL policy for v86 mode has several ramifications on the design of DOS compatibility. If IOPL is set less than 3, I/O-sensitive instructions cause general protection faults. Therefore, with IOPL less than 3, I/O-sensitive instructions must be emulated, and the interrupt flag must be virtualized on a per-VDM basis. However, large numbers of I/O-sensitive instructions in BASIC programs can cause an excessive amount of trapping for providing emulation. Trapping from v86 mode to protected mode at ring 0 is expensive compared to most operations. It is most comparable to a kernel system call for protected-mode OS/2 applications. If IOPL is set to 3, I/O-sensitive instructions work without trapping when executed in v86 mode. However, this allows DOS applications to access the real interrupt flag of the system. If a DOS application disables interrupts and goes into a spin loop, it could potentially hang the entire system unless preventative measures are enforced.

MVDM uses IOPL set to 3 to provide the best performance possible. This setting reduces the trapping overhead, but lets VDMs disable interrupts, a potential integrity problem for the whole system. To make sure that a DOS application does not disable interrupts and go into a spin loop and hang the system, OS/2 uses a *watchdog timer*. A watchdog timer is set with a duration interval; as long as the timer is primed before that interval expires, the timer does not interrupt. If the watchdog timer interrupts, the system terminates the DOS application. Therefore, setting IOPL to 3 allows the system to achieve maximum performance, and using the watchdog timer prevents DOS applications from taking down the system or disrupting protected-mode applications.

IOPL is set to 0 for a single VDM only when that VDM needs to have the interrupt flag virtualized. For example, when some VDD needs to simulate a hardware interrupt into a VDM, it must be able to detect when the VDM can be interrupted. Therefore, IOPL is decreased to less than 3, so that the interrupt flag can be virtualized for a VDM, and the system can detect when the interrupts are enabled in that VDM. IOPL is increased back to 3 when the simulated interrupt is delivered to the VDM.

The software interrupt instructions, INT, INTO, and INT 3, need special handling since the interrupt vector table is never used by the 80386 while executing in v86 mode. All software and hardware interrupts cause the 80386 to switch to protected mode when it is in v86 mode. Therefore, the 8086 emulation component provides a function called *software interrupt reflection* to route these interrupts to VDMs as appropriate.

If IOPL is less than 3, the software interrupt instructions cause general protection faults, and are routed to the 8086 emulation component through the general-protection-fault handler. If IOPL is set to 3, the software interrupt instructions cause control to vector through the IDT. If the gate descriptor for an interrupt in the IDT has privilege level 3, control is passed to 8086 emulation from the interrupt handler at privilege level 0. If the gate descriptor's privilege level is less than 3, a general protection fault occurs, and the interrupt is routed to 8086 emulation through the fault handler.

Software interrupt reflection occurs as follows. A software interrupt causes the 80386 to enter protected mode at privilege level 0. When the system detects that the software interrupt occurred in v86 mode, either through the general-protection-fault handler or through an interrupt handler mapped by the IDT, control is transferred to the 8086 emulation component. The INTO and INT 3 software interrupts are routed to the 8086 emulation component through the IDT by setting the descriptors for their interrupts to privilege level 3. If either of these instructions occurs while IOPL is less than 3, it is routed to the 8086 emulation component through the general-protection-fault handler. All other software interrupts are always routed to 8086 emulation through the general-protection-fault handler.

Once control comes to the 8086 emulation component, the MVDM kernel enters kernel mode. The 8086 emulation component then decodes the instruction causing the control transfer, and determines the type of the interrupt. It locates the destination of the interrupt by scanning the interrupt vector table in the VDM's memory. It builds a simulated interrupt stack frame on the v86-mode stack, and calls *ExitKMode* to dispatch the VDM. When the VDM runs, it begins running in the interrupt handler, with the IRET frame on the stack looking like an interrupt occurred.

There are two ways that a VDD can hook a software interrupt. In some cases, the VDD wants to get control before the interrupt is reflected in the VDM. In this case, a *prereflection hook* is used. In other cases, the VDD wants to allow any interrupt handlers installed by DOS applications to be able to handle the interrupt before the VDD. In this case, the VDD uses a *postreflection hook*. The VDD sets a postreflection hook by placing a breakpoint in the return address portion of the IRET stack frame on the v86-mode stack. When the interrupt handler in the DOS application executes the IRET instruction to complete interrupt service, it causes a fault, and control ultimately vectors to the VDD that placed the hook.

VDM breakpoints are used by the 8086 emulation component to control execution flow when in v86 mode. The ARPL instruction is inserted into the VDM's interrupt vector table and interrupt stack frames when VDM breakpoints are set. Execution of the ARPL instruction in v86 mode causes a general protection fault, and the system ultimately vectors to the 8086 emulation component. VDM breakpoints are used to transition from v86 mode in a VDM to the MVDM kernel running in kernel mode. VDM breakpoints are not like events. Events occur in the dispatch cycle from protected mode to v86 mode. Breakpoints occur in v86 mode, and return control to the protected-mode MVDM kernel.

Protected instructions, such as LGDT and LLDT, are reflected back to the VDM that originated them as invalid opcode exceptions. The same policy is used for invalid v86-mode and real-mode instructions. Other valid exceptions and traps generated by a VDM are routed through the IDT and then reflected to the VDM.

10.4.4 Virtual Device Drivers

Virtual device drivers virtualize hardware and ROM BIOS services on a per-VDM basis. They provide support for the direct manipulation of memory-mapped I/O devices, and the direct programming of I/O ports. They also emulate ROM BIOS software interrupt services, and support the direct manipulation of the ROM BIOS data area by DOS applications. VDDs provide these services by intercepting hardware and software interrupts, and maintaining a virtual hardware state for each VDM. VDDs use *VDHelp* services to hook BIOS interrupts, to trap I/O port and memory-mapped I/O device accesses, and to access system services.

VDDs are trusted modules that execute in protected mode at ring 0. They are flat 0:32 modules, usually written in a high-level language such as C. VDDs use the 32-bit executable format that is designed for OS/2 2.0. They are distinguished from EXEs and DLLs by a special bit in the executable header, and are loaded when the system is started. Each VDD contains a code object, a data object, and an instance data object. The code and data are shared across all VDM contexts and are mapped into the system arena. The instance data object is used for per-VDM memory, and is mapped at the same address in each VDM. VDDs are protected from DOS applications running in a VDM since they are not mapped into the v86-mode-accessible portion of the VDM address space. VDDs are responsible for preventing VDMs from corrupting one another and the system. The memory used by VDDs can be swappable or fixed, and private (per VDM) or shared (global).

The architecture of existing OS/2 device drivers changes because of the VDD architecture. Device drivers, as they were known in the 16-bit version of OS/2, no longer need to be bimodal since the system never executes in real mode. Therefore, they are called in only protected mode on OS/2 2.0. Also, the BIOS and DOS interrupt support necessary in existing 16-bit device drivers is no longer needed since this support is provided by VDDs. Furthermore, the tiling of objects, allowing them to be accessed in real mode and protected mode using the same virtual address, is not required. Therefore, existing 16-bit device drivers have a modified architecture called *physical device drivers (PDDs)*. PDDs provide support for protected-mode applications, and also provide services for VDDs using a private VDD–PDD interface. Because PDDs are used for actual I/O, VDDs remain independent of the physical hardware underlying the virtual DOS implementation. Figure 10.5 illustrates the VDD–PDD model.

The VDD has several simple interfaces. The VDD initialization routine is called when the VDD is loaded as the system is started. There is a per-VDM initialization routine called by the VDM manager when a VDM is created by a user. The per-VDM initialization routine usually initializes the virtual device and the virtual ROM BIOS state; hooks any necessary software interrupts, I/O ports, or memory-mapped addresses; and allocates per-VDM memory. When a VDD is called by a PDD at interrupt time, it is executing in interrupt mode on the interrupt stack of the system. However, VDDs do not

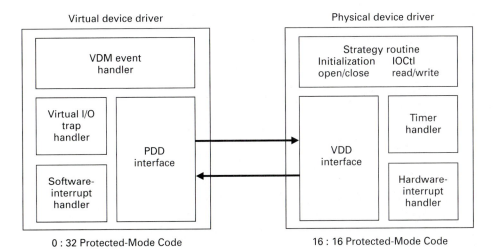

Fig. 10.5 32-bit model for physical and virtual device drivers. (Adapted from *OS/2 Notebook,* Copyright 1990, Microsoft Corporation. Reprinted by permission of Microsoft Press.)

process interrupts in interrupt mode; rather, they defer processing of interrupts until task time. The trap and event handlers of a VDD are called in kernel mode running on the thread stack for that VDM.

10.4.5 Virtual Interrupt Management

The virtual interrupt management services component is responsible for simulating hardware interrupts into VDMs. It performs services similar to software interrupt reflection, but the routing and source of the interrupts is external to the VDM. Each VDM is provided with a *virtual programmable interrupt controller (VPIC)* device by the VPIC VDD. As stated previously, VDMs receive hardware interrupts not at interrupt time, but rather at task time. Hardware interrupts are routed to a VDD from a PDD when they are received in interrupt mode. Typically, the VDD calls *VDHelp* to set a global event handler so that the VDD can process the interrupt at task time, and then returns to the PDD to finish regular interrupt processing. The next time a process attempts to exit kernel mode, the global event handler set by the VDD is called. The VDD then calls VPIC services through VDHelp to simulate a hardware interrupt into the VDM for which the interrupt was targeted, using a local event handler.

The local event causes the VPIC to get control before the VDM is dispatched. If interrupts are disabled in the target VDM, VPIC virtualizes the interrupt flag to determine when the VDM can receive the simulated interrupt. In this case, the VPIC sets IOPL to 0 and dispatches the VDM. When the interrupts are finally enabled in the VDM, a trap occurs because IOPL is less than 3 (IOPL-sensitive instructions are being emulated). VPIC receives control, restores IOPL to 3, and then simulates the interrupt into the

VDM using a mechanism similar to software interrupt reflection. An IRET stack frame is built to simulate an interrupt on the v86 mode stack. VPIC then exits the kernel, causing a dispatch cycle to occur. The next time the VDM runs, it executes the interrupt routine. When the VDM runs its interrupt routine, the V86 mode stack has an IRET frame pointing to the interrupted instruction, and the VDM's VPIC device and interrupting virtual device look like they have just been interrupted.

10.4.6 Virtual DevHelp (VDHelp) Services

The services of the virtual device helper (VDHelp) are used by VDDs to gain access to the MVDM kernel and other OS/2 system services. Unlike the 16-bit DevHelp and FSHelp interfaces, VDHelp is dynamically linked using the 32-bit dynamic linking model. VDHelp is accessed using stack-based parameter passing just like 32-bit APIs. It provides functions that allow VDDs to register for the following:

- Software and hardware interrupts
- Specific I/O traps
- Page faults to memory-mapped I/O devices
- Memory management
- PDD–VDD communication
- VDM state control
- VDM event and breakpoint management
- Virtual interrupt management

VDDs can use VDHelp to hook page faults to memory-mapped I/O devices. They do so by calling the memory manager, so that, when a page fault occurs on certain virtual addresses in a v86 mode address space, control is routed to the VDD emulating the memory-mapped device. Memory can be allocated in either a global or a per-VDM instance context, and aliasing and mapping services are available to allow EMS emulation. Also, there are page management features to enable the virtual-video device driver to perform lazy page copying of the video buffer data during VDM context switching.

10.5 OS/2 2.X WINDOWS 3.X COMPATIBILITY

The 32-bit version of OS/2 provides binary compatibility for Windows 3.X real-, and standard-mode applications. The compatibility is not implemented with a compatibility layer that maps Windows 3.X application requests into OS/2 PM requests; instead, a special VDM is provided that emulates a DPMI server. Loaded into the VDM is a special version of the Windows 3.X kernel that directly services the requests of Windows 3.X applications running in the VDM. Unlike in Windows 3.X, ill-behaved or defective Windows 3.X applications cannot disrupt the entire system, since the Windows environment is encapsulated. OS/2 2.X provides an environment with better protection, memory management, and integration for Windows 3.X applications.

10.6 OS/2 2.X 16-BIT COMPATIBILITY

The 32-bit OS/2 system can run 16-bit OS/2 EXEs and DLLs. It provides support for the entire 16-bit API, including support for loading 16-bit EXEs and DLLs and any associated file formats that the API supports. This support is needed to encourage the migration of users running 16-bit OS/2 on 80386-based computers to the 32-bit OS/2 platform. Also, since OS/2 is such a large system, it is impossible to convert the entire system to a 32-bit system in the first release. Therefore, the system is a hybrid of 16-bit and 32-bit code internally. Such a hybrid system requires that 16-bit and 32-bit code coexist. The system also provides support for calling 16-bit APIs from 32-bit modules. This support is needed since all user-supplied DLLs may not be available in 32-bit format when the product is initially shipped.

10.7 HYBRID SYSTEM STRATEGIES

There are basically three methods that allow a 32-bit API and a 16-bit API to coexist. The first alternative is to have separate 16-bit and 32-bit subsystems. This alternative is difficult to implement because usually some kind of interlock is needed between the 16-bit and 32-bit functions, since they perform similar actions and manipulate the same resources. The second approach is to use a 16-bit system that provides a 32-bit API by mapping the 32-bit API onto a 16-bit API. The third approach is to use a 32-bit system that provides 16-bit compatibility by mapping the 16-bit API onto a 32-bit API. Figure 10.6 illustrates two of these coexistence strategies.

OS/2 2.0 uses all three alternatives. The kernel is mostly 32 bit, with 16-bit interfaces for compatibility with 16-bit functions. Much of the Presentation Manager and utility programs are 16-bit. Therefore, most of the 32-bit PM API is mapped onto the 16-bit API. The intermediate code that provides this mapping functionality is called a *thunk*. Thunks make the transition between 16-bit and 32-bit code, and can map one API function onto another transparently. There are two types of thunks: *16-to-32* and *32-to-16*. The 16-to-32 thunks are used to provide compatibility for a 16-bit API function by mapping it to a new 32-bit API function. The 32-to-16 thunks are used to implement 32-bit API functions using existing 16-bit API functions. Thunks minimize the impact on the system of providing compatibility. Thunks require coexistence of 16-bit and 32-bit memory objects within a single process virtual address space that is used by both 16-bit and 32-bit code. Thunks are discussed in more detail in Section 10.10.

10.8 MEMORY MODEL COEXISTENCE

The differences in the flat and segmented programming environments of the 32-bit and 16-bit systems are summarized in Table 10.1. OS/2 provides a hybrid of the flat and segmented memory models that is used as a foundation for the coexistence of 16-bit and 32-bit code. Each process is given its own 512MB linear address space. Each process also has an LDT to map the 512MB process virtual address space whether the process was created

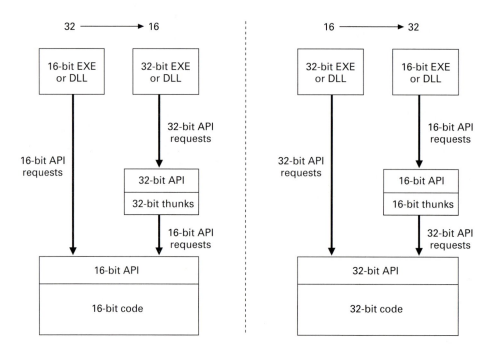

Fig. 10.6   Coexistence strategies for 16-bit and 32- bit API.

Function	16-bit segmented model	32-bit flat model
Process virtual address space	LDT per process	Linear address space per process
Code segment descriptor(s)	D-bit off for 16-bit registers and operands	D-bit on for 32-bit registers and operands
Data/Stack segment descriptor(s)	B-bit off for 16-bit stack pointer in stack operations	B-bit on for 32-bit stack pointer in stack operations
Virtual addresses	16:16 selector:offset	0:32 linear address
Memory objects	Byte-granular segments up to 64KB	Page-granular range of linear pages
Dynamic linking	Far call model	Near call model
API parameters	16-bit WORD	32-bit DWORD
API parameter and structure alignment	WORD alignment	DWORD alignment

Table 10.1   Segmented- and flat-model programming environments.

using the 16-bit or 32-bit version of *DosExecPgm,* and whether or not a 16-bit or 32-bit EXE module was loaded. When a process runs 32-bit code, it executes using the flat-model address space. When a process is running 16-bit code, it executes using LDT selectors that map the flat address space. Therefore, memory objects in this hybrid model can coexist in one process virtual address space, and are addressable by both 16-bit and 32-bit code. It is important to realize that processes and threads are not 16 bit or 32 bit; they merely execute 16-bit or 32-bit code at any instance. All memory objects, including 16-bit segments in the hybrid model, take advantage of paging instead of swapping.

There is also a difference in the granularity of memory objects and memory protection between the two memory models. The 80386 allows 16-bit segments to be packed on a page, since 16-bit programs access memory through the LDT. Accessing memory through the LDT results in byte-granular memory access with limit protection. However, 32-bit code accesses memory one page at a time, since the flat model is page granular. Therefore, if 16-bit segments are packed on partial pages in OS/2 2.0, 32-bit code can access all the segments packed on a single page. This problem is a significant one in shared objects. Therefore, small segments use an entire linear and physical page. As a result, 16-bit modules with many small segments can fragment the linear address space and waste virtual and physical storage. This waste is due to the disparity of memory object granularity between the two memory models. Later in this chapter several strategies for reducing this fragmentation are described.

The 80386 converts addresses between 16:16 and 0:32 by determining the descriptor base address, and adding a 16-bit offset. It converts a 16:16 address to a 0:32 address in software by examining the LDT and extracting the base address from the descriptor for the segment. Unless the LDT is mapped into the process address space, the kernel must be called to convert a 16:16 address to a 0:32 address. However, the LDT can be mapped into the process virtual address space as read-only data, allowing the conversion to occur in user mode without a call to the kernel.

The 80386 converts between 0:32 and 16:16 addresses by having a descriptor map the correct region of linear address space. The base address in descriptors under OS/2 2.0 with paging enabled is a linear address. The 80386 converts a 0:32 address to a 16:16 address in software by creating a segment alias to the specific region addressed. The kernel is required for creating and destroying aliases, since the LDT must be modified.

This approach to converting between 16:16 and 0:32 addresses in software emulates the method used by the 80386 when translating addresses. However, due to the overhead of calling the kernel to manage aliases in the latter case, an alternative scheme that provides fast address translation without the kernel is required to build a mapping layer that provides 16-bit compatibility with acceptable performance.

10.9 LDT TILING

LDT tiling is a technique invented by the OS/2 design team, and used to establish an arithmetic relationship between 0:32 and 16:16 virtual addresses. It is similar to the tiling used in the DOS compatibility support of the 16-bit system, but tiles two different types of virtual addresses, instead of a 16:16 virtual address and a physical address. An LDT can contain 8192 descriptors, and each descriptor can map a maximum of 64KB per segment. Thus, an LDT can map 512MB of process virtual address space. This technique is the cause of the 512MB limitation on process virtual address spaces in OS/2 2.0.

In a tiled LDT, the base linear address of every 16-bit segment is the selector index * 64KB. Each LDT selector is thus forced to map a specific 64KB portion of the 32-bit process virtual address space. Regions mapped by contiguous selectors are contiguous within the process virtual address space. Therefore, each tiled memory object has 16:16 and 0:32 addresses that are related by an arithmetic function. Memory objects are tiled when allocated—that is, when their virtual addresses are selected by the virtual memory manager. Figure 10.7 illustrates the relationship between 16:16 and 0:32 virtual addresses that results from LDT tiling.

Tiled objects are allocated on 64KB linear boundaries within the process virtual address space, and have related descriptors in the LDT that map each 64KB increment of each object. Each tiled object reserves 64KB of linear memory, since a 16-bit segment can be as large as 64KB. Also, 64KB of linear memory must be reserved for each tiled object, since any 16-bit segment can be reallocated up to its maximum 64KB size. Figure 10.8 illustrates a tiled virtual address space.

In Fig. 10.8, three 16-bit segments are depicted: A, B, and C. Segment A is 100 bytes. Therefore, 64KB is reserved for the tiled object, and a single page is committed. As Fig. 10.8 shows, part of the linear page on which segment A exists is wasted; that is, this partial page cannot be allocated as part of another memory object, and must be swapped with segment A, since OS/2 2.0 performs page swapping. Segment B is 5KB, and requires two committed pages to satisfy the allocation. Once again, the partial page not used by segment B is wasted. Segment C is a full 64KB and requires 16 pages of committed memory.

LDT management in the 32-bit system is different from that in the 16-bit system as a result of the LDT tiling algorithm. Unlike the 16-bit system, in which private and shared selectors are interleaved within the LDT in a 3:1 ratio, in the 32-bit system the

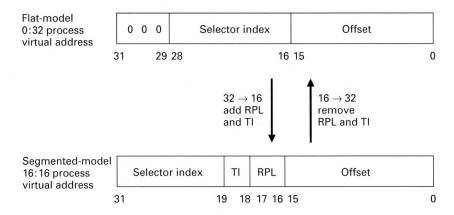

Fig. 10.7   0:32 and 16:16 address conversion.

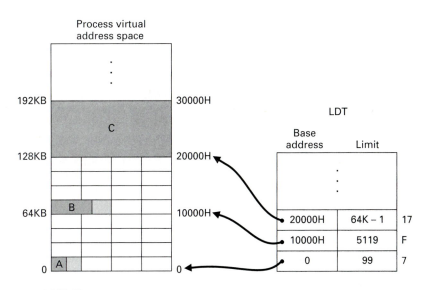

Fig. 10.8   LDT tiling.

private selectors are allocated from the low end of the LDT, and the shared LDT are allocated from the high end. This allocation scheme is necessary because the LDT descriptor allocation strategy must parallel the allocation strategy of the flat process virtual address space. This change in LDT management is transparent to 16-bit applications, since they do not rely on specific LDT selector values.

Allocating the selectors from the top and bottom of the LDT is not feasible in the 16-bit system since it requires every LDT to be 64KB. However, since the 32-bit environment is paged, there is no penalty for this LDT management strategy. LDTs are sparse objects in the 32-bit system. Therefore, a minimal LDT uses 8KB—one page for the private descriptors at the bottom, and one page for the shared descriptors at the top.

All user memory objects that need to be addressable by both 16-bit and 32-bit code are tiled memory objects. All 16-bit segment allocations, whether made at load time or at run time, are tiled. Any 32-bit memory objects that can potentially be passed to 16-bit routines need to be tiled. Since OS/2 2.0 is not all 32 bits internally, all 32-bit objects are tiled by default. This default setting is used because 32-bit applications cannot determine whether a 32-bit API is serviced by thunking to 16-bit code. Therefore, all 32-bit memory object allocations have a *tile option* to tell the system whether the object needs to be tiled. This facility allows forward compatibility with 32-bit OS/2 systems that support the use of memory above the 512MB limit currently enforced. For load-time allocations, there is a *tile bit* in the executable file header that tells the loader whether EXE or DLL objects need to be tiled. There is a *tile flag* available on the 32-bit memory management API calls that allows the program requesting memory at run time to indicate whether or not objects need to be tiled.

Support for a system that provides more than 512MB of process virtual address space and retains 16-bit compatibility requires that the entire system be 32-bits internally. Only then can the system guarantee that 32-bit memory objects never will be passed to 16-bit code as a result of a 32-bit API being implemented using a 16-bit API. If an object is not tiled, it cannot be addressed by 16-bit code. Nontiled objects are not addressable through the LDT. Therefore, the system must be entirely 32-bit internally to extend the 512MB limit and thus to support nontiled objects.

There is a slight difference between the way 16-bit and 32-bit memory allocations are made. This difference lies in how the limits are set inside the tiled descriptors. When a 16-bit segment is allocated, the descriptor that maps the segment has a limit that is byte granular. In other words, the descriptor limit is based on the size specified by the 16-bit requestor. However, when a 32-bit application allocates a memory object that is tiled, the descriptor limit in the tiled descriptor is always page granular. This granularity is used because all 32-bit memory objects are page granular, and their size is always a multiple of the page size.

There are several problems associated with the LDT tiling approach. Any 32-bit memory object larger than 64KB crosses 64KB linear boundaries. When an object that crosses a 64KB boundary is passed to 16-bit code, the 16-bit code cannot address the entire object with a single selector. For compatibility to be maintained, the 16-bit code needs to be able to run without being changed. Therefore, the 32-to-16 thunks ensure that objects passed to 16-bit API functions are addressable. This mechanism is detailed in Section 10.10. Tiling also fails for 16-bit applications that use GDT selectors in 16-bit API calls. This situation is rare, since GDT selectors for user data can be provided only by device drivers using special private interfaces. There is no way for a 16-bit application adhering to the 16-bit API to allocate a segment mapped by the GDT. Another problem with tiling is the fragmentation of the address space by 16-bit applications with many small segments, which wastes virtual and physical memory. The 80386 supports packing of segments on partial pages, but packing breaks the LDT tiling arithmetic algorithm, and poses a threat to system integrity and protection.

The system does provide an optimization to overcome fragmentation for private 16-bit code segments by packing them into a special region of the tiled address space. Since code objects are read-only, they can be packed onto a single page without posing any protection problems. If all private packed objects for a process are isolated in the bottom of the linear address space, the address conversion algorithm does not suffer much degradation, and tiling still works for the rest of the address space. Figure 10.9 illustrates LDT tiling with private code packing.

When a 16-bit EXE is loaded by a call to *DosExecPgm*, the executable code objects from the load module are packed into the low end of the private region. LDT selectors at the low end of the LDT are used to map packed objects. This area of the process virtual address space is not tiled. The thread information block has the linear address of the top of the packed area. The LDT tiling address conversion algorithm is modified to account for packed objects. When a 0:32 address is converted to a 16:16 address, if the address is in the packed region, the LDT is searched for a selector that maps the region. When a 16:16 address is converted to a 0:32 address, the base address from the descriptor is used to create 32-bit address. Both translations require a read-only alias to the LDT to be

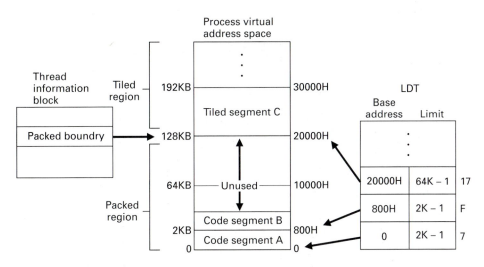

Fig. 10.9   LDT tiling with 16-bit private code packing.

mapped into the process virtual address space to allow the conversions to run in user mode without calling the kernel.

This approach saves physical and virtual memory, but degrades the performance of pointer conversion. The extra comparison to test whether a memory object is in the packed region is not significant, but searching the LDT when converting 0:32 to 16:16 is relatively slow. However, this path is not executed unless a 32-bit API call is thunked to a 16-bit API call, and code pointers are used as parameters in the API call. This situation occurs rarely since code is usually not passed as a parameter in API requests. Processes that originate from 32-bit EXE modules have no packed area in their process virtual address space.

10.10 THUNKS

Thunks are the intermediate code mapping technology used to implement an API function of one model using an analogous API function in the other model. They are transparent to requestors of the API function being mapped, and to the API function being used to map the request. Thunks also allow 32-bit applications to call 16-bit APIs directly. Thunks that implement 32-bit API calls are not built into each 32-bit application, but rather are part of the system. Therefore, applications that use 32-bit API functions that are thunked to 16-bit API functions will benefit transparently from performance increases as more of the system is converted to 32-bit in the future. Thunks depend on LDT tiling to provide an architecture for efficient address conversion between the two memory models.

There are two types of thunks: *16-to-32* and *32-to-16*. The 16-to-32 thunks are used to provide compatibility for a 16-bit API function by mapping it to a new 32-bit API function. They are relatively straightforward to implement, since the 32-bit addressing model is more powerful than is the 16-bit model. The 32-to-16 thunks are used to implement 32-bit API functions using existing 16-bit API functions. The 32-to-16 thunks are a bit more difficult to implement because 16-bit code has difficulty dealing with memory objects that span 64KB linear boundaries in the tiled environment. A 32-bit application can create memory objects that span 64KB linear boundaries. Although it is valid to pass one of these objects to a 32-bit API function, the 32-to-16 thunk that implements the 32-bit API must deal with alignment issues, so that the 16-bit API being used to service the 32-bit API can access the data properly. Both types of thunks exist in OS/2 2.0. The ensuing material about thunks is valid for both types of thunks, but the 32-to-16 case is discussed in more detail.

Thunks must deal with several differences between the 16-bit and 32-bit memory environments:

- Dynamic linking models
- Pointer-parameter conversion
- Stack management
- 64KB restrictions on 16-bit applications

The 32-bit dynamic linking model uses *near calls,* and the 16-bit dynamic linking model uses *far calls.* If a 32-bit application makes a near CALL to a 16-bit segment, a general protection fault usually occurs when the 16-bit code executes the RETF instruction to return to the 32-bit code. This fault occurs because the near CALL pushes EIP on the stack, and the 16-bit RETF interprets the return address as a 16:16 CS:IP. If a 32-bit application directly executes a far CALL to a 16-bit segment, a 48-bit CS:EIP return address is pushed on the stack, since the far CALL is made from a 32-bit segment. Since 48 bits are pushed on the stack, instead of 16 bits, the parameters for the 16-bit code are shifted on the stack, thus breaking compatibility. Also, the RETF executed to return to the caller pops only 32 of the 48 bits off the stack. A 16-bit far call can be made from a 32-bit code segment to a 16-bit code segment, but only from within the first 64KB of the 32-bit segment, since the 16-bit code does not update the high-order word of EIP properly. Therefore, the thunks in OS/2 use a simulated indirect call to make the transition between 16-bit and 32-bit code.

When a thunk needs to transition to the opposite model, it executes a far jump to a stub code segment of the target model. In the case of 32-bit code calling 16-bit code, the 32-bit thunk executes a far JMP instruction to a 16-bit stub segment. The stub segment executes a far call to the 16-bit API function used to implement the 32-bit API function. The 16-bit API completes service, executes a RETF back to the 16-bit code stub, and the stub executes a far JMP back to the instruction following the original jump in the 32-bit code. This approach has no problems with 64KB boundaries, and is transparent to both the 32-bit API caller and the 16-bit API being called by the thunk.

The parameter sizes for the 16-bit and 32-bit models are also different. The 16-bit system uses 16-bit word parameters; the 32-bit system uses 32-bit double words. Thunks must convert between 16-bit words and 32-bit double words by either zero-extending a

16-bit word to a double word, or truncating a double word to a word. Structure parameters also need to be converted by the thunk layer. Structures in the 32-bit model are aligned on double-word boundaries, instead of on word boundaries as in the 16-bit system. Therefore, the structures that are passed input and output parameters to API functions must be realigned and converted to match the model of the API being used to service the request. Furthermore, pointers imbedded in structures are also sensitive to a given calling model, and must be converted. Thunks convert the structures between the two models and understand the semantics of the parameters for each API that is being thunked.

The stack addressing between the two models is also different. The 16-bit API runs using 16-bit-wide stacks that have 16-bit stack pointers. The 32-bit API runs using 32-bit-wide stacks that have 32-bit stack pointers. Furthermore, 16-bit stacks cannot be larger than 64KB, whereas 32-bit stacks have no 64KB restriction on size. Thus, the thunk must construct the correct stack frames and convert between stacks when using one API call to implement another.

Pointer conversion is managed using the LDT tiling mechanism described earlier in this chapter. However, the problem associated with LDT tiling is the inability of 16:16 code to deal with objects that cross 64KB linear boundaries using a single selector. If a 32-bit application passes a converted pointer to an object that crosses a 64KB linear boundary to 16-bit code, the 16-bit code usually generates a general protection fault when trying to access the entire object, or accesses the wrong data depending on the access semantics. Although LDT tiling has benefits in the areas of speed and symmetry, it does not deal gracefully with the problem of crossing 64KB boundaries.

The 32-to-16 thunks in OS/2 implement several strategies, depending on the size of the memory object, for dealing with the 64KB boundary problem. Small objects—those smaller than 129 bytes—can be copied to an aligned temporary buffer on the stack without much performance penalty. However, copying large objects that straddle 64KB linear boundaries is not a feasible option, since it would be too slow. For large objects, OS/2 thunks use a feature called *linear address aliasing*. Linear address aliasing takes the address of an object that spans a 64KB boundary, and the size of the object, and proceeds to create another linear address on a new 64KB boundary that maps the same physical memory. It asks the virtual memory manager to create an alias in the process's arena, and calls the page manager to copy the page table entries from the original object that straddles a 64KB linear boundary to the new object that does not. This process is effectively the same as allocating a tiled segment whose contents are defined by an object that crosses a 64KB boundary. The new linear address is 64KB aligned, and has an associated new tiled descriptor. However, since aliasing must be done by the kernel, it is relatively slow compared to the LDT tiling arithmetic address conversion. Thunks must free aliases when the latter are no longer being used.

Due to guarantees provided by the language tools for 32-bit applications, few cases require aliasing. Statically allocated load-time objects smaller than 64KB are guaranteed not to cross 64KB linear boundaries, as are memory objects that are dynamically allocated using the C run-time library (i.e., *malloc* and *free)*. Stack objects, or automatic objects in the C language, can cross a 64KB linear boundary, but they are handled by the thunk layer. Furthermore, if an application directly calls *DosAllocMem,* creates an object that straddles 64KB linear boundaries, and passes an offset from that object into a 32-bit API that is thunked to a 16-bit API such that the boundary condition is created, then the thunk handles the boundary condition.

There are also 16-bit restrictions based on stack space. The 32-bit API allows stacks to be larger than 64KB. The 16-bit API requires stacks to fit within a 64KB segment. In OS/2 2.0, stack objects are tiled. However, the 64KB boundary can cause serious problems when a stack pointer is converted from one model to the other. The problem is that, as the stack grows in memory toward a 64KB linear boundary, if the stack pointer is converted to a 16:16 address, the stack pointer is already near the bottom or end of the stack, leaving insufficient stack space to complete the service. Therefore, if the stack pointer is within 4KB of a 64KB linear boundary, the stack pointer is bumped down to the next 64KB boundary before it is converted to 16-bits. This strategy ensures the 16-bit code has plenty of stack space. The thunk layer is optimized so that the stack is bumped only once per call, even if execution flows between several API functions that are implemented using thunks.

The following describes the sequence of operations that occur in a typical 32-to-16 thunk. First, the stack is bumped down to the next 64KB linear boundary if necessary. Then, for each input parameter, the parameter is converted to 16 bits, and is put in the stack frame in preparation for calling a 16-bit API function. The conversion of the contents of a stack frame is done by the LDT tiling formula, by copying for small objects that cross 64KB boundaries, or by aliasing for large objects that cross 64KB boundaries. The stack pointer is then converted to 16 bits, and the simulated indirect call is used to invoke the 16-bit API function. After returning from the 16-bit API function, each output parameter is converted to the correct 32-bit syntax specified by the 32-bit API function. The stack is then restored, and the 32-bit API function completes and returns the return code to the 32-bit requestor.

The 16-to-32 bit thunks are significantly simpler than are 32-to-16 thunks, since there are no 64KB boundary problems. However, the 16-to-32 thunks must simulate segment protection semantics in software, since the 32-bit memory model provides page-granular protection. Otherwise, flat-model code could inadvertently or maliciously corrupt memory after converting 16:16 pointer parameters to 0:32. Therefore, before pointers are converted from 16-bit to 32-bit, protection checking is simulated by the thunk.

Thunk creation and coding can be automated. Within the OS/2 project, a thunk compiler was used to generate the code for the thunks used by the system. The thunk compiler uses a C-like high-level language to describe API functions and the relationship between functions. This language describes parameters, types, and conversions that are applied, and tells the compiler how to generate code to map one API function using another.

SUMMARY

This chapter described compatibility in OS/2. It discussed the technologies used to provide DOS compatibility on the 80286 and 80386 platforms. It also examined Windows 3.0 compatibility, and explained how 16-bit OS/2 applications run on 32-bit OS/2.

TERMINOLOGY

application base
A20 line
A20 wrap area
bimodal code
bimodal device driver model
binary compatibility
compatibility
Dev Help(PhysToVirt)
DevHelp(ROMCritSection)
DevHelp(SetROMVector)
DevHelp(UnPhysToVirt)
DosAllocMem
DOS compatibility
DOS emulation
double fault
8086 emulation
80386 DOS compatibility
80386 OS/2 1.X binary compatibility
80286 DOS compatibility
ExitKMode
far call
flat addressing
global event
hook (a software or hardware interrupt)
interrupt table shadowing
interrupt vector table
I/O permission map (IOPM)
LDT tiling
linear address aliasing
LOADALL
local event
migration
mode switching
multiple virtual DOS machine (MVDM)
  technology
near call

OS/2 protected-mode interrupt manager
per-VDM memory area
physical device driver (PDD)
postreflection hook
power-on self-test (POST)
prereflection hook
protection
retention
reuse
segmented addressing
shutdown status
16-to-32 thunk
software interrupt reflection
source compatibility
32-to-16 thunk
thread information block (TIB)
thunk
tile bit
tile flag
tile option
tiled memory
triple fault
VDM breakpoint
VDM event
VDM management
VDM manager
v86 address space
virtual device driver (VDD)
virtual device helper (*VDHelp*) services
virtual DOS machine (VDM)
virtual 8086 (v86) mode
virtual programmable interrupt controller
  (VPIC)
virtualization of DOS devices
watchdog timer

EXERCISES

10.1   Define "compatibility" in the context of OS/2.

10.2   Distinguish between binary compatibility and source compatibility. Discuss the advantages and disadvantages of each. Explain why a software vendor might be reluctant to distribute the source code of its products.

10.3   What does it mean to be "DOS compatible"?

10.4   How is the 80286 switched from real mode to protected mode? How is it switched from protected mode to real mode? What PS/2 capability facilitates switching the 80286 from protected mode to real mode?

10.5   Why is it not possible for OS/2 to run DOS applications in the background?

10.6   What is the A20 wrap area?

10.7   Explain the technique of interrupt table shadowing.

10.8   What is tiled memory? What memory objects are normally tiled?

10.9   What are the limitations of DOS compatibility under the 80286 architecture?

10.10   What features make the 80386 architecture superior to that of the 80286 for providing DOS compatibility?

10.11   Discuss OS/2 2.0's multiple virtual DOS machine (MVDM) technology. Consider protection, support of extended memory options, accessing of block devices, and other key issues.

10.12   Explain the functions of the major components of the MVDM kernel, including VDM management, DOS emulation, 8086 emulation, and virtual device drivers (VDDs).

10.13   Discuss the operation of the VDM manager.

10.14   Distinguish between global and local VDM events.

10.15   Explain the notion of software interrupt reflection as used in the 8086 emulation component of the MVDM architecture.

10.16   Explain what it means to "hook a software interrupt." Distinguish between prereflection hook and postreflection hook.

10.17   Why is it not necessary for OS/2 device drivers to be bimodal?

10.18   Why do VDMs receive hardware interrupts not at interrupt time, but rather at task time?

10.19   How is Windows 3.X compatibility implemented in OS/2 2.X?

10.20   The 32-bit OS/2 system provides three means for 32-bit APIs and 16-bit APIs to coexist. Describe each of these techniques.

10.21   The memory model of 16-bit OS/2 allows for byte-granular memory access. In 32-bit OS/2, memory is accessed one page at a time, and is said to be page granular. Thus, when compatibility is implemented, multiple 16-bit segments could be packed on a single page. What problem would this packing create? How does 32-bit OS/2 reconcile this problem? What additional problem does the solution create?

10.22   Explain the technique of LDT tiling. Describe how LDT tiling affects the maximum size of virtual address spaces in OS/2. Discuss several significant problems associated with LDT tiling.

10.23   Explain why the following statement is true: "Applications that use 32-bit API functions thunked to 16-bit API functions will benefit transparently from performance increases as more of the OS/2 system is converted to 32-bit in the future."

10.24   Why are 32-to-16 thunks more difficult to implement than are 16-to-32 thunks?

10.25   Discuss the differences between the 16-bit and 32-bit memory environments with which thunks must deal. In particular, consider dynamic linking models, pointer-parameter conversion, stack management, and the 64KB restrictions on 16-bit applications.

10.26 Explain the notion of linear address aliasing used with OS/2 thunks.

10.27 Describe the sequence of operations that occurs in a typical 32-to-16 thunk.

10.28 In the context of the MVDM architecture, describe a scenario in which a simulated interrupt must be delayed because the VDM's interrupts are disabled. Keep in mind that, since IOPL = 3, the VDM uses the real IF of the system. Also, remember that VDMs run in the background, and that VDDs can block when servicing I/O traps.

11
Communications

Live in fragments no longer. Only connect.

Edward Morgan Forster

Conversation is but carving!
Give no more to every guest,
Than he's able to digest.
Give him always of the prime,
And but little at a time.
Carve to all but just enough,
Let them neither starve nor stuff,
And that you may have your due,
Let your neighbor carve for you.

Jonathan Swift

315

Outline

11.1 INTRODUCTION

This chapter describes communications in the OS/2 system. An overview of the significant network architectures—*OSI, SNA,* and *TCP/IP*—and the strategies for their coexistence sets the foundation for discussion of the communications role played by OS/2 workstations. OS/2's conformance to key network standards is described in the context of the distributed single-user workstation environment. This chapter also examines *multi-user OS/2,* a low-cost alternative to networks for sharing processing resources.

11.2 NETWORKS

Networks enable computer users to communicate with one another and to share computing resources. Data-communication systems range from small networks that interconnect terminals and computers in a single building, to networks that are distributed worldwide.

Networks are composed of *nodes,* typically *intermediate nodes, end-user nodes,* and *gateways.* Intermediate nodes form the *backbone* of the network for passing data between systems. End-user nodes are points at which users access the network. Multiple networks can be connected using a gateway. Gateways provide protocol translation and interfacing between networks of disparate architectures, and are needed for internetwork service. The *network topology* describes the interconnection scheme of the nodes that compose a network, and the access points available to users.

There are two principal types of data communication network technologies in general use today: *circuit-switched* and *packet-switched* networks. The telephone system is a circuit-switched network. Circuit-switched networks are *connection-oriented*—that is, a private transmission path or connection must be established between users before data can flow back and forth over the circuit, exactly as in a telephone call. In the telephone network, connections are established using dedicated private channels and trunk lines.

Packet-switched network technology transfers blocks of data, called *packets*, across the network. Packet-switched networks are used to connect digital devices, such as host computers, communication controllers, terminals, workstations, and printers. Depending on the scope of the network topology, packet-switched networks range from *wide area networks (WANs)* distributed over large geographical areas, to *local area networks (LANs)* distributed over relatively small areas. On a packet-switched network, packets from multiple users share the same distribution and transmission facilities. The packets are *stored and forwarded* at each network node, along with other packets that share the same communication links.

There are two types of *connection modes* in packet-switched networks: *connection-oriented* and *connectionless.* In connection-oriented mode, a *virtual-circuit* connection must be established between the source and destination before packets are transferred between them. The packets must be transmitted and received sequentially between the source and the destination. In connectionless mode, packets are routed across all connections and may arrive out of order. These packets are also known as *datagrams.* Connectionless datagram transmission is analogous to transmission of mail in the postal system.

As computer technology proliferated in the 1960s and 1970s, major packet-switched networks were created to allow international access to the data stored on computer systems. Networks, such as Tymshare's *TYMNET* and GTE's *TELENET,* were created to serve this need. Both of these networks are based on *X.25*, a worldwide standard packet-switched network architecture.

The ARPAnet network was an experiment funded by the *Advanced Research Projects Agency (ARPA)* of the *Department of Defense (DOD)*. The goal of ARPAnet was to connect major computer resources in universities, laboratories, and companies across the United States. ARPAnet was a packet-switched X.25-accessible network that developed and advanced the state of packet-switching technology. ARPAnet was a pioneer of internetwork connection and routing technology. GTE's TELENET network grew out of the ARPAnet research, as did the TCP/IP protocols.

11.3 OPEN SYSTEMS INTERCONNECTION

The development of packet-switching technology and the existence of many disparate network architectures led to communication problems among these different systems. The *International Standards Organization (ISO)* proposed the *Open Systems Interconnection (OSI) reference model* in 1978 to describe the external behavior of *open systems*. In the context of OSI, an open system is a collection of equipment—such as peripherals, computers, terminals and applications—that obeys a standard set of protocols when communicating with other open systems. Note that the OSI reference model standard describes the external behavior of open systems, but does not describe the internal behavior.

OSI will play an important role in the future of the computer industry. The movement toward standardization will allow a high degree of *interoperability* between existing systems, even if these systems are supplied by different vendors. Furthermore, equipment and hardware will become more of a commodity in the future, resulting in more economical equipment and a greater variety of options for users. Interoperability allows users greater access to networks and open systems. OSI is also playing an important role because of the U.S.government's adoption of OSI in the *Government OSI Profile (GOSIP)* that outlines the requirements for government systems procurement.

OSI is a *layered network architecture,* a concept that originated with IBM's *Systems Network Architecture (SNA)* in 1974. IBM staff realized that the problem of allowing systems to communicate required a two-part solution that would ensure that:

- The data delivered by users would arrive at the destination correctly and in a timely fashion.
- The data delivered to the end user at the destination would be recognizable and in proper form.

Low-level or *network-level protocols* handle the delivery of data between nodes on a network, and *user-level protocols* handle the syntax and semantics of the data so that those data are recognizable by end-user programs. Thus, end users see a transparent pipe for network communication, freeing end-user programs from details about the under-lying network media connecting the distributed systems.

11.4 OSI REFERENCE MODEL

The OSI reference model is a layered architecture with seven layers. The layers group together similar functions, and are organized so that interactions across layer boundaries are minimized. Each layer is effectively shielded from details of the layers below it, and each layer provides services to the layer above it. The layers implement their services to the layers above by using and extending the services of the layers below. Of the seven layers of the OSI reference model, layers 1, 2, and 3 are network service related, and layers 5, 6, and 7 are end user related. Layer 4 is usually grouped with the user-level protocols, but actually shields layers 5 and 6 from the specifics of the network-level pro-tocols. Figure 11.1 illustrates the OSI reference model showing two end-user nodes and an intermediate node.

In Fig. 11.1, the end-user nodes could potentially be on networks with different physical media connecting them. The intermediate node serves as a network gateway and routing node, as part of the backbone of the network.

Protocols allow communication between corresponding layers in connected open systems. Different protocol options may be used in each layer without affecting the layer definition. Thus, a *protocol stack* refers to a cut through the layers for a specific choice of protocols. Each layer provides *service access points (SAPs)* to the layer above. A

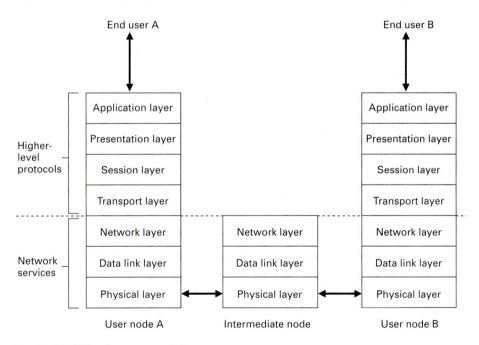

Fig. 11.1   OSI reference model.

service access point is analogous to an API interface to the protocols provided by a layer. Each layer implements its protocols by adding control information to outgoing data as the data move down the layers of the source end-user node. Each layer processes data arriving from lower layers by analyzing and stripping the control information added to the data when they were sent, and then propagates the data up the layers at the destination end-user node.

Layer 1 of the OSI reference model is the *physical layer*. It describes how bits enter the physical medium and how they are received. The following are examples of standards used for the physical layer:

- RS232-C (CCITT V.24)
- CCITT V.35
- CCITT X.21
- ISDN

RS232-C is used for asynchronous communications. *CCITT V.35* describes point-to-point connections across a coaxial connection. *CCITT X.21* is used throughout Europe for supporting X.25 packet-switched networks. *ISDN (Integrated Services Digital Network)* describes the digital physical medium for the next generation of the world's telephone networks.

Layer 2 of the reference model is the *data link layer,* which ensures that blocks and *frames* are transferred reliably and without error across the physical medium. A data link is established across the physical media, and is used by the layers above layer 2. WANs use *high-level data link control (HDLC),* as their protocol for data link control. X.25 packet-switched networks use *LAPB,* a subset of HDLC. IBM SNA networks use *synchronous data link control (SDLC),* a precursor and proper subset of HDLC. LANs use the *IEEE 802.2* standard that describes how LANs accommodate the OSI data link and physical layers. 802.2 provides logical link control for LANs, and supports several major LAN architectures in the following standards: *802.3* for *Ethernet* and the *IBM PC Network, 802.4* for *token bus,* and *802.5* for *token ring.* Together, the physical and data link layers provide point-to-point error-free communication between two nodes on a network.

Layer 3 of the reference model is the *network layer.* It is the topmost layer of the network-specific protocols in the OSI reference model. The network layer performs source and destination routing within a network, and also provides *internetwork routing.* The network layer provides *flow control* and *congestion control* across nodes; it uses the data link layer for moving blocks. In circuit-switched systems, the network layer provides path management and virtual circuits using HDLC or SDLC interfaces from the data link layer. In packet-switched systems such as X.25, the network layer primarily provides *packet addressing* and *routing.*

Layer 4 of the OSI reference model is the *transport layer;* it ensures reliable, sequenced exchange of data between end users. The transport layer is the lowest layer of the upper-level user protocols. It shields the upper layers from details of network connections. It provides flow control and *buffering* to free the upper layers from addressing issues such as network performance, error control, and reliability. The transport layer also can provide *error recovery and detection* and *multiplexing* functions.

The *OSI transport protocol* (OSI TP) specification has five classes, *TP0–TP4,* that are based on the reliability of the network layer. The different classes provide varying amounts of error recovery, error detection, and multiplexing based on whether these capabilities are present in the underlying network-specific layers being used by the transport layer. The standard transport layer supported in most OSI environments is *TP4,* which is the functional equivalent of the *TCP transport protocol* used in TCP/IP networks (see Section 11.5).

Layer 5 of the OSI reference model is the *session layer*. A session is a conversation between two end users. Sessions must first be established by one user calling the other to create a *connection*. Hence, session protocols are connection oriented. Once the session is established, the two users can transfer data, and can disconnect the session when the conversation is over. The OSI session management specification provides for data control and transfer using an established session, and for the organization and synchronization of data flowing over the session connection. *NetBIOS* is an example of a session-level protocol.

Layer 6 of the reference model is the *presentation layer*. The presentation layer manages and transforms the syntax of data units exchanged between end users. It provides a high-level data interchange abstraction for network applications running in layer 7. An example of a presentation layer function is providing *EBCDIC/ASCII transparency* for a terminal emulator that provides a connection across the network. Since the presentation layer presents a format-independent data stream to applications, the terminal emulator program does not have to be concerned about the data format. Other presentation layer functions are the OS/2 and DOS network redirector and device sharing capabilities. The *OS/2 network redirector* is described in Section 11.7.

Layer 7 of the reference model is the *application layer*. Whereas the presentation layer manages the syntax of the data, the application layer interprets the semantics of the data exchanged between end users and applications. Layer 7 defines *application service elements (ASEs)* and *application control service elements (ACSEs),* which define application protocols used by distributed programs. OSI specifies many application protocols that are used by distributed network applications, including

- *X.400 Message Handling*
- *X.500 Directory Services*
- *File Transfer, Access, and Management (FTAM)*
- *Virtual Terminal (VT)*
- *Distributed Transaction Processing (DTP)*

11.5 X.25

The X.25 specification is a three-layer network-level interface for packet-switched WANs. It describes how *data terminal equipment (DTE)* and *data circuit-terminating equipment (DCE)* are connected. An example of DTE is a terminal. Host computers or communications controllers are typical DCEs. DTE connections are provided by the interconnection of DCEs. The network manages the connection between DCEs. The X.25 interface regulates data flow between DTEs and DCEs. The three layers of the X.25 specification correspond closely to OSI reference model layers 1, 2, and 3. Figure 11.2 illustrates the architecture of X.25.

The X.25 specification provides an interface for programs to user DTEs. X.25 is an interface specification; it is not a protocol. The network or packet-level X.25 layer provides virtual circuit and datagram services across logical channels. The multiplexing of data from the logical channels onto one data link saves network resources. It provides channel connect and disconnect procedures, as well as packet-level data transfer and error checking. It uses the *link access procedures balanced (LAPB)* protocol for data link control. LAPB is a subset of HDLC and is used to provide a data link between DCEs and DTEs. This single data link supports the data transferred between all the logical channels defined by the packet layer. The physical layer of X.25 systems is described by the X.21 specification for point-to-point synchronous circuit transmissions. X.21 provides a physical connection between DTEs and DCEs.

11.6 LANS

Networks within a building, a campus, or a set of buildings no more than several kilometers from end to end are classified as LANs. IEEE standard 802.2 describes the relationship of LANs to OSI layers 1 and 2. It has been adopted as a standard protocol for

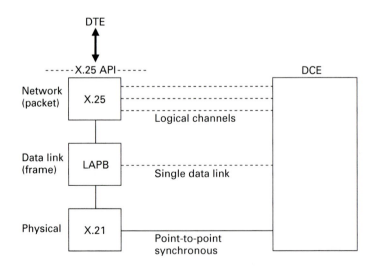

Fig. 11.2 X.25 architecture. (Reprinted from M. Schwartz, *Telecommunications Networks: Protocols, Modeling and Analysis,* Copyright 1987, Addison-Wesley Publishing Co., Reading, MA. Reprinted by permission.)

data link control and physical layers. IEEE 802.2 divides the data link control layer into two parts: the *logical link control (LLC)* and *medium access control (MAC)* sublayers. Figure 11.3 illustrates the IEEE 802.2 LAN standard.

The LLC sublayer defines the 802.2 interface. It constitutes the upper portion of layer 2. It uses the services of the MAC sublayer to provide services to the network layer above. The data link control model is independent of the physical medium and of the MAC. It defines the protocol used to manage one or more logical connections, called *link stations,* through a single physical medium. There are two types of LLC: *connection oriented* and *connectionless.* In connection-oriented service, error recovery is based on a subset of HDLC. In connectionless service, there is no error recovery—it must be supplied by the upper layers. Thus, 802.2 and TP4 dovetail into the OSI LAN strategy nicely, since 802.2 connectionless mode does not provide error recovery, but TP4 at the transport level does.

The MAC sublayer standard covers layer 1 and part of layer 2 in the OSI reference model. It is responsible for maintaining the rules of protocol of the network. It performs the framing, addressing, timing, and error detection for link stations at the logical level. Popular MAC types include

- 802.3 (CSMA/CD)
- 802.4 (token bus)
- 802.5 (token ring)
- 802.6 (metropolitan area networks)

The 802.3 standard describes *carrier sense, multiple access with collision detection (CSMA/CD)* LANs such as Ethernet and the original IBM PC Network. Ethernet was invented by Xerox, DEC, and Intel. When a node on a CSMA/CD network needs to send data, it listens for a window in which a packet can be sent. Once a packet is sent, it either arrives at a destination or *collision* with another packet. The sending node is

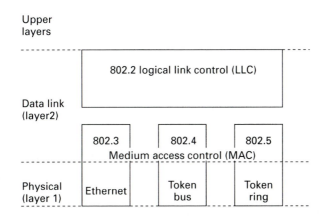

Fig. 11.3   IEEE 802 LAN standards.

notified of the collision and implements a collision detection strategy, usually to resend the packet. Control of access to CSMA/CD networks is similar to what happens when people are talking at a party. If several people start talking at once (collision), they stop, wait, and then restart talking.

CSMA/CD is a random access network scheme with a *contention-based access* mechanism, so large amounts of network traffic can degrade network performance, since collision rates can increase quickly. Thus, it is inappropriate for real-time systems such as those used in factory automation, because it lacks predictable, deterministic responses under heavy loads.

The 802.5 standard describes the *token ring*, developed by IBM Research in Zurich, Switzerland. A node on a token ring network accesses the physical medium when it has a *token*. A token is a bit pattern that permits a node to transmit data on the network. The token ring mechanism effectively provides a type of decentralized polling, where the polling token is passed among peer workstations. Token ring strategies provide more consistent performance during periods of heavy network traffic than do CSMA/CD networks.

The 802.4 standard describes the MAC protocol for token bus networks. The *token bus* is similar to the token ring, except that the nodes are connected using a bus topology instead of a ring topology. 802.6 describes access for metropolitan area networks (MANs), such as those used for cable television (CATV).

11.7 SYSTEMS NETWORK ARCHITECTURE

IBM's earliest projects in data communications connected host computers and terminals in *master/slave hierarchies*. As users required greater access to *host computers* and printers, specialized computers called *communication controllers* were developed. Communication controllers offload communication handling duties from host computers shared by multiple users, and connect different host computer resources. As users' needs for data communication and access continued to grow, IBM recognized the need for a network architecture that would lay the foundation for connecting current and future components to IBM networks. This recognition led to the development of a layered communication architecture in which network-specific and user-specific tasks were separated. IBM's Systems Network Architecture (SNA), introduced in 1974, was the first layered network architecture. Portions of SNA are used in the OSI definition, but the two standards are not the same. SNA is a proprietary IBM architecture originally based on a centralized network model; it now includes a distributed *peer-to-peer* network model. Chapter 12 describes the role of SNA within IBM's *Systems Application Architecture (SAA)*.

The major architectural components of SNA networks are *logical units (LUs), physical units (PUs)*, and *system service control points (SSCPs)*. PUs, LUs, and SSCPs are *network addressable units (NAUs)*. LUs are intermediaries used by end users and programs for accessing the network. End users transfer data across an LU-to-LU connection using sessions. Each node in the network is a physical unit. Examples of physical units are processors, communication controllers, printers, and workstations. Multiple logical units can map to a single physical unit at a given node. SSCP is used to manage network resources, to coordinate LU-to-LU sessions, and to manage subsets of PUs and LUs called *domains*. Figure 11.4 illustrates the layers of the IBM SNA architecture.

At the top of the SNA architecture is the *LU services manager,* also called the *transaction manager*. It is used by applications and end users for accessing the network. End-user programs that use the transaction manager to establish LU-to-LU sessions are called *transaction programs (TPs)*. Multiple transaction programs can share a single logical unit.

The next layer in the SNA architecture is the *presentation services layer*. It performs data transformation, encoding and compression of data, and display formatting. The presentation service layer of SNA is comparable but not identical to the OSI presentation layer. Other layers of the SNA architecture are also similar to layers of the OSI reference model.

Below the presentation services layer is the *data flow control layer,* which performs sequencing and multiplexing of user messages across active sessions. The *transmission control layer* provides end-to-end flow control, called *session pacing* in SNA terminology. It is the bottommost layer of the user-level services that insulates the user-level protocols from the network. The data flow control layer and the transmission control layer together are almost comparable to the OSI session and transport layers.

The *path control layer* has a role similar to the OSI network layer. It performs routing and congestion control for network traffic and data flow between NAUs. Path control multiplexes LU sessions at a node across a given single path, and uses SDLC frames between adjacent nodes to transmit data. SNA data streams can also be routed over X.25 packet-switched networks. The data link control and physical layers of SNA are similar

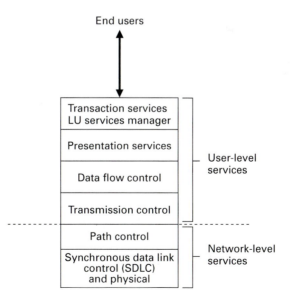

Fig. 11.4   IBM SNA architecture. (Courtesy of International Business Machines Corporation.)

to layers 1 and 2 of the OSI model. They provide error-free transmission of data units across physical connections. SDLC manages synchronous information transfer between nodes joined by telecommunication links.

In the early 1980s, IBM recognized that the future of SNA, and of networking in general, lay in *peer-to-peer distributed computing,* instead of in the centralized network model from which SNA evolved. To meet future requirements, IBM developed *LU6.2,* an architecture for distributed peer-to-peer computing. LU6.2 provides a model that is independent of processor type or operating system. The *Advanced Program-to-Program Communication (APPC)* facility is an interface that enables programs on any SNA node supporting LU6.2 to communicate and to exchange data. APPC and LU6.2 are implemented across all significant IBM architectures from mainframes to workstations. SNA and APPC/LU6.2 play a key role in the Common Communications Architecture (CCA) portion of IBM's SAA.

11.8 TCP/IP

TCP/IP is a set of protocols that evolved to connect universities, laboratories, and companies over ARPAnet. It is a four-layer network architecture that primarily focuses on internetwork connections. Figure 11.5 shows the four layers of the TCP/IP architecture.

At the lowest layer of TCP/IP are data link and physical layers that correspond to those found in the OSI reference model. TCP/IP systems support X.25, 802.2, and many other physical media.

The layer above the data link layer of TCP/IP is the *internet layer*. It is similar to the network layer of the OSI reference model. It is actually a subset of the OSI network layer that has been enhanced to provide *internetwork routing and addressing*. However, the network layer does not provide reliable connection services; rather, it depends on the transport layer to provide reliable connections, error detection, and error recovery. Another protocol used in the internet layer is the *internet control message protocol (ICMP),* used for internetwork control messages.

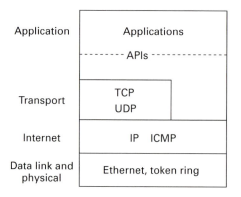

Fig. 11.5   TCP/IP architecture. (From *OS/2 Notebook,* Copyright 1990, Microsoft Corporation. Reprinted by permission of Microsoft Press.)

The third layer of the TCP/IP architecture is the *transport layer*. Two major protocols are used in the transport layer: *transport control protocol (TCP)* and *user datagram protocol (UDP)*. TCP is the equivalent of the OSI transport protocol implemented to class 4 (TP4), since it provides error detection and recovery. It is used in packet-switched networks in which network-level data are not guaranteed to be delivered reliably and in sequence, as in the IP environment.

TCP provides connection-oriented data transfer between users. Data are delivered reliably and in sequence, despite the shortcomings of IP. Like any other connection-oriented protocol, TCP has three phases: *connection, data transfer,* and *disconnection.* TCP transfers stream-oriented data. For example, TCP is used by upper-layer protocols for *virtual terminal* and *file transfer.* Data are delivered continuously by upper layers, and are blocked by TCP into segments for transmission over the network. The other major protocol in the transport layer, UDP, is used for connectionless datagram service with no reliability guaranteed across IP links.

The fourth and uppermost layer in TCP/IP is the *application layer*. Many application protocols are defined that are used by applications running on TCP/IP systems. These are some of the more prevalent protocols:

- *TELNET (terminal emulation protocol)*
- *FTP (file transfer protocol)*
- *SMTP (simple mail transfer protocol)*
- *X/Windows* (distributed window management)
- *NFS (network file system)*
- *Kerberos (user authentification)*

Many of these protocols depend on *sockets,* a basic interprocess communication mechanism originally created in the *Berkeley UNIX* distributions. Sockets provide an IPC abstraction independent of the underlying network and protocols. Sockets are similar to OS/2's named pipes or NetBIOS's interprocess communication mechanisms. However, sockets are a low-level API that require processor-specific information such as knowledge of addressing and byte ordering. Application protocols constructed over sockets must manage processor-specific information for end-user programs.

Sockets are implemented on TCP/IP systems using the TCP, UDP, ICMP, and IP protocols. There are three types of sockets: *stream sockets, datagram sockets,* and *raw sockets.* Sockets are usually programmed in the stream or datagram modes. Stream sockets are used for virtual circuit connections. Datagram sockets are used for connectionless transmissions. Sun Microsystems's *Network File System (NFS)* is built on datagram sockets and UDP. FTP and TELNET are built on stream sockets and TCP.

11.9 NETWORK COEXISTENCE

Network coexistence is concerned with how SNA and TCP/IP—two disparate networking schemes—can be used together and internetworked with OSI. There are two main issues in connecting disparate networks and OSI: *coexistence* and *migration.* Coexistence allows an existing system to support internetworking with another system by integrating OSI support and allowing both types of applications to coexist. Migration implies that users leave their current system to move to OSI. Most vendors consider OSI essential for the future. Vendors are adding OSI support incrementally to proprietary architectures, and are allowing the two to coexist. Thus, vendors are putting themselves in a position to exploit OSI as more OSI products become available, while providing support for installed bases.

There are two main coexistence strategies used in most systems: *stack based* and *service based*. Stack-based strategies have *dual protocol stacks* on a single system. For instance, to allow SNA and TCP/IP to coexist, a system might support SNA and TCP/IP protocol suites simultaneously. An *application gateway* can be used as a bridge to connect the two protocol stacks. However, the stack-based approach is expensive and has poor performance due to the massive protocol conversion that must occur. These restrictions prohibit stack-based strategies from providing end-to-end transmission, and limit them to message support only.

The service-based coexistence strategy is built on *bridges* and *routers*. It is a layer-oriented mapping of two networks. For example, to enable OSI applications to run on a TCP/IP network, we might choose to map the OSI transport layer onto the TCP/IP protocol stack by emulating the OSI TP4 protocol using TCP/IP. This approach is the *transport bridge*. Other types of layer-oriented coexistence strategies exist; for example, *service tunnels* or *routers* essentially perform the same actions as do transport bridges at the network layer or data link layer.

It is interesting to compare and contrast the functionality of OSI, SNA, TCP and IP, and to take a look at how these schemes coexist today. SNA is a full-function network that has had many years to evolve. It provides connectivity, a high degree of network management, predictable performance, and reliability. It has a large installed base, and is a platform for transaction processing and distributed applications through IBM and IBM-connected systems.

OSI is an open architecture backed by many international organizations. Networks that conform to OSI have a high degree of interoperability. This interoperability allows users to choose among hardware and software products custom-tailored to their needs. IBM provides support for OSI in X.25-based WAN and 802.2-based LAN environments. It allows both SNA and OSI to coexist.

OSI and TCP/IP are a bit different. OSI is significantly richer than TCP/IP, especially at the application layer. However, TCP/IP has a huge installed base. As described earlier in this section, OSI applications can be supported on TCP/IP systems using router and bridge technology. Usually, OSI and TCP/IP coexist using gateway architectures. Many parts of TCP/IP are similar to parts of OSI. For example, the IP protocol of TCP/IP is similar to the layer 3 internet network protocol used in OSI. The TCP protocol is similar to TP class 4 of the OSI transport layer. The TELNET application protocol is similar to the OSI VTP protocol, and the file transfer protocol of TCP/IP is similar to the FTAM protocol of OSI. Also, SMTP (simple mail transfer protocol) of TCP/IP is similar to the OSI X.400 and X.500 protocols. Although these application protocols perform similar functions, they are slightly different in implementation. Both OSI and TCP/IP networks can share data links and coexist at physical levels. Figure 11.6 compares OSI, SNA, and TCP/IP.

11.10 OS/2 EXTENDED EDITION

This section examines how OS/2 fits into the role of open systems, and how it supports OSI, SNA, and TCP/IP network interconnection. IBM's OS/2 Extended Edition (EE) includes the *Communications Manager (CM)* and the *Database Manager (DM)*. The CM provides SNA, LAN, and TCP/IP access and connectivity. Other products, such as *Microsoft's LAN Manager* and *Novell Netware,* address similar LAN networking needs.

The CM provides three categories of functions: SNA support, LAN support, and TCP/IP support. The SNA support includes

- 3270 terminal emulation, file transfer, and printer access
- *Emulator high-level language API (EHLLAPI)*
- *Asynchronous communications driver interface (ACDI)*
- APPC/LU6.2
- X.25
- SNA gateway

The CM provides application programs for *3270 terminal emulation*, file transfer, and remote printing. These programs use the EHLLAPI, which is designed to allow applications to access the 3270 data stream. A single workstation can have multiple VM and MVS sessions running at a time. The *ACDI* API provides access to serial communications. APPC/LU6.2, the strategic peer-to-peer distributed programming

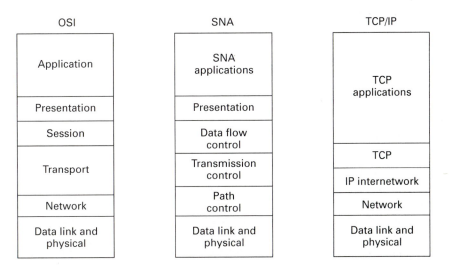

Fig. 11.6 Comparison of OSI, SNA, and TCP/IP.

interface, enables OS/2 applications to communicate with applications running on any LU6.2 system.

The CM provides X.25 support that allows SNA data streams and non-SNA X.25 DTE application data streams to be multiplexed across X.25 packet-switched networks. X.25 is another strategic part of SNA playing the role of defining how SNA systems connect with packet-switched WANs.

The SNA gateway effectively turns a server on the LAN into a multiplexing node that performs communications controller tasks for workstations on the LAN. It allows terminal emulation and APPC programs running on workstations attached to the LAN to access the host system in a transparent fashion. The connectivity of the SNA portion of the CM allows EHLLAPI programs, APPC/LU6.2 programs, and X.25 programs to be distributed over a coaxial attachment, channel-attached to a host, or attached to the host via a LAN using the SNA gateway feature. The APPC/LU6.2, EHLLAPI, and X.25 interfaces are mapped to 802.2 LAN interfaces when running in a LAN-connected environment, and are mapped to a SDLC data link control protocol when running in a coaxial-connected environment.

OS/2 LAN support is packaged in two portions: the *LAN requestor* and the *LAN server*. The LAN requestor is included in the OS/2 EE, but the server program is packaged separately. The LAN requestor allows OS/2 workstations to access files, devices, and programs on a variety of LAN architectures. OS/2 workstations can communicate with DOS, UNIX, VM, and MVS environments. The LAN requestor shipped with OS/2 EE provides

- LAN requestor program
- Network redirector
- LAN API
- 802.2 LLC API
- Network device drivers

The LAN requestor program is a network application that uses the LAN API and OS/2 system services to provide a PM interface for a workstation on the LAN. It allows the user to log in to the network, and thus to access shared resources such as files, printers, named pipes, and messaging services. The *network redirector* is an installable file system that supports redirection of file-level and device-level I/O across the network. Network device drivers that are included with the LAN requestor are 802.2-compliant and support Ethernet, token ring, and IBM PC Network media.

The LAN API provides services for distributed applications to perform distributed interprocess communications for client–server applications, to execute administration and security tasks, and to manage access to network resources. The LAN API provides support for NetBIOS, a layer 5 session management interface, which is mapped onto the 802.2 protocol stack at the data link layer. The LAN API includes two other interprocess communication mechanisms: *mailslots,* and *named pipes* from the OS/2 base. Both of these interprocess communication mechanisms are mapped onto the NetBIOS interface. The network redirector file system driver uses NetBIOS sessions to send local I/O requests to a remote *file server* or *print server.*

The LAN server program is similar to the LAN requestor program, but it has file and device server software that services requests from requestors. Otherwise, the components of the LAN server and requestor are identical. A system running as a server can also be used concurrently as an SNA gateway, an administration machine, and a requestor machine. The LAN server also supports *superserver* configurations with two 80386 or 80486 processors. The LAN server dedicates one of the processors to the network and file system support, while the other processor runs the base OS/2 system.

The CM also provides TCP/IP support. It allows a LAN user to interoperate with systems in a TCP/IP network. The sockets API is supported on the OS/2 TCP/IP stack, and the TCP/IP stack is mapped onto the 802.2 LAN interfaces. The TCP/IP stack has its own data link on the LAN provided through the 802.2 layer. There is no support for allowing NetBIOS applications to run on top of the TCP/IP stack. However, such support probably will be implemented in the future. Of the TCP/IP API and protocols supported, OS/2 TCP/IP support provides sockets, FTP, TELNET, SMTP, X/Windows, Sun NFS, Apollo NCS, RPC, and Kerberos. Figure 11.7 illustrates the OS/2 protocol stacks for LAN, TCP/IP, and SNA.

11.11 MULTIUSER OS/2

Configuring workstations into a LAN can be expensive for small businesses. Therefore, there is a need for low-cost multiuser solutions that allow OS/2 users to share resources and to communicate. Several multiuser products have been developed that allow multiple users to share a single workstation.

An example is *CITRIX Multiuser*. It supports up to 64 users sharing a single 80386 or 80486 OS/2 system, using primarily asynchronous communications. Each user logs

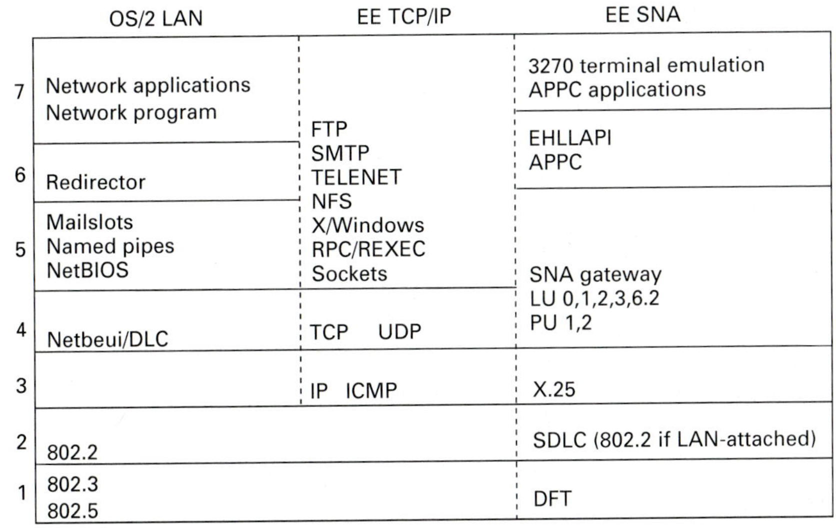

	OS/2 LAN	EE TCP/IP	EE SNA
7	Network applications Network program	FTP SMTP TELENET NFS X/Windows RPC/REXEC Sockets	3270 terminal emulation APPC applications
6	Redirector		EHLLAPI APPC
5	Mailslots Named pipes NetBIOS		SNA gateway LU 0,1,2,3,6.2 PU 1,2
4	Netbeui/DLC	TCP UDP	
3		IP ICMP	X.25
2	802.2		SDLC (802.2 if LAN-attached)
1	802.3 802.5		DFT

Fig. 11.7   OS/2 protocol stacks.

into an OS/2 session using a terminal or computer running a terminal emulation program. Users run OS/2 text-mode applications and can communicate with one another. The Multiuser software incorporates security functions that perform log in, access control list functions, system object permission management, and security auditing.

This solution is a good alternative for the small business, since each user does not need a LAN-configured workstation. If the business later decides to invest in a LAN, the users connected by the Multiuser software can access resources on the network without replacing the terminal connections. Due to the performance of asynchronous communications, most multiuser OS/2 products support only text-mode applications. However, there are many text-based OS/2 applications that meet the needs of these low-end multiuser environments.

SUMMARY

This chapter described communication in the OS/2 system. The evolution and salient features of the primary network architectures—OSI, SNA, and TCP/IP—were explained. Strategies for coexistence of the major network architectures were described. The role of OS/2 in providing connectivity to these platforms was discussed, including the content of OS/2 Extended Edition. OS/2 can handle concurrent LAN access, SNA terminal emulation and file transfer, and TCP/IP access on a single physical connection.

TERMINOLOGY

Advanced Program-to-Program
   Communication (APPC)
Advanced Research Projects Agency
   (ARPA)
application control service element
   (ACSE)
application gateway
application layer
application service element (ASE)
ARPAnet
asynchronous communication driver
   interface (ACDI)
backbone
balanced link access procedures
Berkeley UNIX
bridge
buffering
carrier sense, multiple access with
   collision detection (CSMA/CD)
CCITT V.35
CCITT X.21

centralized network model
circuit-switched network
CITRIX Multiuser
coexistence
collision
Common Communications Architecture
   (CCA) of SAA
communication controller
Communications Manager (CM)
congestion control
connection
connection oriented
connectionless
contention-based access
data circuit terminating equipment (DCE)
data flow control layer
data link layer
data terminal equipment (DTE)
data transfer
Database Manager (DM)
datagram

datagram socket
Department of Defense (DOD)
disconnection
Distributed Transaction Processing (DTP)
domain
dual protocol stacks
Emulator High-Language API (EHLLAPI)
end-user node
error detection and recovery
Ethernet
file server
file transfer
File Transfer, Access, and Management
  (FTAM)
flow control
frame
FTP (file transfer protocol)
gateway
Government OSI Profile (GOSIP)
high-level data link control (HDLC)
host computer
IBM PC network
IEEE 802.3
IEEE 802.4
IEEE 802.5
IEEE 802.6
Integrated Services Digital Network
  (ISDN)
interconnection scheme
intermediate node
International Standards Organization
  (ISO)
internet control message protocol (ICMP)
internet layer
internetwork routing and addressing
interoperability
Kerberos (user authentification)
LAN Manager
LAN requestor
LAN server
LAPB
layered network architecture
link station
local area network (LAN)

logical link control (LLC)
logical unit (LU)
LU services manager
LU6.2
mailslot
master/slave hierarchies
medium access control (MAC)
metropolitan area network (MAN)
migration
multiplexing
multiuser OS/2
named pipe
NetBIOS
network
network addressable unit (NAU)
Network File System (NFS)
network layer
network-level protocols
network redirector
network topology
node
Novell Netware
open system
Open Systems Interconnection (OSI)
  reference model
OSI transport protocol (OSI TP)
OS/2 Extended Edition (EE)
OS/2 network redirector
packet
packet addressing
packet-switched network
path control layer
peer-to-peer distributed computing
physical layer
physical unit (PU)
presentation layer
presentation services layer
print server
protocol stack
raw socket
router
routing
RS232-C (CCITT V.24)
service access point (SAP)

service-based coexistence strategy
service tunnel
session layer
session pacing
simple mail transfer protocol (SMPT)
socket
store and forward
stream socket
superserver
synchronous data link control (SDLC)
system service control point (SSCP)
Systems Application Architecture (SAA)
Systems Network Architecture (SNA)
TCP/IP
TCP transport protocol
TELENET (GTE)
TELNET (terminal emulation protocol)
3270 terminal emulation
token
token bus

token ring
TP4
transaction manager
transaction program (TP)
transmission control layer
transport bridge
transport control protocol (TCP)
transport layer
TYMNET
user datagram protocol (UDP)
user-level protocol
virtual circuit
virtual terminal
Virtual Terminal (VT)
wide area network (WAN)
X.500 Directory Services
X.400 Message Handling
X.25
X Window

EXERCISES

11.1 Explain the use in networks of intermediate nodes, end-user nodes, and gateways.

11.2 Distinguish between circuit-switched networks and packet-switched networks.

11.3 In the context of packet-switched networks, explain the notions of virtual circuits and datagrams.

11.4 Define the term "open system."

11.5 Distinguish between network-level protocols and user-level protocols.

11.6 Explain the notion of a layered architecture, such as that used in SNA and OSI. Describe the advantages and disadvantages of such a structuring approach.

11.7 What is a protocol stack?

11.8 List the seven layers of the OSI reference model. Briefly describe the function of each layer.

11.9 In the context of X.25, define data terminal equipment (DTE), data circuit terminating equipment (DCE), link access procedure balanced (LAPB), and X.21.

11.10 Explain the functions of the two sublayers of the data link layer: logical link control (LLC) and media access control (MAC).

11.11 Briefly discuss the operation of the CSMA/CD, token bus, and token ring local area networking schemes.

11.12 Explain the functions performed by the major architectural components of SNA networks—namely, logical units (LUs), physical units (PUs), and system service control points (SSCPs).

11.13 Discuss the functions of the layers of the TCP/IP network architecture.

11.14 Explain the notion of sockets as developed for the Berkeley UNIX distributions. Indicate the differences among stream sockets, datagram sockets, and raw sockets.

11.15 Distinguish between stack-based and service-based coexistence strategies.

11.16 Compare and contrast OSI and TCP/IP.

11.17 Discuss the capabilities of the OS/2 Communications Manager (CM). Consider SNA support, LAN support, and TCP/IP support.

11.18 Compare the use of a multiuser OS/2 system such as CITRIX Multiuser with LAN-based workstations as a means of enabling users to share resources and communicate with one another. Explain the advantages and disadvantages of each approach. Describe an environment where each might be appropriate.

12
The Future

Pressure from the user community is forcing manufacturers to shy away from proprietary architectures and look more toward open systems. This gives vendors two options: Research and develop now and lead the industry, or be led by the competition later.

Computerworld, April 30, 1990, p. 122

Standards make it easier for purchasers to experiment with equipment embodying new technology and reduce the risk of committing to a technology that quickly becomes obsolete.

Robert B. Reich
"The Quiet Path to Technological Preeminence,"
Scientific American, October 1989

Nothing endures but change.

Heraclitus

We had better wait and see.

H. H. Asquith

Outline

12.1 INTRODUCTION

This chapter describes issues significant to the future of OS/2. Open systems and the Systems Application Architecture (SAA) are described, and the role OS/2 will play in these environments is explained. Other key issues—such as system portability, multi-processing, multimedia, and security—also are discussed. The current state of the personal computer and workstation markets is analyzed, and OS/2's future evolution is plotted based on current trends and requirements.

12.2 OPEN SYSTEMS

The relatively new movement in the computer industry toward standardization of interfaces, and of the systems that provide these interfaces, is called *open systems*. The need to connect disparate systems in distributed environments led to the development of the OSI communication standards described in Chapter 11. Another factor that contributes to the movement toward open systems is the drive to standardize existing implementations of the UNIX operating system. Open systems attempt to satisfy the following goals:

- Maximal portability of applications, data, and users
- Increased functionality
- Vendor independence
- Interoperability
- Lower costs
- Simpler product acquisition
- Coherent network design
- An environment in which custom tailoring is still available through vendor-specific value-added services

These goals have led to standards work in the areas of communications, operating systems, programming languages, and user interfaces. Standards can be classified into four types of specifications:

- Formal standards
- De facto standards
- Standard implementations
- Proprietary implementations

Formal standards are developed by organizations such as *ISO, CCITT, ANSI,* and *IEEE.* These standards are developed by an *open consensus process* that produces a specification that defines the standard. Although formal standard definitions are important to interoperability, a process for testing system *conformance* is also required. The *Corporation for Open Systems* (*COS*) is a nonprofit alliance of major vendors and users, chartered to speed the introduction of interoperable, multivendor products under OSI and other formal standards. IBM is a major COS member.

De facto standards describe implementations with large installed bases that become standards as a result of their prevalence. TCP/IP and SNA are examples of de facto standards. Standard implementations are based on specifications developed by the open process, and produce implementations that can be ported to different architectures. For example, the *Open Software Foundation (OSF)* produces specifications and standard implementations of the UNIX system. *UNIX International* also produces specifications that describe a standard implementation of the UNIX system, but does not produce an implementation. Proprietary implementations include vendor value-added elements, such as internetworking with proprietary network architectures. Proprietary implementations are normally owned, controlled, and defined by a single vendor.

Open systems have interfaces and functionality that conform to available standards; such systems can be manufactured free of proprietary constraints. They are based on formal international standards, and these standards are developed by a consensus process that is open to all participants. The open consensus process ensures that open systems architectures are not proprietary and do not serve the interests of only a specific vendor. This definition of "open systems" is generally accepted in the UNIX community, since it implicitly requires a standard open operating system as a basis for the open environment. An alternative definition for "open system" that most vendors also recognize originates with the OSI standard's definition of "open system." According to OSI, an open system is one in which the external interfaces conform to formal standards. In this definition, since open systems are defined based on external standards, proprietary internal architectures are not an issue, and an open operating system is not required as a basis for interoperability.

12.3 OPEN UNIX

The *UNIX operating system* is viewed as nonproprietary and vendor independent, since any vendor can purchase a source code license and port the system to its hardware. This view of UNIX comes from its unique evolution. UNIX was developed by *AT&T Bell Laboratories*. It was originally written in assembler, but was rewritten in the C programming language before it was widely distributed. The rewritten version enabled it to be ported to many different environments. AT&T was originally prohibited from competing in the computer industry, but it was able to distribute the source of UNIX to many schools and companies. Many ports to different processor architectures followed, each with its own enhancements.

By the late 1980s, over 100 different versions of the UNIX system existed, and the market was extremely fragmented. Among the major variants of the UNIX system were *AT&T System V, Berkeley UNIX 4.3, Microsoft XENIX, Sun Microsystems SunOS,* and *IBM AIX*. Due to the differences in these implementations, and to the movement toward OSI communication standards, people became interested in standardizing the UNIX operating system and related non-operating-system interfaces. Thus, the UNIX market sees open operating systems technology as a critical component to the open systems strategy.

The *IEEE POSIX standard* includes a standard UNIX interface definition, and is based on AT&T System V and assorted enhancements drawn from the most popular implementations. POSIX also includes the X/Windows standard definition that describes the base architecture used to support graphical user interfaces. Currently, the IEEE is reviewing two graphical user interface proposals based on X/Windows, one by UNIX International and the other by the Open Software Foundation.

Another standards body that plays a large role in defining UNIX standards is *X/Open*. Originally, a consortium of European vendors founded X/Open in 1984 to pool their resources in specifying a *common application environment (CAE)* based on de facto and formal standards. Most major UNIX vendors are in X/Open, directly or indirectly. X/Open publishes the *X/Open Portability Guide*, a specification that describes the common application environment. It incorporates formal standards as they are defined, and combines existing formal standards with de facto standards to produce an open systems definition.

In an attempt to produce a standard UNIX definition that meets the requirements of the existing major implementations, AT&T designed *UNIX System V, Release 4*. AT&T chose Sun Microsystems as its partner for producing the system. This agreement upset other major UNIX vendors, since they were in competition with Sun and AT&T, and thought that the evolution of standard UNIX needed to be a more open process. Their concern led to the formation of the *Open Software Foundation (OSF)* to define a rival standard UNIX.

The OSF was formed in 1988 to provide a source of open UNIX systems technology. IBM, DEC, and Hewlett-Packard (HP) are some of the major members of OSF. *OSF/1* is the first UNIX implementation delivered by OSF. It uses *Carnegie–Mellon University's Mach* operating system for the base system kernel. Additional components of the system are provided by the members of OSF. Most members of OSF choose to integrate technology developed by OSF into their own proprietary UNIX implementations, rather than to offer the OSF standard implementation as a whole. OSF uses the *Motif graphical user interface* based on X/Windows for standard access to applications.

OSF addresses the needs of interconnecting open systems with the *distributed computing environment (DCE)*. DCE complements and enhances the upper OSI layers to help application developers and users attain a transparent heterogeneous distributed operating environment. DCE integrates technology for remote procedure calls, distributed directory services, security, and distributed file services.

In response to the OSF consortium, AT&T and Sun formed UNIX International, a consortium of UNIX vendors that promotes *UNIX System V, Release 4* as the standard open operating system. Like OSF, UNIX International uses an open process whereby members can influence the System V definition. However, AT&T owns the System V standard, and documents that standard in the *System V Interface Definition (SVID)*. UNIX International unlike OSF, does not produce an implementation. Licensing and conformance testing of products based on System V is performed by AT&T. UNIX International addresses the needs of interconnecting open systems with Sun Microsystem's *Open Network Computing (ONC)*. ONC addresses goals similar to those met by DCE, and embraces many of the same standards.

Thus, there are two principal standard UNIX implementations—those of UNIX International and those of OSF. Both implementations have similar technical goals, both consortia are members of X/Open, and both systems are based on common standards.

The *X Consortium* is devoted to continued development of X/Windows. X/Windows was developed at MIT with funding from IBM and DEC, and has become popular as the base technology used by graphical user interfaces on most UNIX systems. DEC, IBM, HP, and Sun are leading members of the X Consortium. The X Consortium produces a definition of X/Windows that is used by both OSF and UNIX International.

AIX is IBM's entry into the UNIX market. AIX has been ported to the System 370, the RT/PC, the System 6000, and the PS/2. The contents of AIX are defined by an IBM document called the *Family Definition Specification*. AIX supports X/Windows, OSF/Motif, Sun NFS, TCP/IP, Ethernet, and OSI connectivity. It is based on AT&T's System V, and contains enhancements from Berkeley UNIX and OSF/1. AIX is not a part of SAA, since it does not yet implement all the required SAA elements.

12.4 SYSTEMS APPLICATION ARCHITECTURE

The objective of the *Systems Application Architecture (SAA)* is to tie together IBM's multiple architectures in a manner that ensures consistency across platforms. SAA is a set of software interfaces, conventions, and protocols that provides a framework for developing integrated applications consistent across SAA platforms. It addresses the market's largest installed base, and opens up IBM interfaces that were previously considered proprietary. SAA is IBM's internal open systems path. It represents the largest implementation of the open systems philosophy that exists today.

SAA compliance makes software independent of the system on which that software originated, as long as it is running on an SAA platform. Conversely, UNIX is machine independent, but UNIX application software is dependent on a specific standard implementation of the UNIX system. The benefits of SAA are similar to those of open systems. The portability of applications from the developer and end-user view is a key part of SAA. Also, SAA provides for consistency in environments across systems, and connectivity that enables distributed cooperative processing environments. SAA further improves connectivity by defining an environment in which applications can run across IBM's disparate systems without being sensitive to the underlying operating system. This is in direct contrast to the philosophy espoused by the open UNIX market, in which a standard open operating system is considered critical to the success of open systems across disparate platforms.

SAA is composed of a *base foundation,* and an *interface framework* that describes how the base is accessed by applications. The base foundation consists of *system control programs, application enablers,* and *communications.* System control programs are operating systems, such as VM, MVS, OS/2 Extended Edition, and OS/400. Application enablers are tools such as compilers and database management systems, that assist developers in application development. The communications portion of the SAA base provides functions that connect applications, systems, networks, and devices. Figure 12.1 illustrates the SAA architecture components.

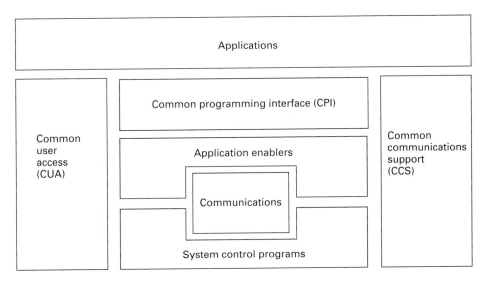

Fig. 12.1   Components of the IBM Systems Application Architecture. (Adapted from *APPC Introduction to LU6.2,* A. Berson, Copyright 1990, McGraw-Hill Publishing Company. Reprinted by permission.)

Outside the SAA foundation, a framework of interfaces is defined that specifies how applications access services provided by the base. The SAA interfaces are divided into three categories: *common user access (CUA), common programming interface (CPI),* and *common communications support (CCS).* CUA allows users to interface with the computer in a consistent manner, regardless of the system. It specifies panels, keyboard layouts, graphical user interface interactions, and controls. CPI details programming language specifications (such as ANSI C) that are implemented across SAA environments. The CCS portion of the SAA interfaces defines common architectures and protocols that interconnect SAA systems. It also provides for the interconnection of non-IBM systems using OSI and TCP/IP protocols.

SNA's LU6.2 is the strategic peer-to-peer distributed application protocol used by IBM systems within SAA. CCS also provides for token ring LANs based on the IEEE 802.2 standard, and for WANs connected using X.25 or SDLC data link protocols. OSI is the strategic vehicle in SAA for connecting non-IBM systems. The *OSI Communications Subsystem (OSI/CS)* program, supported on SAA platforms, supports the government's GOSIP requirements for procuring open systems. The integration of SNA and OSI lets users retain the rich functionality and network management services of SNA, while allowing them to take advantage of new OSI applications. SNA, TCP/IP, and OSI are integrated up to the data link layer within the SAA CCS definition. Different protocol stacks for each of these network architectures coexist above the data link layer. Also, application layer protocol translation programs, or *application gateways,* provide the necessary translation for allowing distributed applications to coexist across SNA and non-SNA systems.

SAA *common applications* are written to the CPI and CUA interfaces. As more common applications become network distributed, they rely more on the CCS component of SAA. Common applications run in all SAA environments with the same user interface. CUA, CPI, and CCS work together so that the underlying SAA foundation does not obstruct consistency, connectivity, or interoperability.

It is interesting to compare IBM's SAA interoperability strategy, and the open UNIX strategy described in the previous section. IBM's approach to open systems and interoperability is the synthesis of vision and practicality. IBM embraces OSI, but is not abandoning the strategic SNA platform with its huge installed base. The IBM approach allows the retention of rich SNA functionality, while acknowledging the desirability and usefulness of the OSI standards. SAA does not require a common operating system, as the UNIX open systems market does, but instead relies on the common interfaces to the SAA base functions to shield applications from the nature of the operating system. This difference between SAA and UNIX-based open systems is the fundamental one.

SAA, like OSI, defines an open system to be one that provides the external interfaces specified by formal standards. As long as the system conforms to these external interfaces, the internal implementation used does not matter. Therefore, in the SAA and OSI definitions of an open system, whether or not the core operating system is proprietary is not an issue. However, in the UNIX market, in which there are so many variants of the UNIX operating system, UNIX vendors realize that it is critical to standardize a single version of UNIX for their open system platforms. Thus, UNIX vendors link the standard operating system to the open systems issue, by taking the position that a single open operating system is critical to the success of open systems. On the other hand, SAA and OSI take the standpoint that, as long as the external interfaces defined by formal standards are obeyed, it does not matter what operating system is used. Ultimately, the two different philosophies have enough in common that they will be able to coexist and to further the strategy of open systems.

OS/2 is the strategic SAA operating system platform for IBM's PS/2 systems. OS/2 is classified as an open system, since it provides connectivity to SNA, TCP/IP, OSI, and DCE environments. Although it can run applications across these heterogenous environments, it is not yet available for other architectures. A key issue for OS/2 will be how to handle the evolution and migration of OS/2 to other processor platforms. Unlike for UNIX systems, there is a single standard for OS/2 systems. However, UNIX vendors view OS/2 as proprietary, since the system design process is not open, OS/2 is not yet portable to most architectures, and OS/2 is not UNIX. As open as UNIX is, there is still not a single standard UNIX implementation on which all vendors agree. The portability of 32-bit OS/2 should give that system the momentum needed to break through the proprietary barriers envisioned by UNIX vendors. It is possible that, in the future, IBM may sell source licenses to 32-bit OS/2, and enable vendors to port 32-bit OS/2 to their own architectures. However, IBM must be careful to ensure that OS/2 remains a standard implementation that meets the requirements of open systems. The 32-bit OS/2 system qualifies as a workstation operating system. It provides the connectivity and functions of both SAA and open systems environments, and will clearly play a major role in the future.

12.5 SYSTEM PORTABILITY

The proliferation of RISC architectures as fast, generic processing engines has fueled the growth of the workstation marketplace. Systems based on the MIPS RISC processor, the IBM POWER architecture, and Sun's SPARC processor are leading the way into open systems in the workstation marketplace. Both IBM and Microsoft have announced that OS/2 will support RISC platforms in the future. The key to providing this support is to finish the task of making the 32-bit OS/2 system portable, and to allow it to migrate from the Intel processor platforms. Several alternatives are being explored for enabling the base system to be portable to other architectures, such as Microsoft's NT system, the Mach system embraced by OSF, and AIX. Regardless of the technology used, applications based on the OS/2 2.0 API are source retargetable, since they are based on the current portable 32-bit API.

OS/2 2.0 is the first release of 32-bit OS/2 technology. Most of the OS/2 2.0 kernel is 32-bit code, and about 60 percent of it is written in the C language. The utilities, the window management portion of the PM, and the device drivers are still 16-bit code. For OS/2 to be independent of the Intel 80X86 processor platform, these components must be converted to 32-bit code. This task entails converting the rest of the kernel to 32-bit C, and isolating machine-dependent portions of the kernel into separate modules. A 32-bit flat-model device-driver architecture is needed to support development of device drivers in C that are portable across different architectures. Portions of the PM, and the utilities, also need to be converted.

Moving OS/2 to a non-Intel platform may require the removal of the DOS compatibility, Windows 3.X compatibility, and 16-bit OS/2 compatibility features. Although many RISC architectures can simulate an 8086 in real mode, and thus some simple DOS applications, this ability does not allow 16-bit OS/2 and 16-bit protected-mode Windows 3.X applications to run on a RISC processor. However, DOS compatibility, 16-bit compatibility, and Windows compatibility may be retained through use of an 80X86 as a coprocessor in the RISC environment.

12.6 MULTIPROCESSOR SYSTEMS

OS/2 already provides some multiprocessing support. The existing coprocessor scheme for LAN superservers allows the network code of the operating system to be run on an 80386 or 80486 coprocessor. It uses a *tightly coupled master/slave relationship* between the processor running the OS/2 system and the processor running the network code. However, it is the evolution of OS/2 toward *symmetric multiprocessing (SMP)* platforms that has interesting implications for the future.

On an SMP platform, any processor can execute kernel and user code, and multi-threaded processes can run on one or more processors. SMP platforms were described in detail in Chapter 3. They can maintain compatibility with uniprocessor programs developed for the same processor. They require efficient shared memory interprocess communications in hardware, and provisions for *processor interlock* to resolve *resource contention.* In an SMP system, peer processing allows processes to be less tightly coupled and less reliant on one another.

There are several technical issues significant to the evolution of a portable OS/2 to an SMP platform. The kernel must be reentrant, since it can be executed by more than one thread at a time on different processors. The kernel may optionally be preemptible, depending on the requirements of the implementation. Other work is necessary in process and thread scheduling, and in memory management. Furthermore, arbitration of resource conflicts between processors must be supplied, as well as shared I/O management capabilities. The MP version of OS/2 must be able to maintain memory and cache integrity across a variety of memory architectures. It will do so by using systemwide tables in shared memory, and coding the kernel to use memory resource locks when accessing shared structures and performing shared I/O. The technical requirements for supporting SMP systems are being addressed in the effort to make the underlying OS/2 system portable.

12.7 SECURITY

Security is important to the future of OS/2 from the perspectives of open systems and distributed environments. Security guidelines have been developed by the *National Computer Security Center (NCSC)* of the Department of Defense (DOD) in the *rainbow* series of documents. Since each of the documents has a cover of a different color, the series uses the term "rainbow," and color names are used as the informal names of the documents. The series includes the *Trusted Computer System Evaluation Criteria* or *Orange Book,* the *Trusted Network Interpretation* or *Red Book,* and the *Green Book* on password management guidelines. A *Blue Book* provides guidelines on magnetic resonance and electrical emissions; a *Yellow Book* describes how to apply the *Orange Book.*

The *Orange Book* contains security standards that specify how manufacturers produce trusted computer systems. It provides criteria used to evaluate the level of trust assigned a system, and also is used as a basis in government procurement specifications. The *Red Book* applies the standards of the *Orange Book* to network distributed environments. Network security services and mechanisms are also defined in the *OSI security architecture.*

Security, according to the *Orange Book,* is provided in two components: *security mechanisms* and *security assurance measures.* Security mechanisms implement controls that guarantee a trusted environment. Security assurance measures provide a certain level of assurance that security mechanisms are designed and implemented correctly. Seven levels of trust are defined by the *Orange Book* specification. They are identified using letters and numbers as follows: D1, C1, C2, B1, B2, B3, A1. Level D1 is the lowest level (no security), and level A1 is the highest level. Levels C1, C2, and B1 define the requirements for security mechanisms, and levels B2, B3, and A1 define the requirements for security assurance measures. Figure 12.2 illustrates the *Orange Book* security levels.

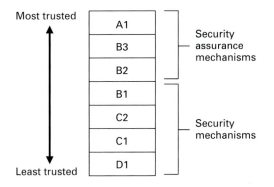

Fig. 12.2 Orange Book security levels.

12.7.1 Security Mechanisms

Security mechanisms are implemented in levels C1 through B1 in the security standard. At the C levels, *discretionary access control (DAC)* is required to provide controlled access to objects by named users or groups at the discretion of the owner. DAC is specified by the creator of an object, and allows the creator to specify what users or groups have a need to access that object. Examples of DAC are the user/group-style permissions of the OS/2 LAN environment and UNIX systems, and the more sophisticated *access control lists (ACLs)* found in CITRIX Multiuser. ACLs allow a finer granularity of control than do the basic user/group-style permissions.

   Accountability is another security mechanism required by the *Orange Book*. Ensuring accountability consists of providing means for user identification and authorization. Accountability is typically provided using passwords or physical identification devices such as badge readers. Accountability also requires that the system to be able to provide an *audit trail* of security-related events.

   Object reuse is a security mechanism that ensures that residual data are cleared from system-provided objects before the objects are reused. Examples of object reuse are clearing of memory buffers, disk storage, or registers when they are assigned to a new user. Discretionary access control, accountability, and object reuse are required at the C1 and C2 levels.

   Beyond the C1 and C2 levels, *security labels* and *mandatory access control (MAC)* are required by the *Orange Book*. Security labels, or *sensitivity labels,* are maintained by the system for each object and user. The labels represent a hierarchy of security levels that are designated using labels—for example, top secret, secret, classified, and unclassified.

   Mandatory access control restricts access to files and system objects through levels and compartments. It relies on security labels to be assigned to objects and users. MAC implements security controls based on the security label hierarchy. Users can access objects only at or below their security level. Users cannot access objects at higher levels even if the ACL or DAC mechanism says the access is valid. MAC supersedes DAC, since it does not allow the creator of an object a choice in applying security mechanisms to that object. In a MAC environment, users also cannot modify objects at lower security levels. This prevents a high-level user from making trusted data accessible to users that do not have sufficient privilege to access those data. Thus, the altering of even low-security-risk data must use a system-enforced security procedure. Mandatory access control is called "mandatory," since its mechanism for preventing trusted data from becoming accessible is a policy of the system, not a policy of the user that created the object. The B1 security level requires sensitivity labels on all objects and mandatory access control.

12.7.2 Security Assurance Measures

The security assurance measures are enforced in security levels B2, B3, and A1 according to the *Orange Book* specification. There are several criteria that are described in the security assurance measures:

- System architecture criteria
- System integrity criteria
- Security testing criteria

The system architecture criteria require protection between the system and applications, and among applications. The system integrity criteria require a means to validate the hardware and microcode of the system itself. The security testing criteria require mechanisms to be tested to conform with the system security documentation. These three criteria are defined differently on the various levels. Level B1 requires an informal model of security policies to be documented. Levels B2 and B3 require system restructuring to meet modularity specifications, and formal modeling of the security system. Due to the modularity requirements, it is nearly impossible to retrofit B2 and B3 security into existing operating system architectures. The modularity requirements also usually hamper the performance of the system, requiring redesign of an existing system and tradeoffs between security and performance. The A1 level requires a mathematically proven model of the security architecture.

12.7.3 OS/2 Security

The existing 16-bit OS/2 system is single user, so security was not a major consideration in its design. The LAN support for 16-bit OS/2 systems has user and group permissions for file system objects and devices that are shared across the network. The CITRIX Multiuser system provides discretionary access control using access control lists. The 32-bit system has parameters reserved in API functions that grant access to shared system objects, such as semaphores, files, and shared memory. The reserved parameters are for access control lists, which will be supported in a future version of the 32-bit system when security is provided in the base system. Future versions of the 32-bit OS/2 system will ultimately progress to the C1, C2, and, at least, B1 levels of security compliance. Thus, OS/2 will be an appropriate candidate in government procurements that demand increased security.

12.8 MULTIMEDIA

Multimedia technology is the integration of television-quality audio and visual capabilities on the personal computer and workstation platforms. With the advent of new technology such as *CD/ROM, musical instrument digital interface (MIDI),* and *digital video interactive (DVI),* multimedia technology is becoming available on general-purpose low-cost systems. The *Interactive Multimedia Association (IMA)* was founded in 1988 as a trade group specializing in video disk technology. It has evolved to a membership of over 170 companies, including IBM, Sony, NCR, Phillips, Intel, Apple, Lotus, and Macromind. The IMA is developing multimedia specifications for hardware and software architectures, based on existing and evolving standards.

Multimedia applications place real-time sequencing requirements on operating systems, because they must be able to perform audio and visual I/O quickly to provide realistic presentations. Audio and video data must be sequenced and synchronized so that audio data sound right, visual data look right, and their combined presentation has the desired effect for the user. Multimedia applications can integrate digital video, digital audio, animation, images, and special effects into multimedia presentations.

IBM has announced multimedia extensions for the 32-bit OS/2 platform that will enable a new class of applications to be developed. OS/2 2.X is the ideal environment for multimedia applications because of its protected multitasking environment, high-performance memory management and IPC mechanisms, and overall system integrity.

SUMMARY

This chapter described issues that will affect the future of OS/2. The open systems market and SAA architectures will play a significant role in defining how OS/2 interconnects to other systems. OS/2 will also be portable to other architectures, and will support symmetrical multiprocessing architectures. Security qualification of OS/2 is an important future requirement that will enable OS/2 to participate in government procurement. Multimedia applications will take advantage of the flexible and robust foundation of OS/2, and will allow users to interact with the system using integrated audio and visual media of television quality.

TERMINOLOGY

access control list (ACL)	Berkeley 4.3BSD
accountability	*Blue Book*
ANSI	Carnegie–Mellon University's Mach
application enabler	CCITT
application gateway	CD/ROM
AT&T Bell Laboratories	CITRIX Multiuser
AT&T System V	common application environment (CAE)
audit trail	common communications support (CCS)
authorization	common programming interface (CPI)
base foundation	common user access (CUA)

conformance
Corporation for Open Systems (COS)
de facto standard
digital video interactive (DVI)
discretionary access control (DAC)
DOD security level
Family Definition Specification
GOSIP
Green Book
IBM AIX
IEEE POSIX standard
Interactive Multimedia Association (IMA)
interface framework
International Standards Organization
  (ISO)
mandatory access control (MAC)
master/slave relationship
Microsoft XENIX
motif graphical user interface
multimedia
multiprocessor
musical instrument digital interface
  (MIDI)
National Computer Security Center
  (NCSC)
object reuse
open consensus process
Open Software Foundation (OSF)
open system
Orange Book

OSF/1
OSI Communications Subsystem
  (OSI/CS)
OSI security architecture
portability
processor interlock
Red Book
resource contention
RISC
security assurance measure
security label
security mechanism
symmetric multiprocessing (SMP)
system control program
System V Interface Definition (SVID)
Systems Application Architecture (SAA)
tightly coupled
*Trusted Computer System Evaluation
  Criteria*
Trusted Network Interpretation
UNIX
UNIX International
UNIX operating system
UNIX System V, Release 4 (SVR4)
X Consortium
X/Open
X/Open Portability Guide
XPG/3
X Windows
Yellow Book

EXERCISES

12.1 Discuss the advantages and disadvantages of the open systems approach.

12.2 Briefly explain each of the following types of standards: formal standards, de facto standards, implementation standards, and proprietary implementation standards.

12.3 Why has UNIX evolved to such a special position of prominence in the open systems arena?

12.4 Explain the roles played by each of the following consortia in the open UNIX arena: UNIX International, the Open Software Foundation, and X/Open.

12.5 Discuss IBM's Systems Application Architecture (SAA).

12.6 Explain the function of each of the following SAA interfaces: common user access (CUA), common programming interface (CPI), and common communications support (CCS).

12.7 Argue why SAA may be called IBM's "internal open systems approach." Explain how SAA provides for connecting to external open systems. Say how crucial you believe SAA's role will be in the worldwide open systems arena.

12.8 What is the fundamental difference between SAA and UNIX-based open systems?

12.9 How does OS/2 fit into IBM's SAA strategy?

12.10 What are the keys to increasing the portability of OS/2?

12.11 How does porting OS/2 to RISC platforms affect OS/2's compatibility features?

12.12 Describe the sequence of steps that would be used to port OS/2 to other processors (other than Intel 80X86 series) once OS/2 has been converted to 32-bit code and has been restructured.

12.13 What features does OS/2 already provide in support of multiprocessing?

12.14 What technical issues are significant to the evolution of a portable OS/2 to a symmetric multiprocessing platform?

12.15 Distinguish between security mechanisms and security assurance measures.

12.16 What discretionary access control (DAC) mechanisms are provided by OS/2 and CITRIX Multiuser?

12.17 In the context of *Orange Book* security, explain the notions of accountability, object reuse, security labels, and mandatory access control (MAC).

12.18 Discuss each of the following criteria described in the *Orange Book* security assurance measures: system architecture criteria, system integrity criteria, and security testing criteria.

12.19 What is multimedia technology? What demands do multimedia applications place on the operating system environment?

Bibliography

(An84)   Anderson, J., "Irresistible DOS 3.0," *PC Tech Journal*, Vol. 2, No. 6, December 1984, pp. 74–87.

(An87)   Anderson, J., "Twilight of DOS," *PC Tech Journal*, Vol. 5, No. 8, August 1987, pp. 180–193.

(An90)   Andleigh, P. K., *UNIX System Architecture*, Englewood Cliffs, NJ: Prentice-Hall, 1990.

(Ar83)   Archer, R., "The IBM PC XT and DOS 2.00," *Byte*, November 1983, pp. 294–304.

(Ar87)   Armbrust, S., and T. Forgeron, "Multiple Tasks," *PC Tech Journal*, Vol. 5, No. 11, November 1987, pp. 90–106.

(Ar87a) Armbrust, S., "Porting to OS/2," *PC Tech Journal*, Vol. 5, No. 11, November 1987, pp. 140–148.

(Ba86)   Bach, M. J., *The Design of the UNIX Operating System*, Englewood Cliffs, NJ: Prentice-Hall, 1986.

(Be86)   Beley, J., and B. Preppernau (Eds.), *MS-DOS Technical Reference Encyclopedia*, Redmond, WA: Microsoft Press, 1986.

(Be90)   Berson, A., *APPC: Introduction to LU6.2*, New York: McGraw-Hill, 1990.

(Br87)   Brown, E.; E. Knorr; and C. Bermant, "Personal Systems Revealed," *PC World*, August 1987, pp. 212–223.

(Bu83)   Burton, K., "Anatomy of a Colossus, Part II," *PC Magazine*, Vol. 1, No. 10, February 1983, pp. 317–330.

(Ca90)   Cashin, J., "Open Systems Market Sees OSI Gain Speed," *Software Magazine*, February 1990, pp. 71–74.

(Ca91)   Cashin, J., "OSF's DCE Attempts To Add OSI Services," *Software Magazine,* March 1991, pp. 87–90.

(Ch88)   Chang, P. Y., and W. W. Myre, "OS/2 EE Database Manager Overview and Technical Highlights," *IBM Systems Journal,* Vol. 27, No. 2, 1988, pp. 105–118.

(Ch87)   Chester, J. A., "IBM and OS/2 Take on the Clones," *Infosystems,* Vol. 34, No. 8, August 1987, pp. 34–36.

(Ch91)   Chiong, J., "UNIX Can Play a Key Role in Network Management," *Computer Technology Review,* January 1991, pp. 29–33.

(Ch89)   Christopher, K. W.; B. A. Feigenbaum; and S. O. Saliga, *The New DOS 4.0,* New York: John Wiley & Sons, 1989.

(Cl89)   Clouse, R., "Security Technology: Standards for Trusted Systems," *Unisphere,* July 1989, pp. 43–45.

(Cl85)   Claff, W. J., "Moving from the 8088 to the 80286," *Byte,* Vol. 10, No. 11, 1985.

(Cl84)   Clune, T.; R. Malloy; and G. M. Vose, "The IBM PC AT," *Byte,* October 1984, pp. 107–111.

(Co90)   Conklin, D., *OS/2 Notebook,* Redmond, WA.: Microsoft Press, 1990.

(Co88a)   Cook, R. L.; F. L. Rawson III; J. A. Tunkel; and R. L. Williams, "Writing an Operating System/2 Application," *IBM Systems Journal,* Vol. 27, No. 2, 1988, pp. 134–157.

(Cu83)   Curren, L., and R. S. Shuford, "IBM's Estridge," *Byte,* November 1983.

(Da89)   Davis, S. R., and W. L. Rosch, "386 Multitasking Environments," *PC Magazine,* Vol. 8, No. 4, February 1989, pp. 94–140.

(De90)   Deitel, H. M., *Operating Systems,* Second Edition, Reading, MA: Addison-Wesley, 1990.

(De86)   Derfler, F. J., Jr., and W. Stallings, "The IBM Token Ring LAN," *PC Magazine,* March 1986, pp. 197–206.

(Du87)   Duncan, R., "Character-Oriented Display Services Using OS/2's VIO Subsystem," *Microsoft Systems Journal,* Vol. 2, No. 4, September 1987, pp. 23–33.

(Du87a)   Duncan, R., "Porting MS-DOS Assembly Language Programs to the OS/2 Environment," *Microsoft Systems Journal,* Vol. 2, No. 3, July 1987, pp. 9–17.

(Du87b)   Duncan, R., "OS/2 Multitasking: Exploiting the Protected Mode of the 80286," *Microsoft Systems Journal,* Vol. 2, No. 2, May 1987, pp. 27–36.

(Du87c)   Duncan, R., "OS/2 Inter-Process Communication: Semaphores, Pipes, and Queues," *Microsoft Systems Journal,* Vol. 2, No. 2, May 1987, pp. 37–50.

(Du88)   Duncan, R., "An Examination of the DevHelp API," *Microsoft Systems Journal,* Vol. 3, No. 2, March 1988, pp. 39–55.

(Du89)   Duncan, R., "Taking a Realistic Look at DOS 4.0," *PC Magazine*, Vol. 8, No. 1, January 1989, pp. 329–334.

(Du89a)   Duncan, R., "Comparing DOS and OS/2 File Systems," *PC Magazine*, Vol. 8, No. 3, February 1989, pp. 321–332.

(Du83)   Dunford, C., "Interrupts and the IBM PC, Part 1," *PC Tech Journal*, Vol. 1, No. 3, November/December 1983, pp. 173–199.

(Ed89)   Edelstein, H. A., "OS/2 Meets SQL," *PC Tech Journal*, Vol. 7, No. 2, February 1989, pp. 62–75.

(Fa86)   Fawcette, J. E., "80386: The Megabyte Manager, *PC World*, February 1986, pp. 238–243.

(Fi83)   Field, T., "Installable Device Drivers for PC-DOS 2.0, *Byte*, November 1983, pp. 188–196.

(Fi85)   Finger, A., "IBM PC AT," *Byte*, May 1985, pp. 270–277.

(Fl87)   Fleig, C. P., "The Well-Connected PC," *PC World*, August 1987, pp. 192–199.

(Fo86)   Foard, R. M., "Multitasking Methods," *PC Tech Journal*, Vol. 4, No. 3, March 1986, pp. 49–60.

(Ge88)   Geary, M., "Converting Windows Applications for Microsoft OS/2 Presentation Manager," *Microsoft Systems Journal*, Vol. 3, No. 1, January 1988, pp. 9–30.

(Ge87)   Getts, J., "A PC Geneology," *PC World*, August 1987, pp. 200–205.

(Gi87)   Gillman, J., "Compatibility and Transition for MS-DOS Programs," *Microsoft Systems Journal*, Vol. 2, No. 2, May 1987, pp. 19–26.

(Gr84)   Greenberg, K., and K. Koessel, "AT: The PC's Powerful Partner," *PC World*, December 1984, pp. 234–250.

(Gr86)   Greenberg, K., "A Candid Conversation with William Lowe," *PC World*, March 1986, pp. 137–143.

(Gr88)   Greenberg, R. M., "Design Concepts and Considerations in Building an OS/2 Dynamic-Link Library," *Microsoft Systems Journal*, Vol. 3, No. 3, May 1988, pp. 27–48.

(Gr84a)   Greene, B., "The Evolution of the iAPX 286," *PC Tech Journal*, Vol. 2, No. 6, 1984, pp. 118–136.

(Gr91)   Grimshaw, M., "LAN Interconnections Technology," *Telecommunications*, February 1991, pp. 25–32.

(Gu88)   Guttman, M., "Building a Foundation for Presentation Manager," *Computerworld Focus*, June 1988, pp. 31–33.

(Ha87)   Hansen, M., and L. Sargent, "Increase the Performance of Your Programs with a Math Coprocessor," *Microsoft Systems Journal*, Vol. 2, No. 3, July 1987, pp. 59–69.

(He88)   Heller, V., "OS/2 Virtual Memory Management," *Byte*, Vol. 13, No. 4, April 1988, pp. 227–233.

(Hi90)   Hindin, E. M., "LAN APIs—Getting in Touch with Network Resources," *Data Communications,* February 1990, pp. 89–95.

(Ho84)   Hoffman, T. V., "Analyzing the Advanced Technology," *PC Tech Journal,* Vol. 2, No. 6, December 1984, pp. 40–56.

(Ho90)   Holliday, J. E., "Thunking 16-Bit Controls for 32-Bit Applications," *IBM Personal Systems Developer,* Summer 1990, pp. 44–54.

(Ho87)   Hoskins, J., *IBM Personal System/2: A Business Perspective,* New York: John Wiley and Sons, 1987.

(Ia88)   Iacobucci, E., *OS/2 Programmer's Guide,* Berkeley, CA: Osborne Mcgraw-Hill, 1988.

(IB84)   IBM Corporation, *DOS Version 3.00 Technical Reference:* IBM, May 1984.

(IB85)   IBM Corporation, *Disk Operating System Version 3.10 User's Guide:* IBM, 1985.

(IB86)   IBM Corporation, *IBM RT Personal Computer Technology:* IBM, 1986.

(IB86a)   IBM Corporation, *Disk Operating System Version 3.20 Reference:* IBM, February 1986.

(IB87)   IBM Corporation, *Operating System/2 Standard Edition Users Reference:* IBM, 1987.

(IB87a)   IBM Corporation, *Operating System/2 Technical Reference,* First Edition, Volume 1: IBM, 1986, 1987.

(IB87b)   IBM Corporation, *Operating System/2 Technical Reference,* First Edition, Volume 2: IBM, 1986, 1987.

(IB87c)   IBM Corporation, *IBM Personal System/2 Customer Reference Guide:* IBM, April 1987.

(IB88)   IBM Corporation, *Systems Application Architecture An Overview,* Third Edition, File Number GC26-4341: IBM, February 1988.

(IB89)   IBM Corporation, *OS/2 1.2 Control Program Programming Reference:* IBM, 1989.

(IB89a)   IBM Corporation, *OS/2 1.2 I/O Subsystems and Device Support Guide:* IBM, 1989.

(IB89b)   IBM Corporation, *OS/2 1.2 Programming Guide:* IBM, 1989.

(In83)   Intel Corporation, *iAPX 286 Programmer's Reference Manual:* Intel, 1983.

(In86)   Intel Corporation, *80386 Programmer's Reference Manual:* Intel, 1986.

(In87)   Intel Corporation, *80386 Hardware Reference Manual:* Intel, 1987.

(In89)   Intel Corporation, *i486 Microprocessor:* Intel, 1989.

(In89a)   Intel Corporation, *i860 64-bit Microprocessor Programmer's Reference Manual:* Intel, 1989.

(In91)   Intel Corporation, *An Introduction to the DOS Protected Mode Interface:* Intel, 1989–91.

(Ke88)   Kessler, A., "OS/2 LAN Manager Provides a Platform for Server-Based Network Applications," *Microsoft Systems Journal,* Vol. 3, No. 2, March 1988, pp. 29–38.

(Ki88)   Killen, M., *IBM: The Making of the Common View*, Orlando, FL: Harcourt Brace Jovanovich, 1988.

(Ki90)   Kirk, M. J., "Open Operating Systems," *British Telecommunication Engineering*, Vol. 8, January 1990, pp. 234–243.

(Ko88)   Kogan, M. S., and F. L. Rawson, III, "The Design of Operating System/2," *IBM Systems Journal*, Vol. 27, No. 2, 1988, pp. 90–104.

(Ko90)   Kogan, M. S., "OS/2 2.0 Overview," *IBM Personal Systems Developer*, Spring 1990, pp. 16–22.

(Ko90a) Kogan, M. S., "OS/2 2.0 32-Bit API," *IBM Personal Systems Developer*, Spring 1990, pp. 23–30.

(Ko90b) Kogan, M. S., and R. Tycast, "OS/2 2.0 Tools and Program Development," *IBM Personal Systems Developer*, Spring 1990, pp. 31–35.

(Ko85)   Kolod, M., "IBM PC Disk Performance and the Interleave Factor," *Byte*, 1985, pp. 283–290.

(Kr88)   Krantz, J. I.; A. M. Mizell; and R.L. Williams, *OS/2 Features, Functions, and Applications*, New York: John Wiley & Sons, 1988.

(La88)   Lammers, S. (Ed.), *The MS-DOS Encyclopedia*, Redmond, WA: Microsoft Press, 1988.

(La83)   Larson, C., "MS-DOS 2.0: An Enhanced 16-bit Operating System," *Byte*, November 1983, pp. 285–290.

(Le89)   Leffler, S.; M. McKusick; M. Karels; and J. Quarterman, *The Design and Implementation of the 4.3BSD UNIX Operating System*, Reading, MA: Addison-Wesley, 1989.

(Le88)   Letwin, G., *Inside OS/2*, Redmond, WA: Microsoft Press, 1988.

(Le88a) Letwin, G., "Dynamic Linking in OS/2," *Byte*, Vol. 13, No. 4, April 1988, pp. 273–280.

(Le82)   Lemmons, P., and T., Roger, "Upward Migration: A Comparison of CP/M-86 and MS-DOS, *Byte*, July 1982, pp. 330–356.

(Le87)   LePage, R., "The Road to MS-DOS," *Macworld*, August 1987, pp. 108–113.

(Li88)   Linnell, D., "SAA: IBM's Road Map to the Future," *PC Tech Journal*, Vol. 6, No. 4, April 1988, pp. 86–105.

(Li89a) Linnell, D., "Cooperative Communications," *PC Tech Journal*, Vol. 7, No. 2, February 1989, pp. 52–61.

(Lu84)   Luhn, R., and R. Cook, "80286: Intel's Multitask Master," *PC World*, Vol. 2, No. 12, 1984, 248–254.

(Ma84)   Machrone, B., "IBM Nurtures a Network," *PC Magazine*, Vol. 3, No. 22, November 1984, pp 135–141.

(Ma88)   Malloy, R., "DOS 4.0," *Byte,* IBM Special Edition, Fall 1988, pp. 75–78.

(Ma85)   Marrin, K., "Realtime and Multiuser Operating Systems Target IBM PC AT," *Computer Design,* December 1985, pp. 135–143.

(Ma86)   Mashey, J. R., "What's All the Fuss About RISC?," *Unix Review,* February 1986, pp. 37–50.

(Mi84)   Miller, H., "3.00 and Counting," *PC World,* Vol. 2, No. 11, 1984.

(Mi90)   Miller, M. J., "OS/2: The Right Stuff?," *Infoworld,* Vol. 12, No. 13, 1990, pp. 51–57.

(Mi86)   Mirecki, T., "Expandable Memory, *PC Tech Journal,* February 1986, pp. 66–82.

(Mi88)   Mizell, A. M., "Understanding Device Drivers in Operating System/2," *IBM,* 1988.

(Mo91)   Moad, J., "Where IS Stands on OS/2," *Datamation,* January 15, 1991, pp. 30–33.

(Mo89)   Morris, R. R., and W. E. Brooks, "UNIX Versus OS/2: A Graphic Comparison," *PC Tech Journal,* Vol. 7, No. 2, February 1989, pp. 106–118.

(Mo88)   Morrow, G., "The IBM Micro Channel I/O Bus," *Micro/Systems Journal,* Vol. 4, No. 2, February 1988, pp. 18–26.

(Ne88)   Newcom, K., "The Micro Channel Versus the AT Bus," *Byte,* IBM Special Issue, Vol. 13, No. 11, Fall 1988, pp. 91–98.

(No83)   Norton, P., *Inside the IBM PC,* Bowie, MD: Robert J. Brady, 1983.

(No84d)   Norton, P., "The Dissection of DOS 3.0," *PC Magazine,* Vol. 3, No. 21, October 30, 1984, pp. 105–107.

(Om85)   O'Malley, C., "What You Should Know About MS-DOS," *Personal Computing, August,* 1985, pp. 43–51.

(Or91)   Orfali, R., Harkey, D., *Client-Server Programming with OS/2 Extended Edition,* New York: Van Nostrand Reinhold, 1991.

(Pa83)   Paterson, T., "An Inside Look at MS-DOS," *Byte,* June 1983, pp. 230-252.

(Pa85)   Patterson, D., "Reduced Instruction Set Computers," *Communications of the ACM,* Vol. 28, No. 1, 1985, pp. 8–21.

(Pa90)   Padovano, M., "Federal UNIX Means Secure UNIX. Here's How.," *Systems Integration,* September 1990, p. 27.

(Pa90a)   Panza, R., "Open SNA," *Interoperability,* Fall 1990, pp. 25–31.

(Pe86)   Petzold, C., "Enlarging the Dimensions of Memory," *PC Magazine,* January, 1986, pp. 120–136.

(Pe88)   Petzold, C., "The Graphics Programming Interface: A Guide to OS/2 Presentation Spaces," *Microsoft Systems Journal,* Vol. 3, No. 3, May 1988, pp. 9–18.

(Pe88a)   Petzold, C., "Utilizing OS/2 Multithread Techniques in Presentation Manager Applications," *Microsoft Systems Journal,* Vol. 3, No. 2, March 1988, pp. 11–27.

(Pe88b)   Petzold, C., "Multiple Threads Make Better OS/2 Programs," *PC Magazine,* Vol. 7, No. 12, June, 1988, pp. 289–307.

(Pe88c)   Petzold, C., "Exploring the OS/2 .EXE File," *PC Magazine,* Vol. 7, No. 9, May, 1988, pp. 329–341.

(Pe88d)   Petzold, C., "Introducing the OS/2 Presentation Manager," *PC Magazine,* Vol. 7, No. 13, July 1988, pp. 379-394.

(Pe89)   Petzold, C., *Programming the OS/2 Presentation Manager,* Redmond, WA: Microsoft Press, 1989.

(Pe90)   Petzold, C., "Computing in the 1990s: Why Windows 3.0 Is Only a Short-Term Solution," *PC Magazine,* November 27, 1990, pp. 469–472.

(Ph84)   Phraner, R., "The Future of UNIX on the IBM PC," *Byte,* 1984, pp. 59–63.

(Qu88)   Quirk, K., "Model 80 Flagship," *PC Tech Journal,* Vol. 6, No. 4, April 1988, pp. 62–73.

(Re84)   Redmond, W. J., "Managing Memory: A Guided Tour of DOS 2.0 Memory Management," *PC Tech Journal,* August 1984, pp. 42–62.

(Re90)   Reinhold, A.; E. Burgdorf; C. Cobleigh; and R. Kressman, "TCP/IP," *IBM Telecommunications System Bulletin,* December 1990.

(Ro88)   Rosch, W. L., "IBM's PS/2 Model 80-111: A Dream Deferred," *PC Magazine,* Vol. 7, No. 8, April 26, 1988, pp. 93–100.

(Ro90)   Rose, M. T., "Transition and Coexistence Strategies for TCP/IP to OSI," *IEEE Journal on Selected Areas in Communications,* Vol. 8, No. 1, 1990, pp. 57–66.

(Ro84)   Roskos, E., "Writing Device Drivers for MS-DOS 2.0," *Byte,* February 1984.

(Ru84)   Rubin, C., and K. Strehlo, "Why So Many Computers Look Like the IBM Standard," *Personal Computing,* March 1984, pp. 52–65, 182–189.

(Ru88)   Ruddell, K., "Using OS/2 Semaphores to Coordinate Concurrent Threads of Execution," *Microsoft Systems Journal,* Vol. 3, No. 3, May 1988, pp. 19–26.

(Sc72)   Schroeder, M. D., and J. H. Saltzer, "A Hardware Architecture for Implementating Protection Rings," *Communications of the ACM,* Vol. 15, No. 3, March 1972, pp. 157–170.

(Sc88)   Schmitt, D. A., "Family Ties," *PC Tech Journal,* Vol. 6, No. 6, June 1988, pp. 124–132.

(Sc88a)   Schmitt, D. A., "Converting DOS Programs to OS/2 Protected Mode," *Micro/Systems Journal,* Vol. 4, No. 3, March 1988, pp. 24–34.

(Sc87)   Schwartz, M., *Telecommunications Networks: Protocols, Modeling and Analysis,* Reading, MA: Addison-Wesley, 1987.

(Se88)   Seybold, A., "OS/2 Represents Future of Micro Operating Systems," *High Technology Business,* July 1988, pp. 58–59.

(Sh85)   Shiell, J., and J. Markoff, "IBM PC Family BIOS Comparison," *Byte,* November 1985.

(So87a)   Somerson, P., "Personal System/2 Gives Life to a Smarter, More Agile DOS," *PC Magazine,* May, 1987, pp. 48–51.

(So87b)   Somerson, P., "DOS Lives," *PC Magazine,* July 1987, pp. 175–182.

(St89)   Stephenson, W. D., "Open Systems Interconnection (OSI)," *IBM Telecommunications System Bulletin,* September 1989.

(Ta82)   Taylor, R., and P. Lemmons, "Upward Migration Part 2: A Comparison of CP/M-86 and MS-DOS," *Byte,* July 1982.

(Te87)   Tevanian, A., "Architecture-Independent Virtual Memory Management for Parallel and Distributed Environments: The Mach Approach," Pittsburgh, PA: Carnegie-Mellon University, 1987.

(Ti90)   Tillman, M. A., and D. Yen, "SNA and OSI: Three Stategies for Interconnection," *Communications of the ACM,* Vol. 33, No. 2, 1990, pp. 214–224.

(Tr88)   Tropp, W., and S. Wright, "The DOS–UNIX Union," *PC Tech Journal,* Vol. 6, No.1, January 1988, pp. 78–91.

(Ty90)   Tyler, J. G., "Multiple Virtual DOS Machines: A Better DOS," *IBM Personal Systems Developer,* Spring 1990, pp. 36–44.

(Ut86)   Uttal, B., "Inside the Deal that Made Bill Gates $350,000,000," *Fortune,* July 21, 1986, pp. 23–33.

(Va87)   Valigra, L., "OS/2: Turning Off the Car to Change Gears," *Microsoft Systems Journal,* Vol. 2, No. 2, May 1987, pp. 61–66.

(Ve87)   Vellon, M., "The OS/2 Windows Presentation Manager: Microsoft Windows on the Future," *Microsoft Systems Journal,* Vol. 2, No. 2, May 1987, pp. 13–18.

(Vi87)   Vigorita, H., "Memory Addressing on the Intel 80386," *Micro/Systems Journal,* Vol. 3, No. 6, November/December 1987, pp. 18–21.

(Wa84)   Waite, M.; J. Angermeyer; and M. Noble, "Climbing Around in the DOS Directory Tree," *PC Magazine,* Vol. 3, No. 11, June, 1984, pp. 275–288.

(We86)   Weinreich, M., "A First Look at the 80386," *Micro/Systems Journal,* September/October 1986, pp. 34–37.

(We84)   Wells, P., "The 80286 Microprocessor," *Byte,* November 1984, pp. 231–242.

(Wh87)   White, E., and R. Grehan, "Microsoft's New DOS," *Byte,* June 1987, pp. 116–126.

(Wh90)   Whitten, N., *Managing Software Development Projects,* New York: John Wiley & Sons, 1990.

Index